D1564344

Jump Jim Crow

Jim Crow Rice.
Courtesy of the Harvard Theatre Collection,
The Houghton Library.

JUMP JIM CROW

Lost Plays, Lyrics, and Street Prose of the First Atlantic Popular Culture

W. T. Lhamon, Jr.

Harvard University Press
Cambridge, Massachusetts
London, England
2003

Library of Congress Cataloging-in-Publication Data

Jump Jim Crow : lost plays, lyrics, and street pose of the first Atlantic popular culture /

W. T. Lhamon, Jr.

p.   cm.

Includes bibliographical references and index.

ISBN 0-674-01062-0 (cloth : alk. paper)

1. African Americans—Literary collections. 2. Social classes—Literary collections.
3. Popular literature—United States. 4. American literature—19th century.
5. Blackface entertainers—History. 6. African Americans in literature.
7. Social classes in literature. 8. Minstrel shows—History.
9. Rice, Tom, 1808–1860. 10. Blacks in literature.
11. Race in literature. I. Lhamon, W. T.

PS509.N4J86   2003

810.8′0896073—dc21   2003041736

Contents

STREET PROSE

Preface: Slipping the Yoke

"Hickman, are you a minister man or a minstrel man?" "I'm both, I'm afraid—but remember, the Word is tricky!"

—Ralph Ellison, *Juneteenth*

Jump Jim Crow became a book because I wanted to find how early I might trace evidence of white fascination with blackness in the Atlantic world. The trail threaded back through the Civil Rights era, which determined my consciousness. Through rhythm 'n' blues and Swing to the Jazz Age and the Harlem Renaissance. Past *Shuffle Along* in 1921 and Bert Williams's and George Walker's *In Dahomey* on Broadway in 1903. Back past the troubling antics of black Billy Kersands jamming billiard balls in his mouth after Reconstruction. Back past white actors scandalizing blackness in minstrel shows through the mid-nineteenth century. Earlier and more popular than all these, I found, were the narrative dramas about a character named Jim Crow. Who was he? How did his story come about? What were his uses?

Black people—then white people and both together—had slowly built up a cultural icon around the folk trickster called Jim Crow. Particularly on the sea islands of Georgia, but also elsewhere, people danced out Jim Crow's gyrations. There were songs about him. Then there were extravaganzas expanding the actions told in the verses. Then there were skits becoming dramas that cleared room on the stage for Jim Crow's cackle. The white actor turned playwright who hauled this black trouble into view was Thomas Dartmouth Rice.

Rice's popularity ran wild between 1830 and the early 1850s, while he acted his plays all over America and Britain to huge audiences, usually of mixed race. No one published any of his dramas in his lifetime, however, and the few skits printed later were missing crucial scenes. Until now, therefore, not one Jim Crow play has appeared in print as Rice played it. *Jump Jim Crow* puts this evidence on the table. Here is the moment when blackness first became widely popular in America.

Handwritten prompt scripts, crumbling newspaper ads, and faded playbills were waiting, buried in archives on both sides of the Atlantic.

They yielded details necessary to reclaim the performances and their context. To read this material is to figure out what Jim Crow meant when the lure of an alternative, tumultuous blackness became powerful, before opponents could monitor its effects.

When Americans were winding up to the Civil War, "Jim Crow" meant the opposite of what it indicates today. "Jim Crow" then referred to free and runaway African Americans moiling together with volatile European Americans. Tracing back this allure delivered a deep paradox: before the concept of "Jim Crow" stood for America's justly despised segregation laws, it first referred to a very real cross-racial energy and recalcitrant alliance between blacks and lower-class whites. That's what the trickster Jim Crow organized and represented: a working-class integration—a jumping, dizzy Jim Crow movement. And that's what those who proposed segregation laws were determined to outlaw.

The Jim Crow movement in the years leading up to the Civil War fitted itself around a jiving jasper whose popularity proved the ragged energy in an interracial *mobility*. It quite consciously opposed authority that pretended to *nobility*. Almost immediately, by the middle of the nineteenth century, elites developed practices and governments devised racist laws to police the scary ferment that Jim Crow trucked into view.

The liveliness in these plays as they originally existed frankly surprised me. The images of black humanity conjured by the earliest Jim Crow materials are broad, subtle, street-sophisticated, frequently slyly learned, and always complexly humane. They are funny; they show good reason for their original popularity. Most startling of all in these plays and lyrics by white men is the creative power that the black characters evince. Jim Crow, Ginger Blue, and Bone Squash are never on the edge of the composition, as such figures were in earlier paintings and literature by whites that touched on blacks' plight until Stowe's *Uncle Tom's Cabin* (in 1851–52) and Melville's "Benito Cereno" (1855) scrambled to catch up with blackface activity in their era's popular theatre. These early blackface plays were not only a resource for fiction and polite theatre, but also a model that other forms tried to bring back alive.

In the plays printed here blackened actors grab center stage, hold it, and defend it. They speak more cunningly than their stilted white counterparts. They achieve their own ends—distinct from white ends—and win audience approval for taking care of business. They are active within the unbalanced power and social strain of their era—tensions both lampooned and seriously addressed in the plays and songs. And against all odds they win their contests. These blackface plays by T. D. Rice are the earliest American written portraits of blacks by whites that center blacks positively. Those who believe there is cumulative power for ritual theatre have logic to argue that this robust image of black attraction for working white culture excited the segregation laws that nabbed the name of what they censored: "Jim Crow."

When and why did this white fascination with black culture come together in distinctive form? No eureka moment, no absolute threshold began it. Still, two things changed after the popularity of Jim Crow displaced its preceding inchoateness. First, Americans developed a figure to express the way they imagined race, in various ways. Second, people in all classes became more culturally canny. Their contentions sharpened around the edges because Jim Crow's staged turnings taught not only how he slips out of control, makes trouble, and raises Cain. The process also clarified how cultural meaning is broadcast, defeated, but seeps back through the cordons that try to control it.

More than a century before Ralph Ellison would name the strategy, these plays push to "change the joke and slip the yoke." Their wit smudges and budges the line between invalidity and validity, exclusion and joining, nobody and somebody. Ellison's phrase and essay by the same name (published first in 1958, reprinted in his *Collected Essays*) identifies nothing not already prominent in the early antebellum plays and songs *Jump Jim Crow* presents. That is, the black folk character Jim Crow had already changed the joke by the time T. D. Rice staged his tricks. Black vernacular culture, the blackface players who followed its principles and figures in the 1830s, and codifier Ralph Ellison all knew that yokes are not easy to slip and that the practice is not foolproof. Slipping the yoke may even turn itself into a new oppressive mode that fosters its own stereotypes. Even so, ridiculing yokers to empower jokers reliably earns anarchic respite.

Why this story now? Why stir up the origins of Jim Crow as rubric and rite when we might forget and move past it? Because forgetting these open-handed plays only ensures that as a society we will be more stunned and less understanding when their concerns return in different guises—as ragtime, jazz, and bop, rock and rap, for instance. Those American popular forms that are about racial formation and difference become angrier the more they suffer disdain, scorn, and repression.

Putting aside origins feeds the basic democratic problem—which is how we might appreciate and include all our parts.

The Jim Crow plays display how politically disfranchised and economically excluded Americans have long felt attraction for black ways of moving through trouble. That's why I hope with Ralph Ellison's Hickman that the gestures and voices of minstrel men recovered in *Jump Jim Crow* might increase our understandings of the perverse exclusions of the Atlantic world, and in that understanding help minister to them.

Americans quite early fused their anxiety about slavery with their celebrations of supposed black forms. Trying to enact this diagnostic Atlantic trauma is what made Irish immigrants like Dan Emmett play at being black; Ukrainian Jewish immigrants like Al Jolson black up and sing Mammy songs; the Gershwin brothers compose a folk opera about crippled Porgy and addicted Bess; Memphis boys like Elvis take up Little Richard's line of work (which Penniman learned in a minstrel show, doing a transvestite act called Princess Lavonne); and Puerto Ricans in the Bronx (like Big Punisher) and trailer park kids from Detroit (like Eminem) rap in rhyme. Spike Lee's summary of the problem in *Bamboozled* (2000) revealingly ends in the violence and self-loathing that stems from this self-fulfilling circle of blackface hate.

There is no way to slip the blackface yoke when the acknowledged history of the process lacks its hopeful early moves. *Jump Jim Crow* provides an earlier and quite different—even enthusiastic—version of the American obsession with blackness. Here black figures take control of the stage as their pleased white audiences applaud their further excitements. The world of the Jim Crow moment was not as severely limited as it became already in the minstrel era around the Civil War and Reconstruction. By the time Al Jolson played *The Jazz Singer* (1927) his blackface character oscillated merely between grin and frown. The mentality of the early Jim Crow plays is not as viciously despairing as it has now become in Spike Lee's films. Can we comprehend a time when a tricky Jim Crow offered encouragement to blacks and his disaffected white followers? If so, we might hope to sunder our current controls, pursue a broader sense of possibility, and approach mutuality again.

Illustrations

JUMP JIM CROW

❧ INTRODUCTION ❧
An Extravagant and Wheeling Stranger

Your daughter . . . hath made a gross revolt,
Tying her duty, beauty, wit, and fortunes
In an extravagant and wheeling stranger
Of here and everywhere.
> —Roderigo to Brabantio,
> Shakespeare's *Othello* (1.1.132–136)

LATERAL SUFFICIENCY

More than a century and a half ago a white man named Thomas Dartmouth Rice became for two decades the most popular actor of his era, in the United States and Britain. He grew up a youth of no means, no parentage now traceable, in New York's most ethnically mixed neighborhood—the Seventh Ward—along the East River docks. He apprenticed as a ship's carver. How could a man with these resources leave so many footprints along Atlantic shores? By blacking up and imitating black men.

Some might say his fame was a freak. It made no sense. The man was lucky and historians ought to ignore him as an anomaly. Others might claim, rightly enough, that his success embarrasses everyone involved and, therefore, historians ought to condemn him. Others might claim, as I do, that the sense Rice made acting the figure he called "Jim Crow" bridged vernacular to high cultural activity in the Atlantic. I'll show how this connection set rolling those industries that provoke and profit from cultures cycling up from the social bottom. Rice coded positive desire into the inevitable stereotypes that deformed his gestures.

In fact, what Rice achieved with his plays and songs was not anomalous, but has recurred in cycles ever since, borne in the moves and styles of daily performance as well as formal productions on stage and screen, record and network, novel and poem. Imitating perceived blackness is arguably the central metaphor for what it is to be an American, even to be a citizen of that wider Atlantic world that suffers still from having in-

[1]

stalled, defended, and opposed its peculiar history of slavery. Blackface performance underlies so much popular and therefore canonical culture in the American Atlantic, it deserves study. Insofar as blackface is racist, it deserves condemnation. But insofar as it also gives evident form to such countertendencies as cross-racial attraction or mutuality of class, it requires commentary and explanation. These roots of enduring cultural strands are too little acknowledged. They feed a cultural paradox that is surprisingly inventive, even liberating. What Rice achieved early and bequeathed to later culture both saps and sets stereotypes.

When he began, what T. D. Rice did was unusual. Then it mushroomed into a pop craze. Then it settled into convention. Many actors emulated Rice on the stage. Offstage and in their daily lives, multitudes adopted the physical and vocal turns Rice raised to the popular level. The song and dance Rice performed and the plays he made formed a crux among ripening cultures. He developed a totemic relationship to varied publics, from those that clapped his performance into existence, even identified with it, all the way over to those who hated it.

Those who took up what he represented were at least as partial to him as those who followed Edwin Forrest, Fanny Kemble, and Madame Vestris. These performers were popular, but the commitment Rice evoked was significantly different. Rice knitted together publics who were normally separated or opposed outside the theatre's fantasy space. Every night he blacked up, he embodied a character who stitched filiation across class, region, even nationality, and race. Beyond his considerable mimetic genius, the quirky grace of his dance, and the radical theatricality he worked out, these social seams Rice interwove were consequential. They troubled other people—which is what ultimately caused his own trouble.

Rice avoided the riots, rumors, and scandals that attached to Forrest, Kemble, and Vestris. Nevertheless, his work spawned controversy sufficiently deep to rehearse abiding fault lines that still diagnose American identity. That's why, while the other stars of Rice's era have faded away, Rice's principal character, Jim Crow, lives infamously on, personifying American racism. No other American cultural figure stirred a legacy that endures such widespread censure as well as continual appropriation.

How elites in his time blamed him and how people offload on his legacy today are in fact quite distinct. When Rice started translating black experience for whites in 1830, Jim Crow was not a stablehand or hostler, as the legends then proclaimed—and as current historians have until very recently still claimed. Instead, Jim Crow was a regional folklore character—an outrageous fiction—and he was already making skittish even the blacks who invoked him.[1] Within a few years, Rice and his approving publics turned Jim Crow into an inaugural icon of international popular culture. From a local figure whom rice and indigo workers down the coastal Carolinas to the Caribbean used to express and explore their hopes and fears, Jim Crow burgeoned into a complex of meanings that publics fought to control wherever they spoke variants of English. But Jim Crow proved too slippery and multisignificant to police. He slipped, shucked, and talked his way out of every confinement. Even the Devil could not pin down the Jim Crow figure in Rice's play *Bone Squash Diavolo.* Devil to Bone: "You're like a 'lasses candy in a shop window. You run away on all sides" (Act II, scene 4). His melting instability is exactly what bosses held against Jim Crow's public. And that's why polite culture aimed its big guns of disrepute against Jim Crow. Elites could not entirely outlaw common people, but they could try to make taboo their cultural activities.

Several factors converging in the case of Jim Crow boosted his controversy and his ramifications. Global dispersal of capital and people throughout the seventeenth and eighteenth centuries, accelerating dramatically in the early nineteenth, was chocking ethnic overlays into such whole regions as the Caribbean Basin as well as metropolitan wharves and markets throughout the western Atlantic. The human consequences included unprecedented uprootedness and anomie. This was the moment when disparate Atlantic consciousnesses quickened into a ripening Atlantic culture. Caroll Smith-Rosenberg quickly pegged the North American feel for this process when she wrote that for the half century between 1790 and the 1850s, "three massive revolutions—the commercial, transportation, and industrial—swept through American society . . . By the 1840s, the world that colonial Americans had carefully crafted lay in fragments. Yet the form the new order would take was not . . . clear. Conflicting economic, social, and ideological systems battled for hegemony. The obsolete coexisted with the novel."[2] Poor people shuffled these broken old and unfamiliar new pieces more desperately than those who enjoyed relative comfort.

Potentially the most anomic cohort of all was blacks. As Sterling Stuckey and others have shown, however, New World blacks contradicted this likely anomie. After their middle passage, they built "black" identities to compound and articulate Ibo, Yoruba, and Hausa self-concepts. In so doing, African Americans presented themselves to themselves, as to others, in ways that could travel and endure. These new selfhoods were fables of identity, necessary to blacks, obviously, but also attractive to others. Why to whites? Because blacks were pioneering ways through extreme versions of the same forces that were also discomfiting whites. Therefore black strategies seemed like good guides. This attraction across race to black culture, if not so often to black men and women, has proved a recurrent fact of Atlantic popular culture. In the Atlantic during Rice's immediate era, the metaphor of blackness came to signal a worst-case condition that others who were neither black nor fully empowered could join and deploy to signal their own disaffection.

The evidence of the songs, street prose, and plays collected in this volume is that poor and disaffected whites, like Rice and others who were later alive to the energy of *infra dig* culture, latched onto these fables of blackness to mark their own dispersal and disruption around the Atlantic. These ragged white publics hoisted Jim Crow to flag their own, even their mutual, condition.

When Jim Crow swooped cackling into metropolitan North American consciousness in the early 1830s, then into Atlantic Europe later in that decade, his dramatic figure contagiously shaped the dire contentions of low audiences. Low-black and ragged, runaway and self-sufficient, reaching for the spoils but not the responsibilities of middle-class modernity, Jim Crow tilted the balance of what was attractive in the social drama. From black models, he produced another way to figure out race and raggedness in his contemporary life. He bodied forth a figure that was simultaneously white and black, and whose location fudged class, for his adherents were not confined to the lumpen core, but included counter-jumping clerks and members of the middle class whose mothers did not know they were out. That is, Jim Crow demonstrated the allure of the low, both to those who were indeed low and to many who were not.

In terming Jim Crow "an inaugural icon of international popular culture," I mean to distinguish him from the local popularity associated with Charles Mathews, Pierce Egan, and Jack Sheppard in England or with George Washington, Rip Van Winkle, and Davy Crockett in the United States. Before Jim Crow, on both sides of the Atlantic, these legendary figures summed up separate regional sorts. Precisely because elites scorned him everywhere in the slave-trade Atlantic, however, Jim Crow became a potent symbol for disdained peoples to rally around in London as well as New York and New Orleans. That gathering was the magnet for the distinctive industry that organizes and speaks in the name of those bottom-up tendencies people now associate correctly with transnational popular culture.

Jim Crow's popularity also structurally opposes the canonical tool to which popular theatre had housebroken Shakespearian production. Two and a half centuries into Shakespeare's cultural fate, the Bard had become a model of transcendent ideals that seemed to naturalize elite status in the States. Shakespeare's sensitive registry of rude mechanicals and rustic manners was not what drove people to produce his art in the early nineteenth century. Rather, one important reason Shakespeare was then culturally useful was the way producers could show his plays subsuming low persons and manners—could bend the plays to serve an ideal of courtly hierarchy. This top-down push on theatre in general of course stimulated an opposing shove upward. This countertendency was what Jim Crow, his dance and his popular following, originally ventilated.

In the blackface scenes that Rice consolidated, and which found their conduit in the blackface lore cycle that followed upon his productions, there developed an engine sufficiently alluring to clear out alternative space within the residual fogs of top-downness. Rice stepped outside the pattern that had naturalized elite status, making it the only staged cultural model. He translated and manufactured the allure of the low. His appeal from below translated wildly in so many domains that it countered the longing for courtliness that had earlier seemed proper. There developed around the charisma of Jim Crow a new entertainment business hoping to control it. A new industry eagerly hacked out a body of plays and lyrics. The aim was to capture the overlapping publics then forming to warm themselves around such sketches. But these publics were never quite in sync. That is, while some cohorts were ridiculing black talk, others were committing to its perceived sass and sharp coinings. These and many more responses were what the Jim Crow fetish compounded and kept in motion.

Many performers, texts, subindustries, and audiences turned now to lumpen tokens for inspiration and identifying gestures more than they pushed toward courtly ideals. As in Rice's play *Virginia Mummy*, indeed, the grandness of the historical past and efforts to revive its life were becoming risible. By turning to Jim Crow's wheeling song, these new publics turned away from the way Shakespearian actors rendered Othello's stately cadence. After blackface, it was never again credible to impose a single model of desirable cultural activity. Through blackface an alternative vector of social identification, a slumming from within, became thinkable because vital players acted it out all across the Atlantic. It caused an axiomatic and diagnostic shift in modern culture that has taken an embarrassingly long time to acknowledge. It marked the entry not of any authentic blackness into American and Atlantic culture, and not of an exclusively working-class position, *per se*, but of a relational opposition that has used racial and class markers to stage a continually sliding disaffection from the dominant culture.

By calling Jim Crow an icon of *international* popular culture, I mean that mingled form toward which industrial dislocations pushed modern life. Something newly hybrid spawned in the alienations, democratized knowledge of others, and class resentments when press gangs dislocated the working poor around the Atlantic. The manuscripts in this book and the behavior they scripted flag the instant when various rogue cultures gathered critical momentum and aligned themselves around blackface as a mutual mark.

This emergent alignment created a culture with gall sufficient to stand up to the imperial reach of early nineteenth-century capital. Transnational capital formations used peoples and resources on all the Atlantic shores, but popular lore early in the nineteenth century also suddenly—if briefly—yoked together sufficient mass, self-awareness, and bravado to reach across the basin. This first Atlantic popular culture linked exploited peoples in counter-forms of in-your-face recalcitrance. Of course it was not revolutionary. But these Jim Crow plays, songs, and street prose demonstrate that underclass culture was certainly able to represent itself. This proven ability to mount its own cultural fables was one way the Atlantic mobility maintained itself on the evermore precipitous field they were inhabiting.

After the mid-nineteenth century, this self-definition through Jim Crow is what the middle class successfully undermined, partly by insisting along with Marx that the poor "cannot represent themselves, they must be represented"—meaning, also along with Marx, We must represent Them.[3] By then the plays, which no publisher had properly printed, were less and less frequently performed, and more and more warped into minstrel skits. These deformations seemed to prove that both the original plays and the form of life they dramatized deserved censure. Readers of the plays here will now be able to judge for themselves.

When the inaugural performances were bodying forth their texts as a living gesture in the 1830s and 1840s, this popular culture had taken advantage of two related opportunities. First, it plied still-vital, still-remembered folk gestures—the wheeling turns of the black Jim Crow dance itself, for instance—to mark space against industrial pressures. Second, the figure of blackface performance was sufficiently novel—and so outrageous to official culture—that it compounded under its sign disparate impulses opposing the scornful merchantry. "How is you gwan to paint me, Massa, like a sign?" Ginger Blue asks Captain Rifle in *Virginia Mummy*. And Rifle replies, "No, like a mummy—white, black, green, blue, and a variety of colors" (scene 3). Of course Ginger Blue is right. A hundred years before the Soviet theorist V. N. Volosinov noted that "differently oriented accents intersect in every ideological sign [and thus a s]ign becomes an arena of class struggle," Rice was producing his body as a lightning rod for ideological contest. Through his embodiment of Jim Crow, Rice became a living fetish in overlapped social spaces.[4]

Gross Revolt

Jim Crow is at issue. Without either praising or scorning Jim Crow, I want to understand his first permutations. My topic is the arc of development that the folk and then the dramatized figure of Jim Crow survived during the push coming to shove over his meaning. How did that conflict ink his body before institutionalized readings of his meaning warped into laws and practices now justly despised? I try to understand the figure's inauguration completely enough not to exonerate American racism, which is the enduring central fact of Atlantic history that none of us can escape, but must always acknowledge. Rather, I want to deepen the sense of tragedy one feels upon seeing how those who controlled public space increasingly bent Jim Crow to their purposes. *Jump Jim Crow* shows that the earliest blackface plays were already ambiguous art. *Bone Squash Diavolo*, *Virginia Mummy*, *Flight to America*, *Yankee Notes for English Circulation*, and *Otello* had multiple meanings that included admiration for perceived blackness. The scripts had enough play to make them particularly useful for organizing heterogeneous publics. In flocking to see Jim Crow, disparate types discovered their mutual affinities. Around Jim Crow's mask the dispersed riffraff of a quickening industrialism began to act out their own parts in a new play in which the insubordinates were mixing among themselves but not melding with the previously dominant. They understood their fetishized Jim Crow radically differently than did the dominant culture that policed the public spaces in which Jim Crow danced. What this never-quite-melded alliance saw in Jim Crow remains unrecorded and that's what the texts gathered in *Jump Jim Crow* access.

Here is the fundamental evidence left us: T. D. Rice's own prompt scripts and variant songs, along with corroborating prose from his publics. *Jump Jim Crow* illuminates the "gross revolt" exhibited when Desdemonas loved Othellos on stage or in the streets—and which Jim Crow furthered with the rude negation of pomp and propriety his own wheeling stranger jubilantly displayed. The early Jim Crow was a symbol of demotic brotherhood played in black. That was the main reason people with power suppressed, besmirched, then finally outlawed it.

A few earlier white actors in America, including Edwin Forrest, had occasionally appeared in blackface to portray American blacks as marginal, laughable, and ephemeral. This general role I will refer to as Sambo. But T. D. Rice recognized and performed a substantial black character that was central, comic, and durable. This role was Jim Crow; it was different from Sambo. The fearful reality in Jim Crow ignited contention then and continues to bother people now. Before Rice shambled onto stages and into consciousnesses where Jim Crow's presence had never before been known, that trickster persona had been prickling African Americans. The African tales of buzzards and crows are doubtless forebears of the African American Jim Crow. When African legends crystallized into the African American trickster remains unknown. Before the nineteenth century, however, Jim Crow's vernacular gimp and pluck had already shaped a recognizable song and dance. This dance was sufficiently practiced that it gathered its own momentum quite independent of Rice's theatrical nicking and was wholly able to survive it. Thus, despite the incorporation of Jim Crow to blazon Atlantic laboring values, and despite all the consequent taboos, blacks in the Georgia sea islands

Figure 1. "Mr. T. Rice as the Original Jim Crow," *by Edward Williams Clay.*
Courtesy of the Harvard Theatre Collection, The Houghton Library.

in the 1970s were still dancing their own Jim Crow, and their practice
has since spread north, west, and south.[5]

When the 1820s turned into the 1830s, T. D. Rice activated this black
folk figure by performing it as a song and dance in blackface, bare toes
out, with a worn, torn costume—pretty much as he imagined a runaway field hand might have done it (see Figure 1). This was a heavily resisted and considerable achievement, for as much as he was able, Rice
brought raggedness into the theatrical house. After Rice died in 1860,
Bone Squash Diavolo and especially *Virginia Mummy* became vehicles for

such minstrel troupes as the Christy Minstrels and for Charles White, one of their derivatives. That's when the deformation and dilution process I have described occurred. Well after the plays' original success, Charles White adapted them for publication in the 1870s, along with a hundred other minstrel skits.[6] But these flaking print editions now available on microfilm were hardly as Rice performed them. Nearly everyone assumed the original plays were lost.[7] But I found eight handwritten prompt scripts in the British Library and another at the New York Public Library.

Racial degradation is what most people presently associate with the term "Jim Crow." They now give it the meaning that Richard Wright exposed in "The Ethics of Living Jim Crow" (1937, frequently reprinted) and that C. Vann Woodward studied in *The Strange Career of Jim Crow* (1955). In any case, racism was not what originally angered educated whites about the Jim Crow plays. That early anger occurred a century before Wright's essay began to associate Jim Crow with sympathies becoming systematic for our time. The first people to shun matters associated with Jim Crow were much more worried about other issues than racial degradation or segregation. Whether black boys could check books out of Southern libraries, could vote, or were being lynched—such powerful incidents as Wright used to illustrate the ethics of living Jim Crow —those issues had not yet, in the 1830s, deeply affected the circle of people with sufficient social power to spurn others meaningfully. Wright and Woodward were consolidating a set of meanings for the new word "racism" that were *just at that time coming into general use*, and did not have the same systematic meaning before the first few decades of the twentieth century. In fact, adherents of the National Socialist Party in Germany coined and proudly applied "racism" for their own beliefs as they rose to power. The word "racism" was not used at all before the 1930s, and was not used widely until after World War II.[8] The figure Jim Crow emerged, therefore, about a century before people began systematically conceiving racial issues the way people overwhelmingly do now. Of course, components of what we now call racism existed before our era's invention of the label, and some of those parts existed in antebellum America. Nevertheless, people think about racial issues more confidently, more self-righteously, when they have a ready, systematic terminology. Having the term "racist" at one's disposal draws a line: you're one, I'm not. It turns a tangle into a binary. It is a powerful weapon with many uses, including self-purification. But handy terminology guarantees neither deeper behavior nor fuller analysis.

Elites first repudiated Jim Crow not because he was racist, but because he was not racist enough. Jim Crow was a charismatic figure who had become an alternative to the Noble Moor. Bad enough that clerks were compact with costermongers, and that both signaled their fondness with black gestures when they danced Jim Crow, but when women went for Jim, too, it was Katie, bar the door. Unlike Othello, Jim Crow had no hold on dignity and was not about to commit suicide at the end of his play and disappear. Elites felt threatened because it was an epidemic the way working white people flocked to these unpredictable, these *unmoored* traits. Jim Crow had children. He multiplied physically and symbolically. The phenomenon of Jim Crow spread beyond its home, went beyond itself. This public applauding Jim Crow was living in much more racially mingled neighborhoods and sharing much more integrated life experiences than those who were able to declare taboos and write dictionaries. Already living belly to belly, white on black, black on white, poor people were not the ones most keen to keep the colors separate. It was people in power who most needed that social division. More important, they could propagate and codify their beliefs.

Were these claims to go on trial, exhibit A on their behalf might well be remarks about Desdemona by John Quincy Adams, the ex-president. His comments are part of a now-visible fraction of a cumbersome system of signs and plots that in the early nineteenth century managed what the words "racism" and "racist" rapidly sort today. Efficient terminology now supplants the clanking mechanisms of the past. The words "racism" and "racist" control acceptable attitudes about strangers that plays, performers, producers, publics, and commentators cranked out for centuries. Othello and Desdemona embodied, enfolded, and excluded the attraction and repulsion of vagrant others. They worked through what current terms summarize.

Adams mulled over his ideas in his journal during the early 1830s, then published them in the spring of 1836. The fundament of the play, he wrote in "The Character of Desdemona," was Desdemona's "unnatural passion" for a "sooty-bosomed . . . thick-lipped wool-headed Moor."[9] Not Iago, not Iago's use of what people now call racism, not a flaw in Othello, but rather the *marriage* of Othello and Desdemona was what Adams considered "the primitive cause of all the tragic incidents of the play." Samuel Coleridge had named this process earlier. That is, Adams was continuing Coleridge's hunt for motives within what people of good will in the era could only repress as a "motiveless malignity." Iago seemed motiveless because there was no convenient name for the emotions he was systematizing. Today one says that Iago was racist, or that he used racism on his behalf, and is done with it. The period while Adams hunted through these motives coincided precisely with the years Rice was incorporating the Jim Crow figure into theatrical display. Rice's actions traveled in precisely the opposite direction from Adams's writing. Rather than attending to blacks to exclude them, as Adams intended to enforce, T. D. Rice was primarily copying black gestures to identify himself and his public *with* them.

Others also took part. James Henry Hackett seconded Adams's essay and its tone. Hackett played Shakespearian, Yankee, and coonskin types at the same time that Rice was delineating blacks.[10] In 1863, Hackett wrote: "The great moral lesson of the tragedy of *Othello* is, that black and white blood cannot be intermingled in marriage without a gross outrage upon the laws of Nature; and that, in such violations, Nature will vindicate her laws."[11] By burnishing Adams's remarks, Hackett and many others showed that the Adams family's revulsion was ordinary in their circle. These thoughts articulated the preexisting disgust such men (and at least Adams's mother) felt about cross-racial intimacy.[12] They imposed their abhorrence on the Othello story, deploying Othello as its figure. They illustrate how representatives of dominating cultures enforce stereotypes where ambiguity and even countervailing meaning in fact reside. Adams and Hackett became spokesmen precisely because they simplified the urgent complexities of their era. For their privileged readers, they found comforting ways through thickets of contention.

Hackett and Adams considered their opinions for years before expressing them carefully. Calling race-mixing a "gross outrage," in the way Hackett underscored Roderigo's "Gross revolt," was one typical way American liberal intellectuals worked through race and love. That Adams would also successfully defend the Amistad's slave mutineers may now seem paradoxical. But twenty-first-century paradox was nineteenth-century convention. Powerful people of European descent, including some abolitionists, could despise peoples of African origins, *qua* people. They could imagine physical intimacy across race with sharp disgust, even while they argued passionately against enslavement in the abstract, just as John Quincy Adams and Harriet Beecher Stowe did.

The texts in *Jump Jim Crow* indicate that Adams's outrage was not a core response shared evenly across class and region, like the ability to sing "Yankee Doodle." Although one surely finds working-class racists in dockyards and poor wards throughout the western Atlantic, there was regularly enough cross-race intimacy, cohabitation, marriage, and cultural creolization to make the opinions Adams and Hackett expressed anomalous or "un-American" by any statistical standard. There were local reasons for varied proportions of racial intimacy in poor areas of Charleston and New Orleans, or Boston and Philadelphia, that distinguished them from New York City and Brooklyn; nevertheless, in all these cities poor people of every hue and trade swapped attitudes face to face, as intimately as possible.[13] But this frank intimacy was worlds apart from the attitudes of the elites for whom Adams and Hackett spoke. In his diary for 6 October 1839, the same year that the Amistad case broke, Adams noted that James Hackett had written him a letter. The actor had "very recently heard of [my] analysis . . . of the tragedy of *Othello*," and inquired "where he can procure it." Adams then quite remarkably confessed to himself, "this extension of my fame is more tickling to my vanity than it was to be elected President of the United States."[14]

Extravagant and Wheeling

John Quincy Adams's view demoted Shakespeare's Othello, after whom the play was named, to an invisible subhuman whose feelings are of no account, whose own story is insignificant and outrageous. Adams's ideas and the public they represented made Desdemona's insubordination to her father the central concern. For the patriarchy of the Northeast during the antebellum years, the play is not about Othello as he sees himself and as Desdemona sees him. Instead, the story is about "The Character of Desdemona" deserting the patriarchy for its opposite: for *"an extravagant and wheeling stranger"* (1.1.135).

Shakespeare puts this telling phrase in Roderigo's mouth. Adams approvingly quotes it. I emphasize it to recall that the racial markers which Rice redeployed for his staged character were far older than he. They were older than ex-President Adams, than the United States, than African American culture. By putting these markers back in motion, remixed in precise ways that upset what was then the conventional use of the Othello and Desdemona figures, Rice excited fears that still plumb ancient social differences. His strategy was the template that Lenny Bruce, Richard Pryor, Eddie Murphy, and Chris Rock would reactivate in our own era. Jim Crow probed enfranchised values where they were most vulnerable. He haunted the dreams of such senior advocates as Brabantio or John Quincy Adams, who might have woken in the night with cold sweats: "This accident is not unlike my dream," says Brabantio, "Belief of it oppresses me already" (1.1.141–142).

If actor Hackett's subscription to Adams's ideas tickled the statesman's vanity, rogue T. D. Rice sapped the composure of their whole circle. Rice embodied that wheeling stranger—orally in his thickly marked dialect, and physically in his limping dance. After every one of the hundreds of verses he improvised to "Jump Jim Crow," Rice told friend and foe alike that Jim Crow stood for all wheeling strangers. Their creed was his chorus:

> I wheel about an' turn about
> And do jis' so,
> And ebry time I wheel about,
> I jump Jim Crow.

Jim Crow was nothing if not the whirling dervish that has always troubled the likes of John Quincy Adams. And then, late in his career, Rice quite literally became the wheeling stranger, anew. That's when he brilliantly reworked the old Othello story of the Mediterranean basin for the much larger and even more multicultural Atlantic. He came forth with his own variant, pushing particular features found in no other version, that would destroy Brabantio's dreams even more radically than had Shakespeare's Othello. Rice performed his burlesque opera *Otello* first in 1844.

Here and Everywhere

Despite all these connections, neither T. D. Rice nor Jim Crow attacked John Quincy Adams or James Henry Hackett directly. Rather, the Jim Crow craze diffusely countered elite scorn for low publics. It fought the war of the flea and ant—biting its host here, there, and everywhere, but mounting no substantial battlement that superior forces might storm. The dramatized Jim Crow figure began having a wide impact beyond its original Gullah constellation because its popularity in the metropolis demonstrated that elites could not decree all value.

The wheeling stranger and the patriarch relate oppositionally. The patriarchy judged the mob from on high; the mob nudged their judges from below. Disdain met something like *updain* in the Jim Crow plays. Disgust encountered *upgust*, and abhorred this rough insubordination. There is not yet a settled terminology for this pattern.[15] Except that it occurred in metropolitan centers as well as rustic frontiers, this welling up against felt scorn is close to what James C. Scott has analyzed in peasant culture "infrapolitics." Scott means the "wide variety of low-profile forms of resistance that dare not speak in their own name."[16] In certain situations of the western Atlantic, this refractoriness takes on what Eric Lott terms "white ventriloquism through black art forms."[17] Lott was characterizing a period that followed 1842 and the increasingly formulaic minstrel show, so I run the risk of overstating the division between the lowest groups if I apply "white ventriloquism" to the 1830s. *Ventriloquism* grants the earliest puppeteers too much acumen, perhaps, and the puppets a passivity that the facts of the 1830s do not support. Neither in the skits nor in reality did black subjects stand still and let themselves be spoken through. Even so, *ventriloquism* memorably names the way mudsill publics activating their consciousness across the Atlantic world latched onto a version of "blackness" to speak their values.

My desire has long been to discover, steaming up from the most disdained white workers, some term of their own that displays their kinship with black charisma and recognition of the creolized culture that results from that transracial and international identification. A New York newspaper for 1833 handed me such a term in its announcement for one of Rice's earliest skits. The paper says Jim Crow, himself, called his topic nothing less than "the *Ethiopian Mobility*."[18] Indeed, in order to minimize prejudice, perhaps we should return, along with Thomas Pynchon in his novel *Mason and Dixon* (1997), to this late seventeenth-century coinage, "mobility." The term, like the crowd, then conveniently opposed the nobility, but without the cartload of negative meaning later driven on board when users shortened the word to "mob."

The emergence of the distinctive outcast voice of the Jim Crow songs and plays has had real consequence in their own era as in ours. In their day, the mobility figured out a consciousness that gradually, tentatively defined itself in relation to its opponents. The Jim Crow songs and plays show not only an emerging consciousness within the low caste, but also an awareness of the uneven capacities of the wheeling stranger and the patriarch to affect each other. The patriarch had power. The stranger had cunning. And today, their texts evince the origin of that cultural resistance which has plagued mandarin sensibilities during every successive stage of industrialism. Here is the voice of the *mobility* that mandarins shunned as the mob, socialists defined as the *lumpenproletariat,* and which remains unwarranted by any "moral economy," to use E. P. Thompson's enduring phrase.[19] Too skittish to stand and be saddled, they wheel away estranged.

The nettle in the ethic Jim Crow elaborated—he called it his "slashing"—was just this independent agency. The mobility are by condition and often by choice outside the "social dialectic of unequal mutuality" that warrants the relationships of other poor classes—farmer to mill owner, factory worker to boss—within Atlantic systems.[20] Jim Crow was a quick-quipping runaway who mocked slavery but he also pestered those who would enter into middle-class aspirations or grasp at dandiacal pretensions. Rice showed his congenial publics that images of black runaways and jitterbug dancers could figure them. His own terms were gestural—visual and musical. His mercurial canniness anathematized both the extant Atlantic systems, industrial and agricultural, factory and plantation. Both systems tried to contain Jim Crow. He burst out of both. His songs and plays demonstrated both the confinement and its bursting. They were diagnostic and prescriptive.

During the mid-nineteenth century, many Atlantic intellectuals tried to name, if not always understand, the emerging mobility. With varied insight, they attempted to place this pesky group from the outside. Theodore Parker sermonized them as "the Dangerous Classes." Marx scorned them as the "lumpenproletariat." And Melville reckoned them a "piebald parliament." Melville's coinage was an early reach toward doubleness in demotic speech that was modeled most fully in the popular theatre of his time.[21] "Piebald" was a compound pun that supplemented *crow.* The second syllable in *piebald* intensifies the first syllable's reference to *magpie*, a gregarious black-and-white scavenger in the same *corvidae* family with crows. Cultural crows, Melville was covertly announcing, were his world's unacknowledged legislators.[22]

When the curtain lifted on Rice's *Bone Squash Diavolo* as early as 1835, Rice's actors in piebald blackface graphically compacted a good bit of the doubleness, disdain, and incipient self-awareness of the mobility. Already fifteen years before Parker, Marx, and Melville, they positioned themselves on the inside, with a concerted outlook. Their first song concluded with,

> I'm de Nigger dat do de whitewashing, oh
> I'm de Nigger dat do de whitewashing, oh
> > On de scaffold I stand
> > Wid de brush in my hand
> And de genus shines out wid de slashing, oh.[23]

Sure of their situation on that ambiguous scaffold—site of painting and punishment, spectacle and structure—they point out their double genus and genius from the start: get this if nothing else. These lyrics of primary attitudes about denigrated identity circulated around the Atlantic with the people who spawned them. Today, African Caribbean musicians at home and abroad, calling their style *ragga*, invert to a positive badge the English "raggedy" translation of the German *lumpen*. Rice represented that multiplicity and menace early on, but it is telling that he never tried to alter the term already active in black folklife: Jim Crow. He tried to bring in that out caste, their moves, their codes.

That out caste has always had complex oral codes. Occasionally, as in the case of the Jim Crow song and the plays that engage it, the codes achieved a fugitive recording in performance scripts. But even these have oscillated wildly between cult favor and official scorn. The list of disdained popular culture texts begins with "Jump Jim Crow" (as early as 21 May 1830), *Oh! Hush!* (20 July 1833), and *Virginia Mummy* (22 April 1835), by Rice. It continues with Frank Chanfrau's "Mose" plays in the 1840s. It winds into the minstrel show that was already turning scabrously racist by the 1850s as it rounded the bend toward the Civil War. As early as the 1840s, however, blackface impulses were leaching into literature, as in the references to Rice's plays in George Lippard's *The Quaker City* (1844–45). Frederick Douglass's first autobiography (1845) repeats, as his own opening, that first line of the most widely reprinted "Jump Jim Crow" variant which Rice had been singing even then for almost fifteen years.

Jim Crow:

> Come listen all you galls and boys,
> I's jist from Tuckyhoe.

Douglass:

> I was born in Tuckahoe.

Hawthorne belittled Jim Crow as a gingerbread boy, easily devoured, in *The House of the Seven Gables* (1851). In *Moby-Dick*, published in that same year, Melville's Ishmael represented his voyage on the *Pequod*, quite literally, in the display type of a theatre bill. The famous shaving scene at the center of Melville's "Benito Cereno" (1855) tried to live up to the grave humor that Dan Emmett and Eph Horn had been performing on the minstrel stage for a decade and a half. This same blackface-derived scene would still be reincarnate in Charles Chesnutt's "The Doll" (1912).[24] Stowe's *Uncle Tom's Cabin* (1852), Delany's *Blake* (1861–62), and Twain's *The Adventures of Huckleberry Finn* (1884) deeply engage blackface.

Ethiopian Mobility

Especially when subordinate groups discover their identity against fear and disgust, as did the blackface public, they must define themselves in full view of their oppressors, communicate their kinship among themselves, reach out to potential sympathizers, and articulate these internal needs within the external controls all at once. They must hide in public, even while they are broadcasting themselves. Like lizards bloating their red throats in courtship rituals, alert always to blue jays hunting them from above, the predicament of the mobility staging itself is stunning, delicate, and dangerous.

The culture of the mobility always plays warily to at least two audiences. Rice's blackface plays show how a population on the lam explains itself to itself while the dominant, sedentary population commits close misunderstanding. For example, here is the *Courier & Enquirer*'s whole blurb for *Life in Philadelphia*, with their full embedding of Jim Crow's "Ethiopian Mobility":

> Jim Crow bears his blushing honors thick upon him and comes in for a Benefit tonight, giving us another novelty in his *Life in Philadelphia, or, How They Do Go On*, a farce written with great spirit, for the purpose of introducing what Jim Crow calls the Ethiopian Mobility of Philadelphia in all their glory—supper, champagne, bustle and balls. Jim Crow sustains the prominent character of a North Carolina negro undergoing his initiation into the mysteries of high life under the tutelage of Bonaparte, a Philadelphia Swell, capitally personated by Mr. Hanson. Many of the situations are strikingly ludicrous, the acting is excellent, and elicited the merriest bursts of laughter.

The middle-class *upward* mobility is already imposed on "what Jim Crow calls . . . Ethiopian Mobility." The middle-class journalist here lays his dream of joining one's tormentors right over the quite distinct ideal of *lateral sufficiency* that is in fact diagnostic of the mobility, and which Rice's character and his play are in fact promoting. Ragged Jim Crow is the character the play leads the audience to approve. The play is in fact lampooning the dandiacal pretensions of the characters who pursue champagne, bustles, and balls.

The mobility's dilemma: in order to organize its far-flung membership and recruit new adherents, it had to display figures of its condition; but to expose its values to its scorners was dangerous. The partial solution was to raise up perplexing, coded figures in ambiguous interactions that pundits might receive as images of their own hopes. That's what was happening with *Life in Philadelphia* as the *Courier & Enquirer* reported it. I do not say it was intentional, this misunderstanding, but the faux universality that middle-class analysts imposed on the phenomenon —as if to say, everyone wants to be like us—provided the mobility a chance to reflect on themselves within the dominating culture. Such misdirection requires bluff actors, however, and more discipline than any group can continually muster. Thus, lateral sufficiency within dominance has always proved a difficult margin to articulate and inhabit, much less extend. Trying to work it out gave enduring tension to Rice's plays.

GUMBO CUFF AND THE
NEW YORK DESDEMONAS

One rarely finds justifications for the mobility's cultural aesthetic because they could not stand and declare their intentions. Early on, while T. D. Rice was still learning how to play his roles, however, a New York literary magazine, the *Mirror*, stunned him with a sardonic attack on his play *Oh! Hush!*, in which Rice was playing a black man named Gumbo Cuff. "'Gumbo Cuff' is one of those finely tempered, susceptible beings," wrote the *Mirror*, "which Shakespeare, in his 'Othello' . . . must have conceived. Let no one, however, suppose that Mr. Rice has taken a hint from Shakespeare; far be it from his original genius to borrow an idea from any body; and . . . we deem it no more than justice to inform the reader, that 'Gumbo Cuff' is not founded upon Shakespeare's Othello." The writer is "Colonel" George Pope Morris, publisher and editor of the *Mirror*, minor poet and playwright. Although I have removed most of his remarks, his wordy irony remains apparent. The long review's gloved hand fisted up in the end, when Colonel Morris urged audiences to riot and run Jim Crow out of town: "We are staunch friends of *native* talent, and this must be our apology for the present notice of the opera of *Oh! Hush!* We are very sincere in wishing manager, author, actors, musicians, supernumeraries, and others engaged in its production, all the success they deserve—which is a sound and glorious pelting from the stage, to the exhilarating melody of *'Jump, Jim Crow!'*"[25]

The conclusion delivers the barb that pained Rice. Its nativism patrols the narrow corridor of what was American in the theatre. Sensing here a new claimant—arguably the very themes and distinctive voice that history would show has most rigorously probed and refracted American culture—Colonel Morris moved quickly to mow it down. Already at age twenty-five, Rice was facing boundary scourges from the new cultural machinery set up to censor acts such as his. Morris exemplifies the way gentlemen of property and standing instigated rough music that they would then blame on the mobility.[26]

In his earliest plays—*Oh! Hush!*, *Life in Philadelphia*, and *Love by the Bushel, or, Long Island Juba*—Rice confined himself to ethnographic skits showing interactions among the "Ethiopian Mobility" set in its oyster houses, street markets, and low interiors. As he piled characters and capers on these kernel scenes, it was surely the mood of the sting that Colonel Morris published in the *Mirror* that incited Rice to move beyond black ethnography, penetrate behind the lines of the dominating culture, and take on the manners of the middle class. Thus, *Bone Squash Diavolo* added to its black characters a white Yankee devil, replete with a tail. *Virginia Mummy* supplied a raft of pretentious white characters whom Rice's black figure ridiculed for being self-aggrandizing, cruel, and stupid. In these mixed plays, Rice's blackface character is an excluded and disdained foil to the failures of established sectors in society. Attacks such as Morris's spurred Rice and his public to represent their embattled positions more widely.

By the time the *Mirror* published Colonel Morris's screed, Rice had struck out on his own from the Bowery for theatres southward—Baltimore, Washington, and Charleston—all part of his scheduled circuit. He had performed *Oh! Hush!* at the Bowery for large audiences right through the last half of August and on through mid-September. A bill at the Bowery on 19 September 1833 had begun with *Othello* (James William Wallack in the lead) and concluded with *Oh! Hush!* Perhaps that juxtaposition was what roused Morris's complaint in the *Mirror.* That Rice's opera was a hit among working publics, and beyond, was certain. One feels Rice's confidence in the way the young actor talked back to Morris in a long, feisty, and telling letter he sent the *Courier & Enquirer* the following week. I give the entire letter because it is the only defense of his work I know he penned, and because it displays the pressures his work breasted:

No. 1
   To the Editor of the Courier & Enquirer.
   "Cock-a-doodle-doo!"
      Jim Crow!
   Crow Castle, October 11, 1833.

   Sir,—The conductor of the *New York Mirror* has chosen to be very angry with me for having succeeded with the audience of the Bowery Theatre. He has, more than once, threatened to launch his thunders but could not remember my name. In his last number, his recollection has returned, and he comes out with a blast—against which my unfortunate head can scarcely hope to keep any longer above water. But as even the "Poor Nigger," in our glorious country, has a right to speak for himself before a jury ere he yield up his life to the more powerful—Jim Crow, who like his *brudder* actors—if he would "Live to please, must please live"

—also begs leave, as farmer Ashifeld [sic] says,[27] to *argufy the topic*, a little, with the editor of the *Mirror*, before he acknowledges that he ought to be driven from the stage—as the gentleman so liberally desires.

I own the attempt is a very rash one, to break a lance with the *Mirror*, especially since the direction has devolved entirely upon its *military* leader —the only civil members of the firm having left the country.[28] Pardon me, Colonel of the Printing office! I really forget your name—is it Pluck? Colonel Pluck[29] is the mighty spirit which cannot forget its warlike propensities even in the pursuits of literature; but, while, like Camden,

> One hand the sword,
> And one the pen employs

ceasing to remember which is which, starts up in the midst of an essay, runs a man through with—a goose-quill! Pardon me, I implore, most fulminating of the critic tribe, if I humbly ask leave to be heard in my own defense, and venture to protest against utter damnation, even though from you!

If your mortal enmity has arisen from my having selected other papers for perusal in *Oh! Hush!* to the exclusion of the *New York Mirror*,[30] I can only excuse myself on the score of having forgot there *was* such a paper, until your artillery roused me to the recollection! I candidly own, that, neither in the song of *"Jim Crow"* nor in the Opera of *Oh! Hush!* have I aimed at so high a flight as the legitamcy [sic] of other native productions —*Brier Cliff*, the Militia Muster or the *Kentuckian*, for example.[31] I have merely sought to give a sketch of the lowest classes, something in the same style with *Tom and Jerry*,[32] so long the favorite of the stage in England as well as in America; which, I am told by those who have traveled, is itself imitated from a style of humble life drama, exceedingly popular even among the audiences more fastidious in their tastes, of other countries. I assure the public that my object in doing this, was to emulate my friend and their favorite the Colonel, and hold the Mirror up to nature;[33] and if my Mirror shows a *black face*, (charity forbid it should ever show a black heart) it must be none the less true to nature, than Dr. Meredith[34] and his "gallinippers,"[35] in a certain play which Colonel Pluck, notwithstanding his short memory, very likely may remember better and longer than anybody else ever will.

I am sorry that the niggar affectation of white manners should be so annoying to the *Mirror;* but there was a precedent for this sort of "high life below stairs" in the farce of that name, which was famous even before Colonel Pluck was ever heard of.[36] And I do not see why Colonel Pluck should be so anxious to warn the New York Desdemonas against Gumbo Cuff, by repeating to them, over and over again, that neither Gumbo Cuff nor Jim

Crow are equal to Othello; and therefore that the aforesaid Desdemonas ought to bid their husbands or their lovers to hiss, and to pelt both Gumbo and Jim off the stage; for neither Gumbo or Jim could ever aspire to rival the Colonel with the ladies,[37] although it is a poor compliment to the ladies on the Colonel's part, to suppose that they can be best satisfied in having nothing to look upon but the *Mirror*,[38] and if dandyism is rendered contemptible in their eyes by its copying the blacks, may not the copy render a service to society by inducing the ladies to discourage its original in the whites? This is the moral benefit of all caricatures, of which Gumbo Cuff puts in his claim for a share.

And so far as the negro manner and character is concerned, Colonel Pluck may be assured that the representation is as carefully studied from life as any ever brought upon the stage, even the most renowned drama of *Brier Cliff.* If he needs evidence of this, I am ready to produce it; and, before I admit that in my humble labors to amuse a public who have so kindly fostered me, I deserve to be hooted out of house and home, I will endeavor, provided Colonel Pluck desires it, to justify my Opera by a parallel with *Brier Cliff;* of which, should he wish to pursue the correspondence, I will in my next letter favor the public with a description and full history. At present, however, I have only to hope that I may not be called into the field again, for it is too much for a peaceful citizen—whose most exalted ambition is, even if he were

> De Presemdent of dis United State,
> To drink mint julop, and swing pon de gate[39]

—to expect that his unhappy little *Crow* quill can be a fair match for the tremendous *Goose*[40] quill of a gunpowder editor, and especially one of such profound politics and Quixotic daring as the poor redoubtable Colonel Pluck.

I am, Mr. Editor, with perfect veneration for yourself, and yet more for Colonel Pluck, the Ethiopian Vocalist, and severely criticized Dramatist,
  JIM CROW.

Throughout this rejoinder, Rice relates more easily with blacks than with the whites who read and write the *Mirror*—naturally enough, since whites, not blacks, are attacking him and his work. He insists he has the rights of the "Poor Nigger" to speak before a jury and employs black locutions. As Rice speaks through blacks he also claims their mudsill status for his own. He never requests nor assumes higher status than society allows its lowest figures. Grotesquerie of blacks is his vehicle, not his target, as he shows when he hopes black dandyism will "discourage its original in the whites."

Rice ridicules Morris's title and lambasts his imagery. All across the tonal spectrum, however, Rice is angry. The Colonel hid his own aggression, until the end, behind his presumption of natural rightness. But Rice unmasks this posture. He gives us a Colonel smiling to control representation. The Colonel tries to drown him, but Jim Crow remains high and dry. Knowing he is jousting on a tilted field, Rice must fight his war of the flea the only way a "Dramatist and Ethiopian Vocalist" can. His shield is hide-and-seek irony. He greets disdain with updain.

Morris's proposal of a shivaree against *Oh! Hush!* in his magazine also used *Othello* for thinking race. He showed less overt disgust toward Othello, the character, than Adams and Hackett did. But Morris shared their certainty that the play's main issues concerned Desdemona's proclivities—those "New York Desdemonas." Morris feared the Desdemonas might be more attracted to Gumbo or Jim Crow even than to Othello.

The primary service of *Othello*, as received and performed at least in the western Atlantic, was to housebreak Othello by rehearsing fantasies of his incorporation, madness, and induced suicide. Because this taming was tricky, requiring frequent reiteration, *Othello* was one of the most performed plays by the most performed playwright in America through the late eighteenth and early nineteenth centuries—and it was the most parodied.[41] By the early nineteenth century, these embodied reveries drilled into Anglo-American culture through *Othello* were institutional. To be sure, they required periodic buttressing in such statements as Adams's, Hackett's, and Morris's. But a tone of agreement saturates their remarks and constitutes the contemporary orthodoxy. What made these sentiments fantastic and necessitated their repetition was exactly the problem they figured: not everyone was invited to the table, not everyone was orthodox. Rice rubbed that nub.

When Rice's decidedly unmoored blacks twisted their way on stage with their own rough music, the artillery poseurs came out to blast away more pointedly. With Jim Crow facing them, Othello suddenly looked preferable, and the New York literary senators found new missions for their general. Therefore, throughout his career, there were reasons why Rice avoided playing *Othello*. Yet as his work matured and peaked, as the struggle he mounted to represent the mobility lost momentum, the Othello story bristled with more particular meaning for him. When Rice finally mounted his own version of the play, he brought it home, set it in the streets and slave markets of New York, had Otello speak the local dialect, changed the ending, and sowed seeds of further issue. He turned the story inside out. The Othello who conventionally ran missions for the state became the mobility's Otello. Rice mocked the conventional opera, mocked the whole mission of slaughtering outsiders to gain the favor of Brabantios. He made his streetwise Moor and New York Desdemona bring to life real problems that the ancient Othello story conventionally repressed. I shall return to this tale, much as Rice did himself, after I have tried everything else—after testing the strengths and incapacities of Jim Crow in the wide Atlantic.

CHANGE THE JOKE AND SLIP THE STEREOTYPE

> Be careful, Ginger Blue, you isn't fooled like de white folk—get up in de mornin' and wonder why dey can't find demselves.
> —Ginger Blue to himself, *Virginia Mummy*

Much recent scholarship uses minstrelsy to test theoretical suppositions about white and black identities, gendered performance, and class formation. Beyond a tendency to freeze these categories, and to assume a necessary teleology in them, a root problem in that scholarship is its lack of knowledge about the performances that instigated the blackface craze. Because none of the earliest plays was ever published as the first audiences saw it, no one has heard the "Yah! Yah!" of Jim Crow's underclass scoffing and until now no one has been able to study the whole development of blackface forms.

Dating from the early to mid-1830s, these texts constitute some of the first American working-class plays, first distinctly American plays and musicals, and first plays of crossracial identification anywhere in the Atlantic. Set and staged in frontier towns, then moving to seaboard metropoli, these plays supplanted an English farce and melodrama tradition. They stirred a lumpen vernacular with a new Black Stage English that was surely more accurate, certainly more vital and fetishized, than the extant English approximation. These plays launched all their breakthroughs off what Peter Wood has called the "kneebone bent" of African American dance gestures.[42]

Stereotypes abound in the plays. Mad Scientist, Blackey, Nigger, Rhubarb-pounder, Jackanapes, Hottentot: these slurs about roles and ethnicity in *Virginia Mummy*, alone, spatter like shards from anti-personnel bombs. That play feels like a Lenny Bruce routine arriving more than a century early. The degradations are old and deeply embedded. They were certainly thriving before Atlantic blackface began.

In these plays, both blacks and whites casually use racial epithets. Whites assume blacks are stupid, superstitious, lazy. Blacks fulfill these expectations as cover, all the while referring to whites as trash and treating them like monstrous idiots. This shock of the old holds further surprises. Stereotypes in the early blackface plays gave nuance to all sorts of interaction among poor folk. O'Leary, the Irish servant to Dr. Galen in *Virginia Mummy*, can't pronounce "rhinoceros." His fellow servant, an English painter hired to portray Galen's experimental subjects, calls O'Leary a "thick skull'd rhubarb pounder." Nevertheless, O'Leary rapidly turns the tables on the Englishman: "Get out, ye dirty rattlesnake portrait painter. You aren't fit to white-wash a parish school house fince." Here O'Leary carries the sympathy of the play and its public. The rhubarb pounder changing the portrait painter into a fence painter shows how ethnic targets have always known how to "change the joke and slip the yoke," as Ralph Ellison would memorably phrase this process. Target characters see right through the stereotyping strategies and redirect them back at the perpetrators.[43] These plays shock their audience with the alternating current that runs through stereotypes.

The plays in this volume often engage stereotypes not so much to destroy them—a hopeless task—as to laugh at their insufficiency. In limiting a complex situation to a demeaning part, a stereotype inevitably reminds its targets of the perpetrators' vulnerabilities—their need to see others in narrow falsification. Stereotypes maintain, therefore, as a kind of shadow behind their imposition, the precise dimensions that the perpetrators wish to suppress. White plantation jokes stereotype blacks as lazy and stupid. But black plantation jokes show compound opposites —the very traits the white jokes were designed to hide. In black plantation jokes, therefore, Massa is confused, ridiculous, pretentious. Likewise, in the Jim Crow plays anthologized here, white authority figures have tails, are self-regarding or preposterous poseurs. The blackface character boots the behind of authority every chance he finds—which is frequently. Thus Rice slips the yoke on the mobility by making the ostensible authorities the butt of the joke. This method suggests an independent demotic authority rising among the mobility themselves.

What shape does this recalcitrance take in the plays? From the mobility's vantage, the stereotypes in the Jim Crow plays worked against the mandarin ideology. What many commentators in the second half of the twentieth century have assumed worked to derogate blacks, in its own era actually had a more complex effect. Everyone then understood that early incarnations of blackface disrupted and interrogated elite mentalities to their detriment. Blackface confounded the elite capacity to control the mobility.

Although commonly referring to white bosses as "Massa," not one of Rice's characters is ultimately confined, defeated, or mastered. Jim Crow, Gumbo Chaff, Ginger Blue, and Bone Squash—they all outwit and supersede their white employers. In songs like "Gumbo Chaff," "Blue Tail Fly," and "Sitting On a Rail," Massa dies and goes to hell, where he belongs. "Jim Crack Corn, or The Blue Tail Fly"—which Rice and Dan Emmett both sang and which became a modern campfire singalong—is about the singer's relief that he escapes blame when his master dies in a sliding chain of Lacanian signifiers revolving around a horse's ass, a ditch, and a blue-tail'd fly:

> De poney run, he jump an' pitch,
> An tumble massa in de ditch

In "Sitting on a Rail," we find these aggressive lyrics:

> My ole Massa dead and gone
> A dose ob poison help him on
> De Debil say he funeral song.

Ginger Blue rises alive from the coffin-like sarcophagus in which he is wrapped in *Virginia Mummy*. Bone Squash outwits the devil, sends him back to the flames below, then ascends in a balloon at the end of his play, escaping all who would confine him. In *Flight to America*, Jim Crow successfully escapes enslavement on a Virginia plantation, runs off to New York, where he gives a speech at a ball celebrating the freedom of the slaves and, at play's end, sails off to England.

But bursting bondage and telling truth to power are just two parts of the relationship Jim Crow and his mates establish with the employing and entrepreneurial sectors. Also significant in these plays is the stubborn momentum of the culture they are figuring out. This momentum showed that they had their own independent culture, despite its oppositional relationship to the dominating powers. Often their stories are less about bringing down what's on high than about the persistence of disdained life following its own processes, crossing the cultural field in its own way. Even if this persistence does not result in strikes and demonstrations, does not stand up to face off against the opposition, its plain momentum demands respect.

Violent resistance to opposition is only one way an attacked culture maintains its ways. In his songs and dances, then his plays, T. D. Rice was putting his shoulder to wheels of gesture, tune, and tale that had long been looping independently. Before he shaped and transferred these matters to stages where literary editors and national politicians could see them, affiliations like those in his performances had been mining and mapping the worlds of the mobility. They had also been sapping patriarchal structures. When analysts lever up this momentum to see how it crosses other ways of being in the world, it may seem culturally and socially resistant. And it often is. Sometimes, however, people with strong leanings are simply living out patterns that preceded the contemporary controls. Then their popular ways are not so much consciously against the politics of their harriers as they are intent on fulfilling the directives that set them flowing.

Although Rice's plays notice and lambast interrace hatred, the primary opposition they express is not racial. Instead, in play after play that Rice assembled from the sources around him, he asks poor whites to align themselves with blacks against the civil sense that it was "a gross outrage" to do so. To cheer on T. D. Rice's Jim Crow was precisely to nudge along the "extravagant and wheeling stranger" who was the recurring nightmare of the patriarchy. But this time it was to applaud a ruder, more mobile incarnation than the Brabantios had feared before. That's why Brabantio's class was furious about Jim Crow and anything that so much as smelled like burnt cork.

The fragrance the early republic's elites feared was mechanics' rights. Nor was their connection either gratuitous or one-sided. It was real and understood outside their own circle. The early playbills of blackface performance insist on this specific linkage. A couple of years after he began jumping Jim Crow, for instance, T. D. Rice had boosted his repertoire with an additional song about runaway slaves. During a final performance in Louisville "before his departure for New York," as announced by a playbill, Rice would sing Extravaganzas of "Jim Crow," "So Clar de Kitchen," and the new songs "GUMBO CHAFF, What can Read, Write, and Cipher," and "MECHANICS' RIGHTS, or Six O'Clock Boys."[44] We have no lyrics for the song "Mechanics' Rights," but the words for "Gumbo Chaff"—oh, rich name!—sample the moment's insouciance:

> Now old Massa build a barn to put de fodder in,
> Dis ting and dat ting an' one ting anodder;
> Thirty ninth Decembur time come a rise ob water,
> An' it carry Massas barn much farder dan it ought to;
> Then old Massa swear he cuss an' tare his hair,
> Becase de water tuck de barn off he couldn't tell where.

> Now old Massa die on de 'lebenteenth of April,
> I put him in de troff what cotch de sugar maple,
> I digs a deep hole right out upon de level,
> An' I do believe sure enough he's gone to de debil,
> For when he live you know he light upon me so,
> But now he's gone to tote de firewood way down below.[45]

Old Massa's gone to hell, Gumbo's loose on the world, and the "six o'clock boys," those mechanics by day, are ready to join Gumbo's chaff soon as the bell strikes six. For all those mechanics, Rice was imagining, bringing into view, then dancing on, the master's grave. In the mobility's imagined afterlife, Massas saw wood for the devil while the Gumbos roam free.

It is always surprising when political affect in artful performance coincides with a public awakening to itself. Especially when there are few earlier signposts, it is difficult to represent a faction's unconscious. Nevertheless, when the coincidences do occur, publics are grateful. One way such an affect occurs is when an artist shows a new group that its individual feelings constitute an ideology. Ralph Ellison's effect in the early 1950s makes one example; many readers felt he spoke on every frequency for them. Bob Dylan's relation to disaffected people in the 1960s is a second, for he seemed to overhear an inner self they might have preferred to have. Publics developing around figures like KRS-One and Rakim made further examples in the 1990s. The effect of Jim Crow in the 1830s was more distinctive than these recent examples because, then, transracial affiliation was virtually unprecedented. Jim Crow provided the template.

All popular drama passes a censor whether or not the Lord Chamberlain, or some other local body, vets it. No popular form is deposited in the vaults of memory and frequent production if it does not vivify home truths that already lurk in an audience's consciousness. In Rice's case, factional performance was certainly not something he started out to do. He fell into his practices. It dawned gradually on Rice, his publics, and their opponents that factions were forming that needed reactions. To every phase that Rice passed through while enacting Jim Crow, there were counter- and parallel formations from opponents, audiences, theatre entrepreneurs, other performers, and journalists. Novelists, for instance, varied and improvised Rice's impulse to perform Jim Crow. They represented that fascination along a spectrum from the trivial to the monstrous. We have noted that Douglass, Hawthorne, Melville, Delany, Stowe, and Twain all used minstrel imagery. Before any such transfusion could occur, however, the figure of Jim Crow had to be discovered, translated, conveyed, conventionalized, and made popular. Jim Crow had to become a stimulus around which people in the Atlantic agreed to contend. These changes occurred in phases.

THE PHASES OF JIM CROW'S RUNAWAY STAGE

If the skin were parchment, and the blows you gave were ink
Your own handwriting would tell you what I think.
—Shakespeare's *Comedy of Errors* (3.1.13–14)

First there were Rice's apprenticeships, in New York and on frontier stages in the Gulf States and the Ohio Valley (1827–1830). He crossed into a second phase (1830–1833) when he started jumping Jim Crow, quite literally figuring Jim out. The song and dance came first, but they were too unruly for the extant repertoire of the American stage to accommodate. A third phase (1833–1836) occupied Rice while he learned to incorporate Jim Crow, bringing this essential outsider into plays of his own design. He had to make plays that would not reject, but pivot on,

Jim Crow's turbulence. These first three phases all occurred in the western Atlantic.

When Rice traveled to England in 1836, he carried Jim Crow into wider filiations that began a long fourth phase (1836–1844). During this period, he painted a portrait of Atlantic-wide working-class social relations all around the states and Great Britain (with short hops to Paris).[46] As a transnational star, he was bringing into popular view an international underclass that was increasingly aware of itself and its challenge to established power. He acted his original American plays in tandem with new Jim Crow scriptings from British playwrights. The title of the 1839 play *The Foreign Prince*, which William Leman Rede wrote for Rice, indicates some of the characteristic British interpretation. If the English were going to marry their daughters to Jim Crow, they insisted he be of African royalty, certainly not from New York's Five Points.

Now that Jim Crow had his own momentum, now that hivings off the initial figure were happening, setbacks started. During this fourth phase, conventional reaction to Jim Crow hardened. Rice's brilliant remaking of the Othello story as a musical *Otello* (1844) culminated this turmoil. *Otello* melded New York street dialect and black gesturation with the British acculturation of the alienated, foreign prince. Also during these years, circus entrepreneurs were learning to merge the newly robust racism gelling in society with some conventions from blackface performance and present them in theatres as the quite distinct minstrel show. This new form of blackface, conventionally dated as beginning during the winter of 1842, inverted Rice's positive connections to "blackness" and made them abhorrent. The richness of *Otello* might well be understood as Rice's complication of the minstrel show's commodified circus stereotypes.

During a final fifth phase (1845–1860), spent entirely in the United States, the inertia of social misreadings overcame the meaning of Jim Crow. Age and paralysis overwhelmed his nimble jumping. Rice subsided into the early stagings of *Uncle Tom's Cabin*. He was inhabiting a part Harriet Beecher Stowe had tamed from the unsettling stances he had translated into white view two decades before her novel. With his lively inventiveness now reduced, the meaning of Jim Crow passed into the hands of the very salesmen the figure initially challenged. What had been radical in Jim Crow was now warped into the Jim Crow car on the train, the Jim Crow water cooler at the bus station, Jim Crow elections and schools, the ethics of living and lynching Jim Crow. If there was any hope for the original trickster Jim Crow that Rice had transferred from African American performance, it lay now in underground transmission. It lay in gestures and impulses of a subtextual lore cycle. Rice died in 1860, age 53, his signature palsied and faint, listing his occupation on his will as "comedian."[47]

Phase One. Were You Ever Tarred and Feathered?

His earliest notices show Rice had a talent for biting beneath the skin, sometimes genially, often not. Joe Cowell recalled a time when Rice was a frontier actor in Alexander Drake's company. In Cincinnati in 1829, Drake's troupe were living rough, boiling potatoes in costume helmets, roasting coffee on the metal sheets they shook by night to produce thunder, stirring the beans with gilt daggers. After this company played *School for Scandal*, Cowell remembered how "a tall scrambling-looking man with a sepulchral falsetto voice, sung 'Giles Scroggins Ghost.'" The voice and demeanor were what jogged Cowell's memory. The year before in New York, he had seen this same scurrying fellow, then just "one of the supernumeraries," steal the show at the Park Theatre: "this man, *without a name*, was the only person the audience appeared to notice; and the next day [the principal actors] had made a formal complaint against this extemporaneous jester, and insisted on his not being again employed. His name, I found, was Rice, and not long after he 'Turn'd about and wheel'd about / And jump'd Jim Crow,' to his own profit and the wonder and delight of all admirers of intellectual agility."[48]

The young jester's "intellectual agility" gravitated mostly to farces about displacement. By accident or aggression, Rice's character appears where he should not be and is not wanted. In Mrs. Inchbald's *A Mogul's Tale*, he rides a balloon across lines of exclusion into a seraglio. As the servant Jerry in Somerset's *A Day after the Fair*, Rice did six roles of rough music that drive a stockbroker from his house, so that Jerry and his girl may occupy it.[49] He played *The Irish Tutor*, faking scholarly identity to gain access to a big house and a tutor's salary. In *The Lottery Ticket*, he played Wormwood—a clerk devoted to upsetting everyone else in the play. Mrs. Corset, a staymaker in *The Lottery Ticket*, complains to the town's lawyer that Wormwood "never really lets anyone alone."

Lawyer: Yes, he sits upon my stomach like a nightmare.

Staymaker: Then why not let him go?

Lawyer: Did you ever get a burr on your clothes?—Did you ever pop your hand into a pot of pitch;—or were you ever tarred and feathered? This fellow, Mrs. Corset, sticks to me like any of these things.

Staymaker: He is really a common nuisance; he never lets any body agree, but sets every body together by the ears.[50]

Rice was early incorporating this tar into his persona even before he smeared it on his face to become Jim Crow. This "burr on your clothes" traveled, too, beyond Rice and his era—it was diagnostic in the attitudes of the transatlantic counterculture. This traveling burr allowed the impulses that Rice pulled together to survive their later entrepreneurial corruption. This burr rode on the cuffs of those who most tried to stamp it out. It had the brilliance of weeds.

Phase Two. In Shifting Sides He Is Inexhaustible

> I'm so glad dat I'm a niggar,
> An dont you wish you was too.
> —Early published "Jim Crow" lyrics (1832)

The second phase of Rice's transformation developed in the extended Ohio valley—from Pittsburgh to St. Louis. He realized then that his improvisations on black servant roles, which were increasingly clustered around a figure he was learning to represent as "Jim Crow," could not fit into the extant drama. Traveling with Alexander Drake's and Noah Ludlow's companies, and sometimes barnstorming on his own in even smaller towns, he was undermining the limits of sedimented North American stereotypes.

As early as December 1828 in Mobile, Alabama, playbills featured Rice for his comic songs between each evening's play and farce.[51] Somewhere along the way, and certainly by 21 May 1830, in Louisville, Kentucky, the generic comic songs hatched specifically as "Jim Crow."[52] Learning to dance Jim Crow was a process, the record shows clearly. It was no sudden appropriation of a song from a single model, as contemporary journalists were soon telling it. Rice's version of Jim Crow began as interpolations that annoyed the local theatre critics even while they excited audiences. Rice soon built this figure into a character who had to stand alone because there was no place for him within the extant repertoire. A black character who could hold the stage in slave states as well as free, in Louisville and Pittsburgh at first, later in New Orleans and New York, was going to be a creature of compound identity. Rice sustained this complex by propagating verses so quickly that no one could pin a fixed reading on Jim Crow.

Rice at first played Sambo roles in diverging sorts of plays, from Frederick Reynolds's English seduction farce *Laugh While You Can* (1799) to *The Kentucky Rifle, or A Prairie Narrative*, which Drake's company was performing in 1830 when Rice first danced "Jim Crow." Further, Rice played Procles, the agent provocateur in Richard Shiel's *Damon and Pythias*. A critic for the Louisville *Public Advertiser*, writing as "Lope Tocho," objected that "Procles was rather too comic for a soldier" and sniffed that Rice thought "it necessary, to introduce *local sayings and bye words*, in order to create a laugh."[53] A week later, early October 1830, commenting on *The Padlock*, Lope Tocho observed that "Our friend Rice in *Mungo*, was all that could be wished, though, notwithstanding our former remarks relative to localities, he entered, singing a *Kentucky corn song*."[54] Later it would be the role; but at first it was the way Rice played any role that got up the nose of convention. Why was Rice deforming these stereotypes and irritating those who preferred them pat?

In Isaac Bickerstaffe's early comic opera, *The Padlock* (1768), Mungo is the black servant, one of the first blackface roles in English stage history after *Othello*. Like many of Rice's early roles, Mungo penetrates off-limit zones; he helps the young lover past the padlock to the old money-bags' young wife. Charles Dibdin, the comic opera's lyricist, acted Mungo in the original productions and his song "Dear heart! what a terrible life am I led!" indicates the tenor of the role:

> Dear Heart! what a terrible life am I led!
> A dog has better, that's shelter'd and fed;
> > Night and day 'tis the same
> > My pain is dere game;
> Me wish to de Lord me was dead.
> > Whate'er's to be done,

> Poor Blacky must run;
> Mungo here, Mungo dere,
> Mungo every where.
> Above or below,
> Sirrah, come, sirrah, go;
> Me wish to de Lord me was dead.[55]

Well beyond the theatregoing public, "Mungo here, Mungo dere, Mungo everywhere" became the saying *du jour* for mad-hatter scurrying. By countering this pathos with his own "Kentucky corn song," Rice contested the childish Black Stage English Bickerstaffe composed and Dibdin sang into currency. Rice was launching a savvier rendering of American blackness. He Kentuckified black stage diction away from Mungo's faux Caribbean. Then he displaced the pitiful mood in which Mungo's pathos nested. Jim Crow and Gumbo Chaff would proceed to amend this pitifulness that colonial playwrights had been etching into theatre-goers' consciousness.

As opposed to Mungo, Rice's Jim Crow is a free agent, proudly black, sometimes childlike but never childish, and certainly not pitiful. He outwits the powerful whites around him in order to create a blackened version of working-class melodrama, streamlined as comic burletta, seductive with songs. His audience will not identify with a white character. They will identify instead with a white man's embodied desire for blackness.

Rice's apprenticeship, as in *The Padlock*, bequeathed him plays that, at best, *pitied* black characters. This inherited repertoire stuffed the characters he cared about beneath furbelows of plotted conventions. They larded all that with vestigial roles from social classes of only the most tenuous relevance on the west side of the Atlantic, or, for that matter, in London south of the Thames. Rice responded by sidestepping the confines of this behest. He came on solo. His song and dance increasingly became standup comedy. "The Extravaganza of Jim Crow," as he billed it, hammered the quirks and mores of each town that would suffer his act. For the old conventions, he substituted what then seemed like simple blackface; he used that blackface to license himself as a fool talking truth to local power. In these extravaganzas he was explicitly furthering, but turning back on itself, Roderigo's and Brabantio's sneer: "*Extravagant . . . stranger.*" His tactic is like the revolutionary chant "Black is Beautiful" that SNCC activists shouted in 1964, and the strategy of queer theory in the 1990s.

Barring the many inklings toward his famous song and dance, the earliest performance I have located whose advertisements specify "Jim Crow" occurred on Friday evening, 21 May 1830 in Louisville.[56] That night, Sam Drake's troupe billed Rice as Sambo in an unrecovered American play called *The Kentucky Rifle, or A Prairie Narrative,* based on a story by William Leggett. That Friday and Saturday, and then on Monday, Sambo stepped forward and sang "Jim Crow." This pleased the crowd enough that on a Friday two weeks later, for his benefit performance, Rice sang "Jim Crow" in four distinct topical versions: "1) Jim Crow's Trip to the Theatre" (words by a Gentleman of this city); 2) Jim Crow's Trip to New Orleans (words by Pickiune Butler, of New Orleans); 3) Jim Crow's Trip to Washington (words by a Gentleman of Indiana); 4) Miss Dina Crow (words by a poet living in obscurity)."[57]

Rice would return to this pattern of communal production throughout his performance years. Many composed lyrics to "Jim Crow," and collaborated on the Jim Crow plays. This community was interracial, for Pickiune (a.k.a. Picayune) Butler was a black street singer in New Orleans. Rice explicitly underscores his contribution, upfront from the beginning and throughout. He will later point up his relation to Old Corn Meal, another New Orleans black songster. Despite—or perhaps because of—their electoral and cultural disfranchisement, this community is politically insistent. It sends its representative to Washington again and again: "Jim Crow's Trip to Washington" remains in Rice's bills for at least another three years.[58] Its variants, often telling Andrew Jackson how to run the country, appeared throughout the published Jim Crow broadsides. Jim Crow is already struggling with Dinah Crow in these early performances, as he will be all through the years before the Jim Crow plays acquire a firm shape.[59] Early and late, the song and dance of "Jim Crow" promulgated attitudes that shied just short of stating politics; they were "clearly meaningful yet nonpropositional."[60] This nonpropositionality in blackface performance was one feature enabling it to become a movement in popular culture. Absorbing this soft ideology, audiences were more likely to think they were developing their own politics, rather than accepting creeds dictated to them.

The Kentucky Rifle could not contain the Jim Crow figure within its Sambo stereotype. Stereotypical Sambos did not travel from New Orleans to the District of Columbia and back again, talking sass to presidents. Sambo was easygoing. He predictably observed protocols; he was settled in his character. Sambo might spat with Dinah but not fight with men, black or white. Jim Crow, however, began contentious and grew riotous; his lyrics show him fighting "white dandies," Jersey blacks, and Philadelphia Sambos. Stereotypic Sambo did not beat opponents into "a little grease spot," taunt whites for failing to be "full as black as me," nor applaud racial revolution as a "bold stroke for de niggar"—all of which Jim Crow sang in his early lyrics. Jim Crow took on the editor James Watson Webb, whose *Morning Courier and New York Enquirer* had been hostile to every hue of lower-class aggression.

Jim Crow moved like a free man, crowed like a dandy cock, enjoyed the liberty of every public conveyance from steamship to bus and train, sitting where he wished. He took occupation of the public sphere. Jim Crow addressed, even challenged, men of every rank and color. Dressed like a ragamuffin, Jim Crow behaved like a sovereign. Because he was so unstable, Jim Crow was the single figure most problematic for the lower edge of the culture to work up in plays or stories, and for the culture's richer part to fasten down in its newspapers and courts. This transgressive power of Jim Crow is what the political regime of Jim Crow laws in the South projected on all African Americans, of every class, and thus used to contain them as a category following the North's betrayal of Reconstruction.

The second phase of Rice's career lasted a year and a half, between that first jumping of 21 May 1830 and 17 December 1832, when he played *Love in a Cloud* in Boston. This is the instant when Jim Crow found a skit snugged especially for him. Rice had looked far and wide for appropriate fits. I have been able to verify at least sixty-five *different* plays in which Rice acted during this phase (that is, *not* counting the same plays titled variously). All the while audiences were encoring his dances, he could find no plays that gave good fit to his capers. These sixty-five plays run the whole gamut of the Anglo-American popular stage, from the most ephemeral of homebred pieces *(The Kentucky Rifle)* to hoariest Shakespeare, but the bulk are English farces *(Lovers' Quarrels, or—Like Master, Like Man)* and legendary history *(William Tell)*. In short, Rice worked his way through the repertoire of the day playing servants or underlings. In all, he was cheeky, a provocateur, a loose screw, a runaway. In *Julius Caesar*, Rice played the slave, Pindarus. After slaying his owner, Cassius, his last words would have been: "Far from this country Pindarus shall run, / Where never Roman shall take note of him" (5.3.49–50).

A quick catalogue of Rice's Shakespearian roles during this phase shows some of the attributes he would nab for Jim Crow. In *Lear* Rice played Oswald; in *Romeo and Juliet* he played Peter, the servant of a servant, whom the musicians scorn as "a pestilent knave" (4.5.145); he parodied Forrest's Shylock in *The Merchant of Venice*; in *Macbeth* he played Hecate, head of the witches; in *As You Like It* Rice was Touchstone; in *Catherine and Petruchio* (Garrick's adaptation of *The Taming of the Shrew*) Rice played Grumio, Petruchio's abused straight man.[61]

Between all these plays, grabbing help from collaborators across the racial spectrum, Rice was always expanding his song and dance of Jim Crow. In this early phase, he had not established the near monopoly on Jim Crow that others would later cede him. Whites like the child actor Sam Cowell and the mature George Nichols danced Jim Crow—Cowell in New Orleans, Nichols throughout the Ohio Valley.[62] Picayune Butler and a street songster called Old Corn Meal were blacks performing Jim Crow in New Orleans in these years.[63] George Nichols, Picayune Butler, and Old Corn Meal intersected in New Orleans in 1830 when Nichols was performing Jim Crow in the city with two circuses, first Bailey's and then J. Purdy Brown's. T. D. Rice also did a short stint during November 1830 in Purdy Brown's Theatre and Circus while it was competing with Alexander Drake's troupe for audiences in the Ohio Valley.[64] Thus, Brown's circus was another petri dish for the culture of Jim Crow. Certainly, this vernacular nexus documents a mutual swapping back and forth among these white and black performers of an already-growing blackface repertoire. Looking back from the vantage of his documented theatrical appearances in New Orleans, in 1835, 1836, and 1838,[65] it is evident that T. D. Rice also modeled himself on Old Corn Meal. When he performed a skit titled "Corn Meal" in New Orleans in 1836, he made the homage clear.[66]

Old Corn Meal's singing drew customers to his vendor's pushcart. There are dozens of references to him in the city papers beginning 12 May 1837 and continuing until the obituaries on 22 and 23 May 1842. These references both patronize and appreciate his talent. His song "Fresh Corn Meal" must have been a variant on the calls for "Fresh Stroh Bare" with which black vendors thrilled me still in Baltimore during the early 1960s. And Old Corn Meal also sang "My Long Tail Blue,"

"Sich a Gettin Up Stairs," and, his greatest hit, "Old Rosin the Bow."[67] All these songs were also in Rice's expanding repertoire; he would use them well in his plays.

Old Corn Meal's talent was a precursor of the instability that Richard Penniman, performing as Little Richard, exploited 120 years later in the same city with roughly the same sort of audience, at about the same point in a subsequent cycle of the same lore. That is, Old Corn Meal's voice, like Little Richard's on "Slippin' and Slidin'," was in itself free-floating and wildly indeterminant. The contemporaneous visitor Francis G. Sheridan, an English diplomat, documented Old Corn Meal's radical quaver. Sheridan described its immediacy: it begins, he wrote, "in a deep bass & at every other 3 or 4 words of his song, jumps into a falsetto of power. . . . It has precisely the same effect as one of our street duets where the Man & Boy alternately sing a line." Sheridan quickly noted, first, the English duets were not nearly so lively and, second, Old Corn Meal sang both parts himself. New Orleans' local commentators wrote that the singer could "make his voice 'wheel about and turn about' . . . from tenor to bass and from bass to falsetto" so quickly that it was best to speak about his "voices" rather than his voice.[68] This redoubling oscillation across man and boy is precisely what the white songsters were trying to live up to when they took their turns on stage and in circus rings. The newspaper writers copying the language from the chorus to "Jump Jim Crow" were also cottoning to these mutualities across modes.

Here, too, a pattern was seeded to crop repeatedly in the springs of the lore cycle. With his fame and act maturing, Rice went to New Orleans and performed a skit in February, 1836 based on Old Corn Meal's street performances. A little over a year later, on Saturday night, 13 May 1837, Old Corn Meal drove his horse cart around the fanciest stage in town, the new St. Charles Theatre. His appearance on stage integrated a louche play titled *Life in New Orleans*—the sort of drama then popular in New York and Philadelphia. These plays gussied up images of ethnicity and style for public peeking and turned their audiences into flâneurs for a night. The show was sufficiently successful to be repeated the next Tuesday, 16 May. In that second performance, Old Corn Meal's horse fell off the stage and had to be killed.[69] This disaster no way finished off Old Corn Meal's theatrical presence. A year later, the New Orleans *True American* pushed an opinion that other papers had been urging: some entrepreneur, Yankee or other, should make a fortune by putting Old Corn Meal on the stage up North and abroad. Could he go to London, sug-

gested the *True American,* "he would make a fortune and consign the
memory of Jim Crow to the tomb of all the Capulets."[70] In January 1839,
the actress Fanny Kemble described blacks dancing on her husband's
plantation, St. Simon's Island, along the south Georgia coast. I have just
"seen Jim Crow," she writes, "—the veritable James: all the contortions,
and springs, and flings, and kicks, and capers you have been beguiled into
accepting as indicative of him are spurious, faint, feeble, impotent—in a
word, pale Northern reproductions of that ineffable black conception. It
is impossible for words to describe the things these people did with their
bodies."[71]

These remarks early lock in a fundamental (if spurious) authenticity
of black folk performance that passes along parallel to white "contortions." This lock occurs even as Old Corn Meal is contradicting her assertion of an authentic purity by copying Rice's "Sich a Gittin' Up Stairs"
and even as Kemble is almost simultaneously noting that her black servants are experts at "transparent plagiarism" of "Scotch or Irish airs."[72]
Did she imagine—do we think—these plagiarized airs remained unab-
sorbed on either side?

Kemble's dismissal of imitative "springs, and flings, and kicks, and capers" and her plumping for the "original" makes one long to know what
this dance that caught fire around the Atlantic basin was really like. The
fullest description I have found is asynchronous because it comes from
County Cork a few years later, during what I am calling the fourth phase
of the development of Jim Crow. Nevertheless, because Rice moved from
one phase to the next not by changing or shucking his aspects, but by
compounding them, I believe the following description inventories the
transactions that characterized early phases of Jim Crow's development:

This [Jim Crow] part is comic, and without escaping the vulgar, comes
close to the idiotic. [Rice] personated the mixed cunning and stupidity of
an American nigger, and though nauseous the character of human being
may be when degraded to the caste of a *filthy fool,* still James Crow miti-
gates your abhorrence by many touches of low and amiable pleasantries.
The song from which he derives his name and celebrity is paltry and vulgar—the air brief and pretty; but it has a feature that belongs to few songs
—it is mostly made up of dancing. Half of each verse is chorus, and then
all the chorus motion—so that it is of compound and really complex character. Mr. Crow's agility in describing the evolutions that the words en-
join—for he addresses himself in the imperative mood "Jump Jim Crow,"
—is truly magnificent. He has all the velocity of a dancing master, with

the quaint capers of a cleave-boy—the bewitching grace of Douvernay, in partnership with the sylph-like movements of Taglioni. He varies his jumpings to an infinite extent, starting with different steps, and terminating with different positions each verse. Then there are eight verses to the song, and it is encored six times; which draws deeply upon Mr. Crow's ingenuity to vary the pantomime, and re-model the extravagance of this grotesque transaction. And so he does; for each bound he gives is other than the last, which proves that motion is commensurate with space, and of course illimitable. But Mr. Crow sings different songs, and tickles the upper gallery with similar effect in each. This establishes his flexibility, and satiates the gluttonous cravings of a mob, who are sure to gormandize every fun in a new form.

The words Jim Crow are a nom de guerre—the real name of the performer is D. T. Rice [sic]. In person he is good looking, but on the stage he is lame . . . and observe, nature unkindly afflicts born fools with some co-operative deformity. [I]n language he is obscure, ridiculous, yet cunning; in antics he is frisky—in grimace frightful, and *in changing positions or shifting sides he is inexhaustible*, endless, marvellous [sic], wonderful.[73]

Jim Crow's tireless jiggling inspired the reviewer's own reversals; irony permeated early nineteenth-century journalism, but Jim Crow's conflicting affects roused more than usual doses of sardonic description. The whiplash tone here mirrored contrarieties in its subject and well shows Rice's struggle to translate lumpen blackness into the grammar of European-derived roles. He "shifted sides" from Sambo and Mungo to Touchstone and Grumio, Gumbo Chaff to Hecate, Ginger Blue to Wormwood, adding vignettes and tones from street life, until the parts so intercut and mulched each other that they generated new contexts: "fun in a new form" for the mobility to "gormandize."

First "Jump Jim Crow" expanded to epic lengths, and he sang the song as a skit, an "extravaganza." In Baltimore, at his own benefit during the fall of 1832, he performed "'Jim Crow' in all his varieties[:] Description of Baltimore—Trip to Centre Market—Peep at the Play—Discovery in the Almanac—Glance at Mrs. Trollope—Life in Kentucky." As he had upon leaving the frontier, he also sang that night "the Extravaganzas 'Gumbo Chaff' and 'Clar De Kitchen.' " Another performer sang "the celebrated song called the '*Shamrock*,' written by Mr. Rice, and recently sung in Philadelphia before 2,000 patriotic Irishmen." Yet another player sang "an entire new Song, written expressly for the occasion by Mr. Rice, called the '*Baltimore Railroad*.' "[74] At the Warren Street Theatre in Boston that December, Rice sang "*Jim Crow* (with a variety of new versions: Farewell to Boston, Science of Jim Crow, Stroll on Bunker Hill, Hit at Mrs. Trollope, Deeds of Washington, Description of Boston, Peep in de Almanac, View at de Nullifiers, A Crack at Hagar," and more, as well as "Clar de Kitchen, Or, Old Verginy Neber Tire."[75] These songs were spinning out of him like fireworks from a Catherine wheel, and they were progressing toward scripts.

Rice was now a new sort of star. Like Edwin Forrest, he was an American within a system that primarily featured English players, Italian acrobats and singers, or French novelties. Beyond Forrest, Rice was working Atlantic gestures and tunes rather than Roman history *(Damon and Pythias)*, tragedy (Lear and Shylock), or indigenous others *(Metamora)*. Forrest seems to have been sympathetic to roles of dark others, from Cuffee in Sol Smith's *The Tailor in Distress* to Metamora. But he presented them as exotics. Rice was bringing whites to the black figure and showing how blackness figured them out as a new public. Rice was headlining all over the country, including the large Eastern theatres from Charleston to Boston. More important, he often squeezed encored turns between the conventional plays, showing their alternative literally from within their midst. He was in the theatre, drawing on its resources, even as he pointed beyond its achievements to a lateral sufficiency not yet exacted.

This second phase climaxed when Rice realized a limit of his fad. This limit was not a loss of momentum, for audiences were, if anything, ever thirstier for Crow quips and gestures. Rather, the climax came from the separation that middle-class commentators were trying to enforce, especially in those apparently sympathetic—but deeply aggressive— remarks insisting authenticity lay elsewhere, in Old Corn Meal's songs or the "veritable" antics of Pierce Butler's slaves that Fanny Kemble admired. Rice needed protective context for his act, a shell for his kernel. He had to show what sort of integration was possible. If his regional fad was to consolidate a wider movement, Rice needed to articulate his gestures within theatrical conventions.

Phase Three. The Words "Jim Crow" Are a Nom de Guerre

Rice rapidly began to construct plays that could reincorporate what the Cork journalist had called a "filthy fool" and scorned as a separate caste. Rice was licensing that fool, bringing outcasts under cover. He was giving the fool protection by putting him into sociable relation with others. This reapprenticeship was on different terms than when the Park Theatre in New York banished Rice for stealing scenes. Now instead of punishing his adventitious quirks, the new demand was that he fulfill them.

This third period in the life history of Jim Crow plays commenced in late 1832. That's when Rice performed a play rudimentary as a potato with the leaf mold still clinging to its thin skin. In its prehistory, this play had several names. At first, 17 December 1832, in Boston, he called it *Love in a Cloud, or, The Misty Lovers.* When he brought it to New York early the next year, it became *Long Island Juba, or Love by the Bushel.* The "cloud" in the first title referred to the skit's climactic plot turn and racial inversion. Rice's character, whom he played eventually under the name of Gumbo Cuff or Gumbo Chaff—is hiding in the flour cupboard from Sambo Johnson, Esq., a second suitor of Dinah Rose, "the Prima Donna." When Sambo moves to kiss Dinah Rose, Gumbo Cuff bursts irate from the cupboard to fight his competitor. His revelation upsets the flour bin and all the players dust one another in whitening puffs—returning them to the "misty" white condition of most audience members. "Long Island Juba," in the second title, tagged the black dancers who crossed the East River from Brooklyn to Manhattan's Catherine Market to dance for money and eels in the challenge dances and cutting contests that Rice had observed as a boy. The subtitle, "Love by the Bushel," referred to the setting—an oyster cellar furnished with bushels of oysters.[76]

Over the next seven months these rude trials coalesced into *Oh! Hush!,* first performed at Francis Wemyss's Walnut Street Theatre in Philadelphia, 20 July 1833.[77] This variant of Rice's first play was the one Colonel Morris attacked that autumn in his New York *Mirror.* The core of *Oh! Hush!,* as of each earlier variant, was the blackface song "Coal Black Rose," which George Washington Dixon made popular on the minor New York stages and printed as early as 1828. In the fall of 1829, while Rice was barnstorming western and southern hinterlands, Dixon remained in the metropolis extending the song at the Chatham Theatre. When Dixon named Rose's predicaments in the interlude he called *Love in a Cloud,* he apparently established the convention of the blackface wench: male actors representing black women in drag.[78] Especially since white actresses played white female parts, this role doubly degraded black women.

The black wench did not, however, derive from *Love in a Cloud* (or *Oh! Hush!*, which it became), but from W. T. Moncrieff's stage adaptations of the black club scenes in the London play *Tom and Jerry*. Moncrieff's stage directions specified that white male actors would cross-dress to play the roles of the fast black women Sally and Flashy Nance. Dixon followed that precedent, directing that coal-black Rose, but not the white women in his play, would be in drag. Rice followed these protocols only in *Oh! Hush!* When Rice occasionally included drag roles in subsequent plays, they opposed the conventions of *Tom and Jerry* and of Dixon's example. For instance, Jim Crow dresses as a woman to obtain information in *Flight to America;* and the character Pippin in *Yankee Notes for English Circulation* also goes into drag for similar reasons. In both cases the point is neither to mock gender nor to add coarseness to a despised character.[79]

Long before Rice was in a position to put on the play, Dixon had turned the love contest between two black workers for their beloved Rose into an imitation of white chicanery. Still revolving it around the cupboard-bursting scenes that the song "Coal Black Rose" established, Dixon now called the play *The Duel or Coal Black Rose.* In this version, he outnumbered Rose and her two black suitors with an additional seven white characters.[80] These several new layers of nonsense muffled the black allure of the play and demonstrated that blackface remained subsidiary to shock, which was Dixon's speciality. In his scrapbook of the Philadelphia theatre, Charles Durang delivers a telling anecdote regarding Dixon's dependence on outrage. Dixon "made people laugh," Durang reports, "even in the cholera panic, in reading the report of cases and deaths, as reported from the Health Office daily from the railing of the Independence Square. Crowds used to assemble every morning to listen to George Washington Dixon's cholera bulletin, and his amusing commentaries thereon."[81]

Even though, as a minor member of his troupe, Rice was not yet able to produce the play, he was singing "Coal Black Rose" as an entr'acte at least as early as 9 April 1830, a month before "Jump Jim Crow" was named in a playbill.[82] But when he started pushing the skit toward *Oh! Hush!*, it roused rather different class and race politics than Dixon projected. In all his versions of *Oh! Hush!*, as with the other plays Rice performed in this his most productive phase, Rice focused on blacks. Whites were always marginal in Rice's plays, particularly so in these stateside early plays. There were real reasons why Rice rather than Dixon incensed Colonel Morris. Laughing at cholera epidemics was one thing; pushing whites to the margin while centering black raggedness was quite another.

Of all his plays, Rice remained least committed to *Oh! Hush!* Yes, *Oh! Hush!* clearly confronted and vanquished the stereotype of Sambo. Dixon had played Sambo when he did the play, but Rice played his opponent Gumbo Cuff, who raises his hands in victory as the curtain comes down. Despite beating Sambo, however, their fight shows conflict within a brotherhood that Rice wants to champion, not mock, and *Oh! Hush!* does not challenge whites. In Rice's version the sole white character, the watchman, was often a disembodied voice off stage. Thus, *Oh! Hush!* is different from all of Rice's other blackface plays in which one way or another blacks overcome whites. *Oh! Hush!* amounts to performed ethnography, perhaps pulled together by Philip S. White, a writer who became better known for his temperance tract *The War of Four Thousand Years.*[83] The play's appeal stems from its olio of songs—scenes 2 and 3 are almost entirely sung—and its slapstick: Cuff falls in the flour trying to shoot Sambo; Rose slams Cuff with her frying pan; and Cuff knocks out Sambo with his fiddle.

These early attempts to build plays that would protect the Jim Crow role did not come forth immediately or immaculately. Like the song and dance, they were an uneven, corporate effort. Each play in Rice's initial trio jettisoned false starts, dubious jests, and flat material for stinging dramatic bricolage. Each of Rice's American plays is (as his character's name came to indicate here) a *gumbo*—an octopus's feast. Gumbo Cuff nabbed lines and scenes here and there wherever he could find them, from lithographs, headlines, quackery (men on the moon and mummy revivification), and such pleasures of the moment as ballooning and spectacles (the Indian chief Black Hawk's and President Jackson's visits to town), all stirred together with the turns of black dance, theatrical allusion, and rave phrasing:

> De Kentucky niggas dey libs on mush,
> But de Philadelphia niggas, dey say "Oh, Hush!"
> So I wheel about, &c.[84]

Rice chocked codes so hyperbolically into these plays that they still retain cagey evocations. Changing the name of Dixon's play from *Love in a Cloud* to his own *Oh! Hush!* altered the emphasis from helpless subjects to charismatic recalcitrance. Such small changes sedimented during their multiple performances while these plays were in constant development, improvised over a period of years. Especially mercurial during this early phase, Rice was engaging in guerrilla theatre designed to hit and run. He disarmed with laughter. Because he was a target, Rice stayed in extravagant, wheeling motion. Correctly enough, I think, people of his era took his dodginess as aggression.

→←

Rice's next two plays turned wry on social hierarchies, black as well as white, by inserting Jim Crow's ambition into further tight nooks, then raising the pressure. The result was that the low character remained the center of interest, relying on his wiles, as others tried to clamp him down. Since the mobility had no defense in these scenes except wit, everybody up and down the social scale had at Jim Crow, and he at them. Think of roadrunner cartoons set not in the wild but in the close laboratories of mad scientists: that's the volatile scene of these burlesques. These next two plays, *Virginia Mummy* and *Bone Squash Diavolo*, along with the later *Otello*, are of his extant plays the ones that Rice himself most created.

However funny *Oh! Hush!* was in performance, that skit lacked heft. Thus it is significant that *Virginia Mummy* and *Bone Squash Diavolo* delivered the "intellectual agility" that Joe Cowell had discerned in the frontier apprentice. The anonymous author of the prose piece "Life of Jim Crow" correctly termed these plays "informances." Both punned language and ideas. Both informed the public they culled. In sporting with form, *Bone Squash Diavolo* went further than *Virginia Mummy*, but both turned hard away from the simple riff that *Oh! Hush!* had preserved. In these two plays, T. D. Rice nestled Jim Crow's needling genus/genius under protective cover.

Virginia Mummy opened first in Mobile, Alabama, on 22 April 1835, for Noah Ludlow's benefit.[85] In this spot of unlikely nurture, none of the name players in town appeared with Rice; his ten other cast members were spouses to the leading players mingling with the company's walking men and women. Despite this humble beginning, *Virginia Mummy* became a permanent part of Rice's repertoire and a long-lasting play past mid-century. Rice took it to London and around Britain during his first two European visits and he played it continually when he returned to the States. This was Rice's play that other actors most appropriated. The Christy Minstrels and the famous black actor Ira Aldridge both performed elaborate versions in the 1850s—the Christy troupe chiefly in New York City, Aldridge throughout England, often on the same bill with *Othello*. *Virginia Mummy* was still in regular production in Philadelphia in 1864. And Charles White published his two versions more than a decade later.[86]

The immediate theatrical model for *Virginia Mummy* was William Bayle Bernard's *The Mummy* (1833), a soon-forgotten play for the Falstaffian actor John Reeve in London's Adelphi company: a rejected suitor desires access to the cruel and greedy guardian's house so he can court a willing ward; the young suitor uses the object of greed to enter the guardian's domain; then the lovers sport. In *Virginia Mummy*, a scientist, Dr. Galen, bans a young soldier, Captain Rifle, from courting the scientist's ward. When Rifle sees Galen's newspaper advertisement for a mummy, the soldier hires a voluble black hotel waiter, Ginger Blue, to hold his tongue and dress as the decoy. Rifle masquerades as the mummy's Egyptian owner: in that way they penetrate the household so that Rifle can court young Lucy, the ward. Rifle and Lucy immediately cavort offstage, leaving Ginger Blue centered on stage with his multiple masks and disguises to adopt, adapt, and shuck as necessary. The differences between *Virginia Mummy* and *The Mummy*, then, stemmed from Ginger Blue's blackness: his sly assessments of leverage, nimble defenses, and winning aggressions.

It was as rare in the 1830s as it is now for a performance to stage a genuinely "illustrious stranger." That term was what Galen called Ginger Blue but, as usual, Galen's double-speak was inadvert. Ginger was really strange to Galen and he might have been illustrious, too, if only Galen might have seen him as he was. But Galen did not, and neither could the contemporary critics. Galen and the commentators classified Ginger Blue as a freak outside the history of the theatre when Rice was insisting, to the contrary, that the officious world was anomalous, and his blackened world was everyday sense:

> *Galen:* There you are, illustrious stranger, cold and silent as a block of
> marble.
>
> *Ginger:* Why, I'm sweating like a race horse. . . .
>
> *Galen:* Could you but speak, what scenes you would relate about your

ancestors, and wonders would you tell to this world, what happened in yours!

Ginger: I'd tell you who eat up your breakfast.

Ginger's public hears him well, but Galen and others in the enclosing
dominant world experience him as dumb. These plays had radically uneven effects in the publics that paid them attention.

Rice also mined extra-theatrical lore in *Virginia Mummy*. A fascination with mummies had seeped into deep strata of British and American
culture. The night that Rice started jumping Jim Crow at the Bowery
Theatre, and continuing throughout his run, Peale's Museum in New
York advertised in the morning papers, just below the theatre ads: "The
Egyptian Mummy, which was received direct from Thebes, is one of
the greatest curiosities of antiquity." All over America, contemporary
crowds came to these static exhibits.[87] Even more dramatic were the
unwindings of mummies in public by men of science wielding scalpels on
stages for large audiences. Rice engaged the meaning of these spectacles.
He directed attention to the black victim who came to life through no
fault of the operator—but rather to spite the professional seemingly in
charge.

Dr. Thomas Pettigrew, who later vaccinated Queen Victoria, made a
celebrity practice of "unwrapping Egyptian mummies in public before
large and appreciative audiences. His methods were far from scientific.
As he himself records of a mummy unwrapped on 6 April 1833: 'It was a
task of no little difficulty and required considerable force to separate the
layers of bandages from the body; levers were absolutely necessary.'"[88]
Nearly all the comic business in *Virginia Mummy* comments on wacky
science and quack orientalism—from the admonishing and swaddling of
Ginger's "Wirginian" traits, right up to his turbulent disclosure, after
all, as "the nigger that lives at the hotel."

By making the mummy a black character, Rice harnessed a double
meaning. "'Mummify,'" writes the British Museum's mummy curator,
"comes from the Arabic word *mummiya* meaning bitumen or pitch, and
arose from a misunderstanding; badly embalmed bodies of the Late period (after 600 BC) were filled with molten resin . . . their blackened and
brittle appearance . . . suggested that they had been dipped in bitumen."[89]
Thus, mummies looked like characters daubed in burnt cork and like
characters smeared with tar. Rice saw that the fascination with mummies

was a polite displacement of an ongoing obsession to plumb and punish black strangers. Rice also connected this to the ancient practice of dressing mummies. In the final process of mummification "the whole body was coated with molten resin to toughen it and render it waterproof. But before the bandaging began the last cosmetic touches were applied . . . Often the whole body was painted, with red ochre in the case of male mummies, yellow for females."[90] When Rice dressed himself as the black victim, Ginger Blue, the practice ratcheted up several notches of tension.

What neither Rifle nor Ginger know at the outset, while outside, is that Galen has invented what he fondly believes is "the elixir to make a marble statue speak." Making the stone past speak, imagining how it will speak and who will hear, and how the past can be figured out and by whom—these matters were of real moment in the world Galen thought was monocultural. The monumental past hides its secrets from what Galen considers "this degenerate race of mankind." Never mind that he believes King Crusoe was a Norwegian who discovered America. Still Galen wants to transmit his fuzzy truth to new generations.

Throughout *Virginia Mummy*, the white and ridiculously authoritative characters assume they can frame, paint, curate, and sample a steady reality. Ginger Blue consistently slips out of and mocks this confidence. Rifle acts as a painter to falsify Ginger's reality; Ginger asks, quite revealingly, "is you gwan to paint me . . . like a sign?" Because Rifle paints him over as a piece of desirable history, Ginger can penetrate Galen's laboratory. Galen then hires Charles as a further painter to document Ginger in the manner of the rest of the scientist's natural history displays. Following these successive representations of Ginger, Galen calls in a schoolmaster to narrate and interpret the mummy's story once he "wakes" and starts speaking dead languages. These competing translators and painters are re-presenting an actor whose blackface and pre-painted layers already call obvious attention to their theatricality.

Fully developed in Rice's theatrics is his awareness that symbols convey different meanings to different audiences and the impossibility of prescribing their meaning. A sign points to an open possibility, but a mummy is apparently contained. The point of the play is that what was thought mummified is alive and kicking. Ginger Blue copiously refuels. He kicks, bites, butts, entraps, and sends howling those who mistreat him. As in the world upside down, marginal Ginger commands center stage. This mummy certainly comes alive, but neither in the sense that

Egyptians embalmed or that Galen intended. Instead, what Rice resurrects here is changed and meaningful to the present: a sign after all.

Virginia Mummy goes so far over the top mincing secure representation that ridiculed convention is a core theme. By extending Ginger's gambols, the Christy Minstrels pushed these ideas even further when they adapted them in the 1850s. In their version, the portrait painter leaves the stage for a moment; Ginger says, "dat paintin' feller wants an expression—I'll gib him an expression." Holding the frame on its easel from behind, Ginger jams his face through the painting's center. The painter returns thinking he can touch up the canvas without looking at its "ugly" subject. He dabs at what he thinks is the portrait, but daubs instead Ginger's severally-layered masks. After a while *"Ginger makes faces at him"* and scares the painter, who runs around the stage screaming, Ginger following him until the painter faints. Ginger covers him with the canvas and returns to his box. Upon waking, the painter tells the scientist he was scared stiff by "a moving as well as a striking" image.

Like Jim Crow jumping and wheeling, like Gumbo Chaff lighting out for New Orleans, like Old Corn Meal's radically oscillating vocal register, Ginger's jumping in and out of the box models all the subsequent frame-bursting images of blackface performance. The Christys' decision to have Ginger bust through the surface and terrify his painter was, from angle one, a crazy implausibility feasible only in farce; from angle two, a keen culmination of the play's logic. From angle three, Ginger's erupting from the frame enacts what is challenging about this new popular culture. Ginger Blue's blackface came right out of the frame, moving and striking especially those dabsters who supposed they had it pat. The reality Rice projects is refractory and resourceful, disenfranchised but not powerless. Neither the conventions of the past nor preposterous mad science will tease out Ginger's liveliness. Lumpen energy is practiced at making its way across the tilted field of domestic control.

Jim Crow performances organized a new public surprisingly wider than many had realized, but it was not all-inclusive. Jim Crow had edges. The figure continued to anger those whose values he did not represent. Putting Jim Crow in plays made his talismans penetrate many places that had locked them out, but they could not enter everywhere. Jim Crow, like crows before him, was a black bird and more than a bird. He was a way of forced entry and destruction, a tool of stealth: "Well, I'll break in," says Antipholus of Ephesus in Shakespeare's *Comedy of Errors*, "go borrow me a crow" (3.1.80).

Quite overt violence often met Jim Crow's penetrations. To have his way with the illustrious stranger, Galen brings knives, saws, augurs, and gimlets to open arteries, bore a hole in the mummy's head, or sew up his mouth and lance him in the back of his neck (scene 4). Dr. Galen's theatrical preparations echo the concomitant spectacles of Dr. Pettigrew and his forceful openings of mummies. Readying to cut Ginger-as-the-mummy open, Galen treats him as a block of marble. The attitude toward this stranger is different from what greeted his predecessors. Not even Brabantio was so fatuous as to imagine a stranger still and cold. The Renaissance patriarchy employed Othello's vitality to fight Turks. Galen imagines this illustration of the past will sit still and talk of Solomon and Sheba.

Not only drawing on mummy spectacles in its own era, *Virginia Mummy* also weirdly prefigures future mummy display. Once Ginger is swaddled, painted, and cooped in his coffin-like sepulcher (from which he will arise), once Rifle has used Ginger to crowbar into Galen's house, then further violence plays out, as surely as tar babies pull fools into their traps. Galen's servants all want to snitch literal pieces of the action. Susan checks Ginger Blue's temperature by sticking her finger in his mouth; Ginger bites her. O'Leary tries to cut off Ginger's toe to send to Mrs. O'Leary in Ireland; Ginger kicks O'Leary over; and O'Leary runs off, shouting "I'm kilt! I'm kilt by a dead man." Then Charles tries to cut off the mummy's finger; Ginger head-butts him. These capers are prodigal even for farce.

But life imitates farce. The British Museum later named its most famous mummy "Ginger," purportedly after its color. But anyone knowing Ginger Blue's fame in London must suspect he is the eponymous figure. Unlike Ginger Blue, who proved able to protect himself, the Great Russell Street Ginger suffered grotesquely: "the top joint of one of his forefingers . . . mysteriously vanished from the British Museum over a weekend in March 1900, within twenty-four hours of the body first being unpacked."[91]

Ginger Blue's meaning was likely to disappear, too. The more confinement the meaning suffers, the more vulnerable it is. Ginger could jump in and out of his box, but he was still stuck in the house of received form. The large point of *Virginia Mummy* is its transgressive entry into places and consciousness where such blackened material had not gone before. Ginger sasses authorities and holds the attention of the audience. He shoulders aside Rifle, literally displacing him into courting trivialities, while Ginger gorges sugar and the public gorges on him. Rifle engages Lucy; Ginger engages history and the arts and sciences of representation.

When all is said and applauded, however, *Virginia Mummy* still sputters out in the resolutions of farce.[92] Rifle snags the girl, and she him; Galen is chastened but free to mount more foolishness in the future; and Ginger returns to the hotel. His victory? He understands and dramatically displays how citizens, like servants, are made into cartoons: "ready dried." He has shown how to recognize and plunder those stereotypes: he can "sarbe himself." He has centered the stereotype, making it the subject. His defeat? Claim what we will about *Virginia Mummy*, there is still a formal deference at its end to the way things work.

→←

I stand on two corners at once, and a little round into Broadway.
—Bone Squash, to himself

No deference to the way things work remains at the end of *Bone Squash Diavolo*, Rice's next play. It is radical work that returns as in *Oh! Hush!* to an almost wholly blackened cast. Its one white character is a devil. *Bone Squash Diavolo* avoids most of the dubious limitations of *Oh! Hush!* by building on the enviable charisma of the central black protagonist. Bone Squash is a chimney sweep whose name suggests his combinations. He will be hard and soft, a sentimental rake along the same lines as the legendary English dandy the pronunciation of his name echoes and mocks: Beau Nash.

Unlike the other two plays founding Rice's theatrical fame, the gestation of *Bone Squash Diavolo* is precisely recoverable. Its rhizomes extend toward earlier plays, now lost, that had grown toward it—*Life in Philadelphia* (1833), *Where's My Head* (1834), and *Discoveries in the Moon, or, Herschel out Herscheled* (1835).[93] Funneling these three plays together into *Bone Squash Diavolo* gave it exceptional saturation.

The specific changes leading up to *Bone Squash Diavolo* occurred enough in public that we can still recover their evidence. These changes constituted a hinge for Rice and the public he was forming as it formed him. Elite disdain continued—expressed all the more bitterly now that everyone could see how Jim Crow danced out welling public moods. To support him now, Rice was able to marshal verifiable actors, producers, and writers, whose names are on record. Particularly important to him were emotional reinforcements from Francis Wemyss, a producer in Philadelphia and Pittsburgh. Wemyss was an important instigator for each of the three plays Rice consolidated in this phase of his career. To Wemyss's American Theatre on Walnut Street, Rice had brought not only his increasingly rabid social commentaries, biting all sides, embedded in the songs of Jim Crow, but also *Oh! Hush!* (as we have seen) and *Virginia Mummy.*[94]

Although significant traces of earlier plays remain in *Bone Squash Diavolo*, it was born during the economically sound summer of 1835 in Philadelphia, not yet sliding toward the 1837 recession. Throughout the country, Rice was the hot ticket. Whigs were attacking him. He troubled literary Young Americans in New York. Although they would later rue their enthusiasms, egalitarian poseurs in the Democratic papers were backing him. Quite beyond his motley crew, Jim Crow excitement was gathering its own momentum, and these pressures were visibly emboldening Rice's performances. Those are some of the reasons James Rush indulged in an angry, private screed against practices at the American Theatre the moment Rice arrived that summer.

James Rush was a doctor, son of the esteemed physician Benjamin Rush. Socialite and collector, the younger Rush wrote a treatise on the voice, and was a patron of the Library Company of Philadelphia. On the back of a theatre bill for the Walnut Street Theatre for 24 June 1835, Rush scrawled a long comment. The front of the bill marks a significant turn: Dummy Allen's benefit performance as he bid farewell to the stage forever. And the bill also proudly announces that Jim Crow Rice is engaged to appear. Rush's own handwriting on the bill's back shows elite frustration biting its tongue as it witnessed the demotic wave cresting. Rush holds his nose while he records his anger for "posterity":

Preserved as a specimen of the elevated condition of the Philadelphian drama in the year 1835. This theatre is situated at the North East corner of Walnut × Ninth Street, is managed by Weemys,[95] an Englishman who hates every thing American, and yet puffs his theatre as the *Patriotic House of the City*.

The business tells two things. One, his knavish good will to the people of the United States, & the other the state of taste in the City of Philadelphia—for this was the second theatre in the Town and the one which pretended to patronize American genius, so that if posterity will take the Bill on the other side of this leaf as a specimen of what American Genius employed itself upon, in the year 1835 it will not say much for the *National*, of taste, whatever it may conclude the manner of it was. This theatre[,] however though[t] the *patron-boards* of American genius, was not the *Fashion* in Philade[lphia].

    James Rush

    June 24, 1835

    This bill being this day thrown in at my office door, No. 179 Chesnut Street.[96]

This bill and Rush's comments on it nicely token the hardening attitudes now inverting each other.

Here was a passing moment quite changed from Colonel Morris's public attack on *Oh! Hush!* not two years earlier in the New York *Mirror.* The desire of James Rush to express attitudes he does not print might be merely personal. It might betoken a Philadelphia reserve. His self-censored frustration might also reflect Rush's assessment that the patriarchy must now wait out these prevailing belches in American theatrical taste. For all his private confidence that his "Fashion" would ultimately prevail, in 1835 Rush shows that what Wemyss provoked at the theatre was in command. This clout was new.

While they were playing *Discoveries in the Moon* in early September 1835, Rice and the actors at the American Theatre, Walnut Street, were assembling and rehearsing another play far more complex than anything else in his stock. Bills first announced "a petite opera of *Bone Squash Diavolo*," then it grew to "The Grand Opera in Two Acts" when the paper and playbills apologized that *Bone* would not "be played until Mr. Rice returns from Boston." This deferral on 12 September was the result of a letter Rice ruefully dashed to Wemyss the day before: "I regret sincerely that a combination of circumstances render the representation of my new opera tomorrow night an impossibility. We have to sing nearly fifty songs and choruses, all in a very imperfect state, at present, and in fact, I myself am not proficient . . . I have no fires, no rockets, and various other properties necessary for the last scene."[97] *Bone Squash Diavolo* therefore was evidently first produced at the Warren Theatre on 25 September 1835.[98] Rice then played Bone Squash at the Bowery Theatre in New York for the month beginning on 14 October before bringing the play home to the Walnut Theatre in Philadelphia for the week beginning 1 December.[99]

Any character named Bone is likely to be hounded; certainly women, cardsharps, and a Yankee worry this Bone. Friends of both sexes target him and so does the devil. The Faustian element in *Bone Squash Diavolo* simmered long before it crystallized in the play developed at the Walnut Theatre late in the summer of 1835. A protoplay performed under the title of *Life in Philadelphia* two years before had Rice playing not Bone but Hector Skere Debil.[100]

Another mutual element that *Life in Philadelphia* and *Bone Squash Diavolo* shared is a scene that descends verbatim from a set of drawings by Edward Williams Clay, themselves titled *Life in Philadelphia*.[101] While visiting in England, Clay had recently drawn a series of prints illustrating mostly black flâneurs in two- and three-person relationships parading outrageous class and gender markers. Issued separately between 1828 and 1830 in both London and Philadelphia, these came to be known as *Life in Philadelphia* and moved around the Atlantic world on cartes de visite, frameable prints, and stationery. "Dead Cut" (see Figure 2) was one among nine images that *The New Comic Annual* reprinted as illustra-

Figure 2. "A Dead Cut," *from the series* Life in Philadelphia, *by Edward Williams Clay. Courtesy of The Library Company of Philadelphia.*

tions in a narrative composed anonymously to articulate their sentiments. The agitated form of *Bone Squash Diavolo* blasts this inherited
story of slack, bemused comfort.[102]

"Dead Cut" shows a bootblack addressing a couple of dandy blacks,
captioned: "You must be mistaking in de person black man." This scene
reappears intact in *Bone Squash Diavolo*, retained even in the severely
shortened one-act version:

> *Mose:* Why, de laud a mercy, Spruce, when did you ribe from
> Philadelphy?
>
> *Spruce:* You are mistaken in de person black man, dis 'nt he.
>
> *Junietta:* Who does the impertinent Nigger mean, my lub?
>
> *Spruce:* He tinks I am de gemmen he blacks de boots for.

High-falutin' Spruce cuts friendly Mose dead. But at scene's end in the
play, while everyone flees the legendary constable Hays, Mose and his
friends trip Spruce and run him over with a wheelbarrow. The play provides lumpen justice lacking in its two sources (Clay's graphics and the
New Comic Annual story constructed to narrate them).

How the play's characters rehearse the cut has ramifications in memory and banter throughout. Indeed, the word "cut" recurs in nine epi-
sodes of *Bone Squash Diavolo*, triangulating the necessity in street culture of *performance* ("cut de pigeon wing"), *status* ("Wouldn't I cut a swell
in Broadway" and "I'd cut a splash to kill old people"), and *escape* ("see
him cut when de constable is coming"). One way and another, performing a cut is the art on which street survival depends. Being cut hurts—as
Mose knows when he recalls "Spruce Pink, what cut my 'quaintance this
morning." But being able to cut others is to escape being formulized.
Missionary preachers "skin and cut, and clear out when [they're] hard
run" and, indeed, this is Bone's practice at the end.

No one is harder run here than Bone, who must escape the devil four
different times. He escapes up the chimney at the end of Act I and tears
his coat in half to escape at the end of Act II, scene 2. He cuts the devil's
tail off to make his third escape. And finally he cuts the rope that tethers
his balloon to the devil. Bone sends the devil home while rising himself amid exploding rockets at the spectacular finale. Bone is a trickster
like Jim Crow. He has an asocial character not easily approved. Bone
Squash is louche and loose, a gambler and rounder. A loner even in his

crowd, Bone counsels his lovers to be patient, "I'll marry you both to-morrow" (2.1).

Rice here makes swift allusion to John Gay's *The Beggar's Opera* (1728), which was still standard fare in the theatre when Rice was com-ing up. Macheath's promises to Polly and Lucy a century earlier activate Bone's vows to Junietta and Janza. Bone is the champion for the other layabouts in his crew, as Macheath was in his. And just as Macheath's crew turn on him, so too Bone's confederates, Jim Brown and Mose, hap-pily gyp him with loaded dice (2.2). Moreover, Rice solves the infamous problem of Macheath's release at the end of *The Beggar's Opera*, but with-out Gay's contrivance. Gay sends in a reprieve. Rice sees to it that the play shakes Bone free, its very instability accessing the uncertainty of its characters' lives.

Bone makes easy compact with Duckellegs, Junietta's father. It is not just that Pompey Duckellegs is a preacher who, like Bone, cuts when hard run. Both have escaped Southern slavery. Both share tic phrasing appropriate to their wordy cons: both spend considerable energy to "splain" their schemes. Thus, while fractiously rooted in English the-atrical traditions, Bone Squash derives also from southern vernacular. Yet, Rice bit both hands that fed him. He not only remade the inherited Black Stage English that London theatre bequeathed his trade, but also mocked its forms of farce and plot. First, Rice's play *Life in Philadelphia* became *Bone Squash Diavolo* after Daniel Auber's *Fra Diavolo* had be-come a favorite comic opera in London (1830), New York (1831), and at the Walnut Street Theatre in Philadelphia (1834). Second, the title, the main character, and at least some of the content changed after the Hay-market Theatre in London had produced Douglas Jerrold's hit play *Beau Nash* (16 July 1834), about a rake and gambler's rise to social prominence at Bath.[103] Rice alludes indirectly to these sources in his titles, and the re-lationship is wry, too, when it is not a direct thrashing. Since there is no Faustian theme in *Fra Diavolo* and no further thematic relationship be-tween Auber's and Rice's operas, the connection is a winking bait-and-switch aggression. They have nothing in common but singing and com-edy. Yet on Monday the Fourth of July, 1836, before Rice had opened in London, William Bayle Bernard, an American playwright who had lived long in the city, wrote a letter to a journalist asking him to puff *Bone Squash* as "a burlesque upon Fra Diavolo."[104]

The connection to *Beau Nash* is more pointed. Jerrold's barbs had fallen heavily against the vulgarity of the theatre. Unlike James Rush in Philadelphia, Douglas Jerrold in London frankly proscribed perceived theatrical vulgarity in public and print. The difference between Rush's timidity and Jerrold's confidence suggests the earlier and larger success of the mobility in the western Atlantic. Jerrold's character Claptrap despises popular entertainments that even then threatened traditional theatre. Claptrap calls the puppet-master of Bath "the professor of motions" and notes, further: "If you'd pass for somebody, you must sneer at a play, but idolize Punch. I know the most refined folks, who'd not budge a foot to hear Garrick, would give a guinea each, nay, mob for a whole morning, to see a Greenlander eat seal's flesh and swallow whale oil."[105] Jerrold aimed at metropolitan imports that preceded blackface—at the tumbling Bedouin Arabs (or, as the gallery sweeps named them, "the Bedgown Arabs"),[106] the French monkey acts, Hervio Nano the man-fly, and similar exotic attractions then seducing audiences into illegitimate theatres. Nevertheless, what Rice professed above all was, exactly, *motions*. And his uncanny abilities would surpass Jerrold's fears. Rice's blackface motions would make people mob not only for a morning but for seasons of their lives. What Jerrold abuses, Rice organizes. What Rice was creating, indeed, was precisely the American Punch and Judy, sweeps and slaves devising their own backtalk that might at times rise to counterpunches.[107]

Beau Nash concludes languorously with a happy marriage that solves its social contentions. Marriage is not in the cards for Bone Squash, however, despite his lust for its benefits through most of his burletta. Agitated form is his end, and he takes that literally over the top in the last scene. Contrary to the efforts of Ginger Blue in *Virginia Mummy* or Gumbo Cuff in *Oh! Hush!*, the drama in *Bone Squash Diavolo* and in most of the plays thereafter is initially about the Jim Crow figure's struggle to improve his standing in the world. Bone is willing to sell himself to the devil to rise, so that he can marry the fanciest woman on view. But then in each play the Jim Crow character comes to his senses and throws it all over at the end. In *Bone Squash Diavolo*, Bone specifically rejects the marriage he had desired: "Oh ladies, do not tease me so / But please to let me go."

By trying the alternatives, Bone Squash learns the hard way to value what I have been calling lateral sufficiency. This is the switch that Rice pulls after the baiting references to his contemporary sources—*Fra*

Diavolo, the *Life in Philadelphia* etchings, and *Beau Nash*. Auber's and Jerrold's plays both finally snuggled in with the status quo. Not Bone, who rises in the balloon in the final tableau of his play, tossing out his shoes and hat, those fancy trappings that his soul-selling had financed. He returns to the rags his audience wore or fancied. The play reveals that his rise in the world, proposed marriages, and presence in this mockup of Italian opera were all traps. The formal frenzy shakes him loose from his pretenses and returns him to the unmoored spirit of mobility—for which the ballooning craze of his time was a fitting metaphor. The poet William Cowper caught the mood exactly when he worried that balloons and their free-floating tendencies would provide "the annihilation of all authority."[108]

As Bone realizes the consequences of his deals, the last two scenes of *Bone Squash Diavolo* shudder increasingly like a gyroscope with grit in its pivots. Bone sings in his last scene that he has "fled de track and can't come back." Seeking a form for that breakaway dream, *Bone Squash Diavolo* works toward it in scene 5 and finds it in the unique last scene. American popular culture will not match this centrifugal shudder for another century, until Busby Berkeley choreographs camp excess in Hollywood, and Ratliff italicizes Flem Snopes outwitting the devil in Faulkner's *The Hamlet*. Bone's final tableau does not maintain the social resolution of its models but discovers instead a counterpunching opposite of resolution. If I am not to shrink from the spirit of the play, I must say the play delivers its dream of ejaculation that has been Bone's constant need throughout. Ever since he foolishly signed the devil's paper with bootblacking so that he could make love with Junietta and Janza, Bone has been pleading with the devil for time not to marry, per se, but to "take de benefit of de act." The devil is the devil, we must say, just because he (like the constable he parallels) impedes this lust that conventional plays of the era can neither name nor enact. Against that repression one has to understand the play's conclusion: it is a slow, gaudy ejaculation shown as a blobular balloon rising, flares exploding, and long choruses danced out in a friskiness that crosses gender. This is not death, not transcendence, not a trip to heaven; it is too vulgarly lively for that. This is life released, a seeding of attitude.

Bone's crew is with him at the end and he is returning to their underlying ragged condition, free of the promises made to the devil, his lovers, the dice loaders, and the minister. This theatrical instability registers the several pressures on the play's public and ejects Bone, their champion, from the premises of received form. These are major contributions to the ballad opera that John Gay instituted with *The Beggar's Opera* (1729), the play that occasioned the division between patent and illegitimate theatre altogether, thus instituting most of the themes that someone like Rice would be able to consider.[109]

Bone Squash Diavolo releases the ballad opera from the problems symbolized in the important argument over *The Beggar's Opera* between William Empson and Michael Denning. Does Macheath enact a phony "cult of independence" (Empson) or an "ideology of the gang" (Denning)?[110] Gay coded both possibilities into his play because he was painfully conflicted in his connection to both Robert Walpole and Jonathan Wild, prime minister and chief crook. Gay needed both to validate his social schizophrenia. The shape of *The Beggar's Opera* is an exact figuration of the outsider-courtier trying to achieve independence via the constitution of an outsider gang that is simultaneously formed around two instincts: 1) the world of the gang with its apparent freedom will support neither plays nor valuable life; and 2) thieves and politicians weigh the same on the scales of justice. As a courtier-outsider, himself, Gay was inescapably beholden to the powers he critiqued and could not escape them.

The last scene of *Bone Squash Diavolo* manifests a greater freedom, in itself and in the world it engages: it springs a different sort of agency free. Bone returns to being the trickster champion in lumpen rags. The underworld in his play is one that the public applauding Bone can see and inhabit. Like Rice himself, Bone Squash is attracted to rising in the world. He wants to marry up, suit up, climb down and out of chimneys, enter parlors, win his bets. But he does not need to do all this to live; in fact, he gained these activities by a Faustian deal that promises his death. Furthermore, Rice has discovered and helped inaugurate a public for his ragamuffin champions who appreciate and prefer their models without dandiacal ambition. The radical theatricality of the last scene of *Bone Squash*, with its madcap chorus and centrifugal dance, shows the entire collectivity on the stage working through its Faustian temptations to rise beyond its known sufficiencies. The terror of this ascent, rendered in comic excess like a dream out of control, is what frees Bone and his public. Their equilibrium spins off its pivots and rolls to a new place that is not so much new terrain as old ground seen anew, and appreciated better for the frights endured. There is a place elsewhere, indeed it is this one.

The ending of *Bone Squash Diavolo* shows that the scorned, disreputable conventions of blackface can have a substantially different relationship to forms others, like John Gay more than a century earlier, invented to position themselves, and to resolve matters in their favor. Disdained cultural forms necessitate conclusions that *cut* languorous resignation, the courtier's desperate ambivalence, and dandiacal posing. Ejaculation, ejection, and evacuation climax the motions the mobility profess. Their sum is breakaway form.[111] Lower the curtain right there. Take this play abroad.

Phase Four. Here Comes the Black Anomaly

> I shall ride about in three hackney coaches—one for my cane, 'toder for my hat, and the third for myself.
> —Jim Crow in *The Foreign Prince*

At first in London, and all the summer and fall months that Rice played the Royal Surrey Theatre, located at St. George's Circus south of the Thames, anything seemed possible. And everything happened quickly. His extraordinary success at the Royal Surrey Theatre began the fourth phase of Rice's march across Atlantic stages. In this moment what had seemed a national popular culture went transnational, thus revealing different dimensions in its popularity. As the triumph continued, new and conflicting plays entered the Jim Crow repertoire, and that's when Jim Crow's logic fuzzed. As varying hands wrote over his actions and gave him new accents, the concentrated power of what Jim Crow meant to people started spinning off in varying directions.

Bone Squash Diavolo opened at the Surrey on 9 July 1836 and jammed the house until the 14th, when a bill announced that it would play "every evening until further notice." Indeed, *Bone Squash* ran continually until *Virginia Mummy* opened on August 1. Same success. *Virginia Mummy* played that week, then alternated with *Bone Squash* for another week.[112] The papers then reported at mid month that Rice was "touring the continent." His jumping there must have been even speedier than usual, because Rice was wheeling back at the Surrey on the 18th, doing *Bone Squash* again through the rest of August 1836. Now reports of Rice's cheek with royals circulated back home. The *Evening Star* and the *Spirit of the Times*, two American papers, embellished a long story about Rice and his New York friend Tom Flynn, who had accompanied him in these early London days as an informal manager, impersonating effete royal behavior at Vauxhall to the delight of *hoi polloi*.[113] A later report also detailed a trip to Paris in which Rice offered a grand sum "for a seat in the car of Mrs. Graham's balloon, which carried up the Duke of Brunswick lately in London." She snubbed him, preferring to keep her spare seat for dukes. But the balloon "upset and precipitated his Grace and Mrs. G. to the ground; the lady's life was in imminent danger for some days after the accident, and the Duke narrowly escaped with whole bones, being pitched out head foremost from a height of nearly twenty feet."[114] *Mutatis mutandi*, this is the delight that dances into view in blackface songs when the pesky blue-tail'd fly bites the north end of Massa's southbound horse, tumbling Massa into the ditch, breaking his neck, sending him to hell. Same delight, but the royals survive.

T. D. Rice played *Bone Squash* right through the first ten days of September 1836.[115] On the fifth of the month, a bill announced he was also rehearsing a new role, which turned out to be Joseph Graves's *Black God of Love*, now lost, which opened at the Surrey on 12 September. The first of many English plays composed especially to feature Jim Crow, *Black God of Love* was like many of his efforts popular everywhere in the house except where the critics sat. This time Rice was inclined to agree, letting it be known that for all the success of the play in London, "in New York salt petre wouldn't save it."[116]

Later in the month, Rice played Mesty, short for Mephistopheles Faust, in W. H. Oxberry's adaptation of Captain Marryat's novel, *Mr. Midshipman Easy*. Mesty was mentor and sidekick to young Jack Easy, a breeches part played by a Miss Martin. Miss Martin was also playing Psyche in *Black God of Love*, and both dramas were on the same bills. Thus Rice's black characters would have been intimate and loving on the same night with the same actress playing both a white man and a European goddess.[117]

The London and New York papers lamented and crowed, respectively, that Rice was earning unprecedented money. The *Spirit of the Times* proudly put their London correspondent's letter (dated 22 July 1836) on the front page: "Rice has made a decided hit at the Surrey Theatre—he can command his own terms at any London Theatre. At the Surrey he has $75 a week, exclusive of benefits."[118] They may well have derived their intelligence from this scandalized notice in a London paper the week before: "RICE, the American buffoon, is "Jumping Jim Crow" to the tune of seventy pounds per week, and a free benefit! We saw this 'apology for a man,' a few evenings since, and notwithstanding our disgust, could not forbear laughing at the fellow's impudence. He is as great odor as ever with the carpenters, bricklayers, snobs, and sweeps of the sixpenny gallery. We rejoice to hear that his days, in this country, are numbered."[119] In fact, the numbers of his days were as large as his earnings, doubtless because his act smelled of contention. Rice would not leave England for more than a year—he sailed home 30 August 1837—and he came back like a bad penny. He returned to play fifty-three weeks between 1838 and 1840, then played another six months in 1842–43. Before his first run was over, *The Spirit of the Times* proudly reported even grander figures:

> Nothing since the days of Garrick or Kean has equalled the popularity of this *"Virginia Nigger."* He is, by all accounts, coining money, and by no means among the loafers of the metropolis: Dukes and Duchesses; Lord Lieutenants and Field Marshalls, and we shall not be surprised if the youthful Queen herself should send an invitation to Rice to jump Jim Crow for her at the Palace. In looking over a file of Irish papers, we were struck by the unexplainable attractions of his sooty face and garments of rags and tatters. Mr. and Mrs. Wood could not draw a house, and Macready had to quit the field for Jim Crow. We find on one occasion, at Dublin, the Lord Lieutenant and suite were present, and $1800 in the house, one clear third of which goes to Jim Crow. On his fourth night he had $1400 in the house, and in Cork had $1900 in the house, and all the boxes taken before 12 o'clock.[120]

When Rice returned in 1838 to London, his novelty had lessened and so had his weekly wages. But the figures remained newsworthy when compared to anything but his own previous figures. A London paper noted at the beginning of his second visit that "Mr. Rice, the famous representative of Jim Crow, enjoys a salary of £60 a week for singing and jumping after the nigger fashion. He has £40 for his services at the Adelphi and £20 more for his nightly performances at the Pavilion in Whitechapel. What were the salaries enjoyed by Mrs. Siddons and John Kemble to this!"[121]

These multiple appearances in one night were a special feature of Rice's London presence. He was yoking audiences together that were not customarily drawn to the same representational culture. Like Pacman and G.I. Joe, action heroes of subsequent media for whom Jim Crow was one great uncle, Rice was eating the opposition and muscling his way out of the low theatres aiming for the top. He began appearing twice in one night in different theatres in districts separated by geography and status toward the end of his Surrey days, while he was transferring to the Adelphi. The Surrey's audience was primarily the working youths of its South London neighborhood—the costermongers, sweeps, carters, and journeymen that made the polite reporters sniff out his lumpen fragrance. The Royal Adelphi on the Strand reached a relatively urbane public, whose clerks, counterjumpers, and other ambiguous collar-wearing workers set the tone.

The Adelphi hired Rice away from the Surrey, luring him with W. L. Rede's strong play *Flight to America*, which he opened at the Adelphi on 7 November 1836.[122] A month later, during mid-December, he continued nightly in *Flight to America* at the Adelphi, but also sang "Jump Jim Crow" and performed both *Virginia Mummy* and *Bone Squash Diavolo* at the Surrey. Following these Surrey performances early each evening, Rice caravaned up the Waterloo Road from St. George's Circus, still in corked character, parading across Waterloo Bridge with the bulk of the Surrey audience in torchlighted tow, thence to ride his white horse across the stage of the Adelphi, delivering abolitionist speeches on the New York set of *Flight to America*.[123]

This ragtag rite constituted a remarkable moving tableau, lighting the mobility's penetration of the West End's public sphere. This singing and dancing crew enacted rudimentary transfusions of gestural turns, winking language, and rough charisma. It injected into wider London the same material with which the Jim Crow character was transfusing the theatre world's extant repertoire. The mobility's march from the Surrey to the Adelphi substantiated implicit patterns of acculturation that the plays themselves proposed. Motifs and stage moves were escaping the lighted spaces and moving through the dark outside. Then, during the summer of 1837, at the end of Rice's first stay, the two theatre companies merged in what they billed as a "Grand Union" for a temporary alliance.[124]

This yoking had symbolic meaning. Champions of chimney sweeps and costermongers mingled with favorites of flâneurs and clerks. At least for part of each night's bill, mostly white performers and publics chose runaway slaves and refractory free blacks to represent their mutual conditions to themselves and to social groups outside their own. Beyond this interweaving of class and neighborhood affiliations in London was the readily apparent challenge of the Jim Crow figure's dispersed genealogy in much of the new repertoire. In *Mr. Midshipman Easy, The Foreign Prince, Flight to America,* and *Yankee Notes for English Circulation,* Rice's character was born an African prince—or pretends to that status—before he was sold to America. Then he either comes to England because that island abolished slavery *(Mr. Midshipman Easy* and *The Foreign Prince)* or ends the play lighting out for English freedom *(Flight to America* and *Yankee Notes for English Circulation).* The American plays had set up and explored a wide overlapping area fusing regions, classes, and colors—where characters crossed and recrossed their usual separations, mingling attentions and interests. The English Jim Crow plays considerably broadened that overlap. Jim Crow wandered across oceans now, rather than regions. Now he passed from commoner to royalty and back again. Emerging here is a conflict between the demotic impulse, as it existed in the early American plays, and the dilution of the demotic when the scripters insist on a preapproved honor: African royalty in rags.

Between the summer of 1836, when Rice opened *Bone Squash Diavolo* at the Surrey Theatre in London, until the fall of 1844, when he performed *Otello* at the Chesnut Street Theatre in Philadelphia, the last major extant play that he tuned to his presence, Rice acted in at least twenty-two different plays, on both sides of the ocean.[125] Those that were written for him, that stayed in his repertoire, and that have survived are:

Flight to America (by William Leman Rede, opened at Royal Adelphi, 7 November 1836);

The Peacock and the Crow (by Thomas Parry, opened early in February 1837 at the Adelphi);[126]

Jim Crow in His New Place (by Thomas Proclus Taylor, opened 31 December 1838 at the Adelphi);

The Foreign Prince (by William Leman Rede, opened 18 February 1839 at the Adelphi); and

Yankee Notes for English Circulation (by Edward Stirling, opened 26 December 1842 at the Adelphi).

A sixth play was *Otello*. Rice himself changed this play from the decade-old burlesque by Maurice Dowling, writing considerable new dialogue and giving it unprecedented new characters and issue when he opened it at Wemyss's Chesnut Street Theatre in Philadelphia on 28 October 1844. All these plays are in *Jump Jim Crow*. Except for *Otello*—whose authorship is many-layered, deeply sedimented, and exceptional—these plays were all written *for* Rice by English playwrights with a relationship to the Adelphi theatre. Except for *Otello*, all attempt to nestle Jim Crow within the Adelphi ideology. *Otello* tries to wrestle the main character out of the Adelphi ideology. Going one way or the other, all address acculturation.

In the theatrical concoctions staged along the London Strand at the Adelphi, how would the dream of acculturation play out? Would British society integrate into its ongoing theatre the mobility embodied in Jim Crow? Would publics on either side of the ocean work through a new emotional plot in their stagings of secular rituals to absorb this ragged trickster? Of course not: the inertia of the English stage proved harder to budge than the American version across the Atlantic. Jim Crow's laughter and the nips of his "Blue Tail'd Fly" songs neither drove English conventions from their stage, nor substantially loosened its ideology. But there is also a longer, still unresolved answer. Rice framed the issues for this longer answer in his post-Adelphi play, *Otello*. This last of the original plays I have found he wrote is, at least in part, about the failure of the Adelphi integration, and an answer to it.

Rice engaged the English scene in his first Adelphi play differently than he would in *Otello*. In *Flight to America*, Jim Crow is a runaway slave who has fled a Virginia plantation to New York City, where his owner chases him down. Young English lovers—theatre addicts in love with ballerinas, as it happens—who are in flight to New York from marriage-arranging guardians in England, take Jim Crow under their wing. They buy him from the slave owner and trundle both him and his bride back to abolitionist England. At the play's happy conclusion all characters have freed themselves from their variously abusive patriarchies. This congratulatory ending characterizes the Adelphi dramas. Within Adelphi terms it certainly makes sense for Jim Crow to accept the conclusion. In leaving behind the country of his bondage, he carries off the trophy of Sally Snow, the "finest woman in New York," whom white as well as black characters covet.

Although this conclusion is happy for Crow and Snow in the West End, it is smarmy politics. The unaccommodated allure of Crow and Snow throughout the play hardens into an inferior foreignness at the end, when Jim Crow jumps over a broomstick to marry Miss Snow. They accept patronage from English flâneurs and their ballerina brides. This asserted European competence and Jim Crow's succumbing to it contrasts with the endings of Rice's earlier American plays, which produce scenes of Jim Crow's come-again inevitability amidst middle-class white bumblers. The American structure of oppression creates an excluded figure as a continually lurking problem: "dey'll find [Ginger Blue] ready dried, smoked, and painted, to sarbe himself up." None of the English plays manifests this challenge. The Adelphi ideology finds a place for the black characters that removes their worry and, in their meaningless absorption, negates even the sweet menace they managed in slavery-endorsing America.

One example of this erasure comes in the culminating Adelphi play, Edward Stirling's *Yankee Notes for English Circulation* (1842). Hiccory Dick is Rice's blackface character, working as a waiter in a Saratoga Springs resort hotel. He falls for the hotel barmaid, light-skinned Miss Zip Coon, and she for him. But Louise Coon is also not guiltless of flirting with all the English men cornering and kissing her—in scenes that invariably register what various characters declare is devilish madness, as at the end of the first scene: "The house is going mad, they're all bitten." The anguish of watching these transracial capers is primarily what Hiccory promises at the conclusion to write up and take to England as Yankee notes for English circulation. He will then become an American witness in the smug English tradition of prim commentary on American mores, running from Fanny Kemble's *Journal of America* (1835) through volumes by Harriet Martineau, Frances Trollope, and the then just-published *American Notes* (1842), by Charles Dickens.

This is a different direction for the man whose early lyrics attacked what the mobility and most lower-class Americans regarded as Mrs. Trollope's hateful snickery. In October of 1832 he had sung a "Glance at Mrs. Trollope." In February 1833, Rice had performed a "Hit at Mistress Trollope." At the moment he had joined the Bowery Theatre's sketches of *Life in New York* in 1834, one of its most advertised skits was its lambasting of Mrs. Trollope's family circle (see Figure 3). And the prose autobiography of Jim Crow published in 1835 and again in 1837 had set

AMERICAN

THEATRE.....BOWERY.

LAST WEEK!!!

OWING TO THE UNPARALLELLED SUCCESS OF

LIFE IN NEW-YORK,

And the great anxiety, nightly manifested, to witness

MAJOR JACK DOWNING,

That piece will be repeated every Evening until the arrival of Mr. Forrest.

The Manager is happy to announce, that an engagement has been effected with

Mr. Rice, the Celebrated Jim-Crow,

To appear in the above piece for a few nights, for whom several NEW SCENES have been Expressly Written.

On Thursday Evening, May 22d, 1834,

Will be performed a New Local Entertainment, called

Life in New-York,

Or, the Major's Come

EMBRACING THE VARIOUS PROMINENT FEATURES IN ITS PURSUITS & AMUSEMENTS
Which continues to be received with the most enthusiastic cheers.
SCENERY by DUKE WHITE............MUSIC by ST. LUKE.
The whole got up under the direction of MR. ANDERSON.

Frank Dashaway,	warranted sound, and free from Vice,	Mr. G. Jones
George Wheatfield,	a green one at home, but ripe when transplanted,	Flynn
Old Evergreen,	an evergreen,	Gale
Ezekiah Edify,	a careful Guardian, spirituously spirited,	Farren
Old Dashaway,	Too fond of his son to make a good father,	McClure
MAJOR JACK DOWNING,	well known in the city, but better understood at Washington,	Mr. GATES
Jack Nasey,	a knowing one for a novice,	Taylor
Harry Holdstakes,	a loafer, better known than trusted,	Conner
Tom Mason,	an exception to the general rule,	Stevenson
Dandy Crooks,	Too well known to need description	Hanson
OSLUMBER,	a night mare,	ANDERSON
Ned Nobody,	a hard character, struggling for importance,	Collins
Captain Bowbell,	making a haul out of the Yankees,	Wheatley
Jem,	Loafers occasionally employed as	Lewis
Sam,	Government Stone Cutters.	Addis
Spouting Owl-it,	a stage struck hero, good colour for Othello,	
Caesar Scrapeclean,	a low niggar of high birth,	Blackleg
Tailor,	Mr. Flim | Cato Oakstick,	Mr. Bloson
Frenchman,		Mr. Jean Crapeau
Lucy Winlove,	a sentimental young Lady, but not backward in her pursuit of a good husband,	Mrs. Flynn
Rose Evergreen,	More spirit than sentiment	Herring
Mrs. Dashaway,	a Lady of Liberal expenditure	Stevenson
Miss Volatile	Rather flighty	Gale

Freno hman,........ --................ ... Mr Jean Crapeau
Lucy Winlove,----a sentimental young Lady, but not backward in her pursuit of a good husband,.....Mrs. Flynn
Rose Evergreen, --- ....-----More spirit than sentiment ....Herring
Mrs. Dashaway,.... -------------------......a Lady of Liberal expenditure........................Stevenson
Miss Volatile, . ---------------- -------------- Rather flighty -------------------------------------Gale
MRS. TROLLOPE,.........and Family Group, by a well bred Lady of Foreign distraction, and her appendages
Master of Ceremonies,-------------------------- | La Fooli.............................. Miss Johnson
Antonio, ...---------------------------------+----------------------- Irish
  With many others, well known but too numerous to be mentioned,
                                  LIFE IN THE COUNTRY,
      Chorus—" Lo, brightly the Morning."   City Temptations and Youthful impulse.   *Three Cheers for Life in*
      New-York. An old fashioned Rail Road. Chorus—" Away to the City, gay delight."
                              HUDSON STEAM BOAT LANDING.
      Chorus—" Coach, Coach."   Major Jack Downing's March.   Arrival of a Private Character of Public Notoriety
                                       Prejudice.
                                    TATTERSALLS.
              Chorus—" Who'll buy a Mare to Run or Trot."   A City Outfit.
                                     BROADWAY.
      A Green One among the Girls.   Appointment.   The Quickest Method of Getting Rich.
                                  MISS VOLATILE'S.
              Lucy in a new character..... Duet—" With my Hat cocked aside."
      BALL ROOM, in all its Brilliance........Mr. St. Luke has kindly volunteered to take the management of
      the floor on this occasion.
                 PAS de DEUX, BY MR. ST. LUKE AND MISS JOHNSON.
      The Major and Mrs. Trollope,—Family Groupe.   Unhappy Blunder.   Chorus—"Oh what a lubly nigger wench.
                                 LIFE AT PALMO'S.
              Duet,—" Oh Pescator dell onda,"........Mrs. Herring, and Mrs. Flynn.
                                    BROADWAY.
                        Raising a Breeze,......Careful Watchman.
      LIFE AT FIVE POINTS.—Black spirits and white, red spirits and grey, Mingle,mingle, mingle.
      Chorus—" JIM CROW."----Professional Refugees and Black Professors... Danger of getting into Bad Com
      pany.   Quintette—" Hark, where Old Hays and Massa Sparks."
                              LIFE IN THE WATCH HOUSE.
              The Major in durance vile...........Yankee Ingenuity."
                            INTERIOR OF BOWERY THEARE.
      Water Witch,...........Van Beverout,—-........Farren,--Nathan,--Sowerby.
              SURPRISE !!! ....wise saws, and wholesome advice.
      FULLER'S GYMNASIUM. In order to give every effect that this successful entertainment is capable of
              receiving, the Manager has engaged the Celebrated

Mr. Barret,

      who will exhibit some most extraordinary Gymnastic Feats in this Scene.
              LIFE AT THE FARO TABLE......A Friend in Need.
              LIFE AT NIBLO'S, and GRAND FINALE........." Yankee Doodle !!!

During the piece, Mr. Rice the Celebrated Jim Crow will appear in several New scenes written Expressly for him.

Previous to which, a new Farce called

Which is the Prince?

Sir Paul Mainchance,-----------------Mr. McClure | Crump,....................... Mr. ..Addis
Mr. Wm Lightfoot,----------------------Collins | Snipe,.......................................Lew s
Captain Lightfoot, --------------- ----G. Jones | Hornblower,-----------------------------Add's
Sir John Fox,.................-- ------ ......Flynn | Julia,...... ....Mrs. Flynn
Dulcimer Staf,....................................Gates | Biddy,...... ....Herring

Mr. Forrest having arrived
  From New Orleans, will make his First Appearance on Monday Evening.
A New Farce, written expressly for Mr. Rice, is in rehearsal and will be speedily produced, called

              Where's my Head

              J. W. BELL, PRINTER, 17 ANN STREET.

Figure 3. Life in New York *playbill, Bowery Theatre, 22 May 1834. Courtesy of the Harvard Theatre Collection, The Houghton Library.*

70 · Introduction

itself up to correct the skewed pictures of Americans that the "foreign-ificated deatrical ladies" wrote. Right at the Adelphi itself, in late September and early October 1839, Rice had been playing in *The Kentuckian*, a play devoted to ridiculing Mrs. Trollope. That play's manuscripts show how her character was first called Mrs. Wollope; but that name has been crossed through and Mrs. Luminary written over: one sort of cartoon topping another.[127]

Thus for Hiccory Dick to join Boz and the Luminaries in their critique of American caprice is, any way one finds to spin it, a kink in the trajectory of Jim Crow. The character of Jim Crow has become less nationalistic and more cosmopolitan, more compound and increasingly overt, for instance, in his abolitionist stance. Is this switched direction new? Or does the twist point up complexity always lurking in the staging of the mobility? What seemed nationalistic in the American context —the attacks on Kemble and Trollope—may have been more "Don't Tread on Me," more anti-bluestocking, than pro-American. These riptides that churn the Adelphi texts do not settle into an ideology that conforms to twenty-first-century expectations. Jim Crow was a complex totem for nineteenth-century audiences. He responded to social and imaginative pressures that were different from ours even though his legacy helps contour the values we now sort. In eras in which nationalist ideologies ruled, Jim Crow seemed to figure America. In our avowed global era, Jim Crow may seem to prefigure an emerging transnational lumpen ethos.

✦

All safe and sound
To our wives we come
Wid de sprigs of laurel
In battle we won.
  Den drink, my boys,
  Dar's notin' to pay. *[repeat]*

—Rice's *Otello*

As early as 12 June 1833 the managers of the Chesnut Street Theatre in Philadelphia announced a forthcoming one-act "Othello, by Jim Crow."

On the scheduled night, however, the other players did *Richard III* and Rice simply jumped Jim Crow.[128] *Othello* was of course often on the bill in theatres Rice was playing, but I find no record that Rice himself played the Moor at all for another eleven years. All through his peak popularity, from 1833–1844, Rice stubbornly proposed Jim Crow as an alternative to Othello's black presence—for Othello had come to represent the establishment's use and abuse of blackness. Rice intended Jim Crow to gyrate out of that control and rehearse blackness in a zanier register. That was the plan. Not until after his English visits, after bringing several Adelphi plays back home, after rising and falling with them around both the States and Britain, did Rice play the Othello story—but then with original turns.

As he arrives in Cyprus, Rice's Otello gloats about his victory, and not only over the Turks. There has been no consequence for any of his risks: *"Dar's notin' to pay."* He has proved his value, proved his right to Desdemona. He believes he has achieved his acculturation. This is the play's hinge, just before Iago's snare takes him down. It is a moment Rice's popularity prepared him to plumb as a man, an actor, a playwright —for Rice also had laurel sprigs by the bushel. The newspaper consensus claimed him the highest paid actor on two continents. But, beneath those earnings and despite that acclaim, he had no more wrapped the cultural franchise around the mobility than he had acculturated Jim Crow. And at age 33, in the summer of 1840, he had suffered the first bout of a recurring paralysis that made him cancel months of performance. This illness grew gradually worse until his death.[129] Rice had come to know fairly quickly, as he would also show Otello realizing, that one pays a great deal to rehearse the root divisions of culture.

Rice defaulted to the Othello story when it was inescapably clear that Jim Crow would suffer continuing disdain similar to the Moor's. Jim Crow had not, after all, survived his scrapes and sprees with "notin' to pay." That was a young husband's dream. The reprisals against his pesty maneuvers were ready to spring well before he came on the scene— rather like the "steel traps and spring guns" old Podge loaded and locked at the beginning of *The Peacock and the Crow.* Rice had arrived at the point where a mature husband, as Otello becomes in Cyprus, discovers the payments are overwhelming. The mandarin strategies developed over the centuries for subsuming Othello were quite prepared to baffle Jim Crow, too. The Othello juggernaut careened with too much momentum to displace. Powerful audiences conflated Jim Crow with Othello no matter how much Rice negated the connection. Jim Crow might well win guerrilla battles at low-end theatres in towns across America. The earliest paperbacks, those songsters, might all change their content from sailors' chants and patriotic tunes to "Ethiopian" songs by the early 1840s. The blackface rage that Rice inaugurated might be morphing into blackface variety by the late 1830s and naming itself the minstrel show by the winter of 1842. But the larger laurel—the massive social changes his plays and songs imagined and the transracial community whose franchise he was enacting—was receding across the horizon. So Rice entered into the Othello story himself and took it apart.

There had been clues for some time that playing Othello was tempting Rice. What must have convinced him to counter the power of the Othello story was the inability of Jim Crow's rude patter to shift the base of Atlantic racism. Even in those plays ostensibly written for him, Jim Crow was losing ground. In the Adelphi plays the racial slurs against Jim Crow continued, even picked up frequency. The external confusion of the two roles, as when Knickerbocker critics mistook Jim Crow to be a crude emulation of Othello, began appearing across the Atlantic even inside the Jim Crow plays. Jim Crow could ride across the stage on a white horse shouting abolitionist slogans in *Flight to America*, but even in this first and most ambitious Adelphi play his chants could not stop the racist slurs. "All dese Othello fellow make very bad husbands," announces Pirouette in *Flight to America*.

When he finally entered into the story, therefore, Rice had accrued distance from its meanings, but he had also acquired a body of associations that shared Othello's fate. When Rice played the Othello story, his knowing public could see in his role both Jim Crow's mingled success and his failure escaping the ancient fable. His bragging that there was "notin' to pay" was an inversion that many in his public would have recognized indicated its opposite. Rice made his cheeky new representation of Othello reckon the costs of whirling blackness through white dominance—just as Iago warned in a line Rice tempered nail-hard for his version: "I'll sarve this black chap out, else I'm not white." In *Otello*, Rice finally closed the connection between Brabantio's scorned wheeling stranger and the character that wheeled about as Jim Crow. And he mounted all this as a formal burlesque on the Italian operas which the Brabantios of his own era attended.

The formal target in Rice's *Otello* was Rossini's *Otello* (1816), first performed in New York in 1826 during the formative years of Rice's earliest theatrical dreaming. For his model, however, Rice turned to an English blackface burletta by Maurice Dowling. W. J. Hammond first performed the title role of Dowling's musical play at Liverpool's Liver Theatre in 1834. Rice would have seen it in London after Hammond became co-manager with Douglas Jerrold of the Strand Theatre in April 1836. That same year Rice also converged on London, making his way just down the road to the Adelphi. Hammond and Jerrold opened Dowling's *Othello Travestie* in May for a long run that lasted into September and launched the Strand Theatre's enduring popularity.[130] Rice's play partly follows Dowling's scenic structure, but increasingly departs even from that.

Dowling had changed to rhyming couplets the muscular free verse Shakespeare assigned Iago. Shakespeare's Iago typically confined couplets to final lines of interior monologues at scene ends. But Dowling spread this emphasis throughout most of the play, for every character, and Rice sustained the leakage. Couplet rhymes are a regular part of the larger leveling by which popular forms frequently sneer back at canonicity. Disturbing the peace today at traffic lights all across the land, similarly insistent rhymes blare out of every hip-hopping car radio. In that sense, then, this pumping rhyme is both beyond and determines the points I have to make here. By maneuvering to propagate these couplets, Rice colored the familiar, inherited phrasings. Shakespeare's Iago:

> Three great ones of the city,
> In personal suit to make me his lieutenant,
> Off-capp'd to him. (1.1.9–11)

Rice's Iago:

> Three great men of the City—aye and wise men—
> To make me one of Venice's Excisemen
> Tried all their interest and walked some miles
> From one to t'other, even doffed their tiles.

Beyond the couplets, Dowling's shifts and Rice's elaborations on them are apparent here. Rice's Iago complains not that Desdemona has preferred Otello to him (as the Mediterranean sources preceding Shakespeare had it), not that Otello has preferred Cassio for lieutenant (as in

Shakespeare's *Othello*), but that he has to be a soldier at all: "I don't," he says, "like being shot." Shakespeare paved this path that Dowling drove, but Rice speeds around its bend, now adding lines about aldermanic graft and mayoral reversals. Rice inserts an urban politics, undeveloped in his sources, that continually betrays the mobility. His New York Iago, cynic that he is, wants to leap out of the homosocial mobility into the constabulary. Iago blames Otello for thwarting this desire.

The diagnostic break that Rice makes with Dowling, however, is a matter of speech: dialect melding with, and displaying, urban pressure. These Othello texts successively overwriting one another display this material action. It is a practice of merger and disruption, one idiom drawing on another to break it down and reassemble them together. This is the process of the lore cycle, by which canonical and vernacular cultures together mulch motifs, stories, gestures, and other traces of the past for continual recycling. This overwriting is not replacing but repositioning. It adjusts ratios of dominance and resistance, finding new niches for play, new ways to describe, inhabit, and shift the old restraints.

Watching the Othello story turn in time, one may see successive generations thawing, and returning to use, elements that earlier generations chilled. These moving ratios exemplify the way popular cultures sustain themselves and dog the progress of canonical momentum. But there is a further reason to follow these ingredients of class and ethnic idiom as they mix but do not dissolve. Particularly at this stage of the merger there is concern for the fate of individual parts of the complex recipe. Actors preparing to stir together a new cultural kinship are displaying here two conflicting impulses—a worry about losing their distinction and also a keen cross-cultural attraction. Here these are matters of dialect. The same problems in this early blackface theatre also come embodied in makeup, mask, and family offspring. That way, cultural issue becomes emotional, human issue.

Rice moves in that direction at the moment Iago delivers the street noun that the play's pronouns have deferred. In all the Othello plays, Iago's opening speech teases innocents in the audience who strain to find out whom Roderigo and Iago hate. Shakespeare held back naming the subject until Iago's coy "his Moorship" in the very last line of his speech (1.1.33). Dowling peppered his earlier delivery by calling Othello "Mister Blacky." Rice also delivers early. But his New York Iago ups the ante of Shakespeare's irony and Dowling's sneer with the epithet, "nigger."

Nor, in *Otello*, is Iago a lone user of this crackling tone. Roderigo and Brabantio continually pile on the slur everywhere Dowling used neutral references ("wight," "rascal," "black man," "chap"). Even Desdemona weighs in when, at the nadir of her husband's despair over Cassio, she tries to joke about Otello's "snowball face."

Although none of the play's characters yet displays our own era's characteristic anxiety and aggression in using these epithets, "nigger" had already become a divisive marker, just as "white," too, was in 1844 its hardened contrafact. Brabantio uses "white" three times in a racial sense, Iago twice, and Otello once. In addition to the many other degradations about hair, lips, and fetishes, Brabantio four times utters "nigger," Iago, Roderigo, and Otello twice. Both times Otello uses the word he is connecting to Desdemona—once when quoting her response to his wooing stories (scene 3), then when he worries in the final scene that she will betray others of his kind. In using "nigger" next to Desdemona, Otello emphasizes his consciousness of their difference. The same might be said about the play at large: its flaunted extremes display its conscious difference from both its predecessors and its mates on the contemporary hoardings.

This hard difference between *Otello* and even its own era's other burlesqued versions of *Othello* catalyzes Rice's theme and its cultural impact. Dowling specified that his Othello came "from the Republic of Hayti,"[131] and his Haitian Othello strewed pidgin rudiments that passed for Caribbean English on the Liverpool and London stages ("Me no got interest in the excise department, / Him not much place in piping time of peace"). Erasing this demeaning babble, Rice wrote drastically altered dialect. Rice tolled "nigger" regularly as a clock tower, located Otello's origins in the slave South, inserted New York's Five Points into his accent, and bolstered Otello's vibrant lexicon with rampant coinages. Where Dowling lapsed coy ("Mister Blacky"), Rice substituted cracking idiom that audiences high and low knew was the talk of an American mobility positioning itself against the upper crust.

Even more than earlier variants on the Othello story, the title character is estranged, utterly alone in a world of hate, tangled in snares of petty politics while he "done de state some sarbice." That even his wife jokes about his skin color is merely the beginning. When Otello approaches the sleeping Desdemona to kiss her a last time, she wakes in a spasm and kicks him over, asking "is it you, Otello?" Speaking truly through the slapstick tragedy, he answers, "It am indeed dat much-abused poor fellow." That's one extreme of *Otello*.

Another extreme is this idiom that Rice assigns to Otello, and that Iago imitates in his own speeches. These characters' blend of blacktalk with Bowery b'hoy argot is important because their dialect predates by several years Frank Chanfrau's staging of a white Mose as the proto-typical b'hoy in his *A Glance at New York in 1848*. Thus, the b'hoy cohort was already coming into being around blackface before Chanfrau. This consolidation through black performance was just as the billboard ads for the Chanfrau plays verified—white youths clustering around young blacks dancing for eels.[132]

This creolized street talk stages and speaks for the transracial public Rice has been organizing. Otello is *their* agent in the play. The disdain he suffers on the boards is the contempt a good part of his audience endures offstage. Interweaving these then-realizable dialects changes the affect of the play, and must be fundamental to our understanding of it. These two changes—more extreme estrangement and a hard-working creo-lized argot—make the difference between a play that it hurts to experi-ence and one that we should encounter despite its pain and ours. Rice is deploying rather than enjoying the social hurt.

Rice followed Dowling's play until the precise instant he had to repre-sent Otello's talk in Iago's paraphrase. Despite his flattening couplets, the American street vernacular Iago speaks is sufficiently nuanced to in-dicate its several strands. It weaves together Iago's hatred, blacktalk (both in quotes and paraphrase), and working-class white argot. This braiding is subtle. It does not bracket black speech as the ham-fisted pidgin that English playwrights had been composing for Jim Crow, and that Dowling piped intact into *Othello Travestie*. Rather, the New York Iago limns a much more acculturated blacktalk. The *Otello* script slowly warms to this bricolage, first giving snatches of Otello in quotes: "'sarved me out.'" Then, in the lines following the divisive epithet "nigger" (which acts as the fulcrum in the speech), we can hear Otello talking through Iago without quotes—in his verbs (he *do*, he *hab*) as in his articles (*dat* department, *de* ticket). We hear Iago deploying Otello's dialect and we hear him dropping out of it as he finishes his anecdote, even though he is still paraphrasing Otello, but (after "quarter dollar a day") in his own voice: whitetalk.

It certainly is not only Iago who can imitate and absorb the speech of others. Otello, too, contracts phrases that mark "white" popular speech. In the exact way Chanfrau would famously tag b'hoys a few years later, Otello's emphatic "no mistake" marks his own intimate involvement with lumpen culture. Certainly Brabantio and the Duke speak in *Otello* of "no mistake," but it only seems to be the same expression. They embed their phrase quite differently from the characteristic cross-racial lower-class emphatic utterance.

Such intensifying remarks have many implications. They cement both the content of their sentence and their speaker's filiation. They tag their cohort just as distinctively as tattoos do, or ballcaps worn awry. Except that they change more rapidly in history, they are as diagnostic as bird calls, and are to humans at least as poignant. Four years following the first performance of *Otello*, Frank Chanfrau staged his landmark play *A Glance at New York in 1848*. Chanfrau's female lead confides to her girl-friend what she likes about Mose, Chanfrau's role. "De way he takes hold of a cleaver," says Lize, "and fetches it down is sinful! Dere's *no mistake* but he's one of de b'hoys."[133]

"No mistake" is plangent throughout *Otello*, from the first scene to its last. The word *mistake* appears not at all in Shakespeare's *Othello*, just once in Dowling's *Othello Travestie*, but six times in Rice's *Otello*. Always in *Otello* the issue is about ascertaining or displaying one's loyalties and kinship. The phrase always arises in ambiguous cases where Brabantio or Otello must explain to others Desdemona's relationship to a man. Her filiative choices—what she *takes*—make all the contenders for her fealty doubt their own decisions and wonder what's due them. The issue in *Otello* is whether these new cultural kinships are more determinative than human families.

The Othello story has always rehearsed the choice of a young girl's fealty and shown the danger that she might choose wrong—that is, out-side her circle. All through its heyday middle-class culture has worried this problem not only in the theatre but perhaps most obsessively in its classic nineteenth-century novels. From Jane Austen to George Eliot, the climactic moment of a young girl's power, her chance to choose within social limits, fascinated readers. Rice in *Otello* contradicted this prejudiced choice, bringing news that wider options existed. *Otello* war-ranted ripe New York Desdemonas to choose others for their sake. That is, the ancient Othello story had raised the fear of an other stealing and smothering Desdemona, but discredited the values behind the otherness.

Those other's values, it elaborately pointed out, were not real. Shakespeare rendered Othello's ideology as superstition: strawberries crocheted in a handkerchief "dyed in mummy, which the skilful / Conserved of maidens' hearts" (3.4.70–71). Othello ultimately learns to blame this superstition as the cause of his downfall and the reason he murdered Desdemona. He judges his earlier self, who could be swayed by such a primitive talisman, to be a "base Indian," a "turbaned Turk," a "circumcisèd dog" (5.2.343, 349–350). He condemns that self to death, stabs himself, and dies. This conversion to the English national ideology is still today produced as exemplary; Othello typifies the mortal cost of rational self-knowledge.

Equally costly, however, is the exclusion of the Mediterranean-African values woven into that silk handkerchief. Rice's *Otello* reaches a different conclusion, a positive estimation of the values its title figure bears. Simultaneously, Rice's version of the story shifts concern away from erasing Otello's influence to tracing and sustaining it. This transfer to Otello's values ranges from hearing his presence in the play's polyphony to visual bricolage having to do with his black face.

Returning to the verbal and aural patterns of *Otello*, however, one hears the play's vital irruptions, often independent of the speech mergers that are displayed both in Iago's imitation of Otello and Otello's larding of his speech with b'hoy talk. Otello's idiom is exciting in itself. He sings

> Ob de sprees dat I get in
> And de scrapes dat I get out
> And how often run away when leff loose
> And how dat I got free
> From de Southern Slabery.

Before Otello and Desdemona realized they were wooing each other, when Brabantio invited him over for dinner, Otello replied, "I'll be up to de trough, Sar, in time." Otello sings to Desdemona that black folks are going to be angry with him for marrying her, but

> What de debil's dat to dem?
> You can't help your complexion;
> Nature made you as well as dem.

Worried that he is not receiving all that Iago knows about Desdemona and Cassio, Otello mutters "More could Iago chat, / If he'd but let de bag out of de cat."[134] When Desdemona pleads that Cassio be sent to verify her honesty, Otello angrily tells her that Cassio's dead: "Send for Michael Debil O—He can't come at all / Kase he hab put him spoon into de wall." And in scene 6, packed into the context of the famous blackface song "Dandy Jim from Caroline," a song that sent up flâneurs both white and black, Rice offloaded some fuming misprisions about the toiletries on a wellborn woman's dressing table. They reveal Otello's complete estrangement, his entanglement with signs and gestures he cannot decode, and his own powerful inventions:

> To lub a wife dat don't lub me,
> I'd rather be a toad, you see;
> And den de face to lib upon
> De wassous ob a demijohn.
>> De Gypsy woman tell me so,
>> I was born to be a General, oh.
>> I looked in the glass and find it so,
>> Jist what de Gypsy told me, oh.

In Shakespeare's *Othello*, the Moor says he would "rather be a toad / And live upon the vapour of a dungeon" (3.3.270–271). Dowling omits this image. But Rice restores it with the outrageous slant pun—dungeon:demijohn. He slides into this brilliant linkage by multiplying and merging the *vapour* of the model with the waters a jar would hold, giving *wassous*. Only to hear botched language in such speeches is to miss, in this case, the way it extraordinarily yokes a radical slam at effete life within enjoyment of Elizabethan language and its snares.

Desdemona's wordplay is less incandescent than Otello's, but her gestural inventions are zanier. Rice rekindles the lively spirit with which the Mediterranean folk sources laced Desdemona's role before Shakespeare intervened to stanch her behavior, thus disabling general male response to it. In the earliest recoverable versions, the Ensign's motive was sexual desire rather than the professional jealousy Shakespeare later made primary.[135] Icing that lust, Shakespeare turned Iago's conniving into the "motiveless malignity" that Coleridge famously judged. Reheating that lust, Rice set the Othello story flowing once more. Rice did not reverse matters back to the Italian sources. Rather, he both increased the professional jealousy, adding the loops within loops of urban politics, *and* compounded the sexual theme. Rice's Desdemona did not simply spurn

Iago, as she had in Shakespeare's sources. She did not turn away only Roderigo as in *Othello*. Instead, the New York Iago promises to claim that Desdemona "jilted the whole neighborhood." In *Otello*, everyone desires Desdemona. They all hope to control whom this Miss takes. It's not just Iago, Otello, Cassio, and Roderigo scrambling for her favor. Desdemona focuses a contest of the younger men against her father's co-hort, too. Rice sharpens the generational conflict through Desdemona as much as when he had Bone Squash sing that he wanted "to cut a splash to kill old people" (*Bone Squash Diavolo*, scene 1).

Through Desdemona's choices, Rice literally gives issue to the latent core of the Othello story. Initial clues come during Desdemona's singing interplay with the chorus in scene 3, when she explains "why [she] loved the Black." Her second verse explains that Otello's wooing tales made her swoon ("so romantic, yet so tender . . . That I fell across the fender"). Here's part of the third verse:

Desdemona
When I came about—ah, me!
Chorus
Rather supple—rather supple . . .
Desdemona
I was sitting on his knee—
Chorus
Loving couple—loving couple!
Desdemona
Greatful for the scrape I'd missed.

We can never be sure, now, if "Greatful" and "scrape" are intentional puns alluding slyly to conception and abortion. Nevertheless, we do know that Rice or his copyist changed the spelling from Dowling's conventional "grateful." We do know the blackface theatre, by 1844 a house with many wings, cemented its seams with conundrums and puns.

These imponderables lead to the extraordinary supplement Rice gave this story. Desdemona's song is pregnant in more ways than one. Whether or not swooning across Otello's knee was the auspicious moment she became "greatful," Rice has bodied forth the seed that the Othello story repressed from its beginning. Otello the man, like *Otello* the play, produces real offspring. For the first time in all the variants on the Othello story, *Otello* delivers an objective correlative for the results of love between Otello and Desdemona. She delivers.

The ecstatic invention between Desdemona and the Chorus is not in Shakespeare. Their song is a tame solo in Dowling. In *Otello* the song erupts outrageously, like the conclusion of *Bone Squash Diavolo.* The device of the Chorus, which brings more agents of the public on stage to provoke the principals, to comment on and produce public attitude, is a convention that Rice uses to reckon character's social warping and to dramatize its crack-up. Here, however, Rice invokes the Chorus as early as scene 2 and reactivates it continually throughout the play, repeating it like the racial slurs and those doubts reiterated in "no mistake." Choric interplay with several characters saturates this burletta, most surreally with Desdemona.

Unlike Shakespeare, Dowling made Othello confirm to the Senate that he married Desdemona, "Yes, one and one am one." Then Rice upends this chaste commonplace in a way that excites Desdemona and the Chorus to their extravagant duet: "Dat am a fact," says Otello, "one and one make one." The different dialect and its different verb indicate a different action. Otello has impregnated Desdemona already and she will give birth to Young Otello. Desdemona is great, full, with child. She has avoided a scrape, in several possible senses, by marrying her lover, and she gives birth. One and one really do make one—not an impotent marriage, not a play too repressed to admit the result of love, but finally a problem child for the play, for New York, for the Atlantic.[136] In Rice's *Otello,* then, the Moor and Desdemona have a baby, whom she brings out of the storm and introduces to his father when they all converge on Cyprus. Otello greets her with a kiss. She says, "Behold this pledge, your image here is seen." Otello must noticeably demur, for Desdemona quickly pivots, saying, "Not this side, love, the other side I mean." This stunning pledge displays and links everything in the play, as in its applauding public.

One side of Young Otello's face was marked black, the other white. It must have detonated extreme tension in the production. Such bisected masks flag a vernacular persistence and crop up frequently in the black diaspora. One can run them back from Wesley Brown's 1994 novel *Darktown Strutters,* through American and Haitian paintings by Robert Colescott and Stivenson Magloire, back past Bruce Nugent's "Drawings for Mulattoes" (1927), through such fugitive surrogates as Desdemona's

Figure 4. Otello *playbill, Cincinnati National Theatre, 9 May 1846. Note at List's end:* "Master Lorenzo Otello (eldest son of Otello and that there may be no partiality, nature has colored him half and half) . . . Master Kent." *Courtesy of the Harvard Theatre Collection, The Houghton Library.*

living pledge, and ultimately across to African masks the Central Pende peoples are sculpting and dancing still today.[137]

The pledge dialogue in *Otello* declares that the child's face visibly emphasizes his constitutive genealogies. They are joined and neither side effaces the other. The playbill for a Cincinnati staging of *Otello* declared, "that there may be no partiality, nature has colored him half and half" (see Figure 4). This child's presence is a profound embodiment of meanings in the Othello story. Young Otello is a picture of the particular hopes for a stand-off merger, joined intact, that were developing in Atlantic vanguards, and which would find their most eloquent statement more than a half century later. In the opening pages of *The Souls of Black Folk* (1903), W. E. B. Du Bois voices the visual premonitions in *Otello:*

> The history of the American Negro is the history of this strife,—this longing to attain self-conscious manhood, to merge his double self into a better and truer self. *In this merging he wishes neither of the older selves to be lost.* He would not Africanize America, for America has too much to teach the world and Africa. He would not bleach his Negro soul in a flood of white Americanism, for he knows that Negro blood has a message for the world. He simply wishes to make it possible for a man to be both a Negro and an American, without being cursed and spit upon by his fellows.[138]

Rice gives his blessing, not his curse, to this image when his stage directions insist that Otello take the child and kiss him.

Staging this kiss isolates and underscores its sharp ramifications:

↝ Otello's kiss acknowledges both heritages at once, rather than one subsuming another. Thus, the play challenges the "one drop" racial regime that, in making all mulattos black, distinguishes U.S. mores from those in other Atlantic societies—Brazil is one, Cuba a second —that allow mixed progeny more latitude for their elective affinities.

↝ Otello kisses the fruit of miscegenation, which was then a realized fact in the streets where both Otello's talk and Young Otello germinated. He thus rubs raw the very spot that nabob interpretations of the Othello story—like those of Adams and Hackett—meant to force. Departing from the play's usual presentation and returning to the latent core deep in the ancient story, *Otello* comments further on the office of the story, then consensual, as it has again become. Otello's awareness makes available how Shakespeare's master text consistently enabled some dominating playgoers to repress their deepest social fears of mixing—and simultaneously disabled out-castes from rehearsing *their* contrary excitement over connections.

↝ As a clear sign, but something absent from common experience, the bifurcated mask asserts the role of trickster. In its doubling or refiguring of the make-up that old Otello wears, Young Otello's meta-mask insists that the players as an ensemble are together figuring a curative ritual. This is a loaded scene, neither entertainment nor a story alone. This problem child has implications for the play and is also the sign of its implications. The problematic mask reminds audiences of the core issues in the play that conventional meanings have effaced.

✦ Young Otello is himself a *"pledge."* He is a promise for the future that is uncertain and that his generators cannot make real by themselves. The generators are Otello and Desdemona, certainly; behind them, however, is the public that the play appeals to at the end, when the Chorus looks from the galleries to the pit, summoning all to "Dance and sing / *'Til the whole house ring.*" They all must raise this pledge together: "De longer den de family grows," Otello sings immediately after kissing Young Otello, "More stronger am de Union." They cannot defend that union in a world that forbids or undermines their being together. Their pledge is both material and not yet certain. Their pledge is tender. It is a new promise, a green shoot, a babe in the city.

✦ The appearance of Young Otello greatly expands and integrates the family resemblances that this play has been about from the beginning, from its first "no mistake" and its first lumpen, ironic-bonding "nigger" set against the sneering epithet of Brabantio and Iago. Every performance of *Otello* at the Chesnut was partially integrated in the compromise then permissible—with the upper gallery reserved for blacks.

Otello's first bill concluded: *"Box 50 cents, Pit 25 cents, Gallery for Colored Persons Only, 25 cents."* This pricing continued throughout the run.[139] The bisected appearance of Young Otello may reflect this segregated integration. It may also represent the being separate together that arts about people in diasporic movement are usually about. It may be a despairing image of people brought only so close together. And it may also be, as I prefer to argue here, an image of twoness in which no generator is lost in the mix. Certainly the image of the child reminds us that both Otello and Desdemona, and both sides of the generating audience wherever they sit in the house, have together issued forth Young Otello.

Welcoming his son leads Otello directly into a crucial song for the play that develops all these claims. To the tune of "The Girl I Left Behind Me," Otello champions joining opposites together. Rice reversed the song's normal expectations. Soldiers conventionally sang "The Girl I Left Behind Me" to lament the loss of lovers they had naively hoped would remain faithful. But at this moment in his play Otello is confident he has overcome loss. He sings it as a victory. The plays on "union" in its

third verse are characteristic of Rice's work. They correlate marital and
national unity with the actors' own urge to merge ("if you like me and I
like you") with the public that this song helps organize.

Politically, T. D. Rice consistently opposed nullification and advocated
the Union—even while he insisted on black freedom by any means necessary—from his first printed Jim Crow lyrics in the early 1830s on-
ward:

> 34
> De great Nullification,
> And fuss in de South,
> Is now before Congress,
> To be tried by word ob mouth.
> . . .

> 37
> Should dey get to fighting,
> Perhaps de blacks will rise,
> For deir wish for freedom,
> Is shining in deir eyes.

> 38
> An if de blacks should get free,
> I guess dey'll fee some bigger,
> An I shall concider it,
> A bold stroke for de niggar.

> 39
> I'm for freedom,
> An for Union altogether,
> Aldough I'm a black man,
> De white is call'd my broder.

South Carolina's Declaration of Nullification was on 24 November
1832. Andrew Jackson responded at length on 16 January. A month later,
Rice was singing "A Hit at Nullification" at Frank Wemyss's theatre in
Philadelphia.[140] One has only to compare Rice's racial politics with, say,
the available radical efforts of his time to put this all in perspective. Even
Thomas Dorr's militant efforts to extend the franchise in Rhode Island
in 1842, heavily supported by radical Democrats like John O'Sullivan in

New York City, did not welcome blacks to the extension, as Rice did.[141] And Rice's sung remarks did not equivocate when he faced south during the countdown through nullification and toward the Civil War: "And dere no station in all de world / Like de state of annexation."

Producing meta-masked progeny that symbolize annexation, and kissing the consequences, are ultimate but not the final liberties *Otello* takes with its parent story. Rice alters the end much as earlier strong versions of Othello's story had changed *their* conclusions. Indeed, disposing of the Moor is really one of the most important functions of the productions that descend from the story's Renaissance variant. Until Rice's *Otello*, the great office of the play was to eradicate Othello's presence one way or another, usually by inducing his guilt and suicide. But if that failed, altering authors called in supernatural cleansers.

Shakespeare's ending had heavily revised his Mediterranean sources —in which the Ensign kills Desdemona and the Moor goes free until Desdemona's family kills him in exile. Instead, Shakespeare had Othello smother Desdemona; then, when Othello realized his Ensign manipulated him into the murder, he tried to kill Iago (but merely wounded him) and quite successfully obliterated himself. Dowling's 1834 *Othello Travestie*, in two acts, has Desdemona's ghost rise from her body when Othello smothers her; this ghost then chokes Othello until Desdemona sits up in her bed, saying she still lives and that Iago was the villain; the characters agree suddenly to follow Roderigo's advice to "let the past be all forgot," and the curtain falls. In his subsequent single-act version, *Othello, According to Act of Parliament* (1836), Dowling rewrote his own rewrite, this time solving the disposal question. This time Desdemona's ghost takes Othello and Iago to Hell, Desdemona stays dead, Roderigo confesses his guilt, and the ghost says he will fetch Roderigo later. The ghost admonishes the audience to learn from the play, promising that the actors will return when required; the trap sinks; the curtain falls.[142]

Amidst all these options and more in his era, Rice played out his *Otello*. The encompassing Othello story was by then no longer a fixed, master text. Its resurrected plasticity was now disrupting what "race" might mean as slavery concluded in the British imperium and, stateside, came to a head in both congressional and porchfront debate. These burlesque productions of the Moor's tale restored his constituent elements to turbulent flow. Shakespeare's tale had articulated the elements in rich array for more than two hundred years; now they were again in friction and play. Now the identification of many in the ragged Atlantic with black charisma was both supplementing the play's cast (with Young Otello) and confounding its conclusion (with Desdemona, Otello, and their mutual pledge all surviving).

Rice's *Otello* ends happily for everyone in the play and its public—except for Brabantio and the cohort connecting to him, the old governors of the state. Young Otello's parents dance united with their peers. The agent of this rapprochement is not a supernatural ghost. Instead, the motley Chorus intervenes at the lowest moment of the principals, right after Otello smothers Desdemona. The Chorus does mock Otello, but the Chorus also enfolds our then fargone stranger back into the scene to the tune of "Old Dan Tucker." Whether or not Otello feels reenlisted he does reach understanding of his situation.

This understanding makes Otello's fate distinct from the reflexive spasms and convenient self-disposal of his model in the Othello story. In Rice's play, Otello's awareness drives him neither to more murder nor to suicide. Otello's understanding takes him quite contrarily to moderation born of the full weight of his rightness balancing the social inertia he has confronted:

> If his wife hab but been black,
> Instead of white, all had been right

Breasting this apparently indelible conclusion, Otello accepts the treadmill. He realizes that a whole social pattern nested and determined Iago's manipulation. There is no sense in Otello that his own values or what others would call superstition are to blame, and he does not conceive of his earlier perplexed self as Indian, Turk, or dog.

This recognition of the larger social momentum may be why, in *Otello*, there is no attempt to slay the villain. No one even pronounces Iago's name after he proposes the plan to smother Desdemona. At the end, the Chorus simply calls him, "the other fellow," making him change places overtly with the wheeling stranger, who, following his understanding, is now brought *in*, while Iago the consummate insider is frozen out. Iago is an agent for this massive blame, this overwhelming and socially coded racism, but he is not its originator, nor its owner, and Otello comprehends these articulated relations. That's what Otello's calm explanation at the end of this play is about, as opposed to the reflex anger at the end of the Othello models and the dervish madness that concluded *Oh!*

Hush!, Bone Squash Diavolo, Flight to America, and *Yankee Notes for English Circulation.* The ending of *Otello* distinctly lacks the thrashing behavior by which Othello had eradicated himself since the English Renaissance. This *Otello* delivers appraisal if not forgiveness. It pledges to visual bricolage that includes blackness and whiteness in substantial and traceable measure.

The State is not all. Its workings are more powerful than Jim Crow believed in his pesky youth, more powerful than Otello had hoped when he fell in love and almost involuntarily began to challenge social mores. But even as he bitterly recognizes the creed that white makes right, he retains his love through the end of the play. Otello never admits his cross-racial love for Desdemona has been wrong—only that nabob offices forbid it to the end of the earth. Otello not only stays within the frame, he no longer tries to burst bonds as he had in earlier plays. Here are no balloons, fireworks, or lunacy. Instead, there is a final dance of commonality and inclusion that works matters through. The play, its actors, and its audience all accept the cross-racial marriage and the child. The "whole house" dances together with Otello, Desdemona, and Young Otello at the final applause. Otello's disposal here is integration.

Otello achieves this integration by understanding his relation to the forces arrayed against the mobility. That's why the two tread mill references in Rice's *Otello* are important: they mark Otello's changes and the play's bitter lesson. In the first mentioning, Brabantio urges the Senate to condemn Otello to the tread mill for mesmerizing Desdemona (scene 3). Brabantio claims Otello's crime was to alter Desdemona's natural attraction to her own color. To the tune of "Ginger Blue" (thus referencing Rice's character in *Virginia Mummy*), Otello demonstrates how natural his winning ways were to Desdemona, as to us. Early in the burletta, therefore, Otello avoids this machine invented in England to torture eighteenth-century prisoners. At the end of the play, however, Otello submits himself to the "treaden mill," that is, to prison. This moment, when Otello understands the extent of power configuring him, is the moment the gong sounds, Desdemona pops awake, and the house forgives him. No suicide, no fleeing, no agreeing to "let the past be all forgot." Here, Otello understands the plight he embodies: there exist no exceptional fates. There is no safe haven.

Whatever scorn Roderigo and Brabantio shared in *Othello* for the "wheeling stranger," however Rice elaborated that estrangement early in

Otello, and despite the tactics Jim Crow had applied during the first stages of his career, nipping at the magnates and their pretensions— there was in fact no alternative to the modern enclosure. Except for slavery, there was no outside. Both Otello and Jim Crow had freed themselves from slavery. All free men, Rice's play dreamed as Desdemona awoke, were folded into common cultural values that were unevenly shared but demonstrably existed for people to wrestle and dance out together. Ultimately there were no strangers in the Atlantic. The stranger had come inside, had brought all his wheeling back home, and his public applauded his living, lively, inclusion.

The radicality of *Otello* as a play is not Otello's breaking out of confinement, but his breaking in to stay. He's in for the duration now: for the production of offspring, for public celebration of his achieved kinship. Young Otello's makeup registers the crossing of cultural and biological kins. Young Otello is the product of many diasporas, biological and cultural meanderings that meet and mingle in particular histories. He codes the circulation of the Othello story, the movements of Africans and Europeans, the migration of fetish ideas that encouraged his parents' attraction to each other. Young Otello materially displays such filiations as vanguard arts can propose, which is to say his audiences still must interpret him. What the pledge and its kissing risks, then, is the spectrum of possible responses. If the entire play did not exist, with its love and insistent choices, audiences would not know if they should laugh at the problem child, scorn him as a freak, kiss him as the pledge of the future, or meld responses around all these feelings. But the play within the crucible of Rice's career is now available. The play *Otello,* its internal wooings between Otello and Desdemona, and its external wooings between Otello's actor and his publics is reconstructed here. Therefore, Young Otello's meta-marking is a challenge that people can ascertain holds his pasts in clarified tension. He embodies aspects of the modern experience that earlier tellings would not touch or admit.

It is true that, after Rice's decade of performing the play, Young Otello again dropped from the encompassing Othello story. This disappearance of Otello and Desdemona's issue shows that the purchase he held on audience attention was small and those who saw him were not strong enough to keep the pledge. Nevertheless, his bifurcated image remains fugitive throughout the cultures that contributed to it. His divided marking showed a public its location at a particular moment. Then it went under, into the mulch, perhaps to cycle to the surface again. The story is not yet over. Not a year after Rice performed *Otello*, Thoreau concluded *Walden* with the discovery of a "strong and beautiful bug" warmed but not yet hatched, buried in the wood of an old table. He wrote, "There is more day to dawn."

Phase Five. Passings and Afterlife

> Folk art and kitsch ought for once to be regarded as a single great movement that passes certain themes from hand to hand, like batons, behind the back of what is known as great art.
>
> —Walter Benjamin[143]

Otello was the last important play that Rice wrote. Between the fall of 1844, when he started performing it, and the fall of 1860, when Rice died, *Otello* joined his other major plays in steady rotation. During this final phase, *Otello* participated in several spectacular conjunctions. *Otello* immediately preceded and followed the suppressed production of George Lippard's *The Quaker City* at the Chesnut Street Theatre in Philadelphia, November 1844. Five years later, Rice played *Otello* (subtitling it then as "The Moor of Orange Street") on the same bill as *Jack Sheppard* at Chanfrau's National Theatre (the old Chatham). Three years after teaming with Jack Sheppard, *Otello* was on the bill with the first staged production of *Uncle Tom's Cabin*—again at the same theatre, now called Purdy's National, 30 August 1852. These conjunctions marked the grading of Rice's cultural work into another mode. By early 1854, Stowe's Uncle Tom had supplanted both Jim Crow and Otello. But Rice, whose family and friends called Tom—was now playing the role that Stowe may have subconsciously named after him. The earliest record I have found for his playing Uncle Tom is 16 January 1854, at the Bowery Theatre.[144]

There were of course many versions of *Uncle Tom's Cabin*, some of them—like the Conway production that Barnum produced—racist to the core. But H. E. Stevens, the Bowery Theatre's own stage manager, wrote the version Rice performed.[145] The *Spirit of the Times* review praised Rice as enacting Tom "more successfully than any of his competitors." The *New York Tribune* reviewer was more specifically excited, re-

porting that this production made "a gross, robust unreasoning sentiment of hatred to slavery in the *very ground tier of society*, that may be the
germ of a tremendous social explosion . . . Let [slaveholders] reckon
upon the quiet of the rumbling volcano. If slavery shall persist in her
blind purpose of defying the philanthropic sentiment of the age, and con-
temning the explosive forces of an outraged humanity, let it beware of
the deep sentiment of human brotherhood that lies beneath the brittle trans-
parencies of all political ties."[146]

Uncle Tom was Rice's last great role. He made it a revolutionary
statement that lived up to the liberatory impulses that followed from this
"deep sentiment of human brotherhood" his Jim Crow performances had
evoked. He and other performers had communicated those impulses so
powerfully that Harriet Beecher Stowe could sense and formulize them
without ever seeing a blackface performance. And then Rice could step
back into her narrative and project it as a "rumbling volcano" from the
"ground tier of society."

The story of Jim Crow as a totemic character documents a profound and
stunningly persistent affiliation across race and class that precedes and
underwrites all the other interests in this material. Without this deep
recognition of African American charisma, and the way it figured everyone else arrayed in movement around the Atlantic, Rice's impact would
have faded along with the facile comedies of his era. Had there not been
this stub of provocative connection among disdained peoples, the Jim
Crow extravaganzas, *Virginia Mummy, Bone Squash Diavolo*, and *Otello*
would have gone the way of plays about parlor love, Yankee peddlers,
and river raftsmen. But Jim Crow was fated for a dynamic hidden life. Although the Jim Crow plays became taboo and dropped from textual circulation for more than a century, lore cycles bootlegged their import into
the daily life of gestures and song fragments. They often hitched onto offensive cliches and stereotypes, but they survived willy-nilly. Few if any
cultural figures high or low are packing nutmegs or growing finger-
nails to gouge eyeballs—those signature actions of Constance Rourke's
other two members of the "comic trio" during the early nineteenth century. But her trio's third member has remained continually vital. Cultural players today dance hip hop all over. People of all hues and nationality around the Atlantic con black dress styles and syncopate popular

rhythms. They cycle through the generations of rock 'n' roll and standup comedy that the staged patterns of blackface worked out. Jim Crow lives all the more enduringly despite the disdain—likely because of it—in ways that peddler and raftsmen never have.

T. D. Rice brought blackness into the house, married it to whiteness, and bequeathed the bifurcated differences that keep American citizens separate together. Members of his succeeding generations regularly survive their dances of attraction, make the whole house ring, and celebrate "this wedding over." Of all the footprints he left along Atlantic shores, the deepest is that Otello and Desdemona's baby looks like us.

SONGS

Before there were Jim Crow plays, there was "Jump Jim Crow," first as a folk song and dance, then gradually as an improvised stage performance that became its own extravaganza. T. D. Rice would sing and dance the song, then pretend to try to stop; his audience would demand multiple encores. This song was unstable in every way. Its few core verses continually changed as they adapted to the performance contexts. They never, for instance, decided if Jim Crow's birth was in Kentucky or Virginia. The chorus was always fully half the song and embodied the need to leap out of itself. And rather than providing an authoritative text, the printed versions increased the song's flux by modeling its improvisation. The half-dozen examples of the song's earliest printed variants given below emphasize their variety and frequent contentions.

Jim Crow was associated also with many other songs. There are seven in this section whose tunes and lyrics Rice uses most often in his plays. They appear in the general order Rice seems to have developed them.

Coal Black Rose[1]

Lubly Rosa, Sambo cum
Don't you hear de banjo tum, tum, tum!
   Lubly Rosa, Sambo cum!
Don't you hear de banjo tum, tum, tum!
Oh Rose! coal black Rose.
I wish I may be cortched if I don't love Rose.

Dat you Sambo?—Yes, I cum.
Don't you hear the banjo tum, tum, tum?
Dat you, Sambo?—Yes, I cum,
Don't you hear the banjo tum, tum, tum?
    Oh, Rose &c.

Tay a little, Sambo, I cum soon.
As I make a fire in de back room.
Tay a little Sambo, I cum soon.
As I make a fire in de back room.
    Oh, Rose &c.

Make haste, Rose, lubby dear,
I froze tiff as a poker tandin here.
Make haste, Rose, lubby dear,
I almost froze a waitin here;
Oh, Rose I almost froze.
I wish I mab burnt if I don't lub Rose.
Cum in, Sambo, don't tand dere shakin,
De fire is a burnin and de hoe cak a bakin.
Cum in, Sambo, and top dat shakin,
De pease in de pot, and hoe cak a bakin.
Oh, Rose, bress dat Rose.
I wish I may be cortched if I don't lub Rose.

Sit down, Sambo, an warm your skin,
Lord bress you, Honey! for what make you grin?
Sit down, Sambo, an' toast your skin,
Lord bress you, honey! for what make you grin?
    Oh, Rose &c.

I laff to tink if you were mine, lubby Rose.
I'd give you plenty, the Lord above knows;
Ob possum fat, and hominey, and sometimes rice,
Cow heel and sugar cane, ebery ting nice.
　　Oh, Rose &c.

What in de corner dare Rose; dat I py?
I know dat nigger Cuffee, by de white of he eye.
Dat not Cuffee, 'tis a tick ob wood, sure,
A tick ob wood wid tocking on, you tell me dat? p'shaw!
Oh, Rose! take care, Rose,
I wish I may be shute if I don't hate Rose.
Let go my arm, Rose, let me at him rush.
I swella his two lip like a black a balla brush.
Let go my arm, Rose, an let me top his win.
Let go my arm Rose, while I kick him on de shin.
　　Oh, Rose &c.

I ketch hold ob Cuffee, I take him by de wool.
I ketch hold ob Cuffee, he try away to pull.
But I up wid a foot an kick him on de shin,
Which put him breafless on de floor, an made de nigger grin.
　　Oh, Rose &c.

He jump up for sartin cut, dart an run,
Now Sambo follow arter wid his tum, tum, tum,
He jump up for sartin he cut dart and run,
No Sambo follow arter, wid his tum, tum, tum.
Oh, Rose, curse dat Rose.
I wish Master Hays² would ketch dat Rose.
Ah Rose cus dat Rosa! I wish I may be hang'd if I don't hate Rose.

*The Original Jim Crow*³

1
Come listen all you galls and boys
I's jist from Tuckyhoe,⁴
I'm goin to sing a little song,
My name is Jim Crow

Chorus:
Weel about and turn about and do jis so,
Eb'ry time I weel about and jump Jim Crow.

2

Oh I'm a roarer on de Fiddle,
And down in old Virginny,
They say I play de skyentific
Like Massa Pagannini.[5]

3

I git 'pon a flat boat
I cotch de Uncle Sam,
Den I went to see de place
Where dey kill'd Packenham.[6]

4

I went down to de riber,
I did'nt mean to stay,
But dere I see so many galls,
I could'nt get away.

5

An den I go to Orleans
An feel so full of fight
Dey put me in de Calaboose,
An keep me dare all night.

6

When I got out I hit a man,
His name I now forget,
But dere was nothing left
'Sept a little grease spot.

7

I wip my weight in wildcats
I eat an Alligator,
And tear up more ground
Dan kifer 50 load of tater.

8

I sit upon a Hornet's nest,
I dance upon my head,
I tie a Wiper[7] round my neck
And den I goes to bed.

9

Dere's Possum up de gumtree
An Raccoon in de hollow,
Wake Snakes for June bugs
Stole my half a dollar.

10

A ring tail'd monkey
An a rib nose Babboon,
Went out de odder day
To spend de arternoon.

11

Oh de way dey bake de hoecake[8]
In old Virginny neber tire
Dey put de doe upon de foot
An hole it to de fire.

12

Oh by trade I am a carpenter,
But be it understood,
De way I get my liben is,
By sawing de tick oh wood.

13

I'm a full blooded niggar,
Ob de real ole stock,
An wid my head and shoulder
I can split a horse block.

14

I struck a Jarsey niggar,
In de street de oder day,
An I hope I neber stir
If he didn't turn gray.

15

I'm berry much afraid of late
Dis jumping will be no good.
For while de Crow are dancing,
De Wites will saw de wood.

16

But if dey get honest,
By sawing wood like slaves
Der'es an end to de business,
Ob our friend Massa Hays.[9]

17

I met a Philadelphia niggar
Dress'd up quite nice & clean
But de way he 'bused de Yorkers
I thought was berry mean.

18

So I knocked down dis Sambo
And shut up his light,
For I'm jist about as sassy,
As if I was half white.

19

But he soon jumped up again,
An 'gan for me to feel,
Says I go away you niggar,
Or I'll skin you like an eel.

20

I'm so glad dat I'm a niggar,
An dont you wish you was too
For den you'd gain popularity
By jumping Jim Crow.

21

Now my brodder niggars,
I do not think it right,
Dat you should laugh at dem
Who happen to be white.

22

Kase it dar misfortune,
And dey'd spend ebery dollar,
If dey only could be
Gentlemen ob colour.

23

It almost break my heart,
To see dem envy me,
An from my soul I wish dem,
Full as black as we.

24

What stuf it is in dem,
To make de Debbil black
I'll prove dat he is white
In de twinkling of a crack.

25

For you see loved brodders,
As true as he hab a tail,
It is his berry wickedness,
What makes him turn pale.

26

I went to Hoboken,
To hab a promenade,
An dar I see de pretty gals,
Drinking de Lemonade.

27

Dat sour and dat sweet,
Is berry good by gum',
But de best of lemonade is,
Made by adding rum.

28

At de Swan cottage,
Is de place I tink,
Whar dey make dis'licious,
An 'toxicating drink.

29

Some go to Weehawk,
An some to Brooklyn hight
But dey better stay at home,
If dey want to see de sight.

30

To go to de museum,
I'm sure it is dare duty,
If for noting else,
Jist to see de sleeping beauty.

31

An dare is daddy Lambert,[10]
An a skeleton on he hunkie,
An likeness of Broadway dandy
In a glass case of monkies.

32

De Broadway bells,
When dey carry full sail,
Around dem wear a funny ting,
Just like a fox tail.

33

When you hear de name of it,
I sure it make you roar,
Why I ax'd 'em what it was,
And dey said it was a boar.

34

De great Nullification,
And fuss in de South,
Is now before Congress,
To be tried by word ob mouth.

35

Dey hab had no blows yet,
And I hope dey nebber will,
For its berry cruel in bredren,
One anoders blood to spill.

36

Wid Jackson at de head,
Dey soon de ting may settle
For ole Hickory is a man,
Dat's tarnal full ob mettle.

37

Should dey get to fighting,
Perhaps de blacks will rise,
For deir wish for freedom,
Is shining in deir eyes.

38

An if de blacks should get free,
I guess dey'll fee some bigger,
An I shall concider it,
A bold stroke for de niggar.

39

I'm for freedom,
An for Union altogether,
Aldough I'm a black man,
De white is call'd my broder.

40

I'm for union to a gal,
An dis is a stubborn fact,
But if I marry an dont like it,
I'll nullify de act.

41

I'm tired of being a single man
An I'm tarmined to get a wife
For what I think de happiest
Is de swee married life.

42

Its berry common 'mong de white
To marry and get divorced
But dat I'll nebber do
Unless I'm really forced

43

I think I see myself in Broadway
Wid my wife upon my arm,
And to follow up de fashion,
Dere sure can be no harm.

44

An I caution all white dandies,
Not to come in my way,
For if dey insult me,
dey'll in de gutter lay.

Jim Crow, Still Alive!!![11]

1

De way to bake a hoe cake
Ol Virginny nebber tire,
Stick de hoe cake on de foot,
And hold it to de fire.
So I wheel about
I turn about
I do just so,
And ebry time I wheel about
I jump Jim Crow.

2

Old Sam Peacock
Stole a side of leather
Well done Sam
Cant you go and steal anoder
So I wheel, etc.

3

Dere's meat upon de goosefoot,
And marrow on de bone,
Dere's pretty gals at our house,
An mamma's not at home.
So I wheel, etc.

4

I listed in de army
An sarve Uncle Sam,
Any other service
Aint worth a damn.
So I wheel, etc.

5

At New Orleans town
De British went to teal,
But when dey see ol Hickory,
Day took to dere heel.
So I wheel, etc.

6

Lord how dey cut dirt,
An didn't stop to trifle.
For dey didn't like de sight
Ob de dam Yankee rifle.
So I wheel, etc.

7

I'm a touch of the snapping turtle,
Nine-tenths of a bull dog.
I've turned the Mississippy,
All for a pint of grog.
So I wheel, etc.

8

I went to New York,
And I tink I cut a swell,
And de first place I stopp'd at,
Was Holt's new Hotel.[12]
So I wheel, etc.

9

I went up stairs
To peep at de nation,
And dere I met Ol Hays[13]

An all de Corporation.[14]
So I wheel, etc.

10

An Alderman got up to top,
And called for a glass ob gin,
Says he, I'm nearer Heaven
Dan I shall ever be agin.
So I wheel, etc.

11

Dey had so many good tings
As true as I'm a sinner,
I tink rader went a head
Ob de Corporation dinner.
So I wheel, etc.

12

Dey bid me help myself
An cut and come again,
An sure I wasnt slow
When dey brought de Campaigne[15]
So I wheel, etc.

13

But I dont admire de liquor,
It berry good for some,
But we gentleman of color,
Always prefer de niggar rum.

14

When I was in Philadelphia,
I had to laugh in de treet,
To see de butcher women
In de market selling meat.

15

Dere you can see women
Slipping on like a sled,
With a tub full of mackarel
Which dey carry on de head.

16

Sister Dinah hab gib a hint.
Dat Avery will swing[16]
An on dat gran occasion,
A verse or two I'll sing.

17

It is his last appearance
I guess upon de stage,
An I tink de naughty feller
Will exit in a rage.

18

Now my verses are de best kind,
And dis I'm sure's no bore,
For ebry time I dance and sing,
De people cry encore.

19

For poets are a poor set,
As you must all know,
For de more dey try to write,
De poorer dey do grow.
So I wheel, etc.

20

Oh I saw a dandy niggar wench,
An I thought dat I should die,
When I saw her wink at me,
An roll round her eye.

21

She was brack as de debbil,
An she hab such a squint,
Dat when she wink at me
I couldn't take he hint.

22

Election's coming on,
An I'll try if I can,
Just be elected for a 'Sembly man.

23

I tink if I get in,
I should suit em to a hair,
An de next ting dey would do
Would be to make me mayor.

24

For de duties ob de Semblyman
I tink is very funny,
For dey only hab to eat dinners,
And spend de people's money.

25

Dey dont mind what folks say,
Tho' it comes from every quarter,
An all de people wants
Is a little wholesome water.[17]

26

But dat don consarn dem,
For what do you tink!
Why water is de only ting
Dat dey do not drink.

27

I stopt at Washington City,
The capital ob de nation,
An I ax'd Massa Jackson
To gib me situation.

28

Says he, Jim Crow,
What can you do?
I can nullify de boot,
An put de veto on de shoe.

29

Says he, Jim Crow,
What can you do for me?
Says I, Massa Jackson,
I can plant a hickory tree.

30

Forty-eleben debbils
Lived in Noah's ark,
Jona was de fisherman
What swallowed down de shark.

31

It rained forty days,
An it rained forty nites,
And Noah's Ark rested
On de Brooklyn Hites.

32

Oh by trade I am a carpenter
But be it understood,
De way I get a liben is
By sawing de stick ob wood.

33

I hab a sneaking notion,
If dere's fun to be had,
Its not in skinning cat-fish,
Or in eating raw shad.

34

I was at a ball de oder night,
A lady tried to faint,
We poured water on her face,
Not tinking der was paint.

35

And sich a nasty figgur,
I'm sure was neber seen,
A face wid streaks of red and white,
Dat before looked berry clean.

36

Dis song is getting long
But will be longer still,
For I am full 'tarmined
To give you your fill.

37

If you want to buy a song,
De one you like you'll meet,
At five hundred seventy two
North Second Street[18]

38

If I were a regular sweep,
I'd set the town a ringing,
So musical my verses are,
For scantimental singing.

39

But de real fun of all is,
And dis you all well know,
Is to gib de scientific touch,
Ob jumping Jim Crow.
So I wheel, etc.

40

I'm a full blooded niggar,
Ob de real old stock,
An wid my head and shoulders
I can split a horse block.

41

I struck a Jarsey niggar,
In de street de oder day,
An I hope I neber stir,
If he did'nt turn grey.

42

I'm berry much afraid ob late,
Dis jumping will be no good,
For while de Crows are dancing,
De *Whites* will saw de wood.

43

But if dey get honest,
By sawing wood like slaves,
Dere's an end to the business
Ob our friend Massa Hays.

44

I met a New York niggar,
Dress'd up quite clean,
But de way he bused de Delphians,
I thought was bery mean.

45

So I knock'd down dis Sambo
And shut up his light,
For I'm jist about as sassy,
As if I was half white.

46

But he soon jumped up again,
An 'gan for me to feel,
Says I, go away you niggar,
Or I'll skin you like an eel.

47

Dere's anoder niggar,
As cunning as a fox.
He's a great steam scourer,
And his name is dandy Cox.

48

I hab a gal in dis city,
She's as quick as a trigger,
And she neber look so handsome,
As when kiss'd by a niggar.

49

A white kiss is good enouff
But it don't sound so keen,
As when given by a brack man,
Wid a great broad grin.

50

When I do kiss the lubly creatures,
I screw my mouth just so,
For it makes me feel so bery good,
Dat I don't know what to do.

51

But I neber kissed a white gal,
And I hope I nebber will;
For you hab to be so delicate,
You cannot get your fill.

52

I went to de chicken coop
An got upon my knees,
I tink I die a laughing
To hear de chickens sneeze.

53

De great Nullification,
And de fuss in the South,
Is now before Congress
To be tried by de word ob mouth.

54

Dey hab had no blows yet,
An I hope dey nebber will,
For it's berry cruel in bredren,
One anoder's blood to spill.

55

Wid Jackson at de head
Dey soon dis ting may settle
For ol Hickory is a man
Dat's tarnal full ob mettle.

56

Should dey go to fighting,
Perhaps de bracks will rise,
For der wish for freedom
Is shining in der eyes.

57

An if de bracks should get free,
I guess dey'll feel som bigger,
I shall consider it
A bo'd stroke for de niggar.

58

I am for freedom
An for union altogeder,
Although I am a brack man,
De white is called my broder.

59

What stuff it is in dem,
To make de debbil brack,
I'll prove dat he is white,
In de twinkling of a crack.
So I wheel about, etc.

60

For you see loved brodders,
As true as he hab a tail,
It is his berry wickedness,
What makes he turn pale.

61

I went to de Camden,
To hab a promenade.
And dare I saw de dretty gals,
Drinking de lemonade.

62

Dat sour and dat sweet,
Is berry good by gum,
But de best of lemonade is
Made by adding rum.

63

At de Swan cottage,
Is de place I tink,
Whar dey make dis liscious
And toxicating drink.

64

De Filedelfia grog shop,
You can see as dey pass,
And dey sell de best ob lekier
For three cents a glass.

65

Some go to Weehawk
And some to Brooklyn heights
But dey better stay at home
If dey want to see de sights.

66

To go to de museum
I'm sure it is der duty
If for notting else
Just to see de sleeping beauty.

67

And dere is Daddy Lambert[19]
An a skeleton on he hunkies.
And likeness of Broadway dandy,
In a glass case of monkies.

68

Dere was one Sam Patch[20]
Who took de ugly leap,
He'd better stay in York,
And be a chimney sweep.

69

An if he minded he profession
An not to fond of de cup
When oders was getting down
He'd sure be getting up.

70

I seen a pretty gal,
Wid a tipet and a muff,
I don't know what her trade is,
But I guess she's up to snuff.

71

She went in de dry goods store,
An winked at de clerk,
She ax'd him to come to her house,
A little arter dark.

72

He went to de three bells,
He watch went up de spout,
Kase de master was in de store,
An he no chance for sourkrout.

73

Dis wicked boy do dat,
All for a painted face,
Which berry soon I see
Will bring him to disgrace.

74

I'm for union to a gal
An dis is a stubborn fact,
Dat if I marry an don't like it,
I'll nullify de act.

75

I'm sure dere be gals enuff,
To hab a fair chance,
An if I don't get a good un,
I'll laugh it off an dance.

76

I'm tired ob being a single man,
An I'm tarmin'd to git a wife,
For what I tink de happiest,
Is de sweet married life.

77

Its berry common 'mong de whites
To marry and git divorc'd,
But dat I'll deber do,
Unless I'm really forced.

78

I tink I see myself on Rail Road,
Wid a wife upon my arm,
An to foller up de fashun,
Dare sure can be no harm.

79

An I caution all de white dandies
Not to come in my way,
For as sure as they insult me,
Dey'll in de gutter lay.

80

De Chesnut street belles,
When dey carry full sail
Around dem wear a funny ting,
Just like a fox' tail.

81

When you har de name of it,
I sure it make you roar.
Why I ax'd em what it was,
And dey said it was a bore.

82

My sister dinah I see
Has made a great debut
But she cannot dance like me
No more den one ob you.

83

She's my sista it is true,
But dat is not de ting,
For what is de use ob wenches
Trying to jump play and sing.

84

Dare's sista Cuffelena,
Now she hab more sense,
Dan to fool away her time,
An at her own expense.

85

And Cuffelena hab got a plan,
Into effect she'll carry.
And dat is to make a match,
And her lubly Sambo marry.

86

But as for poor Dinah,
Its just as mudder said,
She be a bery sassy gal,
Wid a soft piece on de head.

87

She's a tarnal sassy niggar,
As you I guess can see,
Or she would'nt make a fuss,
And try to blaguard me.

88

Now my brodder niggars,
I do not tink it right,
Dat you should laugh at dem,
Who happen to be white.

89

Kase its dar misfortune,
An dey'd spend every dollar
If dey could only be
Gentlemen ob colour.

90

It almost break my heart,
To see dem envy me,
And from my soul I wish dem
Full as brack as we.

91

For I am as true a nigger
As ever yet was born,
An I am little fractious
When I hab a small horn.[21]

92

For I'm of a dancing family,
An I'd radder dance dan pray,
For ob de two professions,
De dancing's de best pay.

93

As I was born in a cane break,
An Dinah in a dough-trough,
I hope you'll see de difference,
And hussle her off.

94

Now before I leave you,
One ting I hab to ask,
If de making ob dese verses
Be not a plagy task.

95

But if you're not contented,
An tink it is not right,
I'll come agen some oder time,
An dance all night.

96

Now white folks, white folks,
Don't take offence,
An when I take a benefit,
I'll treat to stone fence.[22]

97

Farewell, farewell,
But dont cry encore,
You now had 100 verses,
Nex time I gib you more.

98

O white folks, white folks,
I glad to hear you holler,
But I'll not jump Jim Crow 'gin
Unless you hit me wid a dollar.

Dinah Crow

1

O gentlemen an ladies
I'd hab you all to know,

Dat here is Miss Dinah,
A full sister to Jim Crow.
   I wink and smile,
   And play O jist so,
   And ebery one dat see me,
   Admire Miss Crow.

2

All de he niggars
Are full of dere stuff.
But dat Jersey niggar
I tink dey call him Cuff.
   I wink and smile, etc.

3

He call for to see me,
When I was washing in de yard.
And de dandy couldn't see me,
So he luff his card.
   I wink and smile, etc.

4

He cum next Sunday,
To wait on me to church,
But I went off wi Sambo
And left him in the lurch.
   I wink and smile, etc.

5

Sambo is a nice man,
And dresses so neat,
You'd take him for a gemman,
If you meet him in de street.
   I wink and smile, etc.

6

He hab a profession,
An not like de dandies,
You can see him in Market Street,
Selling of de candies.
   I wink and smile, etc.

7

He's got a little table,
An he sits him on a stump,
And he sells to the boy,
De sweet lasses lump.
    I wink and smile, etc.

8

He hate my proud sister
De ugly Cuffelena,
But he berry fond ob me,
His sweet and lubly Dinah.
    I wink and smile, etc.

9

I tink I mus hab him,
Since he mus hab a wife,
An if he do behave,
We'll lead a merry life.
    I wink and smile, etc.

10

While oders in de shoops
Drinking from de glasses,
We'd rather be at home,
Boiling our molasses.
    I wink and smile, etc.

11

If you come to see us,
Sure it make you luffee,
If you only view us,
Making ob our taffy.
    I wink and smile, etc.

12

When de little niggar born,
(For dey sure enuff to cum,)
Den we mean to treat our friends
Wid a pint of niggar rum.
    I wink and smile, etc.

13

I hab a might trouble,
And dat's my broder Jim,
For he's so bery ill-bred,
I can do nothing wid him.
　　I wink and smile, etc.

14

I went to Camptown market
To buy a marrow bone,
Den de butcher fall in lub,
An want to see me home.
　　I wink and smile, etc.

15

An when we arrived dere,
An he laid down de meat,
He bery politely ax
If I were going to treat.
　　I wink and smile, etc.

16

An I thought it be mean,
Since I had ax'd him in,
So I took the colonny bottle
An bought a glass of gin.
　　I wink, etc.

17

I give him a glas,
An he took two or tree sips
An den he wanted to kiss
My lubly pouting lips.
　　I wink, etc.

18

But I soon ax'd no,
An said he'd better hop,
For if granted dat fabor,
He wouldn't know where to stop.
　　I wink, etc.

19

For young gals must take care,
An keep de fellers cibil,
Or berry son dey hab cause
To wish dem to de debbil.
    I wink, etc.

20

De chesnut street gals
Wear der petticoats so high,
Dat too much is exposed
Unto de naked eye.
    I wink, etc.

21

I set dem example
Dey better follow by half,
For I only show de ancle,
Instead of de calf.
    I wink, etc.

22

I seed a feller peeping down,
An I ax'd what he were arter,
Says he, I only want to see
Where dat girl ties her garter.
    I wink, etc.

23

If de gals wear der frock
Up to de moon,
I would advise dem
To wear de trowsaloon.
    I wink, etc.

24

O dis Philadelfy's a wicked place,
To take de stranger in,
For de gals wear de false tings,
And tink it be no sin.
    I wink, etc.

25

I seed an old maid,
An her mouth was so gum'd
Dat she could not eat a cracker,
Unless she had it mumm'd
   I wink, etc.

26

She went down Arch street,
And pawned her clothes for bones,
And now dese false teeth
Is all dat she owns.
   I wink, etc.

27

Wid white paint an red,
An salve for de lips,
And a sham bishop[23] behind,
An a false pair ob hips.
   I wink, etc.

28

Dey rig demselves out,
An promenade all day
An pass demselves off
For a lady gay.
   I wink, etc.

29

Wid dere big cloth cloaks
And little velvet hats,
Dey are in prime order
For to catch de flats.
   I wink, etc.

30

Oder day I was walking
An lemonading in de street,
Wid my shoe laces dangling,
All around my feet.
   I wink, etc.

31

Pompey says to me
De politest ting I can do
Is to ax de lady in de street
If I may tie her shoe.
    I wink, etc.

32

O when I consented,
His heart wid rapture beat,
Lord I thought he would die,
When he looked at my feet.
    I wink, etc.

33

My shoe muddied his trowsers,
Played debbil wid his vest
False bosom did fly open
An expose his naked breast.
    I wink, etc.

34

When he fingered de strings,
His ideas began to creep,
All de while he tie de shoe
His eyes began to peep.
    I wink, etc.

35

Says I, you nasty niggar,
What debbil are you arter.
What make you want to know
Where a lady tie her garter.
    I wink, etc.

36

Dere he was in de open street,
Exposed to de vulgar gaze,
When who show'd de cloven foot,
But de niggar's foe, Old Hays.[24]
    I wink, etc.

37
Den dis ferocious man
Takes Pomp by de collar,
Den he wouldn't let him go,
Kase he didn't show de dollar.
　I wink, etc.

38
Den he took him to de court,
And dere dey did sentence he,
All for to sarve tree month
Out in de penitentiary.
　I wink, etc.

39
After dey hab sentence him,
I couldn't make a muss,
So he hab to take a ride
In Fair Mount omnibus.
　I wink, etc.

40
I didn't begrudge him de ride
But I didn't tink it right,
Dat dey should chain a nigger
Along side a sassy white.
　I wink, etc.

41
O its slippery an wet,
An I don't know what to do,
I cant raise de dollar,
To buy de Indian rubber shoe.
　I wink, etc.

42
Dey are maid for niggars
An I like dem a deal
Kase dey stretch so
To fit de cuffy's heel
　I wink, etc.

43

Between de white an brack,
I'm sure dere is no kin,
Whites tender place is on head,
Negro's on de shin.
    I wink, etc.

44

Sharp nose for de white,
De cuffy hab a chubb,
De way I like a niggars
Is up to de hub.
    I wink, etc.

45

Most white men
Look too pale
Some hab a red nose
Kase dey dring too much ale.
    I wink, etc.

46

White gals hab queer tastes
Some lub anniseed
Some like spruce beer
But gib me Pope's Mead.
    I wink, etc.

47

One day I seed a wench
Dressed out in silk,
Next day I seed her
Selling buttermilk.
    I wink, etc.

48

Lor breesdem hansum niggars
What lib in Shippen street.[25]
Though dey go to pray'r meetin,
How slick an sly dey cheat.
    I wink, etc.

49

When de meetin' it is out,
Den homeward how dey run,
Dey soon doff dere bonnets plain,
To hab a bit of—fun.
    I wink, etc.

50

For sartin sure de gals are rite,
An I tink it is no sin,
If dey slily slip a cross de street
An git a drop ob gin.
    I wink, etc.

51

But dem ob Antony an Church
I had amose forgot;
Dey eber take a stranger in,
And der corn um berry hot.
    I wink, etc.

52

On de fifth of July,
De niggars hab permission,
All for to celumbrate
De gran Bobalition.
    I wink, etc.

53

Den you'll see Dinah Crow,
As de wite ladies do,
Trip de gran Rushun waltz,
Fixt in silver an blue.
    I wink, etc.

54

De composition of dis
Will get me many an admirer,
An I expect a puff
In de Inquirer.
    I wink, etc.

55

De brack ban dey turn[26]
And for musick dey don't lack,
While de niggar captain
Look like a dandy jack.
    I wink, etc.

56

When dey walk till um warm
Dey will get in a room
Gosh! it do de heart good
For to smell de sweet fume.
    I wink, etc.

57

I went to de teatre,
All for too see de show,
An dere was a wite niggar,
Making fun of Jim Crow.
    I wink, etc.

58

Dis ruffled up my temper,
An my hair stood strate out,
Says I, you nasty wite man,
I'll surely break your snout.

59

I see a gran dandy niggar,
On de teatre street he stood
I cotch him next morning early
Sawing a load ob wood.[27]

60

I met a sassy he niggar,
An gib him such a crack,
Dat I split him like a shad
Up and down de back.

61

I mean to git married
An make a mighty fuss

For dere's notting can be sweeter,
Dan to hug, squeeze and buss.

62
I'd like to hab a man,
Wid neat an curly locks
And cut as big a figger
As de "steamer" dandy Cox.

63
Here's a health to de wite gals
But dere's one ting dey lack,
For how dey would be tickled,
If like me dey were only brack.

64
I'm de tip ob de fashion,
As you can easy see.
An de wite gals may take pattern
An fashion arter me.

65
Dey may dress and dey may paint
An look slick as an eel,
But when it comes to dancing,
Dey want de niggar heel.

66
De writing ob dese lines
Hab made me berry sad,
But now dey are done
I am damn glad

67
Now I am done,
I leave you in de lurch,
Whoever steal dese lines
I tink would rob a church.
    I wink, etc.

Jim Crow[28]

I cam from ole Kentucky,
A long time ago,
Where I first larn to wheel about
And jump Jim Crow.

Wheel about and turn about
And do jis so
Ebry time I wheel about,
I jump Jim Crow

I us'd to take him fiddle
Ebry morn and afternoon
And charm the old Buzzard
And dance to the Raccoon
[Chorus]

I landed fust at Liverpool
Dat place of Ships and Docks
I strutted down Lord Street
And as'd de price of Stocks
[Chorus]

I paid my fare den up to Town
And de coach to cut a dash
De Axletree soon gave way.
And spilt us wid a smash.
[Chorus]

I lighted den upon my head,
All in de nassy dirt
Dey all thought dat I war dead
But I laughed and wasn't hurt
[Chorus]

Dis head you know am pretty tick,
Cause dere it make a hole
On de dam macadamis road
Much bigger dan a bowl
[Chorus]

When I got into Lunnon
Dey took me for a savage.
But I war pretty well behaved,
So I gaged with Massa Davidge[29]
[Chorus]

Dem young Jim Crows bout de streets
More like a Raven rader,
Pray good people don't mistake
Indeed I'm not dare fader
[Chorus]

Dem urchin's what sing my song,
Had better mind dar books.
For any how dey cant be Crows
You see d'ar only Rooks.
[Chorus]

De Original Jim Crow[30]

Oh Jim Crow's cum again, as you must all know
For he wheel about, he jump about, he do just so,
   And ebery time he jump about, he jump Jim Crow.
   So I wheel about, I turn about,
   I do just so,
   And ebery time I wheel about,
   I jump Jim Crow.
I kneel to de buzzard, and I bow to de crow,
An ebery time I wheel about, I jump Jim Crow,
   So I wheel about, &c.
I stopt at Washington City, as I came from de West,
An went for to see de great President.
   So I wheel about, &c.
I meet ole Andy at de corner ob de street,
Says he, Jim Crow, an't you gwan for to treat.
   So I wheel about, &c.
So I pull'd out my pocket-book, I didn't mind expense

An went in an got a horn ob good stone fence.[31]
    So I wheel about, &c.
An arter I had treated him to a smaller ob de best
I went to count my money, an found but a quarter left.
    So I wheel about, &c.
Den, says he, Jim Crow, I know what are at,
You cum for an office, an I'll make you my shoe black
    So I wheel about, &c.
De Kentucky niggas dey libs on mush,
But de Philadelphia niggas, dey say "Oh, Hush!"
    So I wheel about, &c.
De New York niggas, dey tink dey are free,
Case dey all out ob de penitentiary.
    So I wheel about, &c.
De New York loafers dey cum here to teal
Dey cum up de market and tole a leg ob veal.
    So I wheel about, &c.
Old folks, old folks you'd better go to bed,
Case you only put de debil in de young folks hed.
    So I wheel about, &c.
A ring tail'd monkey and a ribb'd nose baboon,
Went out de oder day to spend de arternoon.
    So I wheel about, &c.
So den at night dey went to drink dere tea,
De one drank Shoushong, de oder bohea.
    So I wheel about, &c.
I met Miss Dinah, an I gin her a buss,
She slapt me in de face and made a mighty fuss.
    So I wheel about, &c.
Snake bak'd a hoe cake, and set de frog to watch it,
De frog fell asleep, and de lizard come an cotch'd it.
    So I wheel about, &c.
I cum to a riber an couldn't get across,
So I gib half a dolla for an old blind horse.
    So I wheel about, &c.
I druv this horse up a hill, an just as he got to de top
He fell down and got kill'd, an den I couldn't swop.
    So I wheel about, &c.

Dere's Van Buren, he's firmly bent,
To hold himself up for de next President.[32]
    So I wheel about, &c.
Now if I was President ob dese United States,
I'd drink mint julep, an swing upon de gates.
    So I wheel about, &c.
Oh, massa gib me holiday I staid ober time,
So he hung me up and gib me sweet thirty nine.
    So I wheel about, &c.
Oh, Jim Crow struck a man, his name I forgot,
But dare was notin left but a little grease spot.
    So I wheel about, &c.
I'm for union to a gal, an dis is a stubborn fact,
But if I marry an don't like it, I'll nullify de act.
    So I wheel about, &c.
I'm tired ob being single, so I'm tarmined to git a wife,
[F]or what I tink de happiest, is de sweet married life.
    So I wheel about, &c.
I tink I see myself in Broadway, wid wife upon my arm,
An to follow up de fashion, dere sure can be no harm.
    So I wheel about, &c.
Oh, white folks, white folks, I see your up to snuff,
I'm berry much afraid dat you neber get enuff.
    So I wheel about, &c.

Jim Crow[33]

OLD JIM CROW's come agin, as you must all know,
And ebery body say I cum to jump Jim Crow
    Chorus.—Weel about and turn about, and do jis so.
      Ebery time I weel about, I jump Jim Crow.

My name is Daddy Rice, as you berry well do know,
And none in de Nited States like me, can jump Jim Crow.

I was born in a cane break, and cradled in a trough,
Swam de Mississippi, whar I cotch'd de hoopen coff.

To whip my weight in wild cats, eat an alligator,
And drink de Mississippi dry, I'm de very *critter*.

I went to de woods, heard a debil of a howl,
I look'd up a tree, and saw a great owl.

I off wid my hat, stuck my heel in de ground,
And then went to work to grin the owl down.

I grinn'd wid my eyes open, and den wid um shut,
But I could not diskiver dat I stirred de owl a foot.

Den I grinn'd slantendicular, den wid one eye,
'Twould have done your soul good to see de feathers fly.

Den I climb'd up de tree, and I wish I may be shot,
If I had'nt been grinning at a great pine knot.

I'm like de frost in ole December, git my foot widin de ground,
Takes a hook and ladder company to try to pull me down.

And eben when you get me down, I melt and run about,
You'll hab to send for engine, to cum and put me out.

Though you tink you got me out, some heat dar will remain,
Nex morning, bright and early, I'll be blazing up agin.

I've been to old Kentucky, whar I hab you for to know,
Dat all de pretty ladies dar lub Jim Crow.

I've been to Philadelphia, New York and Baltimore,
But when I got to Boston, it beat all I'd seen before.

Dey build most all dar houses out ob brick and stone,
Dey run em up so high, dey almost reach de moon.

Dey talk ob de Philadelphia markets, an de New York markets, loud,
But de ole market, here in Boston, will be seen among de crowd.

No matter what is wantin, in de market you can buy
From a quarter of an ox, down to a punkin pie.

Dare is someting I gwaing to tell you, which I want you all to know,
Dare is a pretty lady here, in lub wid Jim Crow.

Lor bless de lubly creature, I teach dem how to dance,
And show dem de new step, just arrived from France.

Dis is de style of Alabama, what dey hab in Mobile,
And dis is Louisiana, whar dey trike upon de heel.

Here's Virginny double trouble, whar dey dance de corn chuck,
And dere's de real scientific, what dey hab in Kentuck.

Here's de long Island ube,³⁴ or de hunck ober dee,
And here's de Georgia step, by de double rule ob tree.

Here's de kneel to Carleton's daughter, what dey hab in Indian,
And here's de old Mississippi step, and fetch it if you can.

And dare is ole Virginny, she cut a pretty figger,
I neber go dar, kase dey don't respect de nigger.

It was twelve o'clock de udder night, or somewhere dare about,
I took my finger for de snuffers, and put de candle out.

De debil take de noise when de nigger is so tire.
When along came watchman, and hollar, fire!! fire!!

O, I got out ob de bed, put on my close widout much fright,
And started for de fire, in de middle ob de night.

When I got to de fire, I did'nt know what to do.
But I heard a gemman cry, lay hold ob No. 2.

I went up to de Colonel, and ax'd how he'd ben,
He say, you sassy nigger, you lay hold ob No. 10.

I work hard at de engine, den de foreman send for rum,
Jolly, how my eye glisten, wen I see it cum.

When I saw de eatables a comin, says I, if you please,
I'll thank you for a stiffer, and hunk ob bread and cheese.

I take one horn, and den I take anoder,
When I drink more, white man call me brudder.

Den I went down to Ann Street, did'nt mean to stay,
But dey took me to de watch house, and I couldn't get away.

And de tin pot alley, de niggers had a hop,
I went in a little while, didn't mean to stop.

The house was topsy turvy, all turned upside down,
And de niggers had de dance ten foot under groun.

De wite folks get a barrel of flour, and knock'd de head in,
And den de way dey cried fire, I'm sure it was a sin.

De niggers rushed out, as if it was a shower,
And when dey got up stair, dey let'em hab de flour.

And such a set ob niggers, I'm sure was neber seen,
And such fun in white folk, I tink was berry mean.

I was liv'd in ole Virginny, and dey used to gib me
Hoe cakes, sassafras, and shangalanga tea.

De way dey bake de hoe cake, in old Virginny neber tire,
Dey put de cake upon de foot, and hold de foot to de fire.

If nature make me black man, and oder folks white,
I went to ole Boston, where dey learn me left and right.

I went into de cradle, where dey rock'd sweet Liberty,
And dare I saw de names ob those who made their country free.

I went across to Charlestown, and on to Bunker Hill,
Which once de British tried to climb, but found it diffikil.

'Twas dare I saw de Navy Yard, likewide de Dry Dock.
'Twas lin'd by de best ob stone, dug out ob Quincy Rock.

Near it lay de ship ob war, among dem de Constitution,
Which our brave heroes sail'd in, and put England in confusion.

De finest fun dat ever happened, was in de city ob New York,
When dey told de British soger it was time to walk and talk.

Dey did'nt know what to tink ob it, when dey found dey must be gone,
Kase dey hab no shoe or tocking on, and cold wedder comin on.

So dey gaddered up dare fixeds, and 'gan to march away,
And sailed for land ob Johnny Bull, about de brake ob day.

When dey got back to England dey didn't fear de debbil,
Buy dey radder be excused, dan fight wid Yankee rebel.

For dey are are like a piece ob India rubber, you may hit 'em on de
    sconce,
De harder dat you knock 'em down, de higher up they bounce.

Dare's a place dey call de Boson, once fought for liberty,
Dey'd throw de nullifiers overboard, as once dey did de tea.

Dar's two ole sogers, whose names me no forget,
One was massa George Washington, de oder Laughayit.

When de war was ober, and ebery ting content,
De people make George Washington de great President.

Den he put all de States togedder, and tied a string around,
And when de string is broken, boys, dey'll tumble to de ground.

When dey was first set up, dare was only a dozen and one,
But now dare is twenty-four, and a number more to cum.

Dese twenty-four children belong to Uncle Sam,
And hab been bery dutiful, except now and den.

You all know who Uncle Sam is, from de captain to de mate,
He's de fader of de children ob dese Nited State.

He's got a handsome fortune by industry's made,
And now his chief concern is, to gib his children a trade.

He's got one sassy daughter, her name is Caroline,
I'm 'fraid he'll hab to tie her up and gib her 39.

Now as for South Carlina, she'd better keep her passion in,
Or else she'll get a licken now, before she does begin.

Johnny C. Calhoun is courting her, dey say he's got de wedding ring,
And when de weddin' ober, dey are going to make him king.

When he walks up to Caroline, her sun-bright hand to take,
Be careful de wedding ring don't turn out to be an Irish wake.

Dey say South Carolina is a fool, and as for Johnny C. Calhoun,
He'll be worse dan Davy Crockett, when he tried to fool de coon.

Oh, he took up his crooked gun, and fired round de maple tree,
De ball came back in de same place, and hit him on de knee.

O, wite folks, wite folks, I see you up to snuff,
I'm bery much afraid dat you neber get anuff.

Now wite folks, wite folks, please to let me go.
And I'll cum back anuder night and jump Jim Crow.

All de Women Shout Loo! Loo![35]

Hark! I hear de frum-frums blow,
Karemboos from de norf hab come;
We'll blue our beards wid indigo,
And sound de banderer and drum.
    While all de women shout loo! loo!
    Lots ob life at Jim buc too.[36]

Run a thong in de white bull's nose,
Let his tail wid scarlet brush be dyed,
He dance till he crack his horny toes,
When de Musgow gals him back bestride.
    While all de women, &c.

I caper if you'll strong waters bring,
Go fetch you tick lip broder down,
I'm hired a 'jillee man'[37] to sing,
Ole Yussuf's come from Bornow Town.
    While all de women, &c.

A Tibboo Man once steal my corn,
I squash him flat like button ob brass,
I knock my bes wife down dis morn,
She quiz too much at de looking glass.
    While all de women, &c.

Here's sour milk and meal for a Sinkatoo,
A boat brought down a poor dead man,
I can't make a sweet sarce out ob you,
So he must be buried how he can.
    While all de women, &c.

I'm smear'd wid oil—I'm fit to fight,
I've asked a Fortune Teller my luck;
I'm strong as a sea Oss toof to night
And sheep facc Muckna got no pluck.
    While all de women, &c.

If you dance all night your beads 'ell bust,
Lets make a game in de sand wid de beans;
De white Man's brought salt for gold dust,
So we rob his Camel by all means.
    While all de women, &c.

I'm come talk to you regular.
I'm got room for a nice fat bride;
I will get leab from your Papa,
Or else commit my shoes aside.
    While all de women, &c.

De Bandera shall loudly sound,
De singing gals shall scream to night
Come, fling de Bullock's flesh all round,
W'ell shout and roar and feast and fight.
    While all de women, &c.

Clare de Kitchen[38]

In old Kentuck in de arter noon,
We sweep de floor wid a bran new broom,
And arter dat we form a ring,
And dis de song dat we do sing,
    Oh! Clare de kitchen old folks, young folks,
    Clare de kitchen old folks young folks,
    Old Virginny never tire.

2

I went to de creek, I cou'dn't get a cross,
I'd nobody wid me but an old blind horse;
But old Jim Crow came riding by,
Says he, old fellow your horse will die.
    Its Clare de kitchen &c.

3

My horse fell down upon de spot,
Says he "don't you see his eyes is sot";
So I took out my knife and off wid his skin,
And when he comes to life I'll ride him agin.
   So Clare de kitchen &c.

4

A jay-bird sot on a hickory limb,
He wink'd at me and I wink'd at him;
I picked up a stone and I hit his shin,
Says he you better not do dat agin.
   He Clar'd de kitchen &c.

5

A Bull-frog dress'd in sogers close,[39]
Went in a field to shoot some crows;
De crows smell powder and fly away,
De Bull-frog mighty mad dat day.
   So Clare de kitchen &c.

6

Den I went down wid Cato Moore,
To see de Steam-boat come ashore;
Ev'ry man for himself, so I pick'd up a trunk—
Leff off, said the Captain, or I burn you wid a chunk.
   And Clare de kitchen &c.

7

I hab a sweetheart in dis town,
She wears a yellow striped gown;
And when she walks de streets around,
De hollow of her foot makes a hole in de ground.[40]
   Now Clare de kitchen &c.

8

Dis love is a ticklish ting you know,
It makes abody feel all over so;
I put de question to Coal black Rose,
She's as black as ten of spades, and got a lubly flat nose
   So Clare de kitchen &c.

9

Go away says she, wid your cowcumber[41] shin,
If you come here agin I stick you wid a pin;
So I turn on my heel and I bid her good bye,
And arter I was gone, she began for to cry.
    Oh! Clare de kitchen &c.

10

So now I'se up and off you see,
To take a julep sangaree;
I'll sit upon a tater hill,
And eat a little Whip-poor-will.
    So Clare de kitchen &c.

11

I wish I was back in old Kentuck,
For since I left it I had no luck;
De galls so proud dey won't eat mush,
And when you go to court'em dey say O hush.
    Its Clare de kitchen &c.

Gombo Chaff[42]

On de Ohio bluff in de state of Indiana,
Dere's where I live, chock up to de Habbanna.
Eb'ry mornin early Massa gib me licker,
I take my net and paddle and I put out de quicker,
I jump into my kiff. And I down de river driff,
And I cotch as many cat fish as ever nigger liff.

2

Now dis morning on a driff-log tink I see an Alligator,
I scull my skiff around and chuck him sweet potato,
I cratch him on de head and try for to vex it,
But I could'nt fool de varmint no how I could fix it;
So I picks up a brick an' I fotch'd him sich a lick,
But twant nothin' but a pine knot 'pon a big stick.

3

Now old Massa build a barn to put de fodder in,
Dis ting an dat ting an' one ting anodder;
Thirty ninth Decembur time come a rise ob water,
An' it carry Massa barn much farder dan it ought to;
Then old Massa swear he cuss an' tare his hair,
Becase de water tuck barn off he couldn't tell where.

4

Now old Massa die on de 'lebenteenth of April,
I put him in de troff what cotch de sugar maple,
I digs a deep hole right out upon de level,
An' I do believe sure enough he's gone to de debil,
For when he live you know he light upon me so,
But now he's gone to tote de firewood way down below.

5

Den Missis she did marry Big Bill de weaver,
Soon she found out he was a gay deceiver,
He grab all de money and put it in his pocket,
And de way he did put out was a sin to Davy Crocket;
So old Missis cry and 'gin to wipe her eye
For she marry Bill de weaver she cou'dn't tell why.

6

Now one day de sun gone down an' de days work over,
Old Gumbo Chaff he tink he'd live in Clover;
He jump into a boat wid his old Tamborine,
While schoonerhead Sambo play'd de Violin;
De way we sail'd to New Orleans never be forgotten,
Dey put me on de Levy dock to roll a bale of Cotton.

7

When I cotch hold de bale oh! den you ought to seen us!
First time dis child 'gan to show his genus;
I got hold de corner an' I give him such a hug,
An' light upon him like a duck 'pon a june bug,
Oh! you ought to been dare to see de Niggers laff,
For dey swore it was de debil or old Gumbo Chaff.

8

I learn'd to talk de French oh! a la mode de dancey,
Kick him shoe, tare him wool, parle vo de Francey,
Bone jaw Madamselle, Stevadors and Riggers,
Apple jack and sassafras and little Indian Niggers;
De natives laff'd and swore dat I was corn'd,
For dey neber heard sich French since dey was born'd.

9

I leab New Orleans early one day morning,
I jump'd aboard de boat jist as de day was dawning,
I hide behind de wood where de Niggers always toss'um,
And lay low like de Coon when him tries to food de Possum;
I lay dare still doe 'twas rather diffikill,
An dey did'nt find me out 'till I got to Louisville.

10

Dare Jim beats de drum and old Joe's de fifer,
An I is dat child what can read an cifer;
Twice one is five den carry six to seven,
Twice six is twenty nine and eighteen's eleven,
So 'twixt you and me its very plain to see,
Dat I learnt to play de Banjo by de double rule of three.

11

Now I 'rive on our farm on de Ohio Bluff,
An' I tink of fun an' frolick old Gumbo's had enough;
Oh! de white folks at home I very much amuse,
When I sing dis song an tell 'em all de news;
So we'd music all night an dey set up sich a laff
When I introduced de Niggers to Mrs. Gumbo Chaff.

Sich a Gitting Up Stairs[43]

On a Suskyhanner raft I come down de bay
And I danc'd, and I frolick'd, and fiddled all de way.
    Sich a gitting up stairs I never did see, &c.

Trike he to and heel—cut de pigeon wing,
Scratch gravel, slap de foot—dats just de ting.
   Sich a gitting up stairs I never did see, &c.

I went to de play, and I see'd Jim Crow,
Oh! nigger Isam den he swell, for Jim was no go!
   Sich a gitting up stairs I never did see, &c.

I look him in de face untill I make him grin,
And den I trow a backa quid an' hit him on de chin.
   Sich a gitting up stairs I never did see, &c.

Oh! I is dat boy dat know to preach a sarmont
Bout temperance and seven up an all dat kind of varmint.
   Sich a gitting up stairs I never did see, &c.

Nigger hold a meeting about de Colnization,
And dare I spoke a speech about Amalgamation!
   Sich a gitting up stairs I never did see, &c.

To Washington I go, dare I cut a swell
Cleaning gemmen's boots and ringin auction bell.
   Sich a gitting up stairs I never did see, &c.

I call on yaller Sal dat trade in sassenges,
An dare I met big Joe, which make my daner ris.
   Sich a gitting up stairs I never did see, &c.

Says I "you see dat door? just mosey, nigger Joe,
For I'm a Suskyhanner boy what knows a ting or two!
   Sich a gitting up stairs I never did see, &c.

An den I show my science—prencz gardez vouz,
Bung he eye, break he shin, split de nose in two.
   Sich a gitting up stairs I never did see, &c.

Sal holler out—den she jump between us,
But guess he no forget de day wheyn Isam show his genus.
   Sich a gitting up stairs I never did see, &c.

Den big Joe went out, he gwoin to take de law,
But he no fool de Possum—I cut stick for Baltimore.
   Sich a gitting up stairs I never did see, &c.

Jim Crack Corn, or the Blue Tail Fly[++]

1

When I was young I us'd to wait
On Massa and hand him de plate;
Pass down de bottle when he git dry
And bresh away de blue tail fly.
   Jim crack corn I don't care,
   Jim crack corn I don't care,
   Jim crack corn I don't care,
   Ole Massa gone away.

2

Den arter dinner massa sleep,
He bid dis niggar vigil keep;
An' when he gwine to shut his eye,
He tell me watch de blue tail fly.
   Jim crack corn &c.

3

An' when he ride in de arternoon,
I foller wid a hickory broom;
De poney being berry shy,
When bitten by de blue tail fly.
   Jim crack corn &c.

4

One day he rode aroun' de farm,
De flies so numerous dey did swarm;
One chance to bite 'im on the thigh,
De debble take dat blu tail fly.
   Jim crack corn &c.

5

De poney run, he jump an' pitch,
An' tumble massa in de ditch;
He died, an' de jury wondr'd why
De verdic was de blue tail fly.
   Jim crack corn &c.

6

Dey laid 'im under a 'simmon tree,
His epitaph am dar to see:
'Beneath dis stone I'm forced to lie,
All by de means ob de blue tail fly.
    Jim crack corn &c.

7

Ole massa gone, now let 'im rest,
Dey say all tings am for de best;
I nebber forget till de day I die,
Ole massa an' dat blue tail fly.
    Jim crack corn &c.

Settin' on a Rail, or, Racoon Hunt[45]

As I walk'd out by de light ob de moon
So merrily singing dis same tune,
I cum across a big racoon
A sittin on a rail
    sitting on a rail,
    sittin on a rail,
    sittin on a rail,
Sleepin werry sound.

2

I at de Racoon take a peep
And den so softly to him creep,
I found de Racoon fast asleep,
    An pull him off de rail [repeat]
An fling him on de ground.

3

De Racoon gan to scratch an bite,
I hit him once wid all my might,
I bung he eye an spile he sight
    O Im dat child to fight, [repeat]
An heat de banjo to.

4

I fell de Racoon gin to pray,
While up de ground de Racoon lay,
But he jump up and run away,
    An soon he out ob sight [repeat]
Sittin on a rail.

5

My ole Massa dead an gone,
A dose ob poison help him on,
De debil say him funeral song,
    Oh bress him let him go [repeat]
An joy go wid him to.

6

De Racoon hunt do werry quare,
Am no touch to kill de deer
Be Case you kotch him wid out fear,
    Sittin on a rail, [repeat]
Sleepin werry sound.

7

Ob all de songs dat eber I sung,
De Racoon hunt's de greatest one,
It always pleases old and young,
    An den dey cry encore, [repeat]
An den I cum agin.

PLAYS

———◆◆◆———

Here are the extant nine Jim Crow plays that T. D. Rice wrote or that others wrote expressly for him. Except for *Otello*, all turned up in the British Library, where the Lord Chamberlain deposited them after licensing their production in Middlesex or in central London. This censor did not monitor plays performed in Sussex, at the Royal Surrey, where Rice first built his base in England. Thus, unless a play became a regular part of Rice's repertoire, and he performed it in London north of the Thames, a text has not appeared, and I have not been able to reconstruct it. I found *Otello* in the New York Public Library, filed under the name of John B. Wright, the Boston stage manager who copied it out with Rice's permission.

I edited all these plays from the handwritten prompt scripts, founding decisions upon this primary question: what returns the play most closely to the way Rice's own audiences experienced it? Sometimes contemporary reviews describe actions that audiences cheered but that a printed version omitted—as in the case of Jim Crow giving abolitionist speeches while riding a white steed across the stage in *Flight to America*. I restored that scene, for it existed in the prompt script that its author William Leman Rede wrote. Although the often shortened scripts Rice submitted to the licensing office surely manifest what he considered to be the play's core, and are important for that reason, I always preferred a fuller to a shorter play if there was evidence that he regularly performed more scenes. This volume therefore contains the fullest texts I have been able to justify on the grounds of actual performance.

❧ OH! HUSH! ❧
OR, THE VIRGINNY CUPIDS!
An Operatic Olio[1]

Act 1

Scene 1. Exterior, Street. The characters discovered blacking boots. Some sitting down. Sam Johnson *sits on a chair, R., his feet resting on a barrel. He is reading a newspaper, which he holds upside down.* All *laugh and begin to get up as the curtain rises.*

Cuff: Pete, I hab been round to all the hotels today, an' I got so many boots to black by four o'clock dat I don't tink I can do it. Now, den, boys, if you polish dem by dat time, I'll gib you a holiday dis ebenin'.

Pete: Ah! dat's right, Cuff, we'll gib 'em de shine ob de best Day and Martin[2]—but, Cuff, gib us a song.

Cuff [*sings*]:
Come, all you Virginny gals, and listen to my noise,
   Neber do you wed wid de Carolina boys;
For if dat you do, your portion will be:
   Cowheel and sugarcane, wid shangolango tea.

Full Chorus
   Mamzel ze marrel—ze bunkum sa!
   Mamzel ze marrel—ze bunkum sa!
When you go a-courting, de pretty gals to see
   You kiss 'em and you hug 'em like de double rule ob free.
De fust ting dey ax you when you are sitting down,
   Is, "Fetch along de Johnny-cake—it's gitting rader brown."

Chorus
   Mamzel ze marrel, &c.
Before you are married, potatoes dey am cheap,
   Money am so plenty dat you find it in the street.
But arter you git married, I tell you how it is—
   Potatoes dey am berry high, and sassengers is riz.

Chorus

Mamzel ze marrel, &c.

Cuff [*turning round after the song, discovers* Johnson]: I say, Pete, who is dat comsumquencial darkey ober dar, dat is puttin' on so many airs?

Pete: I don't know, Cuff. He stopped here a few minutes arter you went away, an' he's been reading dar eber since. Speak to him.

Cuff [*approaching* Johnson *scrutinizes his person*]: Why, it am Sam Johnson!

All: Sam Johnson!

Cuff: Yes, to be sure it am.

Johnson [*looking through his eyeglass*]: Gemblem, is you distressing your conversation to me?

Cuff: Yes, sar, I is distressing my observation to you inderwidually, collectively, skientifically and alone. [*Seats himself on the barrel.*]

Johnson [*rising*]: Well, sar, den I would hab you to know dat my name, sar, is Mr. Samuel Johnson, Exquire, an' I don't wish to be addressed by such—[*pointing to crowd*]—low, common, vulgar trash! You had better mind your business and brack your filthy boots. [*He sits down again.*]

Cuff [*gets off the barrel*]: I say, Pete, I'll tell you whar I seed dat darkey. He used to work in de same shop wid me for old Jake Simmons, but he drawed a high prize in de lottery, and retired from de 'spectable perfession of bracking boots. De last time I seed him he was down in old Virginny on a coon hunt. I'll tell you suffin' 'bout it. [*He sings:*]

'Way down in old Virginny, 'twas in de arternoon
    Oh! Roley, boley!
Wid de gun dat Massa gib me, I went to shoot the coon.

Chorus

Wid my hiddy-co-dink-er—mi! who dar?
    Good mornin', ladies fair.
Wid my hiddy-co-dink-er—mi! who call?
    Good mornin', ladies all.
He sat on a pine branch, whistlin a tune.
    Oh! Roley, boley!
I up wid my gun, and brought down Mr. Coon.

Chorus

Wid my hiddy-co-dink-er, &c.

Pete: I tell you what, Cuff; speak to him in a little more eliphant manner.

Cuff: Yes, I will. [*Goes over to Johnson in his best style.*] Johnson! [*No answer.*]

Cuff: Mr. Johnson! [*No answer.*] I'll fetch him dis time, Pete. Mr. Samuel Johnson Exquire?

Johnson [*rises and bows politely*]: Sar, I am at your sarbice.

Cuff: Excuse my interrupting you for I see you am busy readin' de paper. Would you be so kind as to enlighten us upon de principal topicks ob de day?

Johnson: Well, Mr. Cuff, I hab no objection 'kase I see dat you common unsophisticated gemmen hab not got edgemcation yourself, and you am 'bliged to come to me who has. So spread around, you unintellumgent bracks, hear de news ob de day discoursed in de most fluid manner. [*He reads out some local items.*] Dar has been a great storm at sea and de ships hab been turned upside down.

Cuff [*looks at paper*]: Why, Mr. Johnson, you've got the paper upside down! [*All laugh heartily*]

Johnson: Well, yes, so I is. Golly! I didn't take notice ob dat. [*He starts with amazement.*] Oh, what do I see? Has de perfession come to dis degraded persition?

All: What is it?

Johnson: Does my eyes deceibe me? Bracking boots on de Canal Street plan for free cents a pair!

All [*grab at the paper, which they tear in pieces, and cry*]: Whar? wharabouts?

Cuff: I say, Pete, I can't see nuffin like dat here. [*To Johnson:*] Mr. Johnson, show me dat. [*Holds the torn piece to him.*]

Johnson: Oh, I can't show you now—it's torn out.

Cuff: It won't do, Mr. Johnson. Say, darkies, don't you tink dat nigger am in lub?

All: Yes, yes! [*Johnson paces the stage in anger.*]

Cuff [*sings*]:
   Sam Johnson, why so solitacious?
    Hah, hah, hah, hah, hah!
   'Tis lub dat makes you so vexatious,
    Sam Johnson, ho!

   Does your lub lib in Philadelphy?
    Hah, hah, &c.
   Oh! is she poor, or am she wealthy?
    Sam Johnson, ho!
   Now, gib him boots and make him travel,
    Hah, hah, &c.
   Oh! chuck dem at him widout cavil,
    Sam Johnson, ho!

[Johnson *exits.* All *throw a perfect shower of boots at* Johnson *as he leaves, and begin laughing.*]

 Cuff: Dar he goes, Pete. I radder guess Mr. Samuel Johnson Exquire
  won't trouble dis crowd any more wid his presence. [*He sings:*]
   De greatest man dat eber libed was Day and Martin
    Johnny, my lango la!
   For he was de fus ob de boot black startin'.
     Chorus
    Johnny, my lango la!
   Did you eber see a ginsling made out ob brandy,
    Johnny, my lango la!
   Did you eber see a pretty girl lickin' lasses candy?
     Chorus
    Johnny, my lango la!
     Full Chorus
   Ah, oh—ah! ah, oh—ah! oh—o—o-o!
    Johnny, my lango la!
   Ah, oh—ah! ah, oh—ah! oh—o—o-o!

Watchman [*crosses in front, or he may sing outside*]:
   Past twelve o'clock and a cloudy mornin'
    Johnny, my lango la!
   Past twelve o'clock and de daylight dawnin',
    Johnny, my lango la!

Cuff [*resumes singing*]:
  Dat's de ole watchman, we're gwine to fool him,
      Johnny, my lango la!
  If he stays outside, de weder will cool him.

Chorus

      Johnny, my lango la!
  Now, cut your sticks, niggers, de daylight's dawnin'
      Johnny, my lango la!
  We'll meet right here quite early in de mornin'

Chorus

  Johnny, my lango la! [all exit R. and L. singing very piano]

✦

Scene 2. Exterior of Rose's House—Dark Stage. Staccato music.

Johnson [*enters with guitar to serenade*]: Tank heaben! I hab got clar ob
    dem ruffian darkies at last. I neber was so grossly insulted in all my
    life. Dey nearly spiled my best clothes, and——but let me see, I
    promised to gib my lubly Rosa a serenade dis ebenin', and if I can
    only find de house. [*Goes up to house.*] Yes, here is de house—I
    know it from a tack in de door. [*Sings:*][3]

Song: "Lubly Rosa"

  Oh! lubly Rosa, Sambo has cum
      To salute his lub wid his tum, tum, tum.
  So open de door, Rose, and luff me in,
      For de way I lub you am a sin.

Rose [*appears at Window and sings*]:
  Oh, who's dat knocking at my door,
      Making such a noise wid his saucy jaw,
  Ise looking down upon de stoop,
      Like a henhawk on a chicken-coop.
          So clar de kitchen.

Johnson:
  'Tis Sambo Johnson, dearest dove,
      Come like Bacchus, God of Love;
  To tell his lubly Rosa how

He's quit his old perfersion now
So clar de kitchen.

Rose:

Oh, hold yer hat and cotch de key,
    Come into de little backroom wid me;
Sit by de fire and warm your shin,
    And on de shelf you'll find some gin.
        So clar de kitchen.

[*She drops the key.* Johnson *catches it in his hat and exits into the House.*]

Scene 3. Interior of Rose's House. Table set—cups and saucers for two and two chairs.

Cuff [*enters L. and sings*]:
            Song: "Coal Black Rose!"
I wonder whar de debil my lubly Rosa's gone,
    She's luff me half an hour sittin' all alone.
If she don't come back an' tell me why she didn't stay wid me,
    I'll drink all de sassengers and eat up all de tea.
                Chorus
    Oh, Rose! you coal black Rose!
    I neber lub a gal like I lub dat Rose.

Rose [*enters R., and sings*]:
    Now, get up, you Cuffy, an' gib me up dat chair,
        Mr. Johnson'll play de dickens if he cotch you sitting dar.

Cuff:

    I doesn't fear de devil, Rose, luff alone dat Sam,
        If dat nigger fool his time wid me, I'll hit him . . . I'll be—
                                    [*breaks a plate*].
                Chorus
    Oh, Rose &c.

Rose:

    Now, get you in de cupboard, Cuff, a little while to stay.
        I'll give you plenty applejack when Sambo's gone away.

Cuff:

    I'll keep my eye upon him—if he 'tempts to kiss or hug,

        I'll be down upon him like a duck upon a bug. [*Rose conducts*

    Cuff *to the closet, puts him in and closes the door.*]

Johnson [*heard singing without*]:

    Oh, make haste, Rose, for as sure as I am born,

        I'm trembling like a sweep-oh! on a frosty morn.

Rose:

    Walk in, Sambo, and don't stan' dar a-shakin'

        De fire am a-burnin', and de hoecake is a-bakin'.

Johnson [*enters L., looks around the room, and converses* ad libidum;[4] *he then discovers the table, starts with surprise and sings*]:

    From de chairs around de table and de two cups of tea,

        I see you've been to supper and had some company.

Rose:

    'Twas de missionary preacher, dey call him Dr. Birch,

        He come to raise a 'scription to build hisself a church.

    Come sit you down, Sambo, an' tell me how you've bin.

    [Johnson *laughs*]

    Why la bress you, honey, what does make you grin?

Johnson:

    I'd laugh to tink if you was mine, my dear, my lub, my Rose,

        I'd gib you eberyting dat's nice, de Lord above knows,

    Dar's possum fat an' hominy, and sometimes—

Cuff [*sings out from the closet*]:

                                 —Rice![5]

Johnson:

    Cowheel an' sugarcane an' eberyting dat's—

Cuff [*sings out from the closet*]:

                                 —nice!

Johnson [*gets up, comes front and sings*]:

    I thought I heard a noise, Rose, it come from ober dar.

Rose:

    It was de plaster fallin' down upon de chair.

Johnson:

But it hollered out rice! as sure as I'm Sambo.

Rose:

It was dat nigger Cuffy up stairs, dat jumps Jim Crow.

Johnson:

I wish I was a glove, Rose, upon dat lubly hand,
I'd be de happiest nigger ob all in dis land.
My bosom am so full ob lub—'twould soon find some relief
When you took de glove to wipe your nose instead ob a
handkerchief.

Chorus

Oh, Rose, &c.

Rose:

My love is strong, and of it strength dar's none but you can tell.

Cuff:

Half past twelve o'clock and all's not well.

Johnson:

Dat's de old watchman took me up de udder night.

Cuff:

Half past twelve o'clock, dar's gwine to be a fight.

Chorus

Oh, Rose, &c.

Rose:

Johnson, now you'd better go, for you see it's gettin' late,
An' missus will be comin' home from de freminate.

Johnson:

Well, gib me one kiss, Rose———[*tries to kiss her.*]

Rose:

Why, Sam, what is you at?

Johnson:

Why I'll hug like a grizzly—what de debil noise am dat?
[*In trying to get the gun down from shelf, Cuff falls down and spills the flour over him.*]

Johnson [*goes up stage, brings Cuff down front, and sings*]:

Who is you and from whar did you cum?

Rose:

Oh, it am dat nigger Cuff—foreber I'm undone.

Cuff:

Ise been out whitewashin' an feelin' a little tire,
   I merely cum to ax Miss Rose for a shobel-ful ob fire.

Johnson:

Tell me, you saucy nigger, how you do on dat shelf?

Cuff:

I was pretty well, I thank you, pray how do you find yourself?

Johnson:

Come, no prevarication, or I'll smash dat calibash.

Rose:

Oh, Johnson, be advised by me—he's noffin' else but trash.

Johnson:

Is dis your constancy, Miss Rose, you tell me ob all day?

Cuff:

Why de wench she am dumbfounded, and don't know what to
   say.

Rose:

I neber saw his face before—his berry sight I hate—
   I believe he am a runaway from de nullifying state.

Cuff:

Say, tell me Mr. Johnson, what dat nigger 'jaculates.

Johnson:

Why, she says you am a runaway from de nullifying states.

Cuff:

Dat's enuff to make a jaybird split his shin in two,
   For here's my free papers dat I carry in my shoe. [*shows his
   papers*]

Chorus

Oh, Rose, &c.
By dat darkey's peroration and his sarcarmastus grin,
   I'll bet he gets a lickin' afore he does begin.

Johnson:

Be off, you common nigger.

Cuff:

>   Not until we hab a fight.
> And Rose, don't you interfere, I'll show dis moke a sight.
>   [*Clinches Johnson and they fight.*]

Rose [*screams, seizes frying pan, and strikes Cuff over his head, breaking the bottom of the pan*]:

> Fire, help! murder, suicide, all sorts ob death!

Johnson:

> Stand off, you common nigger, gib me time to draw a breff.

Pete Williams [*and others enter*]:

> What's de matter, Rose, dat you gib dat Injun yelp?

Rose:

> Why, it's Cuffy killin' Sambo, and I was cryin' out for help.

Pete [*raises and supports* Cuff, *while some one does the same to* Johnson]:[6]

> Cuffy, is you much hurt?

Cuff: Oh, no, I'm only drawing my last breff. You'd better take me to de hoss-pistol.

Pete: Why, Cuff?

Cuff: Oh, I don't know; but I hardly tink I shall live mor dan twenty-five years longer. [Cuff *and* Johnson *have now regained their feet.*]

Johnson [*starts*]: Why, Cuff!

Cuff: Why Johnson!

Johnson [*sings*]:

> Rose, my love, pray tell me how this cum so.

Rose:

> Well, dear, I will, since you really want to know:
> You see he sweeps de street, and blacks de gemmen's shoes.
> But when he gets de liquor in, he don't know what he does.

Cuff [*sings to Rose*]:

> If I'd a married you, Miss Rose, I'd surely had a curse,
>   I offered for to take you for better or for worse;
> But I was blind wid lub, your faults I couldn't see,
>   You is a deal sight worser dan I took you to be.

Chorus

Oh, Rose, &c.

Johnson [*crosses over to* Cuff]:

Mr. Cuff, I ax your pardon.

Cuff:

Mr. Johnson, dar's my hand.

An' Rose, I'm glad to find my head was harder dan your pan;

But dar's no use to keep up grievances, since love am all by chance.

So jest hand down de fiddle, Pete, and let us hab a dance.

[*Spoken*] Come, darks, take your places and I'll saw de catgut.

[*They* All *form and go through a reel.* Cuff *gets excited while* Rose *and* Johnson *are dancing, and, jumping up, he breaks his fiddle over* Johnson's *head.* Rose *faints and is caught by* Some One. Johnson *falls at her feet.* Cuff *stands with uplifted hands.* All *form picture. Curtain.*]

The End.

❧ VIRGINIA MUMMY ❧
A Farce in One Act[1]

Scene 1. A Room. Enter Captain Rifle *followed by* Waiter *with baggage* LH

Rifle: Let me have a commodious room, fellow; patent sofa[2], and gum elastic[3] bath.

Waiter: Yes, Sir. [*Exit* Waiter LH]

Rifle: Well, here I am once again, once more inhaling the balmy atmosphere that gives the life, the joy, the animation to my retrospections: I am afraid Lucy will scarcely know me—for a two years' campaign on our western frontier changes a man's complexion, as a chameleon does its color. I will first see if there be letters from my old dad at the Post Office. [*calling waiter; enter* Ginger Blue LH]

Ginger: Did you call me, master?

Rifle: I call'd the waiter, are you he?

Ginger: I ar one of dem.

Rifle: I ar one of dem! And how many does it take to make one of dem?

Ginger: Dar's where you hab me. I guess it take a right smart change, anyhow.

Rifle: Well, you are an original.

Ginger: No, I'm a Wirginian.

Rifle: Ha! ha! ha! Come here. Can you go an errand for me?

Ginger: If you isn't sent nobody else.

Rifle: What do you ask me that for?

Ginger: 'Cause if dere's two, we'll be sure to quarrel about de pay when we come back.

Rifle: But suppose I do not choose to pay you? What then will be the consequence?

Ginger: It will be rather hard to hear you when it rings.

Rifle: Ha! ha! He has a reason for his subtlety, but not experience enough to conceal it. Well, go you to the Post Office, and ask if there be any letters for Captain Rifle and, if so, bring them direct to me. Here, Sir, is a dollar.

Ginger: Look here, you isn't Captain Rifle dat sold Massa a load de coal?

Rifle: No, no, damn it, no; do you take me for a coal merchant? I am Captain Rifle of the Army.

Ginger: Is you a soger?

Rifle: Ask no further questions, but be gone.

Ginger: Well master, I only ax't.⁴ [*Exit* Ginger Blue LH]

Rifle: I am afraid that stupid negro will make some mistake; however, it is but a stone's throw, if I have to go myself. Lucy little thinks her lover is so near, or a welcome in a shape of a billet-doux,⁵ would have dropped from the point of love's own weapon. But how to procure an interview? Her guardian was opposed to me for not reconciling myself to the pestle and mortar, as he styles it. But, no, give me a soldier's life, with *one arm* and *half* a leg in preference to a stuffed Alligator, or a box of pills⁶—but should her affections have changed, oh, fie! To think it! Woman's love is like a falling torrent,⁷ ever constant, and man recedes from nature's dignity when he suspects without a cause. I'll now to my room, change my dress, and devise means to announce my arrival. [*Exit* Rifle RH]

➤◄

Scene 2. Room in Galen's House. Enter Doctor Galen⁸ *and* Charles LH

Charles: Here's the advertisement, and I have given orders to continue the publication 'til further notice—

Galen: That's right, let me see, *"Wanted a mummy"*—excellent. [*reads*] *"Doctor Galen being anxious to try the virtue of his new invented Compound Extract of Live-Forever upon the mortal remnants of Egypt and China, will give the highest price for embalmed mummies. For further particulars, please call at his office, Exchange Building."* This is excellent. Now, if I can only resuscitate life that's been extinct for three thousand years—why, vanish all ye quacks and diabolical impostors! The world shall begin all anew; the glorious battles of Major Pompey and General Caesar, shall be repeated like an opera in a theatre, while I stand upon the mount of Aetna, and pour down my new invented Compound Extract of Live-Forever. [*crosses left*]

Charles: But, Sir, suppose you should try it on some person who has been dead a week, or three days, or, say, one day; and if it succeeds *then* try it on your mummies.

Galen: Why, you impudent Jackanapes;[9] you thing of no penetration, do you think I have studied for twenty-five years to procure an antidote to bring back the life of this degenerate race of mankind? No —tis for the days of King Solomon, King Pharaoh, King Brutus, and King Crusoe.

Charles: I beg your pardon, Sir, but I don't remember ever reading of King Crusoe.

Galen: Who said you did? I never read of him myself. I only heard of him.

Charles: [*aside*] Ha! Ha! Ha! What country, Sir, was this King Crusoe of?

Galen: He was from no country, but from the Norwegian Islands, and the first man that discovered America.

Charles: Well, Sir, was this three thousand years ago?

Galen: More than that, Sir, it was long before the Battle of Stonington.[10]

Charles: [*aside*] Ha! Ha! Ha!

Galen: What are you giggling at, you impudent rascal? Out of the room, out of the room this instant. [*Exit* Charles LH] What is society coming to? Impudence! And ignorance is paramount to everything! No matter. I shan't let him see me perform the operation on a mummy, nor shall he know the ingredients that I use: when I die, I shall *will* the receipt to the college to be performed on me at the expiration of One Thousand Years. Then I will publish a work on my other world peregrinations. [*Enter* Lucy LH]

Lucy: La! Guardian, what have you done to Charles? He is as scared as if he was going to be married.

Galen: An impudent blockhead: when I was diffusing into his thick skull the knowledge of philosophy, he bursts out a-laughing in my face and pays no more attention to me than if I were the cook or butler.

Lucy: Now, guardian, tell me, who is this handsome young man, you have destined for my husband?

Galen: He is a professor of zoological subjects. I saw him this morning. He was busily employed in stuffing a rhinoceros which I intend to purchase to place among my collections.

Lucy: Oh, la! To marry a man with such a profession—he's worse than a grave digger.

Galen: Science and knowledge, before profession.

Lucy: [*half aside*] I wonder where Captain Rifle is.

Galen: What's that you say? You want to know where Captain Rifle is? Dead, I hope. I would not bring *him* to life, if there were not another man in the world.

Lucy: But only consider, my dear guardian.

Galen: I won't consider anything now but mummies. So get along to your chamber, and put this love out of your head. [*Exeunt* RH]

Scene 3. A Hotel. Enter Captain Rifle, RH.

Rifle: How long that fellow stays. I have beat my brains ever since, trying to find out a plan to introduce myself, but not one can I hit upon. Ah! Here comes the fellow, at last. [*Enter* Ginger Blue LH] Why, one would have thought you went to Paris.

Ginger: Can't help what de people tink.

Rifle: Well, did you get any letters for me?

Ginger: No—dere warn't any for you, but here's an armful I buyed for wrapping paper. Maybe some of dem do.

Rifle: Zounds! Was there ever such a perplexing[11] ink bottle?

Ginger: I ax't de man, when he 'spect you goin' to hab some.

Rifle: Well, and what did he say?

Ginger: Why, he say, clear out you damn nigger, and don't ax gemman questions.

Rifle: I'm not astonished at the answer. You will give me the change, and bring the morning newspaper.

Ginger: If I don't bring dis mornin's, I will bring de oder mornin's paper.

Rifle: Bring me this morning's and no other. Here, take this for your blundering trouble.

Ginger: Tank you, Massa, but what you gwan to do wid de oder rest of it?

Rifle: Put it in my pocket. What makes you so anxious to know?

Ginger: Noting, only it might fall out.

Rifle: Do *you get out* and bring the paper. [*Exit* Ginger LH] The rascal seems to be between the two—cunning as well as stupid. Now, let me see. Shall I say a gentleman from the South wants advice? Or shall I say I am a learned Greek doctor come to reside in his neighborhood, and wish to have his countenance?[12] No—I have it—I'll say——[*Re-enter* Ginger, *with paper* LH]

Ginger: Here's de paper, Massa.

Rifle: Well, what does the paper say?

Ginger: I doesn't know, he haven't spoke a word.[13]

Rifle: Give it here! [*reads*] *"Foreign intelligence."*

Ginger: Who is he, I wonder?

Rifle: *"Mummies wanted"* [*reads the advertisement*]. Zounds, this is Lucy's old guardian. I wonder where I can purchase a mummy? I am afraid I shall find them rather a scarce article in market. I have it. I will have a dead body dug up; then smoke it and roll it up in several old sheets, put it into a box stained with a few hieroglyphics, and I defy old Nick[14] himself to detect the cheat. Ginger, come here. Do you know where the undertaker lives?

Ginger: Who is dem?

Rifle: People who attend the funerals.

Ginger: The Lord knows, I doesn't want to know dem.

Rifle: Do you know where I could get a dead body?

Ginger: Yes, I does dat—

Rifle: Where?

Ginger: Ole Massa Sander's nigger shot a deer dis mornin'.

Rifle: No, I mean a human body.

Ginger: A human body—what's dat?

Rifle: A dead man.

Ginger: I knows where you can git a man *dead* drunk.

Rifle: Where, you stupid?

Ginger: Only you pay for de liquor—and de apparition stand right afore you.

Rifle: I can't get any information out of this fellow, I will see the landlord. Stay you here until I return. [*Exit Rifle* LH]

Ginger: I wonder what he gwan to do wid de inhuman dead body. I guess he gwan to make de doctor's stuff. I'll be mighty careful how I drink de wine at de dinner table, else when I gwan to fetch de gemmen's baggage I find myself a dead nigger. Be careful, Ginger Blue, you isn't fool'd like de white folks: get up in de mornin' and wonder why dey can't find demselves. [*Re-enter* Captain Rifle LH]

Rifle: The landlord is not in, and I have thought of a better scheme. Here, Ginger, is a silver dollar for you. How long can you hold your tongue without speaking?

Ginger: Well, I guess I hold him, 'til I git about tired.

Rifle: Can you shut your mouth—not speak without I tell you?

Ginger: Yes. Spose you tell me to speak to people I don't 'sociate wid —how I gwan to do den?

Rifle: Suppose you don't speak at all?

Ginger: Den it be de best way for me to say notin'.

Rifle: So it will. Now, listen [*Ginger goes to door*]. No, no, come here to me; I want you now to make folks believe you are a mummy.

Ginger: Who am dem?

Rifle: You don't understand me. A mummy is a dead man preserved in spices, put into a coffin, deposited in a tomb, and never molders away.

Ginger: And do you want to pickle me up in dat way? Child, de wedder is too hot! Dis ole nigger wouldn't keep from now 'til Sunday.

Rifle: I only want you to have the appearance of it, to make people think you are a mummy, when you are only Ginger Blue.

Ginger: Well, did you ebber hear de like? You is too debbily for de nigger.

Rifle: Come along after me to my room, where I will dress and paint you, and give you a lesson to show you how to keep still.

Ginger: How, is you gwan to paint me, Master, like a sign?

Rifle: No, like a mummy—white, black, green, blue, and a variety of colors.

Ginger: Massa, put plenty of turpentine wid de white paint so it won't rub off. I like to make 'em believe I'm a white man, too.[15]

Rifle: Above all, don't breathe loud.

Ginger: I mind dat, for ebery time I gwan to breath, I put my hand right up to my mouth.

Rifle: Then they will be sure to find you out.

Ginger: Nebber mind dat, I'll swear I'm a mummy.

Rifle: But you must be silent as death and, if you succeed, I will give you a five dollar note.

Ginger: Dat's a whole month's wages, but what I gwan to do when I get hungry? You know de mummies couldn't live widout dey hab de wittles.

Rifle: I will be near, and see that you do not want for anything. But you must try to remember that mummies are dead and never eat.

Ginger: Yes, but I'm a live mummy.

Rifle: Well, anyway, so you answer my purpose. Come, we have little time to lose.

Ginger: I spect you gwan to make a show of me. [*Exit* Rifle, R.H.]

Song—"Jim Crow"[16]

[*Exit* Ginger Blue, RH]

➤◄

Scene 4. Doctor's office. Pallette and brushes on. Charles and O'Leary discovered: Charles painting from a Boa Constrictor which O'Leary holds in his hand. Pestle and mortar on.

O'Leary: Sure, when nature molded the cratur, she had some very whimsical ideas about her when she made such a thing as this.

Charles: I have almost finish'd. Hold up the head 'til I get the color of the eye. That will do.

O'Leary: His eye is like Paddy Cape's light house, seen as well in a mist as in a fog.

Charles: What do you mean by that, you thick-skull'd rhubarb pounder.

O'Leary: Sure, is there any eye there? Isn't it shut up as close as Barney Laughlin's whiskey shop on a Sunday?

Charles: Well, lay it aside, you booby. There's as fine an imitation of an anaconda as two peas.

O'Leary: As two peas! Sure then, one of them must be in a pod.

Charles: How so?

O'Leary: Sure, isn't this one straight out, like a crook'd stick?[17] And isn't the other screw'd up, as if he had the cramp?[18]

Charles: Ha! ha! It is his common position.

O'Leary: Then it's very common, let me tell you. If you want wild animals why don't you paint a rhinosorus?

Charles: Rynosorus! Rhinoceros, you mean.

O'Leary: Well, didn't I say rynosnorus? Och! That would be a beautiful subject.

Charles: Where did you ever see one?

O'Leary: I saw one in the ship I came over in. They had him hanging up in a cage with the canary bird.

Charles: Ha! ha! ha! A rhinoceros hanging up with a canary bird! If you had told that to the sailors, they would have pitched you overboard.

O'Leary: No, they wouldn't have pitched me overboard; they wasn't so desartless of breeding as you are, Mr. Charles; they were gintlemin, as so was the Captain, and so was the steerage pasenger, Mr. O'Leary. [*turning to pestle and mortar*]

Charles: Well, but, Mr. O'Leary, I meant no offence.

O'Leary: Oh! Get out, ye dirty rattlesnake portrait painter. You aren't fit to white-wash a parish school house fince.

Charles: And instead of mixing medicines, you ought to be mixing mortar.

O'Leary: Sure, and haven't I done that already? It was there I got my hand in, or how the divil do you think I could be a doctor, and mixing up things, if I hadn't a little practice?

Charles: And a pretty doctor you are, too; you cannot tell a box of pills from a bottle of Swain's Panacea.

O'Leary: Sure, can't I taste thim, and tell by the effects they have upon the system?

Charles: Ha! ha! Was there ever such a clod? Now, O'Leary, what would you do, suppose you should see a man fall out of a garret window?

O'Leary: What would I do? Why, pick him up, to be sure.

Charles: Ha! ha! ha!

O'Leary: Ha! ha! ha! Och! You may ha! ha! Maybe, Mr. Charles, I won't tell the doctor how you want to be sweethearting Miss Lucy.

Charles: Silence! Here comes the doctor. [*Enter* Doctor Galen, L.H.]

Galen: Now, I shall be able to try my genius, here's a letter from a gentleman just-arrived from Grand Cairo in Upper Egypt that has a mummy taken from the Pyramids 3000 years old.

O'Leary: That's some time before I left Ireland.

Galen: Now, Charles, let the incredulous world tremble, and those who have laughed at my discovery: Down, and beg for mercy.

Charles: When will it be here?

Galen: I expect it every minute. Now, Charles, I want you, as soon as I restore its life, to be ready with pen, ink, and paper to write his history, which I intend to have translated into French, German, Latin, Greek and Choctaw.

Charles: But what language will he speak, Sir? For if it does not speak plain English, I shall not be able to understand it.

O'Leary: If it's the sweet mother tongue, just cast your eye around and you will find O'Leary close at your elbow.

Galen: I have it—go you for the learned schoolmaster who has recently opened school in the neighborhood and he shall be the one to do the business.

Charles [*aside:*] And a pretty business I'm afraid he'll make of it. [*Exit* Charles LH]

Galen: Now, let me see if everything is ready [*goes to box and takes out a large bottle*]. This is the elixir to make a marble statue speak. Now,

O'Leary have every thing in its proper place—my knives, my saws, my augers, gimlets, etc.

O'Leary: Faith, everything will be as ready as the wake of Teddy Rowe.

Galen: I believe I had better add a half an ounce more of alcohol to kill the taste of the asafoetida, and you, O'Leary, get a bottle of Thompsonian No. 6 to rub him down with, in case that change of climate gives him a cold. [*Enter* Susan LH]

Susan: Doctor, breakfast is ready.

Galen: Bring it in here, I have no time now to leave the office. O'Leary remain you here to receive the mummy. [*Exit* Galen *and* Susan L H]

O'Leary: What the devil is he going to do with the mummy? Faith, Charles told me it was a dead man wrapp'd up in a napkin of molasses. I begin to think it's a big fish. [*Enter* Charles LH]

Charles: O'Leary! O'Leary, it's come, it's come, and the owner with it, who is in full dress—the original costume of his native country.

O'Leary: In full dress, the costume of his country—and isn't a full dress the costume of all countries, you Hottentot, and would you have a man go half-naked?

Charles: Now we shall see, I have often read about mummies, but never saw one. Only fancy, a man that lived 3000 years ago.

O'Leary: That's nothing—St. Patrick lived before the world was made.

Charles: Ha! ha! That's as bad as the rhinoceros and the Canary bird. Stand aside, here comes the Doctor and the owner. [*Enter* Doctor, *with bottle, and the* Captain *dress'd in a Persian dress LH—all bow to the Captain*]

Galen: Welcome, Sir, to the young world, as it is call'd in Captain Cook's life.[19]

Rifle: Sir, I thank you, and, ere we part, we will be better acquainted.

Galen: If not, Sir, then have I degenerated with society.

O'Leary: He's got a hat like a washerwoman.

Charles: And an overcoat like a short-gown.

Rifle: How many inmates have you in your house?

Galen: My wife, and my ward, Lucy, and myself. The others you see are my domestics, except this young man who is an artist and has been busily employed in painting my ward's portrait.

Rifle: Sir, I bow submissive to genius.

Galen: But come, Sir, now for inspecting the mummy—

Rifle: Handle it very careful, for it is old and unused to being in its present situation.

Galen: Come Charles, come O'Leary, don't be in too great a haste, take care! Be careful! [*Exeunt* Galen, Charles, *and* O'Leary LH]

Rifle: I see nothing of my Lucy, as yet. But, so far, so well. If blackey only keeps still, I defy them to find out the cheat. [*Enter* Galen, Charles, O'Leary LH, *with mummy*]

Galen: There now, set it down, and let it be open'd immediately. Shut the windows and the doors, so that the spicy fragrance may not escape.

[O'Leary *goes up and shuts window. All commence hammering on the sarcophagus, the* Doctor *with a hammer and chisel at the head,* Charles *and* O'Leary *at the foot*]

Ginger: [*from inside*] Look here! Look here—what de debbil is you about? [*All stagger from the sarcophagus*]

Rifle: Gentlemen! Gentlemen! What are you about?

Galen: Was it you, Mr. Egyptian? Why, I declare I thought the voice came from the coffin.

Rifle: You will knock it all to pieces, Sir. Give me the hammer. [*he opens it*]

Omnes: What a curiosity.

Galen: Don't touch it! Don't touch it: in what a perfect state of preservation! The expression of the eye has all its natural lustre.

Rifle [*aside:*] It worked well! I must continue to retire to some other apartment or I shall burst with laughter.

Galen: Mr. Egyptian, while I am trying the experiment you may amuse yourself in the garden, or library, or with the chit-chat of my ward, Lucy.

Rifle: With all my heart.

Galen: Come, Sir, I will introduce you; this way, if you please. [*Exeunt* Galen *and* Rifle RH]

O'Leary: And is that what you call a mummy? It looks for all the world like a smok'd hog.[20]

Charles: Poor fellow! He little thought, 3000 years ago, that he was to be brought here to recite the adventures of the other world. Now, while I think of it, and as I will not have a better opportunity, I'll go and get my palette, brush, and paints, and take a sketch of it. [*Exit* Charles RH]

O'Leary: Look here! Mr. Charles! Don't leave me alone with this black looking mummy! Och! Sure, and isn't he dead, and what the devil should I be afraid of? I wonder where the doctor is, eh! He's with the gentleman that pickled him. By the powers, what would Mrs. O'Leary say if she was just to have a squint at it? There's nobody nigh. I'll just take my knife and cut off the big toe, and send it in a letter to her. [*As he is about to cut off the toe, the mummy raises his right foot and kicks him over.*]

Ginger: Not as you knows on.

O'Leary: Murther! murther—I'm kilt! I'm kilt by a dead man. [*Exit* O'Leary LH]

Ginger: Whoo! Here I is, pack'd up like a box of sugar; I guess dey tought dey was breakin' into de ballroom when dey took de kivver off. I wish some of de niggers could see me now, dey'd take me for old Santa Claus. Well, I don't like dis laying down all de time. Spose I jis stand him up dat fashion. I guess dat old Irishman, dat want to cut my toe off, must hab tought dat I had de cramp in de leg. I wonder whar de Captain is? Dis must be de doctor's shop. I wonder if I've time to run out and get someting to drink, I don't see nobody comin'. First let me look about. Hallo! What's dis? Dis must be de whiskey [*smells and drinks*]. 'Tis whiskey! I spose de mummies used to drink de whiskey like de oder folks. If I only had a little sugar, I'd make a sort of whiskey toddy. Hallo, what's dis? [*Takes down a box of lozenges*] Dis must be sugar. Now I'll hab a big drink [*drinks*]. Hallo! Somebody comin'. I must git into de sugar trough again.

I'm like a Philadelphy watchman. I've got a whole box²¹ to myself [*gets into box*]. [*Enter* Charles *with palette, etc.*]

Charles: Now for a sketch. Ah, O'Leary has raised it up.

Ginger: What de debbil is he gwan to do?

Charles: I'm afraid I won't be able to hit the dark shades of the face.

Ginger: As long as he don't hit me on de shin, I don't care.

Charles: But, as close as my genius will admit of, I will come to it.

Ginger: Dat save me trouble of comin' to you.

Charles: But I can scarcely realize that it lived 3000 years ago.

Ginger: Eh! eh! Honey, you're right only half of it.

Charles: No doubt it was some great personage, and stood very high in his native country.

Ginger: When I was up de tree—arter de possum.

Charles: Probably a King—

Ginger: Yes, wid a -dom come to it.

Charles: That has led triumphant armies across the plains of Egypt after the retreating enemy.

Ginger: As rader a pack of dogs troo de canebrake arter de bear.

Charles: Now contrast his situation: from a splendid palace to a domicile of drugs and medicines.

Ginger: So I see by dat bottle dare.

Charles: He might have been an artist, and handled the brush.

Ginger: 'Twas a white-wash brush den.

Charles: Or an astronomer, and read the stars.

Ginger: Well, if I did, I guess de book was upside down.

Charles: Or had an ear for music.

Ginger: Jus' gin me a banjo—dat's all.

Charles: Oh! What a field imagination may trace to find out what it is.

Ginger: You put me in a corn *field*, I show what it is.

Charles: I wonder if his race were all that color?

Ginger: I guess you find me a pretty fair sample.

Charles: And such a prodigious height—almost a giant.

Ginger: Yes, almost, but not quite.

Charles: I wonder what his name was?

Ginger: Ginger Blue, all de world ober.

Charles: But that I suppose is mark'd on the coffin.

Ginger: I guess you'll hab to spose it.

Charles: There *are* figures, but I cannot make them out. I would like to touch it; there can be no harm in that. How soft and moist the flesh is, and quite warm. How confoundedly it smells of shoe blacking.[22] I would like to have a finger to keep as a curiosity. I'll just clip one off. No doubt this hand held a sceptre with as firm a grasp as Samson did when he let fall . . . [Ginger *butts him on the head—* Charles *falls*] Murder! Murder! Murder. [Charles *gets up and runs off* LH]

Ginger: Yah! Yah! I guess he won't want anoder finger in a hurry. Dese white folks must all be crazy. Dey talk like de Indians do when dey don't know what to say. I know one ting, I begin to feel pretty hungry, and if de Captain don't come soon, I'll break and put out. Ah! Here he come. [*Enter* Rifle RH]

Rifle: Hallo! Ginger, what are you doing out of the box?

Ginger: I'm arter some cold vittles, is you got any?

Rifle: You shall have some presently, get back into the box; I hear some one coming. I have disclosed myself to Lucy, and she will be ready in an hour, to elope with me. What are you doing there?

Ginger: I'm arter some liquor.

Rifle: Quick! Ginger! Quick! [*Enter* Galen *with a bag of instruments,* RH]

Galen: Ah! Mr. Egyptian, I see you have stood it up. So much the better; I can pour the extract down with greater facility.

Ginger: Dis is de ole fellow, I wonder what he gwan to do?

Rifle: Keep still, you rascal.

Galen: But tell me Mr. Egyptian, what do you think of my ward?

Rifle: She is beautiful!

Galen: She has a fortune to back that beauty. I say nothing, but she had her eye on you all the time.

Rifle: Oh! Sir!

Galen: I'll speak a good word for you, and you must manage the affair yourself.

Rifle: Thank you, Sir, I think I had better join her again.

Galen: Certainly, by all means [*Exit* Rifle RH] I must put a little more alcohol in this to weaken it—for two drops is enough to kill a person [*Ginger very uneasy*]—as it is now in its present condition *rank* poison; nothing could save a man.

Ginger: Den I'm a gone case.

Galen: I'll just step and prepare it, and then be back and try my experiment. [*Exit* Galen RH]

Ginger: Oh, de Lord! I'm gone now! What de debbil did I drink dat stuff for? It will kill me! Oh, de Lord! I'm gwan to die, den I will be a mummy for sartain [*falls on his knees and begins to pray; enter* Susan *with the tray & breakfast*, LH]

Susan: Master told me to bring his breakfast here; now I'll have a peep at the mummy [*Sees Ginger; screams and runs off* LH; *lets the tray fall*²³]

Ginger: [*Jumps up and goes into box*] O, de debbil! Who's dat? Scream like a cat bird. [*Re-enter* Susan LH]

Susan: Oh me! How scared I am! I thought it was in a box. So it is; who could it have been that I saw kneeling there on the floor? Oh, I expect it was O'Leary trying to frighten me. What a timid creature I am, to be sure, frightened at my own shadow. Oh, my! What an ugly thing it is [*starts*] I thought it moved its eye. Pshaw! I won't be afraid. There—I should like to touch it. I will just put my finger in its mouth. [*Ginger bites her finger. She screams and runs round the room, Ginger following.*]

Ginger: Look here—look here— [*Exit* Susan LH.] I cocht de finger in de trap like dey do de wolf. Ha! I smell someting good, dat's de ole doctor's breakfast. I mean to light on it for fear I don't hab anoder opportunity. I'm just about as hungry as a fish hawk—go right in ober head. I wish I had bite dat woman's finger off. I make her gib me a dollar 'fore I gib it back to her. Oh, de Lord! White sugar! [*empties the contents in his pocket*] I lay for de storm. Now I eat enough, I put de rest into de box, in case I hab de appetite. [*Enter* Rifle RH]

Rifle: Come, Ginger. Ginger! Here comes the doctor.

Ginger: Look here, Captain, I want to go home. I've been drink de doctor's stuff out of dat bottle. I afraid I'm gwan to die.

Rifle: Never fear, allay your apprehensions, for the contents of that bottle is nothing but whiskey and water. I took most especial care in pouring out the original elixir and substituting whiskey and water.

Ginger: Well, if dat's de case, I'm saucy Ginger Blue again.

Rifle: Never mind, keep still.²⁴ [*Exit* Rifle LH; *enter* Doctor Galen RH *shaking a bottle*]

Galen: Now for the great experiment.

Ginger: If I drink all dat, I guess I'll be tight.

Galen: But first, I'll eat my breakfast. Hallo! Can I have eaten my breakfast? There's nothing here but empty dishes. I'll be bound, that fellow O'Leary has eat it for me. Zounds, he does nothing but eat, sleep, and drink. He has not only devoured the trout, eggs, and coffee but he has eaten up all the sugar.²⁵

Ginger: How would you like to hab a lump?

Galen: No matter, I'll have a better appetite for my dinner.

Ginger: And if you isn't, I'll help you.

Galen: There you are, illustrious stranger, cold and silent as a block of marble.

Ginger: Why, I'm sweating like a race horse.

Galen: You little think that Dr. Galen is standing before you.

Ginger: Or you little tink dat Ginger Blue is standing behind you.

Galen: But before I bow with reverence as Solomon did before Great Sheba—

Ginger: De same, to you, I hope you berry well.

Galen: Could you but speak, what scenes you would relate about your ancestors, and wonders would you tell to this world, what happened in yours!

Ginger: I'd tell you who eat up your breakfast.

Galen: Those lips, that look so parch'd and dry, perhaps did seal the nuptial kiss to some fair Princess, chaste and fair as the lilly beams of Bright Aurora.

Ginger: De only Prince he kiss was old Aggs, and she's as black as de debbil.

Galen: Where now are your friends that mourned your loss, that saw you embalmed, and saw you laid in the mighty hetacombs[26] of Egypt?

Ginger: I guess some of dem gwan down de river[27]—oh! Eh!

Galen: Not one even to give a nod, but all gone from whence they came.

Ginger: I want to be gwan, ole Massa'll be looking for me.

Galen: But you shall be resuscitated.

Ginger: What de debbil does he mean by suscitate?

Galen: And marry my ward.

Ginger: Dat's what de missionary call de 'malgamation.[28]

Galen: To inject my elixir, I will have to bore a hole in his head;

Ginger: Oh, Lord! Den all my brains come out.

Galen: Or, as the ancient professors did, open an artery [*taking up a large knife*].

Ginger: Oh, de debbil! He's gwan to cut me up like de fig!

Galen: And if that will not do, I'll sew up his mouth and lance him in the back of his neck.

Ginger: Den I had better make haste and eat dis bone.

Galen: However, I shall try every experiment to be fully satisfied of its virtue.[29] [*Enter* O'Leary LH]

O'Leary: Here's a gentleman that has brought another of these pickled mummies, or what do you call 'em.

Galen: Show him in. [*Exit* O'Leary LH] I'll try the experiment on all they bring. Now, if I fail on this mummy, I will be sure to hit it on the other. [*Re-enter* O'Leary, *with* Charles *and* Mr. Patent LH]

O'Leary: By the powers, we'll have a whole army of mummies, by-and-by.

Galen: Stand it up along side of this one. [*They open it*] It has a much older appearance than the first one.

Patent: It has been roughly handled by the sailors on board the ship.

O'Leary: It looks like a dried herring.

Galen: O'Leary, go, and bring the Egyptian. [*Exit* O'Leary RH] And Charles you go and bring Lucy, to see the operation.

Charles: Yes, and get my pencil ready to take the expression while it's dead. [*Exit* Charles RH]

Galen: [*To Patent*] Come, sir, you must want some refreshment. Step this way. [*Exeunt* Galen *and* Patent LH]

Ginger: [*Looking about*] How do you do? Oh! You don't talk like a Virginny Mummy. I wonder whar dey git him. He look like a burnt chuck.[30] I spect dey git him out of de bee-gum.[31] I 'gin to feel berry dry. I guess I take some ob dis, de Captain said he mix him himself. It's too strong ob de water. [*Drinks out of the bottle*] Look here you hab some. Ha! I drink for you myself. I guess if de chap wants to cut off my toe he want to cut off your leg, can't help youself neider. I wonder whar de Captain is? He said he wouldn't be out ob de way, when I wanted him. I hope he ain't run away, and left me all alone. Dey'll be sure to kick me into a real mummy. I begin to feel like de appetite. [*Eats*] I can't help but laugh how de old man look when de breakfast was all gone. He was rather jubious[32] wedder *he* eat it or *not*. I guess I take a little more liquor becase if dey pickle de mummy in de liquor dey ought to put some ob de liquor *in* de mummy. Oh! Here dey all come. [*Gets into box. Enter* Dr. Galen *and* Patent LH; Charles, Rifle, Lucy, O'Leary RH]

Ginger: Dey are gwan to hab Camp Meeting.

Galen: Now, Mr. Patent, I shall begin with you first.

Ginger: Guess dat aren't strong enough.

Rifle: Silence, be quiet.

Galen: I shall first pour it down the throat to warm the system before I open the arteries. He doesn't speak, as yet.

Rifle: Now try mine.

Galen: [*Placing funnel and pouring the liquor*] See! It winks! It moves.

Rifle: Give it some more.

Galen: See, it walks! It moves! Look! Look! [*Running about the stage—* Ginger *following*]

Omnes: 'Tis brought to life—it lives! It lives!

Galen: Now, Mr. Egyptian, ask me for anything! Everything, you shall have it!

Rifle: The hand of your ward.

Galen: Take her, and all her fortune—likewise a bottle of this elixir, which I will prepare. The world shall now acknowledge me! Most reverend mummy, what shall I order for your dinner?

Ginger: I isn't hungry 'case I eat up all de breakfast.

Charles: [*Seizing him*] Curse me if it isn't Ginger Blue, the nigger that lives at the hotel.

Galen: Old Ginger Blue—and are you not a mummy?

Ginger: Not myself, Sar, damn if I am.

O'Leary: Ooh! What a cursed scrape I'd got into, if I had cut his toe off!

Galen: Get me a gun, I will shoot him.

Ginger: What? After bowing before me, as King Solomon did before before de She nigga?[33]

Galen: And you, Sir, who are you?

Rifle: Captain Rifle, and soon will be your ward's husband.

O'Leary: Here comes the schoolmaster, who is to write the life of the mummy. [*Enter* Schoolmaster LH]

Galen: Write the life of the devil! [*Beats O'Leary offstage; knocks Schoolmaster down; paces up and down the stage in a rage.*] I'm mad enough to pound you all into a mummy, and then myself.

Ginger: Den I gib you some ob dis, to reconsuscitate you wid.

Charles: Come, doctor, love has no bounds—prithee, forget and forgive.

Galen: But I shall be laughed at by the whole town.

Rifle: What signifies the folly of the town, so long as you can retrieve the mummy.

Galen: Well, I do forget and forgive; and the next time I try my experiment on a mummy—

Ginger: I hope you make de medicine strong. And should any ob de faculty hab occasion for a libe mummy again, dey hab only to call on Ginger Blue; when dey'll find him ready dried, smoked, and painted, to sarbe himself up at de shortest notice.

❧ BONE SQUASH ❧
A Burletta[1]

Cast of Characters

Bone Squash
Spruce Pink
Jim Brown
Mose
Juba
Caesar
Pompey Duckellegs[2]
Sam Switchell, the Yankee Devil
Amos
Janson
Junietta Duckellegs
Janza Snowball
Milly
    Black Ladies, Niggers, Sweeps, Watchmen

Scenes
Act 1
Scene 1, the corner of a street—grog shop. Scene 2, a street. Scene 3, a house.
Act 2
Scene 1, a street. Scene 2, a cellar in the Five Points. Scene 3, exterior of a barber shop. Scene 4, interior of barber shop in confusion. Scene 5, a street. Scene 6, the whole stage.

Properties
Violin for Brown. Long Pole, with dirty boots, for Mose. Brushes, scrapers. Two boys: blankets and bags for boys. Whitewash pail and long pole for Juba. Patent sweeper brush, etc, for Bone Squash. Red fire. Bottles and glasses. Lobster. Dice box. Barrels. Devil's Tail. Money. Basket. Check for Devil.

Bone Squash

Act 1

Scene 1. Curtain rises to slow music. The corner of a street. Grog shop underneath a cellar. A wheelbarrow, L.H. Pail with whitewash beside the door. Dark stage. Caesar *lying asleep in wheelbarrow.*

Enter Jim Brown *from house.* Caesar *awakes from the barrow. Enter* Mose *and* Juba *from house. Enter* Amos *from cellar. Each character to make himself visible about the last line of the preceding verse. During 3rd verse,* Watchman *enters, L.H. and exits R.H. During 4th verse, the window in shop is opened—a barrel filled with brooms is placed at door. Over door a sign—* "Large bread for sale here." *The* Watchman, *previous to his going off, puts out light in lamp. The business in this scene is very particular, as there is no symphony between the verses of the solos.*

Enter Jim Brown *from house with fiddle.*

Jim Brown:

Oh, hurrah, day's breaking, oh!
Oh, hurrah, day's breaking, oh!
    I'll put up my fiddle
    And go home to bed.
For my head like de debil am aching.
    Oh! [*retires, R.*]

Mose:

We're gwine to hab rain, dat's comfort, oh!
We're gwine to hab rain, dat's comfort, oh!
    De boots must be black'd
    And de shoes must be brush'd,
Else de gemmen won't feel like a dandy, oh!

Amos [*to two young sweeps, who come out as he calls them*]:

Come, gather up out ob de cellar, oh!
Come, gather up out ob de cellar, oh!
    Dar's chimnies to sweep
    And you're both fast asleep,
And not the first cent for your breakfast, oh!

Juba:

I'm de Nigger dat do de whitewashing, oh
I'm de Nigger dat do de whitewashing, oh

On de scaffold I stand
Wid de brush in my hand
And de genus shines out wid de slashing, oh³
[*All join in general chorus, repeating the last verse*]

Jim Brown: Ha, ha, ha! I cannot help my facetious humor to meditate how natur hab rabished her conneasticle endowments upon de human family. Now, for example, while she make me de great musiciana, she only make you a common mechanic. From de fiddle to de base drum, I am what de white folks call *deficient en-mass.*

Juba: Look here, Mr. Brown, I don't know what you mean by de ficient on de bass drum and de fiddle, for I'm one ob dem Niggers dat nebber blow my own trumpet; but you gib me de side wall ob de church, and though I isn't de portrait painter, jist gib me my whitewashing brush, and if de genus doesn't shine out like raccoon from a woodpile, say I can't slacken de lime, dat's all.

Caesar: Look here, Mr. Juba, I'm one ob dose colored gemmen dat nebber says anyting. But when I hear Niggers blazing what dey gwan to do, it always puts me in mind, as if dar was two selfs to a Nigger; the one self did all de work, while de oder self talk about it. But if you jist gib me de gemmen's baggage straight for de City Hotel, and if you don't see a wheelbarrow go by steam, take me up for running on de walk. [*Crosses to* R.H.]

Amos: Well, I must confess, when Niggers introduce wheelbarrows to 'nopolize de conversation, s'ciety am comin' to a pretty spear. I've seen de time when de chronometar was twenty foots below freena, and de fire shake like a frosty mornin' wid de cold. I've seen dem two little jubenile sweeps throw down more cindars dan a Christmas hail storm. [*Retires up.*]

Mose: Well, never mind, gib me a box of Warren's patent shoe blacking, a little old Tom to grease my elbow, and de gemmen I black boots for travel with his own looking glass. [*All laugh.*]

Jim Brown: Your ideas are so indirectly ober de way from one anoder, owing to your professions, dat it puts me in mind ob de Park orchestra, trying to play on overture.⁴ The horn takes up de superana, de triangular takes up de alto, and leab nothing but de solo for de bass drum. And in condition to dat, hear what de great

doctor ob Physgne Combobologist say: he says, dat on de back of
de head, just in de middle ob de craneum, de organ ob music am
very strongly enveloped in de great Paganini.⁵ Now, I've got a
bump dar, big as de great watermelon.

Mose: How did you get dat bump? Buttin' down de fence?

Jim Brown: No, natur gib em to me. Buttin' down de fence?—what
you take a musiciana for, you saucy Nigger? Now, leff me feel your
head; you isn't got no bump like de one I is. You is got a berry big
bump, just oder de ear. And dat's de sign you black de boots. [*All
laugh*]

Caesar: What is dis bump I got here?

Jim Brown: Dat is de bump what holds de brains. [*Feeling his own
head.*] I isn't got dat myself.

Caesar: Why, how you keep your head in shape?

Jim Brown: Why, when natur make me, he make me all for music. So,
you see, de brains hab to gib way for de music.

Song
Air, "I Am de Paganini"⁶
I am de Paganini
And my name's Jim Brown,
I fiddle at de Five Points,
And all about de town.
I plays upon de banjo,
And I beats de brass drum,
Stands upon de clarionet,
B., number one.
Chorus:
I am de Paganini
And my name's Jim Brown
I fiddle at de Five Points,
And all about de town
[*All dance the shuffle*]
Dar's music in de horse shoe,
And in de tin pan,
Music in de cross-bow,
Dat few understan'

Dar's music in de kettle,
When it's boiling on de fire,
Music in all natur,
Jim Brown nebber tire.
            Chorus
[All *dance and exit*, L.H. *Exit* Caesar *with wheelbarrow*, R.]
Enter Bone Squash *with a ring of wire, brush, &c. at back.*

Bone Squash: Sweep oh! Sweep oh! Twelve o'clock and no chimney
yet! I've been way up Broadway, down de National Theatre, round
de Coffee House Slip, and up again, and am merrier now den when
I first started. I wish de debil had de man what first discovered de
coal fires. I doesn't understand de chemistry ob de 'gredients 'nuff
to disqualify dem; but no sooner den de coal smoke get in de chimney, den he right away emigrate out ob de top, and 'waporates into
de native element like———. He doesn't adherify to de sides like de
wood smoke does. I 'spect when dey make de coal, dey put in de hy-
drophobia gas to sort a kind o'purify it. I doesn't know what I shall
do; I 'gin to feel de 'pression in de money market 'siderable. I fear
I ab to jine de temperance s'ciety 'gainst my will. I hab a good
notion to turn preacher. Ah, but den I hab to marry in de white
families, and become demalgamated! Eh! eh! dat I neber do. I wish
I could sell myself to de debil. What? Whew! Wouldn't I cut a
swell in Broadway on a Sunday afternoon! Wouldn't de Anthony
Niggers stare! I stand on two corners at once, and a little round
into Broadway. But I wish I was de debil. Ha, ha, ha! I can't help but
laugh to tink. I wish I was de debil! de idea kind o' so coincidence
wid my fertile imaginations like. Ha, ha, ha!
            Song
    Oh, I wish I could sell myself to de debil
    I'd cut a splash to kill old people.
    I wish I could sell myself to de debil,
        And leff off patent sweeping.
        I'll go an buy a suit of clothes,
        Ruffle shirt and ro'cco shoeses,
        Strip cravat, whitewashed hat,
        And spectacles for de noses.

Oh, I wish I could sell myself to de debil
Crowd in, move off, and pass thro' them all.

Oh, I wish I could sell myself to de debil,
Oh, I wish I could sell myself to de debil,
  And leff off sweeping chimnies.
  Wid de brush and soap,
  So white I'd scrub me,
  Den ladies all would fall and hug me,
  Some would cry and roll dar eye,
  "Oh, de soul, I wish he'd hug me."
Oh, I wish I could sell myself to de debil,
Crowd in, move off, and pass thro' them all.

Oh, I wish I could sell myself to de debil,
Oh, I wish I could sell myself to de debil,
  New York couldn't hold me.
  At de fancy ball,
  You'd see dis child dar!
  I gib a dollar note,
  Jist to hold my coat,
  To clar de ballroom out dar.
Oh, I wish I could sell myself to de debil,
Crowd in, move off, and pass thro' them all.

The symphony is kept up till the hogshead opens, when the orchestra gives one crash with the help of the gong, and the Devil rises. Maroon bursts. Bone falls and shakes violently on his back. Appropriate music, gently receding—lights up gradually.

Devil: Howdy do? Rather guess I heard you say you wanted to see me. Well, here I am, piping hot. How do you like me? Come, gab out; don't show the Injin: let your legs fall down while your body runs away. Why, you're like a frost-bitten crane: you don't know whither to stand up or fall down. Guess you haven't made up your mind, yet.

Bone Squash: I say, is you de debil?

Devil: Yes, a real genuine Yankee devil, or a devil of a Yankee: you may have me either way by paying the discount. Don't believe I'm very particular, rather think not. However, won't be certain. What do you think?

Bone Squash: Why, I'm thinking, What de debil does you want here?

Devil: Come to buy up stock. Sartin sure I heard you say you'd like to sell out.

Bone Squash: Oh, hush!

Devil: Why, how the critter talks. Why, you're like the chap that didn't know when he was hungry, so he always eat beforehand. Well, I am a real fourth-proof devil, and one of the best in the lot.

Bone Squash: What's dat? what's dat? Best in the lot! Why, how many is there ob you?

Devil: Why, I rayther guess there's a mighty smart chance of us when we all muster. Some of them have gone to 'tend on the House of Lords, and some of them have gone down into Russia to keep an eye upon the Emperor, and others are gone to trade, that is, to swap and bargain with the missionary preacher; that's easily done. Them fellows are like a rat with your foot upon his tail, he'll skin and cut, and clear out when he's hard run. Now, some of your New York quality won't keep patience, without they have a whole devil to themselves.

Bone Squash: A whole debil to themselves! Well, how many does de Nigger hab?

Devil: Why, that's according to the quantity of wood he take. If he belongs to the temperance society, we put a devil to every two, and plenty of Newcastle coal; but if he's a real double distilled swell head, he'll burn a fortnight without any fuel, and can take care of himself. After that, we keep him for a torch, to hang in the hall. You'd do for a patent chandelier.

Bone Squash: Oh, de debil! Bone Squash, de patent sweeper, transmogrified into a patent chandelier. How de Niggers would laugh if dey was to hear dat.

Devil: Come, what do you say, you brick dust? How will you trade? You're as long striking a bargain as a Yankee and a Jew would be in swapping their conscience.

Bone Squash: Look here, Mr. Yankee debil, I'm no common Nigger what you meet wid round de market and de wharfs. I'm a gemman of color what libs wid de sweat ob de chin, as de poet says; and if you buy me you must crowd steam and come up to de landing pretty sarcy. You see, I'm a free Nigger.

[*Crosses*, L.H.

Devil: What? a free Nigger? Well, let's see you move again! [*Bone crosses to* R.H.] Well, I rather think you are worth a couple of hundred dollars.

Bone Squash: Well, I rather tink I'm worth a couple ob dem.

Devil: Not as you knows on.

Bone Squash: Well, den I knows one ting—

Devil: What's that?

Bone Squash: I'm off like a ferry boat, when dey cross on de lag.[7] [*Going*]

Devil: Stop! Why, you damned Nigger, you're jist like a salmon—you give one nibble, and right off. I'll tell you what we'll do. I'll give you three, and split the difference; that's more than I'd give for an Indian preacher.

Bone Squash: Well, I s'pose you'll stand the liquor, too?

Devil: Well, get us a pen, ink, and paper, and I'll draw up a bond. You'll have to be your own witness.

Bone Squash: Bery well. You jist lumber here till I gwan in and fetch some. [*Exit*, R]

Devil: Well, if these Niggers ain't the softest ninnies I ever had dealings with. They're like a batch of nothing, touched with a kind of a thing, and it falls into what-you-may-call it. Darned crittur! I don't think he's got brains enough to put a stocking on inside out. Why he's worth five hundred if he's worth a Bushel of Peas.

Re-enter Bone, R.

Bone Squash: Here's de paper. Isn't got any ink, so I brought a Box of Warren's blacking—guess dat will do.

Devil: Where's de pen?

Bone Squash: Isn't got no pen neider.

Devil: Well, let's have the paper. [Bone *hands him* The Hawk and Buzzard] What's this?

Bone Squash: No, stop; don't take dat; dat's de *Hawk and Buzzard.* I patronize dat paper for 'ticular reasons; it seminates de useful knowledge to de gubernal branches ob de community.[8] Dat's de *New York Mirror*; you may hab dat. I only takes dat paper out ob compliment to de ladies.[9]

Devil: [*Dips his tail into blacking, and writes.*] Can you write?

Bone Squash: Yes, and cipher, too.

Devil: Well, let's see what your name is.

Bone Squash: Well, gib me de money fust.

Devil: First, let me know your name.

Bone Squash: Dar it is—Bone Squash!

Devil: There's the rhino.[10]

Bone Squash: What's dis? A check?

Devil: Yes, and any of the brokers will cash it.

Bone Squash: I doesn't deal in paper. I want de real buttons. Isn't you got any of de hard cash? Come, dump up.

Devil: Why I tell you it will pass on 'change like an omnibus. They all know me; I've dealings with all of them. Mention my name and any of 'em will take old Nick's check in less time than you'd light a match.

Bone Squash: Come, let's hab de liquor, and den I'm off to de tailors.

[Devil *puts bond into his pocket.* Bone *pockets the check.*]

Duet

Bone Squash:

> I'm beginning for to fill,
> Like a Baltimore Clipper.

Devil:

> But first before you go,
> Guess you'd better have the liquor.

Bone Squash:

> I'll do dat ting
> Wid de greatest ob pleasure.

Devil:

> Then get into Wall Street.
> They'll shell out the treasure.

Bone Squash:

> And ebery Nigger dat I meet,
> I'll stop him in de street
> And I'll up wid a penny,
> Head or tail for a treat.[11]

> Chorus as Duet

Devil:

> I reckon now you know me,
> You can read me like a book, sir.

Bone Squash:

> You're like a singed cat,
> Much better than you look, sir.

Devil:

> But clothes, you know,
> Never make the gentleman.

Bone Squash:

> Dat am a fact,
> Or I'd been a sort ob one.

Devil:

> Only shut up your mug,
> Till the cash you hug.
> Then you'll open right upon 'em
> Like a Georgia cotton bug.[12]

> [*Chorus and dance. Exeunt* Devil, R.H., Bone, L.H.]

→←

Scene 2. A street in New York. Enter Spruce Pink *and* Junietta, *with a parasol,* R.H. *Light stage.*

Spruce: Well I neber 'sperienced such condensed wedder. De transcending streaks ob de bright effulminating sun pours down upon me like de watery element of de shower bath.

Junietta: My lub, de reason am berry perspicuous. Yesterday, de inky clouds overhung de earth as black as de smoke around de bakehouse; darfore, de heat could not perforate; but in de rotundity ob natur, dem inky clouds hab all distinguished away, and heat dat we ought to hab come down yesterday, we 'spect we hab today; consequently, we hab two days heat in one.

Spruce: By de by, I did not tink ob dat. But come, my lub, let us take some lemonade wid de sassyparilla in it, for if we stand here communicating in de sun, we'll be tanned as black as de common white folks.

Junietta: Anywhere, my dear, for de warm wedder hab so opened de paws of my system dat de perspiration flows jist as copiously as de 'lasses from de hogshead.

Spruce: Dat's a bery good sign.

Junietta: What, my lub?

Spruce: I mean de perspiration, for Dr. Johnson says, you keep de head warm, and de foots cold, and de system will always be lassitudinated.

Junietta: Oh, Mr. Pink, look at dat man on de corner! He actly got a segar in his mouth. Stop till I put dat down in my journal. [*writes*] Mr. Pink, how you spell segar.

Spruce: Che—s-e. Ghar—g-a-r. Segar.

Junietta: Tank you! I always put down ebery 'diculous custom of de white folks. Well, let's go, Mr. Pink, and when I cum back I want to make explahation from de African language.

Spruce: Suffer me. [*Takes parasol and they are about to exit*]

Enter Mose, *with a stick of boots.*[13]

Mose: Why, de laud a mercy, Spruce, when did you ribe from Philadelphy?

Spruce: You are mistaken in de person black man, dis 'nt he.

Junietta: Who does the impertinent Nigger mean, my lub?

Spruce: He tinks I am de gemmen he blacks de boots for.

Mose: Why look here, Spruce, you is rather lofty. I 'spect the New York climate greases wid you?

Spruce: I tell you, you must be sun struck, else you learn better how to 'sault a gemman in company wid de fair sex.

Junietta: Mr. Pink, don't excommunicate wid de Nigger any more! De people will tink you sosheate wid dem.

Mose: Now, old Spruce, you can't fool dis child. I know you as sure as I knowed a box of Warren's blacking. Who is you waiting on now?

Spruce: On de ladies, to be sure.

Mose: Is you leff off scouring?

Spruce: I'll scour you, you audacity black man.

Junietta: Stop, Mr. Pink, till I put dis down in my journal. August 32nd, 'saulted in Broadway, by common black man.

Mose: Who do you call black man?

Spruce: You, you common Nigger. [*Crossing to* Mose, *but is held back by* Junietta.]

Trio

Spruce:

Let me go, don't hold me fast,
I'll run that Nigger through.

Junietta:

Oh, Mr. Pink, I really tink,
De Nigger must be blue.

Mose:

Oh, let him come; I'll neber run.

Spruce:

Did you eber hear de like?

Junietta:

Oh, pray, keep cool, don't be a fool.

Mose:

Put up dat sword, don't strike!

[Spruce *and* Junietta *sing the first part as chorus, while* Mose *holds his sides, and laughs heartily all through.*]

Junietta:

Brack man, I tink you'd better go.
His passion 'gin to rise.

Mose:

If de Nigger draws de sword agin,
I'll slap him 'cross de eyes.

Spruce:

What's dat I hear?

Junietta:

Noting, my dear.

Spruce:

I'll make him eat his words.

Mose:

Spell "Abel" fust![14]

Spruce:

I almost bust.
Your conduct is absurd.

[*Chorus as before. When within the last two bars of chorus,* Caesar *enters,* L, *with wheelbarrow, and exclaims* "Old Hays is coming."[15] *Music hurry. All scamper off.* Mose *trips up* Spruce. Caesar *wheels the barrow over him. All go off laughing at* Spruce.]

➤◄

Scene 3. Pompey Duckelleg's *house. Two chairs—music.*
Enter Junietta *in confusion.*

Junietta: I am almost horrified wid chagrin! 'Sulted by a common black man to de disgustion of Mr. Pink. I wonder where he am? Maybe dat wheelbarrow, when he ran ober him, hab dissecterated his leg, or shoulder arm. [*A knock,* L.H.] Ah! Who is dat? Should dat be Mr. Pink, and my dear fader not at home! I tremble like a catfish for de consequence. [*Knocking*] Ah, again! Ye Gods, decide my fate. [*Music. She opens the door,* L.F. *when* Pompey *enters with basket and lobster, covered*] My dear, dear fader! Whar am you been?

Pompey: Juni, dear, I am jist come from de market.

Junietta: [*aside*] My tears once more am hush'd up still. What am you buy'd my fader?

Pompey: I hab buy'd dat, my child, which am illustratious ob de wile sinner. Behold dis lobster! It am now dressed in de penitent suit ob sackcloth and ashes; but when you put him in de pot, and squeeze de kiver down upon 'em, de devil will boil out ob dem, and he'll hab de vegetated colors ob de rainbow, singed round wid de indigo ob natur.

Junietta: Bery much like de 'flection ob Mr. Pink! What else is you got?

Pompey: I got anoder ting dat my old gums smack togedder at, like a cellar door leff off de hinges. It is de emblem ob Old Virginny, neber tire: it am de coon.

Junietta: Dis de coon?

Pompey: Dat same old coon.

Junietta: It are de coon.

Pompey: It is de coon. [*Chord. Shows it.*] It puts me in mind ob de many moonshiney nights, when I used to go out wid de old Sancho, and kill 'em. I buy dat coon for your wedding supper.

Junietta: [*Faints.*] Oh, my dear fader!

Pompey: What de matter wid my darter?

Junietta: Oh, my dear fader, when you talk to me—

Pompey: Sit down, my dear, I 'splain de matter. Today, I meet Bone Squash. Fortune hab smiled upon him, and he ax me once more to gib my darter's hand. I hab told him I will do dat ting. As soon as he hab done wid de tailor, he will come to claim his bride.

Junietta: It neber can—it neber shall be. Sooner den be Mistress Squash, dat hateful, vulgar name, I exile to Siberia, and live among de Indians. I make de solemn vow to lub Spruce Pink; dey shall not jerk me from him. See, de wheelbarrow gwan ober him! Old Hays hab got him—he hollers for his Junietta in vain—she cannot help him—her cruel fader marry her to Bone Squash! Ha! ha! ha! [*Faints.*]

Enter Bone Squash, *in full dress*, L.H. *Chord*

Bone Squash: Hallo! What's de matter? Is de chimney afire?

Pompey: No, but my darter was so bery impatient to see you and—

Junietta: De intensity ob de sun was so killing hot today, dat it like to strike me dead when I was up in Broadway, and when I hear your romantic name—

Pompey: Dar, dat is all! Dat's all explained.

Junietta: Mr. Squash, you must draw a prize in de lottery.

Bone Squash: Yes, and I've come to draw out your affections. Say, you hab me quick, for I 'spect ere long I hab to emigrate furder south. [*Points down.*]

Pompey: Bone Squash, and my darter Junietta, listen to what I ex-
close. Take her for your oder half, lub her as de possum do de old
coon! Neber cross each other in de path ob felicitous domestica-
tions, as Jonas dat build de Ark say, de debil be sure to hab you.
[*Music, 3 bars. Slaps* Bone Squash *on the back, which makes him start
and tremble.*] Why, what's de matter wid de damn'd Nigger. Is he
got de shakes?

Bone Squash: I don't like to hear you talk about de debil.

Junietta: Dat's right, neber talk about people you hab not de pleasure
of dar acquaintance.

Pompey: Well, well, drop de subject. Mr. Squash, did you 'vite de company?

Bone Squash: Yes, and dey all gwan to Jim Brown's, and den dey all be
here. [*Music piano.*] Ah, here dey come.

[*Enter* Jim Brown *with his fiddle.* Amos, Caesar, Mose, Juba, Janza, Milly,
*and other blacks. The characters advance to the front, and begin the chorus. Dur-
ing the symphony, they all dance.* Pompey, Junietta, *and* Bone *are on* R.]

Chorus
Come, saw upon de fiddle now,
    Old Jim Brown.
        [*Repeat, three times*]
Till we cut de pigeon wing,
    And hab a break down.
Come, pull out your rosin now,
    And grease up your strings.
        [*Repeat*]
Bone Squash, take de lead,
    And we all will begin.

Dance
We don't fear de constable,
    No, by gosh!
        [*Repeat, three times*]
While we dance at de wedding,
    Ob old Bone Squash.
Strike upon de tambourine
    And upon de fiddle, too.

> Oh, neber mind de Nigger,
> If he habn't got de shoe.

[*Dance, as before. The following is the order of dance.* Amos *advances with* Janza *and* Milly, *who dance to* Mose, *etc. The others dance without precision, following down to lights, to begin chorus.*]

Bone Squash: Gemmen, I 'blige to all ob you! 'Low me to introduce to you Mrs. Squash, my wife dat is to be.

Jim Brown: Mr. Squash, I rader tink de last chimney you swept, you bring down de deposits. [*All laugh.*]

Caesar: I guess he come down de wrong chimney, when de gemmen was down to breakfast. [*All laugh.*]

Bone Squash: Why, look here, gemmen: did you neber see one ob de aristocracy before? [*All laugh.*] Gemmen, de ladies will expire to get ready for de wedd'n. [*Music. Exeunt* Pompey *and ladies.*]

Caesar: But, Mr. Squash, tell us how you come so rich.

[*Music. Solo*]

Bone Squash:

> It was de oder morning,
> About de break ob day,
> As I was gwan up Broadway
> I see'd de high prize
> In de window for sale,
> I went in and paid my money on the nail.

> Dis mornin' I found,
> To my great surprise,
> De ticket what I buy'd,
> Drew de big high prize.

> I went to de tailors,
> And buy'd der clothes,
> Paid my money like a white man,
> And off I goes.

[*Chorus.*]

> Pompey Duckellegs, he see'd me,
> And took me by de hand,
> And says, "I want a son-in-law,

And you is de man.
You hab got fine clothes,
And de cash beside,
My daughter Junietta,
Shall be your bride."

After chorus, re-enter Pompey, Junietta, *and all the ladies.*

Bone Squash: Now, let de ceremony proceed. [*Music. A chord.*]

Enter Spruce Pink, L.

Spruce: Stop dem perjured nuptializations.
[*Ladies scream—Gentlemen support them.*]

Bone Squash: Who is dis Nigger?

Spruce: I am the victim of despair.

Junietta: Oh, can I believe my eyes! It is—

Mose: Spruce Pink, what cut my 'quaintance this morning.

Caesar: You ought to see him cut, when de constable is comin'.

Spruce: Oh, you am Caesar, de Nigger who run de wheelbarrow ober
me dis mornin'. Now, my satisfaction calls for revenge.

[*Music.* Spruce *draws his sword cane. A general scream, when the* Devil *appears up trap. Gong and hurried music, blue lights, etc.*]

All: The devil! The devil!

[*All stand shaking with fear. Music for the* Devil *to step, increasing to forte every minute.*]

Devil: Bone Squash, what do you say to emigrating?

Bone Squash: I can't go jist yet. I am gwan to be married.

Devil: So much the better; bring your wife along. [Junietta, *at the word "wife," gets behind her father.*] Won't you come?

Bone Squash: No.

Devil: Then I'll bring you.

[*Music. As the* Devil *raises his fork, the characters scream, and run to* L. *General commotion, men tripping and rolling over each other.* Bone *gets behind the* Devil*—breaks through all. When, in confusion, the* Devil, *tumbles into basket, the lobster catches hold of his nose—he roars violently.* Bone *escapes up the* *chimney. All exit, while* Pompey *beats the* Devil *with a broom stick. Red fire used in the chimney, trap, and wings. Curtain.*

✦

Act 2

Scene 1.[16] *A street, as before*

Enter Spruce Pink *meeting* Jim Brown.

Spruce: How are you after your horrification?

Jim Brown: I don't mind de disappointment of de wedding, nor de debil grabbing Bone Squash, but, my fiddle! Look at my fiddle—de notes of mine no longer vibrate on mine ear. All gone to de debil, along wid Bone Squash.

Spruce: And dat Miss Duckellegs, too. If you believe me, I stand four hours in de sun wid her yesterday—and now to resignate me for a patent sweeper!

Jim Brown: I thought de Nigger didn't buy dem clothes honest. He said he draw a prize in de lottery.

Spruce: I think de debil got a prize now.

Enter Bone Squash.

Bone Squash: Look here Niggers where de debil is—

Exit Spruce *and* Brown

Bone Squash: Whew! De Niggers run away from me as if I was de Cogeramorbus. I wonder whar Missus Squash, dat what to be, is? I guess she kind ob alter her notion now. Well, I is de nastiest looking Nigger I eber did see. I kind ob tink my closhes want brushing. Well, dat's de last chimney I sweep for noting. I don't know whar de debil went, but I spect he cut after some other Nigger, jist to pay the expenses. Eh! Eh! Ah, who is dis come dar? Dat's my old sweetheart Janza Snowball. I jist lay back and sight de movements.

[*Retires* L.H.]

Enter Janza

Janza: Well I'm glad de debil is got 'em. What he gwan to be married to old Pompey Duckelleg's daughter, when he tells me he lub me better den a johnny cake.

Bone Squash: But I'm afraid dat johnny cake is dough.

Janza: Who's dere? Mr. Squash! Why, I tought de debil had you.

Bone Squash: Oh, no. He made a mistake, you see. He came arter anoder Nigger whose name was—

Janza: Spruce Pink.

Bone Squash: Oh, dat's his name! But he could not tink of it, so he axed for Bone Squash and Spruce Pink. Bone Squash sound bery much alike. Bone Squash, especially.

Janza: Den, Mr. Squash, I presume all my lub and fections for you.

Bone Squash: Den let's get married right off.

Business[17]

Enter Junietta.

Junietta: What, Bone Squash came back again?

Bone Squash: Oh, de debil.

Janza: Run, Squash, here comes de oder one.

Business

Junietta: Upon my word, Mr. Squash I tought was in de oder world, when to my stonishment I cotch him right before de door making lub to anoder Lady [*aside*]. Tis well for you, Mr. Squash, I hab neber seen such vulgar things. Oh, I neber shall hab de fortitude to hold you.

Bone Squash: If you only hab patience, I'll marry both ob you.

Song
When two evils am to choose,
Dey say take de least one.
If I gib my hand here,
De oder will be undone.
What shall I do
To get me out dis mess?
Either way I turn,
My bosom all on fire.
Ladies, dry your grief,
And wipe away your sorrow,
And if you mind's your eye,
I'll marry you both tomorrow.

Exeunt

➤◄

Scene 2. Cellar in the Five Points. Bar, with liquor for sale—hogsheads. All discovered. As curtain rises, a general laugh.

Jim Brown: I wonder where Mr. Squash is by dis time? Hallo!

Enter Bone Squash, C. door. Music.

Bone Squash: Here I am, Niggers! [*Solo—music*] "Look at my dandy coat." Come Niggers, I'll stand a treat, and den I'll tell you whar I've been. [*Goes to bar*]

Spruce [*aside*]: Mr. Bone Squash am now a-going it among de Niggers. I take de 'wantage ob his absence, and go hab an explanation wid Miss Duckellegs. Oh! de perfidious woman ob her sex. [*Exit*, L.H.]

Amos: Mr. Bone, guess you've been leaning against a coal yard.

Bone Squash: Oh, leff off your fun, and I'll tell you all about it.

Music—Solo and Chorus.

Bone Squash:

> In a chimney tight,
>   I staid all night,
> And like to die,
>   Wid de soot and smoke.
> While de fire below,
>   It burn my toe,
> And wid de cinders,
>   Like to choke

Chorus:

> And sich a gittin' up stairs
> And a runnin' from de debil
> Sich a gittin' up stairs,
> I neber did see.

Bone Squash:

> Old Pompey Duckellegs
>   Turn'd blue,

And shouted out,
    Young hally loo!
De daughter, she
    Was left alone,
And de oder ladies
    Scampered home.

Chorus:

        And sich a gittin' up stairs, etc.

Bone Squash:

Come now, I'll stand,
    Anoder treat,
And at de ball,
    Dis night we'll meet.
And if de debil
    Should creep in,
De way we'll use him,
    Be a sin.

Chorus:

        And sich a gittin' up stairs, etc.

[*All retire to drink*. Brown *and* Mose *remain in front.*]

Jim Brown: I say, Mose, let us play a game ob luck.

Mose: I've got no money.

Jim Brown: Mr. Squash has, and I'll get de loaded dice.

Mose: Well, you rope him in, and I'll gib you de items.

Jim Brown: Gemman! Let's play, to see who shall hab de most money.

Bone Squash: I've got de most already; but, come, I'm agreed.

[*Music*. Mose *brings a table to C., over the trap. All* shake their boxes.]

        Solo and Chorus
    Smile my fortune!
        Oh, oh, oh!
    I'll play you for a dollar, boys.
        I'm as good as you.
    And I'll win all your money, boys.
        Ha! ha! ha!

And I'll win all your money, boys.
   Ha! ha! ha!

Hear de chinkling
   Oh, oh, oh!
And de merry clinkling,
   Oh, oh, oh!
Here goes for raffle sixes,
   Worse den before.
I'll double down de money, boys,
   Ha! ha! ha!
I'll double down de money, boys,
   Ha! ha! ha!

Smile my fortune!
   Oh, oh, oh!
Smile my fortune!
   Oh, oh, oh!
I'll sweep it like a hawk, now,
   Twelve! Eh, eh!
Wake snakes, and talk now,
   Three, two, one!
Oh, you'll win all my money, boys!
   Ha! ha! ha!

Smile my fortune!
   Oh, oh, oh!
Smile my fortune!
   Oh, oh, oh!
I'll go you all my money, now,
   Make de pile large!
I'll go you all my money, now,
   Make de pile large!
Now, show your black faces once,
   Six! no more!
Only show your black faces, now,
   Worse den before.

I've lost my fortune!
   Oh, oh, oh!

I've lost my fortune!
 Oh, oh, oh!
So gib me back my money, boys,
 Ha! ha! ha!
Oh, gib me back my money, boys,
 Ha! ha! ha!
I wish de debil had me,
 Ha! ha! ha!
I wish de debil had me,
 Ha! ha! ha!
                    [*Hurried music.*]
Enter Devil *through the table.*

All: Oh, debil! He's come

All thrown into confusion. The Devil *leaps from the table, and the characters run out. As* Bone Squash *is about to follow, the* Devil *stops him with his fork.*

Devil: Oh, you damn Nigger; I've got you now.
Bone Squash: Well, I rader tink you'll hab to run for it.
                    [*Music.*]
[*As* Bone *is making again for the door, enter all the characters. The* Devil *seizes one part of* Bone's *coat tail; the blacks being divided, one half seize the* Devil's *tail, and the other half the tail of* Bone. *They struggle violently, when* Bone's *coat tears up the back.* Bone *escapes through the door in flat, leaving his coat tail behind. The characters all tumble. The* Devil *makes after* Bone, *the rest following.*]

All: Go it, Bone!

✦

Scene 3. Exterior of Barber's shop, with a large window to break. Enter Bone *and* Devil, R.H. *The* Devil *tries in vain to throw a rope over* Bone's *head.* Bone, *seeing no other hope left, plunges through the window, the* Devil *after him.* [*Change. Music continued.*]

✦

Scene 4. Interior of Barber's shop, in horrible confusion. Bone *is discovered with half his body out of window. The* Devil *has hold of him by the leg. In the other window, the others are thronged, anxiously viewing the scene.*

Devil: I've got you now like an oyster has a crab, right by the leg.

Bone Squash: Oh, look here, Mr. Yankee debil, stop! I splain the matter!

Devil: Well, gab you, it's nearly dinner time. You call yourself a business man, do you? Why, they'd kick you out of the Exchange, even on Sunday. Why, curse your color, you aren't fit to sell second-hand coffins. You're like a sand clam commission merchant: you'd walk two miles for one, for fear of meeting your creditors.

Bone Squash: Well, look here, look here, who told you to come to de wedding widout de inbertation, and make me pear so diclous 'fore the ladies?

Devil: Well, I rather calculate we didn't say anything about the time. I guess it's optional.

Bone Squash [*aside*]: Dars where he hab me. But look here, Mr. Debil, I believe I shall take de benefit ob de act.[18]

Devil: Oh, get out, only hearken to your gab. Come now, act white, if you are black.

Jim Brown: Bone, put out!

Devil: No, you don't.

[*Music.* Bone *attempts to run, but is tripped up by a noose the* Devil *has fixed to his leg while talking to him. All laugh.*]

Bone Squash: Who tied that rope round my leg?

Devil: I wanted to pull the kinks out. Why, you fire knot chunk, you're like a 'lasses candy in a shop window. You run away all sides. Come, I think we'd better go. The people will be coming out of church, and I don't want to be mobb'd in the street. They're keeping up a milliner's birthday and I'll make sure of you this time.

Winds his tail round him

Jim Brown: Bone, sham sick!

Bone Squash: Oh! Mr Debil, I tink I got de measles.

Devil: Well, here's an antidote. [*Music.* Devil *takes out a long cigar, and begins to smoke it. He lights it from a phosphorus box in his tail.*] Do you smoke?

Bone Squash: No, I tank you. I'm free from all sich wulgar wices. Eh! What a pain I've got in my leg. Oh! Oh! Oh!

Devil: Why, how you talk! Come along with me, and I'll give you a sulphur bath.

Jim Brown: It's all day wid him.

Mose: Squash, is you gwan to take your brush wid you?

Caesar: Mr. Squash, any word to send to Mrs. Squash dat was to be?

Bone Squash: Look here, jist gib me time to speak to my feller citizens.

Devil: Oh, come now; you're like a rent day, no getting you off.

Bone Squash: Well, if I must, I must. Eh! eh!

Music—Solo and Chorus

Bone Squash:

> Listen while I splain de matter,
> Bout my lub, sweet Junietta. [*A start*]
> Tomorrow we gwan to marry.
> And you no longer leff me tarry. [*Start*]
> And I gib my word and honor,
> To meet you on de Five Points corner,
> And go straight along wid you,
> And go straight along wid you,
> But at present must excuse me,
> And tomorrow you may use me
> And tomorrow, and tomorrow,
> Please to leff me stay.

Devil:

> No, I must haste away.

Bone Squash:

> Pray excuse me.

All:

> Ha! ha! ha!

Devil:

> I must use you.

Bone Squash:

> Please let me stay.

All:

> Ha! ha! ha!

Devil:

> I must away

All:

     Ha! ha! ha!

Bone Squash:

     Farewell all my calculation.[19]
     For I'm bound to de wild goose station. [*Start*]
     Farewell, all your fancy balls.

          [*Start.* Brown *gives knife.*]

     Yes, I must confess my sorrow.
     Since I cannot stay tomorrow.
     Farewell all, Bone Squash is gone,
     If you only would excuse me,
     And tomorrow you may use me,
     And tomorrow, and tomorrow,
     So please to leff me stay.

        [*Chorus as before*]

All: Cut! cut!

[Bone *cuts the* Devil's *tail off and escapes. All finish chorus.* Devil *pursues* Bone, *the others following.*]

※

Scene 5.[20] *A Street. Music. Enter* Bone *and all the ladies,* L.H.

     Song and Chorus.

Bone Squash:

     Oh, ladies, pray, don't tease me so,
     But please to let me go;
     Heigho! my pretty gals,
     Please to let me go.

Ladies [*first chorus*]:

      You shall not go!
      You shall not go!

Bone Squash:

     Heigho! my pretty gals,
     Do let me go.

Ladies [*second chorus*]:

      Heigho! My pretty Bone
      You shall not go.

Bone Squash:

> I'm a gwan to Philadelphy,
> Whar I will be safe, I know.
>> *First Chorus.*

Bone Squash:

> I've just escaped de constable,
> Who'd got me safe in tow.
>> *Second Chorus.*

Bone Squash:

> If you keep me here, my Johnny-cake
> Will all be turned to dough.
>> *First Chorus.*

Bone Squash:

> I must break dis link ob harmony,
> And trust to heel and toe.
>> *Second Chorus.*

Bone Squash:

> Let go your hands, and let me troop
> I'm anxious for to go.
>> *First Chorus.*

Bone Squash:

> If you eber showed compassion,
> Now's the time to let it flow.
>> *Second Chorus.*
> [*Exit* Bone, *pulling the girls after him.*]

✦

Scene 6. The whole stage. A balloon ready for ascending. Two little devils filling it with bellows. All the characters discovered on each side the stage for the finale. Music.

> *Enter* Bone Squash, *crazy.*

Bone Squash:

> Save me! save me! save me!

Omnes:

> Oh, what is de matter now
> Wid old Bone Squash? [*Repeat.*]

Bone Squash:

Save me! save me! save me!

Men:

Oh! oh! oh!

Bone Squash:

Sorry dat I sold myself to de Debil.

Omnes:

Sorry dat he sold himself to de Debil.

Women:

Poor Bone Squash!

Bone Squash:

Oh! oh! oh!

Omnes:

Poor Bone Squash!

Bone Squash:

Juny! Juny! Fare you well for ever!

Omnes:

Oh! oh! oh!

Bone Squash:

What dis I see?

Women:

Junietta, lubly dear.

Bone Squash:

What dis I see?

Men:

You promised marriage here.

Bone Squash:

Go whar I will.

Women:

Go whar you will.

Bone Squash:

Spruce Pink can't come here,
He's gone below.

Men:

He's gone below.

Bone Squash:

Tremble and fear.

Women:

Tremble and fear.

Omnes:

Oh! oh! oh!
Tremble and fear.

Bone Squash:

And I scamper down the street,
Ebry Nigger dat I meet,
And I ups wid a penny,
Head or tail for a treat.

Omnes:

And he scampers down the street,
Ebry Nigger dat he meets,
He ups wid a penny,
Head or tail for a treat.

Bone Squash:

Save me! save me! save me!

Men:

Carry him along! Carry him along!

Bone Squash:

Save me! save me! save me!

Men:

Carry him along! Carry him along!

Bone Squash:

Save me! save me! save me!

Women:

Poor Bone Squash!

Men:

Oh! oh! oh!

Bone Squash:

Sich a gittin' up stairs
And a runnin' from de debil
Sich a gittin' up stairs,
I neber did see.

Omnes:

> Sich a gittin' up stairs
> And a runnin' from de debil
> Sich a gittin' up stairs,
>> We neber did see.

Bone Squash:

> Ladies, dry your grief,
>> And wipe away your sorrow,
> And if you mind's your eye,
>> I'll marry you all tomorrow.

Omnes:

> Oh, de Nigger must be crazy,
>> It's bery plain to see;
> De Debil's comin' after him,
>> He can't get free.

Bone Squash:

> When I fust left Kentucky,—

Women:

> With sorrow he grieves for his home.

Bone Squash:

> My heart filled with joy was too happy.

Men:

> Like de smoke from the chimney is blown.

Bone Squash:

>> Den fill de cup,
>> And leff me sup,
> Dar's nothing like good whiskey,
>> I've fled de track
>> And can't come back,
> Darfore I will be frisky.

Omnes:

>> Den fill de cup,
>> And leff him sup,
> Dar's nothing like good whiskey,
>> He's fled de track
>> And can't come back,
> Darfore we will be frisky.

Bone Squash:

        Smile my fortune!

Men:

        Oh! oh! oh!

Bone Squash:

        Smile my fortune!

Men:

        Oh! oh! oh!

Bone Squash:

And I've lost all my money, boy.

Omnes:

Ha! ha! ha!

Bone Squash:

        Here goes for raffle sixes,

Omnes:

        Ha! ha! ha!

Bone Squash:

        Here goes for raffle sixes,

Omnes:

        Ha! ha! ha!

Bone Squash:

        Oh! oh! oh!
        It is my Junietta's voice.

Omnes:

        Ha! ha! ha!

Bone Squash:

Oh, ladies do not tease me so,
But please to let me go.

Omnes:

        Heigho! my boy Squash,
        Indeed, you shall not go.

Women:

        You shall not go!

Omnes:

        Heigho! my pretty Squash,
        You shall not go.

Bone Squash:

> It's too late to repent of my folly now;
> It's too late to repent of my folly now!

Omnes:

> The Debil will hab him,
> He's sure for to grab him.
> And away goes Bone Squash to—

Bone Squash:

> Fill de cup,
> And leff me sup,
> Dar's nothing like good whiskey,
> I've fled de track
> And can't come back,
> Darfore I will be frisky.

Omnes:

> Come fill de cup
> And leff him sup
> Dar's nothing like good whiskey,
> He's fled de track
> And can't come back,
> Darfore we will be frisky.

Bone Squash:

> Come on! Come on!
> Dar's nought can save me,
> De Debil, he's sure to hab me.
> None to pity dis poor Nigger;
> He will hab to groan for eber. [*Gong.*]
> Save me! Save me! Save Me!

Omnes:

> Ha! ha! ha!

[*Enter the* Devil *with torch and a bundle of straw. He seizes* Bone Squash, *and puts him in car of balloon. Balloon ascends, surrounded with Fireworks.* Bone *cuts the rope; the* Devil *falls and* Bone *ascends, throwing out his shoes, hat, etc. The* Devil *falls through a trap, and red fire is emitted from the same. Curtain falls on tableau.*]

THE END

⚐ FLIGHT TO AMERICA¹ ⚐

Act 1

Scene 1. An Inn at Liverpool. Enter six or seven sailors, L. They fix a sign upon a board that shows "The Royal William for New York sails this day." *R. Another board reads,* "Rocket starts from London: Reduced Fares."

1st Sailor: Now, my boys, a fair wind in the offing and once more across the Atlantic we go.

Chorus
Air—"College Hornpipe."²
Ev'ry hand on board, for the wind sets fair.
Soon the tide will serve and our way lies there.
Then never grieve like asses about wives' friends and lasses,
But cheerily my messmates to the quay repair.

Solo
We have emigrants and vagabonds from ev'ry lands.
We have actors, factors, traders, as I understand.
Our ship's at anchor lying with her colors³ gaily flying—
Then away, away to duty, every able hand.

Every soul on board, etc.
Exit all; bells ring.

Enter Waiter, L.

Waiter: Now for another day's work. There ain't nothing worth living for. I came to Liverpool to be quiet, but here I'm harried worse than London. "American packets," indeed. [*looking at board:*] London's emptying itself into New York, and Liverpool acts by way of a conductor. [*bells ring*]

Enter Second Waiter, L.

Second Waiter: There's a chaise! Run, Bob, run.

First: Run? Walker. I'm a waiter, not a runner. What are they?

Second: A dashing young chap and a lady.

First: Runaways, doing the undutiful. Some girl, now, as has run away from a doting father.

Second: Oh! Confound your moralizing—toddle, will you?

[210]

First: I'm a going. This way, Sir, this way—take care of the step, Ma'am. Little does she know of the step she's taken. [*Bells ring, L.*]
Enter Juliette LaBelle *and* Ellen Freegrave, *L.*

Juliette [*who is dressed en homme:*] Look after our luggage and pay the post boy. Get us an apartment, get us some breakfast, and get along.

First Waiter: Pay the boy. Flashy to look at, but I'll have an eye to the trunks.

Bells ring; Waiters *exit, L.*

Juliette: Here we are, my dear Ellen, in Liverpool: our cares and our lovers behind us, life and the new world before us.

Ellen: With the slight intervention of an ocean, called the Atlantic, and the probability of an accident, called a pursuit.

Juliette: The Atlantic! A mere ditch, crossed and recrossed like Twickenham ferry. And, as to pursuit, my dear, "no catchee, no havee"; and, I flatter myself, my disguise is impenetrable.

Ellen: Pray, pray, be cautious! I nearly fainted when you said ugly words to the waiter—how could you, Juliette?

Juliette: Pooh! My love, I must rattle a little to keep up my character. Had we traveled as two silly girls, we should have been subjected to a hundred annoyances. But now I place you under my protection.

Ellen: Pretty protection, truly. But, my dear love, on board the packet, think of the thousand awkward circumstances your assumption of male attire may subject you to.

Juliette: Think of the ten thousand awkward circumstances it will secure us from. Now, no more faintheartedness and no more morality. *"Honi soit qui mal y pense"*⁴ is my motto. I get rid of a booby lover and an importunate uncle; you gain freedom; that's enough.

Ellen: But, surely, my love, you could have got rid of your lover without this step. Indeed, begging pardon of your *amour propre*, I think he was rather disinclined to the match.

Juliette: I'm sure. I did my utmost to make him so. But you don't know all. I was early left a burthen—as he kindly called it—on my uncle's care, with nothing but him and my heels to rely upon. I danced myself into competence, but am yet my uncle's debtor. For the care

and cost of my childhood, he wished me to wed Blinkinsopp and
extorted from him a promise of marriage. Guess my feelings when
my uncle averred his intention of making Blinkinsopp marry me,
instantly, or of proceeding to legal extremities!

Ellen: But, you being unwilling, how could he?

Juliette: As my guardian, he could. Blinkinsopp's fortune was to in-
demnify my affectionate relative for my maintenance and education. Do you think I could endure the thought of forcing myself on
any man, even if I loved him, or of being forced to wed one I did
not? So, here I am: Juliette LaBelle, late of the Opera *premiere danseuse*, transformed into a very natty fellow, hoping to find in Columbia a home and happiness.

Ellen: There's my hand, love. I'm not as bold a venturer, but you will
find me as true, if not as stout-hearted, as yourself.

Duet

Air—"The Dusty Miller"[5]

Juliette:

> Helter, skelter, scramble,
> Gaily will we trudge it;

Ellen:

> Ah, of such a ramble,
> I have fears, a budget.

Juliette:

> Fears, I laugh to scorn;
> Freely let us revel;
> You beside me, I
> Will face the very—[6]

Both:

> Freshly blows the breeze; sailors steer and tack it.
> Quickly o'er the seas, goes the western packet.

Ellen:

> Mind, your Aunt's advice is,
> "Home, oh! Ne'er forsake it."

Juliette:

> It as easy, twice is,
> To give advice as take it.

Ellen:

> "Look 'fore you leap,"
> Said her latest letter.

Juliette:

> "Leap before you look"
> Suits my taste much better.

Both:

> Freshly blows the breeze; sailors steer and tack it.
> Gaily o'er the seas, sails the western packet.
>> *Exit* Juliette *and* Ellen, *R. Bell rings.*

Waiter [*outside, L.:*] London coach, four insides, five out.
> *First* Waiter *enters, L.*

First Waiter: This way, Sir, this way. [*bell rings*]
> *Enter* Monsieur Pirouette, *L.*

Pirouette: Ah! oui oui, I never sall go outside de top o' de coach again. Ma foi, my foots is froid, very. Every ting I've got is froze away, very. Vaiter! Ah, mon Dieu! De English coach is stupid, rascal ting not compare wis ze diligence. Vaiter, vat I sall never be warm again. I am de gooses flesh, all over. Mais my foot is cold, but mon coeur is on fire. Vaiter, I say!

First Waiter: Beg pardon, we must attend to our insides first.

Pirouette: De devil take your insides, Sare. It is my inside I want attended to. I must have some breakfasts.
> *Second* Waiter *enters, L., and crosses.*

Second Waiter: Number five wants coffee, and eighteen, tea.
>> *Second* Waiter *exits, R.*

Pirouette: I beg your pardon, Sare, but Number One want precisely de same ting, if you are so good.

First Waiter: Very well, Sir, that's the way to the Coffee Room.

Pirouette: Garcon, restez ici pour un moment, s'il vous plait. Attendez! Dis is de house for de packet, eh?

First Waiter: Packets! Oh, yes Sir, there's the board.

Pirouette: You dam wood head, I no want the board. I want you. The packet sail from your door, eh?

First Waiter: No Sir, not from our door exactly—from the *quay*.

Pirouette: From the key of your door! Vat do you mean, Sare?

First Waiter: I mean what I say; I can't help it, if you can't understand plain English.

Pirouette: You insult me, I am offensive. You tell to me I no speak plain English. Diablement! I am quite as plain as you.

First Waiter: Well, I don't say as you ain't.

Pirouette: The packet of America, Sare, vat time it sall take fright?

First Waiter: Take fright! What's that?

Pirouette: Vat's dat—you thick head—vat is dat, [*Points to coach-board, L.*] "The Rocket starts"

First Waiter: Oh, start, you mean.

Pirouette: C'est egal!—start and take fright ze same ting, you know him well enough.

First Waiter: Why, it goes today, weather permitting.

Pirouette: I want to know ven he go, whether or no.

First Waiter: That I can't say. It depends on the wind and I know nothing of that 'ere.

Exit waiter

Pirouette: "De wind and knows nosing of that air:" he is stupid—mais the wind sall be very well this morning. I wonder if dat faithless Juliette ave got avay? I sall ron very quick upon her heel. Sacre! Une ingrate. I ave teach her her first *entre chàt.* I show her the grand mysteries of the sublime science. I show her de purpose for which nature designed de foots—ven she know, she scamper away very much. Helas! I sall perhaps never set my eye upon my pupilles again. Dis makes me trieste. I am miserable. J'en suis au desespoir. I will go get some breakfasts. [*Bells*]

First Waiter [*Without, L*]: This way, gentlemen.

Pirouette: Ah, here is all de passengers. Charmant persons—never speak all de night.

Music. Enter several passengers, L., cross and exit R., with coachman, luggage, etc. After them enters Mr. Benjamin Blinkinsopp, *with a traveling cap over a Welch wig, and wrapped in a number of shawls, etc.; he disburthens himself of them during scene.*

Blinkinsopp: Folks talk. Talk about wonderful improvements in traveling—it's all humbug, Sir, regular humbug of the first water—unadulterated humbug—how dare they pop a man 5 foot 11 into a vehicle 4 feet by 3?

Pirouette: I hope you are pretty well, I thank you, after your travel.

Blinkinsopp: No, Sir, I am not pretty well, I thank *you.* I am cursed uncomfortable. But, I say, my outsider, you was an outsider, wasn't you?[7]

Pirouette: Ah, oui, on de top of de outside.

Blinkinsopp: Yes, and I was in the middle of the inside, chewing my own knees and trying to digest the leggings of my indescribables.[8]

Pirouette: You have sleep, I see, by your nightcaps.

Blinkinsopp: Then you see more than I know. Sleep! I've heard of men sleeping in a sentry box, up in a tree, or down in a dry well; but sleep inside a coach, I defy you. A fat fellow was opposite, though, snoring like a rhinoceros, and stretching out his unwieldy legs every moment, kicking the bark off mine. And just as I was about getting the first five of forty winks, roo, too, too, too, the Guard's horn goes, and all one's work to do over again. The inside of a coach! It's the black hole of Calcutta made easy to the meanest capacity.

Pirouette: Ah, mai foi, de inside is nozing to de out.

Blinkinsopp: De out? Why there you can breathe.

Pirouette: Ah, and dere you can freeze—I am cold as vat you call ice.

Blinkinsopp: That's better than being boiled. I weighed sixteen stone when I set out. I'm thin and genteel now. [*looking at board*] Reduced fares! It's reduced passengers they ought to talk about.

Second Waiter: Breakfast's ready, Sir.

Pirouette: I am read for him. Allons Monsieur. [*exit Pirouette*]

Blinkinsopp: Allons. Allez vous s'en. I'm not going to munch bread and butter and swallow slip slop. I've seven lbs. of sandwiches left yet. "The Royal William sails this day"—when was that put up?

Second Waiter: The board, Sir? About a fortnight ago.

Blinkinsopp: Oh "this day" means any day she sails, I suppose?

Second Waiter: Just so, Sir.

Blinkinsopp: Pleasant. I must keep in cog,[9] or my trip to America will turn into a jaunt to Spike Hall or Abbott's Priory. [*Enter* Dalton, *L.*] Well, fellow-sufferer?

Dalton: Rare news: the wind's fair. The packet sails today for certain.

Blinkinsopp: That's the first pleasant thing I've heard. Then we shall get off?

Dalton: Decidedly. But, man alive, what puts you into such a confounded fluster? That I who haven't a penny, with more duns at my heels than hairs on my head, should be anxious to emigrate isn't to be wondered at. But you—young, rich . . .

Blinkinsopp: That's it, you see. You haven't a penny; you're a happy dog. I have some pennies, and I ain't inclined to lose 'em.

Dalton: But what danger is there of your doing so?

Blinkinsopp: Dollops of danger and little to spare. You're a fortunate fellow and don't know it. I'm an unfortunate one and do. Is your nature susceptible?

Dalton: Try me.

Blinkinsopp: I will. I'll unbosom myself. I've a load here. My heart's as heavy as a bullock's. You see, Mister, some folks are born with silver spoons in their mouths, others with wooden shovels.

Dalton: Ladles.

Blinkinsopp: All's one, for that. Now, I was a ladler at first, born in poverty and nursed in—

Dalton: Misery.

Blinkinsopp: No, Sir, in Mutton Lane, Clerkenwell.

Dalton: Romantic vicinity.

Blinkinsopp: Uncommon. Charmingly laid out in the brokery and crockery line. Now, for all I was one of the wooden ladlers, at first, my spoony days were to come.

Dalton: No doubt.

Blinkinsopp: I'd an uncle as no one ever thought of. Brings his body back from New York with a heap of money and the sweetest asthma you ever heard.

Dalton: Ah, I see. You ingratiated yourself with him and . . .

Blinkinsopp: Not a bit of it. He licked me as though he had a right to do it, and mother winked at it cause she said his flogging would be the better for me in the end—which end she meant, I didn't know. So the more he larrup'd me the more pleased she was.

Dalton: But you—

Blinkinsopp: On the contrary, quite the reverse.

Dalton: Well, he died.

Blinkinsopp: Yes, and insulted me in his last will.

Dalton: Insulted you, how?

Blinkinsopp: In these words, "I leave the bulk of my property to my nephew, Ben, because he's too great a fool to earn his own bread."

Dalton: Well, you can forgive that.

Blinkinsopp: Bless you, bear no malice; popped up a tombstone—"tender father, kind relative, best of men"; got my fortune; turned Westender; and now comes the critical point. To the opera I goes and falls in love up to my false collar with one of the sylphs; was introduced to her sly old codger of an uncle; and . . .

Dalton: And what?

Blinkinsopp: Gave a promise of marriage.

Dalton: Well?

Blinkinsopp: Well! Did you ever give such a promise?

Dalton: Half a dozen, I dare say.

Blinkinsopp: Well, there's nothing like being used to a thing but, pray, how many months were yours after date?

Dalton: I don't understand you.

Blinkinsopp: I promised to marry in six months; time's up; my mind changed; he threatened law; so I depart.

Dalton: But wherefore have you forsaken the lady?

Blinkinsopp: Oh, her twisting and twirling was all very well, at first, but I have so much of that cursed susceptibility. And, next season, came Taglioni.[10] I couldn't stand this [*imitates the bound of Taglioni*]. And seeing that I was likely to be in love with every newcomer and, as a moral man, I couldn't marry a fresh dancer every season, I cut and ran.

Dalton: Leaving the poor *danseuse* to break her heart, unheeded.

Blinkinsopp: Dancers' hearts get so bobbed about that they are too slippery to break. Besides, I might cut one when she used to be continually cutting six—eh, Mister?

Dalton: As you are so susceptible, take care you don't rhapsodize into another promise in New York.

Blinkinsopp: Leave me alone. Once bit, you know. Besides, can't there.

Dalton: Can't? Why not?

Blinkinsopp: All the ladies of New York are in the United State already.[11]

Dalton: Well, I must see my luggage safely on board. Your berth is secured you say? [*Blinkinsopp nods*] Well, better fortune attend us in the New World.

[*Exit* Dalton, *R.*]

Blinkinsopp: So say I. But I'm not like some of your snivelers. There isn't a soul in the world I care a farthing about, nor a thing. Yes, one thing—the opera. That's the place for a chap who has taste and susceptibility.

Medley
Air—"Non piu Andrai"[12]
All my eye, all my eye is the Drama,
Tragic dames calling names in gold lamé:
Drury Lane, English Opera, Covent Garden.
I leave when the Opera invites

Air—"Largo al Factotum"[13]
Forth merrily grinning the buffo[14] bounds;
                                    Lah lah etc.
Round, cheerily ringing, the laugh resounds.
                                    Lah lah etc.
Lablache, Tamburini, Grisi, Rubini[15]
Basso, Contralto, Tenor, and alto,
I love 'em all; I love 'em all.

Air—"Suoni la tromba"[16]
Deep rolls the baritone's voice out,
Thundering follows him the burly bass.

Their notes like an organ swelling—
What love, what power, what grace.

Air—"Son vergin vezzosa"[17]
Balm-breathing soprano, dulcissimo, piano,
Each bosom assailing, she triumphs o'er all.
The loves and the graces have taken their places
In her lovely bosom, and come and come at her call

Recitative

Then the Ballet. Oh, carissimo
Pirouetting—kickerissimo

Tarantella

Bounding as light as the gay tarantella,
And twisting and twirling a deuce of a fellow,
Pirouetting, curvetting; I really can't tell, oh!
What wonderful wonders the creature performs.

Exit, R

❧

Scene 2. Room at a Roadside Inn. Enter Old Hickory *and* Slapup, R., *covered with mud.*

Hickory: Here's a mess. I believe I've dislocated my shoulder bone.

Slapup: Well, don't bullock[18] me. I did it for the civility of the thing.
I've driv' that turn-out fifteen year and never had a spill afore.

Enter Waiter, R.

Waiter: Choose any refreshment, Sir?

Hickory: Yes, Sir.

Waiter: What will you be pleased to order, Sir?

Hickory: Clean water, soap, and a towel.

Slapup: Say, young un, how far's this from Liverpool?

Waiter: About thirty miles, Sir.

Slapup: What coaches is there?

Waiter: None, Sir, this ain't the high road.

Hickory: I told you so, but you would take the near cut, as you called
it, down that confounded lane.

Waiter: What, Sir, have you come through Dead Man's Lane? You're very lucky, Sir, to have got safe. They generally knocks down one or two a day there, Sir.

Hickory: Charming neighborhood.

Slapup: Now, don't put yourself in a fluster, old gentleman; we've had a spill but it might have been worse. Have missed the covey we were looking arter, and that might have been better; but we're all right, nevertheless, old one.

Hickory: How do you mean, all right? Hasn't my niece bolted without so much as goodbye t'ye? Hasn't Blinkensopp done the same?

Slapup: Well, perhaps they'll get spliced their own way—and that was all you wanted.

Hickory: No, it wasn't; your comprehension never gets higher than a man's shoulder. You can't guess what's in my head.

Slapup: Nothing but mud, as I see.

Hickory: Pish! Lookee, Master Slapup, Juliette is no blood of mine; what have I to do with my wife's relations?

Slapup: Nothing whatsumdever.

Hickory: Julie's father didn't cut up—not quite as bad as has been thought.

Slapup: I sees it with half a eye. You touched the cole and bred up the girl, kept her safe and, of course, as was proper, did the same by the rhino.[19]

Hickory: Exactly. Now, if she goes a scampering through the world, she'll get picked up by some vagabond that has a taste for looking over old accounts.

Slapup: In course, there's thousands such chaps.

Hickory: They'd talk of refunding.

Slapup: The very worst sort of funding.

Hickory: Now you perceive why I wanted to marry my Julie to a fool, and to receive from him further maintenance and education; then exchange receipts in full of all demands, eh?

Slapup: You're a downy one! What a fine criminal lawyer you'd a make. I'd give a five pound note to see you at the Old Bailey now.

Hickory: Hem! And, now, Master Slapup, here we are, foxed thirty

miles from Liverpool. Your pocket's full of warranty you can't exe-
cute, while the fugitives, whether together or not, are no doubt
crossing the Atlantic.

Slapup: Well, we're provided for that. It's all the go to visit America
now. If they're gone, we'll follow. When at New York, if we can't do
it with civil process, why, you must stretch a point and swear a robbery.

Hickory: Swear! umph! I don't much like oaths and witness boxes.

Slapup: Nonsense, what's a witness box made for, but to enable a man
to purtect his own property?

Hickory: A very sensible remark. Besides, as I paid for all the things
Miss Juliette eloped in, of course she has robbed me. My property
is in America. Now, I've a nephew there.

Slapup: A nephew have you?

Hickory: And if Blinkinsopp don't meet my views, why my sister's
son, Peterkin Pawks of Virginia, may.

Slapup: It's all right, Mr. Hickory, let us pop a comfortable couple
of bottles here under our waistcoats and then follow suit. If we
catches 'em this side the water, well; if not, won't we sarve 'em out
on t'other?

Exit both, R.

➤◄

Scene 3. Deck of an American Packet. Two Cabin Heads. A Chariot made out
and practicable, so that roof as well as inside can be used.

Major *and* Mrs. Mohawk, Miss Mohawk, Juliette, Ellen, Dalton, *and*
other passengers *discovered with* Pirouette. *Borders half down. Music—*
rapid at first, with the bustle of the scene—then settling to glee.

Glee.

Tenors and Basses.

Slow—"The Boatie Rows."[20]
Oh, weel may the boatie row,
  That scuds before the wind.
And safe may the rovers go,
  Who leave their homes behind.

The boatie rows, the boatie rows.
It scuds before the gale.
May fortune hover o'er her bows
And freedom fan her sails.

Everybody, quick—"Yankee Doodle."

On the bounding billows borne,
To the new world steering,
With delight we'll hail the sight
Of freedom's land appearing.
The broad Atlantic bears our prow;
No danger dread we, when, Sir,
Our vessels heart of oak we know,
And heart of oak, our men, Sir.
O'er the bounding, etc.

Juliette: As I live, there's Pirouette, my dancing master first, my lover afterwards. No matter, I'll brazen it out; he will never recognize, in a middy, his "adorable Juliette." [*They go up*]

Major Mohawk: Here we go at a killing pace: fair wind and clear course. Don't be so down in the mouth, Monsieur.

Pirouette: Quest que c'est? Vat is dat downy mouth?

Mrs. Mohawk: It's Major Mohawk's way, my dear Sir, he thought you seemed melancholy.

Pirouette: Melancholy! Ah, Madame, c'est impossible when I 'ave de pleasure to converse wis you.

Mrs. Mohawk: Oh, Sir! All you French gentlemen are so kind to the ladies.

Pirouette: Ah! Oui, mais de ladies have behaved very bad to me.

Major Mohawk: Jilted you, mayhap? Gave you the go bye, bolted off the course, run away?

Pirouette: Several times. Ah, Madame! Ah, Monsieur! I am miserable. You are happy wis dis lady; I have none.

Major Mohawk: Well, why don't you get one?

Mrs. Mohawk: I'm sure a gentleman of your accomplishments might.

Pirouette: You are too good. Mais, Madame, I ave been mari, sall be fifteen, twenty years ago.

Major Mohawk: Lost your wife, I take it.

Pirouette: She run away.

Mrs. Mohawk: Sad work, Monsieur.

Pirouette: Ah, oui, dam bad Madame. I sall keep von academie for de Dans. Mais, my vife, she keep von auberge—de gentilhommes sall come—one, two, three; merchant, officaire, and she go, "How you do, if you please," to one; "I hope you are very houndsome," to anozer; she vas alvays grin. Mais, she was beauty womans. I say, Madame, I sall not have him, you sall never smile but poir moi— then she turn to me wis such a smile—just so. Ah! She was beauty womans. But my rapture was not long. Von morning I go out see my pupille. I return. I say, "Where is Madame?" De Garcon say, by gar, "Madame gone out to walk." C'est bien! I go up stairs—dere is no bed, no chair, no nosing at all. I say, "Garcon, 'ave de tables gone out to valk, too?" And he say, "Yes." And, begar, he say true, dey all go out to valk in a cart.

Major Mohawk: I see she got you in play or pay and wouldn't run the course. You was distanced.

Mrs. Mohawk: And did you never hear of her after?

Pirouette: Ah! oui, begar, she come again six or eight years after him. She say, "Comment vous portez vous, Monsieur." I say, you are dam rascal; mais I perceive three, four little garcons, all so high as dat. I say, "Eha! vere you sall find him and vat you do wis my furniture?" She say, "Ah, monsieur, I 'ave not de furniture, but I 'ave brought you some oder furniture." And de garcons come run about my foots. I say, "Dam, I sall no have de livestock." Dey all run up to me and call me Papa. I say, "Pooh, pooh, no Papa." Den she give me de look, and my heart all over soft. She was beauty womans and I forgive her.

Mrs. Mohawk: There's a lesson for you, wretch, and so you have been happy ever since.

Pirouette: Madame, vat you sall tink? Two or three months apres, begar, she ron away again and leave me wis de little garcons, vat I sall never know.

Mrs. Mohawk: Whatever did you do, Sir?

Pirouette: Madame, I go to les enfants trouves. I say to him, "I ave dese dam Garcons." Mais dey say, "Dey are too big—great deal. If you have leetle one pop him in de basket." I say, "I ave no leetle one —you think all de family are as bad as one anoser?" [Mrs. Mohawk *and* Pirouette *go up*]

Ellen: Then your French lover proves to be a Benedict,[21] after all.

Juliette: The wretch! It only proves, my love, what I have always said —that the fellows, French or English, are all alike.

Dalton: You belong to the New World, I believe, Sir.

Major Mohawk: Raised in Boston; so was she, my daughter.

Dalton: An amiable specimen of the beauty of your native city, Sir.

Major Mohawk: Aye, Sir, Boston's the place. England's very well, but if you was to boil down the whole world you couldn't make another Boston. [*Enter* Blinkensopp, *from cabin stairs, in sailor's trousers and jacket.*]

Blinkinsopp: I won't stand it and I can't lie it. I can't live six weeks in a cabin six feet by four. Steward.

Steward: Well, Sir?

Blinkinsopp: Do you know the gentleman who occupies the next cabin? Is he a long one? If not, give my compliments. I should feel particularly obliged if he'd suffer a hole to be cut from my cabin into his—and not feel offended if my legs occasionally stray into his apartment.

Juliette: As I live and breathe, there is Blinkinsopp, as well as Pirouette.

Ellen: Do they know each other?

Juliette: I neither know nor care. I am only anxious they should not know me.

Dalton: Well, Blinkinsopp, the weather's getting a little roughish— there's a great swell.

Blinkinsopp: Yes, and there's a little one: how he struts in his uniform! Twig his dirk, they shouldn't suffer children in arms aboard ship.

Dalton: That's a pretty creature!

Blinkinsopp: Which?

Dalton: That, beside the young fellow with the hanger[22] on.

Blinkinsopp: Yes. Some hanger-on of his, no doubt. I'll do the agreeable; my confounded susceptibility comes over me again. [*to Ellen*] Hope you enjoy . . . [*She avoids him*] That is, I trust . . . [*She again avoids him*]. Cuts me, I declare! No matter, I'll—

Juliette [*advancing:*] Any thing to say to that lady, Sir?

Blinkinsopp: I, Sir? Why, Sir? No, Sir.

Juliette: Oh! [*coolly*]

Blinkinsopp: He's one of your fire-eaters. Never mind. Try another: *you* feel quite as you wish to be, and han't no nasty all-overishness, which some folks have aboard ship.

Mrs. Mohawk: Oh, Sir, I'm really quite pleased—we've cattle on board, my husband tells me.

Blinkinsopp: Oh, yes, Ma'am, in Liverpool packets, but, if you go from Portsmouth, you take Cowes in the way.

Dalton: There's a buoy.

Pirouette: One of my dear little boys—where?

Mrs. Mohawk: Oh, pick him up, for Heaven's sake!

Blinkinsopp: He won't hurt, Ma'am; that's the fifteenth buoy we've passed since we left Liverpool.

Mrs. Mohawk: How dreadful! That accounts for what one sees in the papers so often, "Mysterious disappearance of a Young Gentleman."

Sailor: By the mark, seven.

Mrs. Mohawk: Seven! Poor little fellows!

Blinkinsopp: No, Ma'am, he's only taking soundings.

Mrs. Mohawk: Soundings! What, are we unsound?

Blinkinsopp: I don't know, Ma'am, I ain't.

Mrs. Mohawk: Is there any danger of leaks?

Blinkinsopp: Not here, Ma'am. Never have any leeks except on the coast of Wales.

Mrs. Mohawk: Oh dear! The ship begins to waggle-waggle; what is the cause of this? [*Ready lights*]

Sailor: Only the pitch of the vessel.

Mrs. Mohawk: Well, I'm sure! Pray, what is he?

Blinkinsopp: He, Ma'am, is the tar of the vessel. Bless me, Ma'am, you look very pale.

Mrs. Mohawk: Pail! Pail! [*Steward hands her down.* Pirouette *has been gradually getting worse, and at last sits down with his head over a foot-bath*]

Pirouette: Mon Dieu! I am sick very.

Steward: Beg pardon, Sir, that's a foot, not a shower, bath.

Miss Mohawk: Will you tell me, Sir, when we're on the high seas?

Blinkinsopp: Yes, Ma'am, the moment I sees, I will. Why, Monsieur, you're done, I see. Aha! you Frenchmen can't stand the ocean. It's a Briton's element. [*Gets sick and leans on Dalton's shoulder*] Rule Britannia. Britannia rules the waves! Holloa! I wish she'd rule 'em a little straighter. [*From carriage on deck, an* invalid *puts out his head*]

Blinkinsopp: Steward, attend to that gent-le-man.

Steward: What's the matter, Sir?

Invalid: Very bad. Want to be ill, and I can't.

Steward: What's the matter with you, Sir?

Blinkinsopp: Very bad. Want to be well, and I can't.

[*Music here begins*]

Steward: Better sit down, Sir.

Pirouette: [*has crawled on the roof of coach*] Ah, Mon Dieu! Oh, I am mal du tete. I am de bad of de head.

Music—"Rise Gentle Moon."[23] *Cloud cloth continues to work. Moon obscured.*

Distant Thunder.

Steward: Better get down into your cabin, Sir.

Blinkinsopp: No Sir, I shall stay here till I see a ship and go back.

Steward: You'll stay here till we ship a sea and go over.

Blinkinsopp: Eh! Give us your hand, I'm only a little giddy. "The Sea! The Sea! the Open——" [*He is taken down*]

Steward [*to Pirouette:*] Better go below, Sir.

Pirouette: Sare, I sall go below, Sare, to the fathomless abyss. I am de-range with my suffering. [*kicks violently*]

Invalid: I'd be very much obliged by your not kicking over my head, Sir, jus' now for—

Pirouette: Mon Dieu! [*invalid draws in hastily*]

Juliette: So we are the bravest sailors among them, [*thunder*] I find. But come let me hand you to your cabin, dear, and say adieu. I hear the roll of thunder. We shall have a storm, I fear, Captain.

Captain: Aye, a bit of a squall, and not long first, I reckon.

Music. Commencement of Steibelt's Storm.[24] *Juliette hands Ellen to the Cabin Stairs. The Storm increases through Chorus*

Captain [*calls through trumpet:*] Hand your top-gallant sail. [*Two boys go up*]

Crew: Aye, aye, Sir.

Captain: All hands to reef topsails.

Crew: Hoy, hoy, Sir.

Captain: Stow the mainsail.

Crew: Aye, aye, Sir.

Captain: Haul in the sheet.

Crew: It's gone, Sir.

Captain: Brail up your driver.[25]

The storm increases. Lightning. Thunder. The sea rolling mountains high. Pirouette kicks in the blinds of the chariot. Invalid pops his head in. Crash. Scream. Through cabins, everybody rushes on deck, some half-dressed; Blinkinsopp wrapped in a blanket.

"Hurry"—Mozart

All:

Now, now, now what the devil is the matter?
Row, row, row, what a cursed noise;
How, how, how shall we stay their cursed clatter?
Now, now, now pull away, my boys.

Speak, speak, speak—let us know, 'od rot 'em.
Leak! leak! leak! Are we going down?
Speak, speak, speak we're going to the bottom.
Leak! leak! leak! What a thing to drown.
  Now, now, now what the devil, etc.
[*Crash. Scream. Everybody faints in everybody's arms.*]

Captain [*through trumpet:*] She rights! She rights!

>‹

Act 2

Scene 1. Exterior. Enter Slapup.

Slapup: Confound your Yankee roads and confound your cattle, what am I to do? There's my vehicle—stuck in the mud, three feet deep. Here! House! Where are you all? Post horses, and another vehicle, directly.

        Gig with Pawks *backs up to gate—he dismounts*

Pawks: Holloa, you're making a pretty considerable row. I reckon you want post horses, do ye? Now who *are* you? Where were you raised? How do they call you? Where are you come from? Where do you want to go to? Are you a man or a help?

Slapup: I'm a man and want help, as you see.

Pawks: You *say* so and I'm inclined for a paction. I've just come from Virginny and have no objection to sell my turn-out to take you your journey.

Slapup [*looking at gig:*] What that crazy concern? No go! Why that'll never get over the beastly swamps with which this part abounds.

Pawks: Beastly swamps! Well, if ever I heard anything to ditto that— there's not a swamp in America's but a perfect pride of paradise.

Slapup: Aye—you think so—but you're a native.

Pawks: A native? What d'ye mean by "native"? I've a notion you're poking fun at me considerable. I just warn you, I'm a reg'lar built Virginian and if you thinks to undervalle us, or our swamps, tarnation take me if I don't lick you elegant.

Slapup: Lick me? Gammon and all, you would! But, however, I don't want no quarreling, nor to offend you or any other Yankee Doodle.

Pawks: Oh, as long as you're affable, I'm as sociable and delightful as is—but I stands no affronts to me or my country.

Slapup: Right; them as don't love their country, let 'em leave it, I say.

Pawks: You *have* left your'n, I think; now *what* are you?

Slapup: That is immaterial to you I suppose.

Pawks: Oh! no ways materal—*who* are you?

Slapup: 'Sdeath, my name's Slapup—my purpose going to Virginia. My vehicle is stuck in the mud yonder—and I wants another to pursue my route.

Pawks: That thing all on one side is the carriage, I reckon. That's in as awkward a fix as ever I see. I knows that swamp well; there's a power of mud, but no great matter of water.

Slapup: Pray, does that swamp go on any further?

Pawks: No—I never knowed it to stir from where it is.

Slapup: I mean, is there more of it that way; and is it sound at the bottom?

Pawks: That's beyond my knowledge—I reckon it is. A power of people have been smothered there—but if any on 'em did find the bottom, I calculate they never made no mention of its being sound or no. There's no post horses here, but the old boss has two elegant behaved oxen, as steps out remarkable.

Slapup: I, who have tooled bits of blood in a tandem, to be drawn by oxen—come that's good. So, Mr. Peterkin Pawks of Virginny, you'll have none of my company.

Pawks: Pawks, did you say? What do you want with him?

Slapup: That's a cursed impudent question, Sir—I have particular business with him.

Pawks: Then I reckon your upset was a lucky coincidence of events— I am Peterkin Pawks.

Slapup: You?

Pawks: The very same. Rais'd in Virginny! Got a plantation and thirty niggers there, and two horses and one uncle in New York.

Slapup: From that very uncle I come, Mr. Jacob Hickory.

Pawks: Well, if I live to eternity, I shall never obliviate this go. [Slapup *gives letter*] There's his pothooks, sure enough. "Capital chance . . . wife and fortune." I approbate that considerable. So, my uncle's sent for me to get me married.

Slapup: Exactly. But take care, you have a rival, I can tell ye.

Pawks: A rival. I'll beat him into immortal smash, if he dares keep his eyes open as the lady walks by. I would—you needn't stare. I've whipp'd the finest fellow in our parts. T'other day I lick'd the oldest man in the place. Look ye here, iron all over, pieced with rock. One of my blows to any man is either long sickness or sudden death.

Slapup: It may be necessary to carry off the lady.

Pawks: I'm no ways objectionable. I'll run away with any thing from sixteen to sixty, with any man in Virginny. As to this lady—she's an Englisher, I reckon.

Slapup: She is, her name "Juliette." The first object is to place her again in the hands of her guardian.

Pawks: I realize you're an agent in this affair.

Slapup: Yes, and no time's to be lost—this very evening she must be carried off.

Pawks: It's never properly dark in New York. Now, in Virginny, it's sometimes so dark you can't see the flashes of lightning.

Slapup: Will that there vehicle of your'n take us?

Pawks: Why, I dubitate, as we're in a hurry, whether we hadn't better walk. My horse has a notion of progressing backwards, and ain't no ways agreeable. Come away! I've a power of things to do in New York—advertise a damned nigger as has run slick away and, what with that and marrying, I shall have my arms full, I calcilate.

Exeunt.

➤←

Scene 2. The Quay of New York. Porters waiting arrival of packet.

Chorus—Negro Melody

The Packet is in sight, my boys, hurra! hurra!
Be ready every porter there, huzza! huzza!
Come bustle, bustle niggers, all run up and down;
Take the plunder from the vessel through the town.
Now don't stand debating; put your shoulders to the wheel.

There'll be plenty in the freighting for the barrow and creel;
Work, work, my jolly dogs, till twilight shadows fall,
Den eb'ry colored gemmen to the party or de ball.
    The packet is in sight, etc.

Billy Brown: What ship in sight, Sar?

Sailor: The Royal William [*gruffily*]

Billy Brown: Tank you, Sar. Deblish fine girl come dis way, who am she?

Copper Charley: Why, you fool, you not know Miss Sarah Snow? The finest woman in New York, 'pon honor.

Billy Brown: Lubly cretur, I declare.

Enter Sally Snow

All: How do, Miss Sarah—hope you very well. [*All bow*]

Sally Snow: I very well; how am you—what! The packet am not come yet?

Billy Brown: You expect some one, some lubber I 'spose?

Sally Snow: No, Sir, a lady of my private acquaintance.

Billy Brown: Beg pardon, I'm sure.

Sally Snow: A lady as am taken the tower of Europe to improve herself in elegant 'complishments. [*Looking about the crowd*]

Billy Brown: You believe her? All trash—no meet any lady. I know who she come to meet, dat dam Jim Crow. Ah! Miss Sarah you am look for Master Crow. I wonder you waste your lubly eyes on dat fellow.

Sally Snow: Neber you mind, Sir. I cast my lubly eyes whereber 'em like.

Crow [*without:*] "Oh! sich a gittin' up stairs, sich playin' on the fiddle / Sich a gittin' up stairs, I never did see."

All: Ah! ah! here's Jim Crow.

Enter Jim Crow

Jim Crow: Yah! Yah! Well, how y'all am? Miss Snow, I am delighted to see you.

Porter: Well, Jimmy, what have you come here for?

Jim Crow: Same as oder gemmen, I 'spose, Sir! Come to see if any gemman wants anoder gemman to carry his plunder for him. Miss Snow you are more lubly than ever.

Sally Snow: Oh, Missa Crow! For shame, Master Crow, in public, and all the white trash looking at us. You make me blush.

Jim Crow: You wasn't at de ball last night, Miss Sarah.

Sally Snow: No, de company was very mixed.

Jim Crow: Iss, very much mixed company and very much mix'd liquor. It was not de select thing at all. Some deblish fine creturs dere but not one to compare to Miss Snow.

Sally Snow: You insinivating cretur! Mr. Crow, I'm afraid you are terrible rake.

Jim Crow: No, no, 'pon honor.

Sally Snow: And you neglect yourself; you're not near so smart as you used to was.

Jim Crow: Smart, this am very good suit of clothes.

Sally Snow: Why, they are nothing but rags and patches.

Jim Crow: Patches? No'm, not patches. I want strong clothes, so, fear it tear, I stick on dese for strengthening plasters.

Sally Snow: But, then, your hat am shocking bad hat.

Jim Crow: Berry good hat—cost me 1s. 9d. No, no, 'em ladies say, white hat become me best.

All: Ha! ha! ha! ha!

Sally Snow: You seem very strange, Mr. Crow. You expect some friends? Some 'lation from t'oder side of de water?

Jim Crow: No I hab no 'lations dere, only one broder, and we no speak.

Sally Snow: Why not?

Jim Crow: He disgrace de family by imprudent marriage [*proudly*].

Sally Snow: I wonder you neber marry, yourself, Mr. Crow?

Jim Crow: Why, Miss Sally, I hab berry good opportunities in some of de first families where I visit; but I hab set my heart on preticklar lady. Besides, I no sure dat I am quite the person to make a lady of nice feelings happy. [*conceitedly*] What you tink, Miss Snow?

Sally Snow: Oh! Mr. C.

All: The packet! The packet!

Music. An instantaneous bustle as the boat comes in sight, and the passengers land; trucks, barrows, etc. in requisition, into which boxes and parcels are placed. During the following, Billy *and* Charley *crowd upon* Crow; *one of the porters lays hold of barrow;* Crow *kicks him.*

Air—"Negro Melody"[26]

Jim Crow:

Get out the way you dam ugly black nigger.
How dare 'em interrupt a man of my figger?
I'd hab you know, though it's what you mayn't be pleased at,
Dat I am a gemman as is not to be sneezed at.
Any gemman want a porter, I would let him know,
There's not a fellow in New York can beat Jim Crow.

All:

Any gemman want a porter, please to let him know,
The idlest fellow in New York is old Jim Crow.

[Juliette *and* Blinkinsopp *land*]

Air—"Sabatiere"

Juliette:

Fortune be praised, I am out of the packet,
Once more on dear terra firma I stand,
What a confusion, what bustle and racket—
A squall on sea, and a riot on land.

Blinkinsopp:

Waves—waves—I'm heartily tired out.
I long for a ramble on heather once more.

Porter and Jim Crow:

Here—here are lads to be hired out;
Say, shall we carry your luggage ashore?

Blinkinsopp: Stop! Stop, amid so many black faces, it won't be easy to find a light porter.

Jim Crow: Iss, Massa, I'm light porter.

Blinkinsopp: I shouldn't have guess'd it. You're a rum one to look at. Hoist up the trunk; I say, you're not light-fingered are you?

Jim Crow: Sar!

Blinkinsopp: Can you recommend me a hotel?

Jim Crow: Iss, Sar, um can, one I frequent myself; berry good society meet dere.

Blinkinsopp: So I should think. [*Porter (mulatto) assisting Crow in putting great boxes into truck, lets one fall.*] Take care, Ebony.

Jim Crow [*to Porter:*] What am you about, Sir? [*to Blinkinsopp*] Must 'pologize to you, Sar, but dis only pupil of mine, and hasn't my finish'd manner. [*To porter*] You dam stupid fellow, you no porter.

Blinkinsopp: Porter—no, I see that by his color; he's not porter, he's only half and half.

Jim Crow: Gib yourself no trouble; I take eb'ry ting under my care; here's my card, Sir.

Blinkinsopp: [*reads*] "Mr. James Crow—Director of 'Sequestrean Establishment." Sequestrean 'Stablishment—what the deuce is that?

Jim Crow: Iss, Sar, what you am call hossler.

Blinkinsopp: Oh! Ostler![27] "Gemman is request to observe as I am raal Jim Crow—as so many 'posters am about."—what's that?

Jim Crow: Them chaps as go about town singing my "Jim Crow."

Blinkinsopp: Mr. James Crow, I am delighted to have made your acquaintance.

Jim Crow: Quite mutual, I 'sure you, Sar.

Blinkinsopp: Now, Mr. Crow, if you're not too much engaged, I should like to secure your invaluable services, whilst I remain in this city.

Jim Crow: Hab no objection to enter into a paction wid you, or any oder gemman. [*takes up barrow*]

Blinkinsopp: Beg ten thousand pardon, ladies, can I be of any service? [*to Ellen and Mrs. Mohawk*]

Ellen: I thank you, Sir, we are already settled.

Blinkinsopp: Good thing the voyage is over—one gets so confounded susceptible aboard ship all this side of the way [*touching his heart*]. I was getting my old symptoms. Why hey-day! [*seeing the barrow deserted*] Crow, I say!

Jim Crow: [*is conversing tenderly with Sally Snow*] Iss, Sar, directly, just one moment, excuse me, little private conversation wid dis lady.

Sally Snow: Adoo, Mr. Crow. We sall meet den at de ball.

Jim Crow: Um, certainly, and 'fore dat, wait while I take um trunk down, and den I come back, and, till then, adoo.

Both: Adoo.

Blinkinsopp: That's a pretty little creature. An image of Venus in copper.

Jim Crow: Now, Sir, I am ready. [*takes up barrow*] Stand out of de way you dam black nigger; let me and t'oder gemman go by. [*One of the porters stands in the way. Crow wheels him off.*]

Sally Snow: Him berry fine man—only him hab such berry shabby clothes. [*Exit R*]

Blinkinsopp: Here I am in the land of liberty, a single man of rather a prepossessing appearance. I wonder if American ladies are susceptible? If so, what will become of poor Jonathan? Let's see, they call England the Mother Country. Ireland the Sister Country, then America must be the Wife or Daughter Country. Yes! I shall get married here, I know it. The very air has an united state sort of feel about it. I am a victim at the altar of Hymen. Talking of high men, where's that damned six feet and a half porter? Here, Jimmy. Mr. Crow, I say— [*Exit, R.*]

Enter Juliette *and* Ellen

Juliette: Confound that fellow Dalton's eyes—he seems to have penetrated my disguise.

Ellen: And what do you intend doing: doffing these garments or rejoining them?

Juliette: I shall do both—paradoxical as it appears, I shall preserve two characters, be now the Agile Danseuse and anon the Swaggering Middy.

Dalton: If in a strange land I can render any assistance I hope, madam, you know that you may command me; or, if you, Sir, from youth and inexperience, encounter any annoyance, I should be happy to lend any aid.

Juliette: He knows all about me, I'm sure [*aside*]. I thank you, Sir, but I'm more used to traveling adventures than you think. However, should I fall into any quarrel, depend upon it—you are the first person I should ask to go out with me.

Dalton: Any quarrel of yours, I should espouse with delight. She is a woman and a lovely one, in danger, in sorrow. Then there is but one course for me: to shield her from the one, to share with her the other. [*exit*]

Juliette: And now my love it's high time we began to think of our affairs. My ci-devant admirers, though they did not recognize me in this dress, of course will readily do so in my own.

Ellen: But, from Mr. Blinkinsopp you have no fear?

Juliette: Oh, no! He has renounced me. You, I think, have made a conquest there. Now, don't hang your head, child, there's no shame in an honest attachment. But I am strangely taken by that fellow, Dalton.

Ellen: But, my love, I heard him confess that he had not a penny . . .

Juliette: Neither have I! We shall be a charming couple. They say that those who wed for money are always miserable; well, then, if we marry without a shilling between us, we must indubitably be happy. So, allons. [*Exit* Juliette *and* Ellen]

Enter Sally Snow, *R.*[28]

Sally: Well, I'm sure, I neber see sich imperence; white trash follow colored lady in dat manner; if Missa Crow catch him, dere'll be debil to pay.

Enter Piroutte, *R, and follows Sally up and down stage.*

Pirouette: Aha! maid, have I at last overtake you? Your little feet are like de black beetles. I wish to converse wid you. You are beauty womans.

Sally: Well, em know dat berry well; all de gemmen say I deblish fine gal.

Pirouette: Oui, oui; your face is like de beauty boot, after he sall have de Day and Martin 'pon him.

Sally: Him berry polite.

Pirouette: If you please, wo'd converse wid you 'pon a tender subject.

Sally: Me know berry well what you want; you got squeaking kindness for me; you want to make love, not proper in 'publican streets.

Pirouette: I wish to explain myself. I have come to settle in New York; you have surprised my heart at de first sight. I am a widow.

Sally: What, I mind dat, tink you, Sar? I lub anoder, much lublier man dan you; tink I descend to chum chum wid white trash?

Pirouette: Charmant, Miss Snow, you melt my heart, you—

Sally: If you 'tempt to come near me, I call a watch, you dirty feller. I wish Missa Crow would come back and give em satisfaction of a lady.

Pirouette: Begar—I sall blackness his eye, pull his head off, and blow his nose.

Sally: It no use to talk to me, Sar, em engaged. Dark lady neber tell white lie: take my advice, keep out of Missa Crow's way. If he see you make lub to me, him so jealous, him shake him ugly little head into him shoes. [*Exeunt, L*]

Enter Mrs. Marigold *and* Blinkinsopp

Mrs. Marigold: I am from the old country, myself, Sir.

Blinkinsopp: Yes, and precious old you were before you left it. [*aside*]

Mrs. Marigold: A gentleman of your appearance will suffer much from these here vulgarians, these Yankees. I've been here some years, but I'm not manured to the country, yet.

Blinkinsopp: You'll find me a very reg'lar man, Ma'am. Rise at eight, swallow a broiled fowl, four muffins, three or four cups of coffee; that carries me through till lunch; then a rump steak stays on my stomach till dinner. I make a fairish dinner, take my three bottles, that does till tea; have a devil'd biscuit and half a dozen broiled kidneys, for hyson's bad on an empty stomach.[29] Then a hot supper at twelve, and that's all I require. Now, Ma'am, I don't care whether I go to an hotel or boarding house.

Mrs. Marigold: Under all circumstances, Sir, I think my hotel would suit you best; he'd eat me out of house and home in a month, if I boarded him [*Aside*].

Blinkinsopp: Hotel be it, then. Moreover, Ma'am. I've hired a valet de chambre; I must put him into livery.

Mrs. Marigold: I've a livery, quite *happery po*, as the French say. It belonged to a nice little fellow.

Blinkinsopp: Little fellow? The man that belongs to me is a devilish big fellow.

Mrs. Marigold: Um, is he a colored man?

Blinkinsopp: Yes, no—if white's black, and black's no color at all; I suppose he is not. He's a nigger.

Mrs. Marigold: Then it's no matter, whatsomever. Them fellows always puts on what's given 'em. You must be very pertickler here, Sir, for your vale de sham will think nothing of wearing your clothes during your abstinence.[30]

Blinkinsopp: If he only wears them during that period, I'm content. All your servants are colored people, I presume?

Mrs. Marigold: Yes, I am the only speciment of British beauty in the house. All the other females carry copper in their faces, as we say.

Blinkinsopp: And you carry brass in yours, as I say. [*aside*]

Mrs. Marigold: Beg pardon for leaving you, but the poor creters have no taste—no Jenny Squaws, as we whom bin in Paris and Lunnun have. Haw rewoir, Mounseer. [*Exit, R.*]

Blinkinsopp: No Jenny Squaws! Hang it, I see nothing else but squaws. That Miss Ellen Seagraves,[31] aboard the packet, she's touched me at the tender part: my confounded susceptibility. I can't help it; I do all I can to keep the women off, but, somehow or other, 'pon my soul, I can't tell how it is, but so it is, and so it always was.

Sally Snow [*without:*]
        Jumbo, laughing, come and say, ha! ha! ha!
        Will no ave me, aye or nay? ha! ha! ha!

Blinkinsopp: Here's another. I shall do a devilish deal of mischief amid the colored population; I shall regularly "astonish the browns."

Enter Sally Snow

Blinkinsopp: How d'ye do? How d'ye do? Do you live here?

Sally Snow: Iss, iss, ha, ha, ha, I am help.

Blinkinsopp: Help, you're a helpmate fit for any man, you're a sweet creature. Here's my damned susceptibility again. [*Buttons his coat*]

Sally Snow: Iss, ha! ha! ha! You're berry funny gemman.

Blinkinsopp: And you're a very pretty brunette! Saints, forgive me. You're a sort of Irish fairy, what they call a Brownie.

Sally Snow: You lub Englis Lady, all white.

Blinkinsopp: Yes, like a turnip; now, you're more of the artichoke sort. Really, when one comes to look, she's devilish pretty, a devilish pretty brown; I feel strongly inclined to a brown alliance. As Hamlet says, "to this complexion I must come at last."[32] She won't do for daylight, but she's a very good wife for the evening, a sort of twilight woman, something between light and dark.

Sally Snow: Heigho!

Blinkinsopp: What's the matter? There she stands; beauty in a brown study.

Sally Snow: I am tink of oder times, make me melancholy.

Blinkinsopp: Melancholy, musing maid—my confounded susceptibility, I can't conquer it; I'll pop the question—my burnt umbre beauty, could you love me?

Sally Snow: Lub you? Me neber try.

Blinkinsopp: Do you think you could?

Sally Snow: Me neber tink about it.

Blinkinsopp: I see, it's the fashion to do these things without thinking.

Sally Snow: No, Sar, me lub colored gentleman.

Blinkinsopp: Well, I only spoke. Bless you, I wouldn't interfere with your whitey-brown felicity for the world—trip along, little twilight. I don't know but black, brown, and white, it's all the same—I am so cursed susceptible.

Duet

Air—"Savage Dance"[33]

Blinkinsopp:

Say my pretty pretty brown-skinn'd beauty,
Would you love and follow forth an Englishman?

Sally Snow:

Aye, and ever feel my dearest duty
Would be pleasing, pleasing him when e'er I can.

Blinkinsopp:

Follow, follow, now my footsteps merrily—
You're the very maid and I'm the man.

Sally Snow:

No, I follow not those footsteps merrily—
I am not the maid nor you the man.

Both:

La, la, lara, etc.

Sally Snow:

I've a lover come from old Kentucky
Who would break his heart if I should prove untrue.

Blinkinsopp:

Gad, if that's the case, it's rather lucky,
You should feel that I am not the lad for you.
March, my merry maid, where love's inviting you;
Strike the tambourine and toss the can.

Sally Snow:

Wander on where beauty's smile delighting you,
Merry, merry maid, and happy man.

Both:

La, la, Lara, etc.

Exeunt dancing, R.

＞＜

Scene 3. Coffee-room in New York; bar seen; tables, rocking chairs, spittoons; men sitting with heels up on tables, reading newspapers, smoking.[34] Major Mohawk and Slapup in front.

Slapup: I don't mean to say nothing against New York, Major, but I can't say as all your roads are smooth as billiard tables, nor your buildings as regular as a box of dominoes. Now our London streets . . .

Major Mohawk: I calculate I know London streets considerable well —and it's a fact, as can't be denied, that people can't see one another there for the smoke, whereas every street here is a perfect glory under Heaven.

All gentlemen: Oh! decidedly—we can testify to that!

Slapup: Well, but Regent Street.

All gentlemen: Wall Street!

Slapup: Oxford Street.

All gentlemen: The Five Points! Aye, aye, we'll convince you, if you'll only listen. [*bell rings*]

All gentlemen: Dinner! Dinner! [*they scamper off pell-mell*]

Slapup: That's what they call starting for the plate.

Enter Jim Crow

Jim Crow [*chuckling:*] I am hir'd, am Gemman now! Got dirty dollars a month; it will take two omnibuses to carry me now. Yah! Yah! I cut all de low fellers I used to be 'quaint with.

Slapup: Here, you nigger.

Jim Crow: Who you call nigger? [*aside:*] Dam white trash! Hab you to know, Sar, dat colored gemblem good as white man, and perhaps a little gooder, too.

Slapup: I say, you, Boots.

Jim Crow: No, Sar, I'm no Boots. I'm retir'd, what um ministers called, resigned.

Slapup: Oh! you've left your place, have you?

Jim Crow: Iss, Sar, duties too severe, injure my constitution. Now, Sar, am companion to a gemman.

Slapup: And uncommon fit for the office; you've seen a great deal in your time?

Jim Crow: Iss, Sir, berry great deal. I was raised in Old Kentucky,[35] and was reckoned the greatest beauty in dem parts. I hab gone through the world ever since, laughing at all misfortin, and content—whatever come. Dey call me Jim Crow, but my proper name is Mr. James Crow, Sar. Now go to your dinner, or you'll hab to put it off till tomorrow.

Song "Jim Crow"[36]
When I came to Lunnun City,
I see gemman quite dark.
His name is Achilles;
He lives in Hyde Park.
　Turn about and wheel about
　And do just so,
　Eb'ry time I wheel about,
　I jump Jim Crow.

In Lunnun, all they wish for,
Or any thing they dream,

Be it marrying or burying,
They do it all by steam.
   Turn about, etc.

Over Lunnun city,
Cupid holds eternal reign:
It thrives in Love Court,
As well as Huggin Lane.
   Turn about, etc.

When wives take to scolding,
And annoy the lordly sex,
They sells 'em in Smithfield,
With ropes around their necks.[37]
   Turn about, etc.

That a shrew should be sold so,
I wonder not, not I;
But the thing surprise me most,
Is that any one will buy.
   Turn about, etc.

Respectables all keep a gig,
But all the vulgar shabs,
Drives about the Lunnun streets
In patent safety cabs.
   Turn about, etc.

Here comes the Old Virginny,
And he want you all to know,
Dat he wheel about
And turn about and jump Jim Crow.
   Turn about, etc.

They make talk about philosophy,
But to you I'll clearly show,
'Tis all comprised in wheel about
And jump Jim Crow.
   Turn about, etc.

When a gemman wants money,
His purse is rather low,
To get it how he'll wheel about
And jump Jim Crow.
    Turn about, etc.

There's a pretty lady yonder,
Sitting in the middle row;
To get a husband, how she'll wheel about
And jump Jim Crow.
    Turn about, etc.

There's Massa Yates,[38] the playhouse manager,
To bring people to his show—
O Golly, don't he wheel about
And jump Jim Crow.
    Turn about, etc.

Since I'm getting rather tired,
So I pray you let me go.
I'll come again another night,
And jump Jim Crow.
    Turn about, etc.

Then the soldier in the battle,
When pursued by the foe—
Golly, don't he wheel about
And jump Jim Crow.
    Turn about, etc.

Enter after song, Mrs. Marigold

Mrs. Marigold: Here, you poor ragamuffin.

Jim Crow: Ragamuven! Dam toopid old oomans. What she mean by dat?

Mrs. Marigold: Mr. Blinkinsopp has sent you these clothes.

Jim Crow: Ha! Ha! Berry stylish, I declare—fine clothes. Miss Sally! Creation Ball! Oh! sich gittin' up stairs and sich playin' on de fiddle!

Exit Jim Crow

✴

Scene 4. Front Chamber. Enter Mrs. Marigold and Slapup, L.

Slapup: And so, Ma'am, you see I've some thoughts of settling in New York, bringing over some prime prads,[39] and teaching the Yankees how to get over the ground.

Mrs. Marigold: You'll find 'em a natrocious set, Sir. No hellegance, no nothing. I came here from Paris and, I declare, at first I was quite putrified at the manner of the popelars.

Slapup: No doubt Ma'am. I should as soon think of putting a thoroughbred into traces with a drayhorse. You have moved . . .

Mrs. Marigold: In a very different spear, I assure you. In Paris, I was one of the haut tun—in New York I condescends to keep the One Tun.[40]

Slapup: Dreadful change, a break down from a racer to a sand cart. [*scream heard*] Hulloa!

> *Enter Juliette in disorder. (She is in female attire)*

Juliette: Was ever anything so unfortunate, that the first moment I ventur'd out, I should meet that odious Frenchman?

Mrs. Marigold: Young ooman, I thinks it by no means proper that you should scream out in that monstratious manner. And, as to your protruding yourself here, it's what I can't allow.

Juliette: Madam, I *am* sorry for any confusion I may have caused. I was suddenly alarmed at— [*screams*]

Mrs. Marigold: She's no better than she should be. Properly deducted females never screams. [*goes up*]

> *Enter Pirouette*

Pirouette: Ah! c'est bien, I ave got 'pon your heel at last! Comment vous va, ma chere ami? You sall ron very well, mais I can ron, too. Oh, Madamoiselle Juliette, for why you sall use me so? Eh? I teach you de danse. I teach every ting in de world dat I know. When you are all so clever as myself, you ron away.

Juliette: I have already told you, Monsieur Pirouette, my heart cannot be yours and my hand, therefore, never shall.

Pirouette: Dis is de reward for my show you de entire chat de a'plomb? Oh! C'est la le diable! I sall cut my troat several times often. I sall go very mad, indeed!

>*Mrs. Marigold coming forward gives a loud scream*

Pirouette: Eh!

Slapup: Don't, madam. Properly deducted females never screams.

Pirouette: Is it possible you are dere?

Mrs. Marigold: Antoine, is, is that you?

Pirouette: 'Tis de voice—you sall not be dead yet?

Mrs. Marigold: No, nor you? Oh! my dear husband!

All: Husband!

Pirouette: Peste: Madame Pirouette ave come again.

Juliette: Is that wretch your husband?

Mrs. Marigold: Marry, come up! Who do you call wretch?

Pirouette: You may mari, come up, or what you please, mais, you sall not ave me.

Juliette: How dare you, Sir, make love to me?

Mrs. Marigold: Oh, fie! Shame, for shame, Antoine.

Pirouette: Taisez vous, I never hear any one I wish not to hear so very much. Arrête vous, I sall not speak wis you.

Mrs. Marigold: Won't you own me after years of parting?

Pirouette: You shameful rascals womans: why you ron away, leave me wis de dam Garcons, vat I sall never know? Eh? Vat you are now, eh?

Mrs. Marigold: Widow Marigold.

Pirouette: Veuve—c'est bon charmant, Marigold.

Mrs. Marigold: But though I'm a Marigold, you will be a forget-me-not.

Pirouette: I sall not have him, ma fois, diablement. Ugly fellow, mais ven she vas ron away, she vas beauty woman.

Juliette: I shall not remain to part a lovely couple or to witness the tenderness of the reconciliation. [*Crosses*] Adieu Monsieur Pirouette, I am very grateful for "your teach me the êntre-chat." And when your domestic arrangements are completed, you will perhaps, tender me an apology. Adieu, widow Marigold. Ha, ha, ha!

Slapup: I say, Ma'am, never hulloa.

exit Juliette and Slapup

Mrs. Marigold: Oh, Antoine, don't be so obstetric, don't.

Pirouette: Oh, she's got the grin.

Mrs. Marigold: Here I am, on my knees—I have left off all my follies.

Pirouette: Non, non—your follies ave leave you off, now you ave got old.

Mrs. Marigold: And you know you was a going to marry agin yourself; but I'll forgive you, if you'll do the same.

Pirouette: Jamais, jamais! The honor of a French gentleman is concern'd. I cannot forgive it, nor you. Je n'onblerai—jamais!

Mrs. Marigold: Never mind, blear eyed Jammy, or any one else—but forget and forgive. I've a comfortable house and home.

Pirouette: And you never go out to walk no more. Comfortable—de maison and furniture; no little garcons. Aha, Madame Pirouette, mon coeur is never cruel. She is no longer beauty womans, c'est egal, perhaps she never ron away, now.

Mrs. Marigold: Antoine.

Pirouette: Dorothea! Ah, ma chere femme, it is past. Dere's de grin. De noble nature can forgive. We sall now part, jamais. Ah, Madame, long time ago you vas beauty womans. *Exeunt*

→←

Scene 5. Street in New York, Crowd of Women, etc. Discovered.

Chorus. Air—"Finale to Obi"[41]

Fifth July Fifth July!
    Eb'ry color'd soul be gay
Banish Care Banish Care
    Strike de bango dance and play
Freedom reigns o'er the plains
    Bobolition for de nigger
Beat big drum, tamborine thrum
On dis happy day
    Fifth July, etc.

Music. Grand Procession of Niggers
Jim Crow on a white horse[42]

All: Silence for Jim Crow!

Jim Crow: Gemmen, I's 'puted to dress you on dis occasion. I wish de task had fall'n into better hands, but, though oder gemmen speak more abler, no gemman could feel more deeper. You, de enlighten'd gemmen, whom I dress, know dis is de day of our Bobolition. Well, gemmen, I make no long rigmarole furder dan to say, the gemmen I 'tend 'pon hab gone out for de day. And I hab trown open his room for a Ball!

All: Berry good, berry good.

Jim Crow: And I shall be berry happy to see as many lubly Lady and Gemmen as can make it convenient to be dere.

Chorus
Fifth July Fifth July, etc.

Procession recommences and is closed in

→←

Scene 6. A street, night. Enter Blinkinsopp, intoxicated.

Blinkinsopp: I begin partially to suspect that I'm inebriated. Mr. Benjamin Blinkinsopp, I've a word or two to say to you: if you are a gentleman, behave as such. You're in a strange country, Sir, and do nothing to disgrace Great Britain. The honor of the nation rests on my shoulders. They're broad enough to bear it; that's one comfort. I'm intoxicated. And if any gentlemen presumes to say I'm not, he utters a falsity. I defy the world, the united, conglomerated globe, to prove to the contrary I'm intoxicated, and what then? This is a land of liberty—it's cursed hard if a man mayn't take a liberty with himself.

"I won't go home till morning."

Talking of home, where do I live? I've clean forgot. I know! I live somewhere, but where? [*and echo answers, "Where?"*]

Watchman passes behind

That's a charlie[43] with a new-fangled beaver.

"Charlie is my darling, my darling, my darling"

He, he, he, I used to wonder what they did with the charlies when our new police came. I see now they sent 'em all to New York. Beg pardon, Sir, can you tell me where I live?

Watch: No, I can't. Hotel or boarding?

Blinkinsopp: Hotel.

Watch: And you've forgot the name, um, is there nothing you can re-member it by?

Blinkinsopp: No, nothing. Stay, yes, it's where "folderol, Jump Jim Crow" was Boots.

Watch: Oh! I know well enough—this way.

Blinkinsopp: Go on, I'll follow thee.

Watch: I calculate you're swizzled.

Blinkinsopp: Something in the air, that affects the head. Come along my Purveyor of Yankee Peace.

> "We won't go home till morning
> Till daylight does appear."

Exeunt together

✦

Scene 7. A Room laid out for Ball; four musicians, L. Enter Crow and Pirouette

Jim Crow: Here you am. Hab de beautiful ball—all de lubbliest creturs in New York am invited. You play de fiddle and I am a berry Paganni[44] myself.

Pirouette: Ah! oui, I sall be away from dat ugly old womans. Mais, I sall be Grand Directeur, arrange everyting.

Jim Crow: Iss, I am do the horrors, and you direct de Ball.

Pirouette: Je suis content.

Knock L. H.; Enter Joe Carr

Joe: Mass Jim Brown and Miss Sophonibba Snapps coming up.

Enter Brown and Miss Snapps

Jim Crow: 'Lighted to see Mr. Brown. Miss Snapps, you am charming.

[Re-enter] Joe: Mr. Charley Copperas and Miss Matilda Muggins coming up. *[they enter]*

Jim Crow: How is dis dat you am not brought Miss Snow?

Miss Muggins: Miss Snow's missus very impedently go out and lock up all her tings and Miss Snow can't come till she get blacksmith to break open chest of drawers for a dress.

Jim Crow: Did you eber hear de like? Must do something to put down de impedence of de white trash. [*knock*]

[*Re-enter*] *Joe:* Mass Julicum Caesar and Miss Cleopatra Squawk, coming up.

They enter

Jim Crow: Oh! Miss Cleopatra, you am more lubly eb'ry time I see you. How, Massa Julicum Caesar, berry well?

Julius: Tol, lol.

Jim Crow: What you am tink ob de meeting today?

Copperas: Oh! Berry respectable meeting.

Jim Crow: Not much eloquence, but berry well, considering. Bobolition fine ting.

All: Oh, berry!

[*Re-enter*] *Joe:* Miss Sally Snow.

Enter Sally

Jim Crow: Oh! You am dere. All de lady and gemmen ab been wait for you.

Sally Snow: Would you believe it? Missee have de imperance to say I shan't come!

All: Oh!

Sally Snow: And refuse to lend me pair of flesh-color'd stockings for de Ball.

All: Oh!

Jim Crow: But I hope you took 'em, wedder or not.

Sally Snow: Of course! How dare white trash treat color'd lady in dat manner?

[*Re-enter*] *Joe:* Miss Lucretia and Mr. Scipio; Mrs. Mignonette and Mr. Pink; and oder Lady and Gemmen.

Enter a number of dancers

Pirouette: Attendez vous—I am maistre de Ballet—dese ladies sall represent de Graces.

Sally, Matilda, Cleopatra: Yes, we am Graces.

Pirouette: Who sall find Young Love amid the roses. [*To Crow:*] You are love.

Jim Crow: Ha, ha, I am Cupid! Berry well.

> *Quadrille commences, in the middle of which a loud knocking.*

Jim Crow: Whar dat? Berry improper for anybody intrude at dis moment. Who dere, Sir

[*Re-enter*] *Joe:* Is Massa, sure as a gun and a whole posse of people wid him—coming up. [*all alarmed*]

Jim Crow: Berry well, let him come in. What bring de white trash home at this time?

> *Enter Blinkinsopp*

Blinkinsopp: Holloa! What's this? I've come next door, by mistake?

Jim Crow: No, Sar, no mistake. Dis is Bobolition day and I gib ball, as most gemmen do. Berry happy, if you join us.

Blinkinsopp: Bravo! That's nigger independence with a vengeance: invited by my own servant to a ball. I've a couple of bottles under my waistcoat and am in for a frolic. What, you there, Monsieur Pirouette? Foot it away, my snowdrops, and I'll dance to the cause of Liberty and Equality, whether black or white.

> *Dance—Tableau and End of Act 2*

>+<

> *Act 3*

Scene 1. A Street. Enter Bill Sticker, pastes up bill and exits. Enter Jim Crow and Copper Charley.

Jim Crow: So you am see, Sar, I lub Miss Snow and mean to change my condition. I shall enter de holy state of hemlock.

Copper Charley: Berry right. Wish you joy, Mr Crow. Miss Snow fine cretur. No doubt, you be berry happy.

Jim Crow: Iss, mutual 'complishments on both sides. Hab you any toughts of madrimony, Mr. Charles?

Copper Charley: Oh! iss, dere a lady living here, who I sometimes cast a glance at, as I pass, deb'lish fine woman.

Jim Crow: Am I hab the pleasure of her quaintance?

Copper Charley: Oh! iss. Keep de tavern down here—de One Tun.

Crow: What, Mrs. Marigold?

Copper Charley: Yes, Sar!

Jim Crow: Yah, Yah, Yah! Marry old woman!

Copper Charley: Old woman? How dare you call 'em so. Dis come of my keeping low company and 'fiding secrets to such trash.

Jim Crow: You black nigger, you—I hab you know, Sir, dat I always conduct proper. Call me low company, Sir! Dere's my card.

Copper Charley: And dere mine, Sar! Meet you any morning—after I have opened shop.

Exit

Jim Crow: Imp'rent common color'd fellow. Talk to me. I break his damned shins for him. Oh! Sally Snow, how happy we am to be and what beautiful whitey-brown piccaninnies we shall hab! Ha, ha, ha, what dat? [*seeing bill*] Some 'vertizement, I 'pose. [*reads it*] "Runaway—a nigger calling himself Jim Crow" Oha! I'm berry ill, it's dat damned Virginny planter I condiscend to be slave to. "Stands 6 feet, 2 inches high—has a foot eighteen inches long and calves turning out the wrong way." What de debil he mean by dat? My calves berry handsome calves! How dare 'em stick up libel on gemman? Dis abuse ob de liberality ob de press is dreadful. I can't stop here! I must cut away, marry my Sarah, and go to England. Ha, ha, Virginny planter no touch me dere.

Song

What a sight am wedding day,
Clothes so bright and all things gay;
Eb'ry friend and each relation,
Eb'ry rank—and eb'ry station.
There will be, dere, young folks, old folks,
Shy folks, spry folks, coy folks, bold folks—
On my wedding day.

Bridegroom come, him berry fine man;
Bridesmaid whisper 'hind a fan;
Den come de bride, all black with blushes;
Up, de lover fondly rushes,
Such a giggling, young folk, old folk.

Enter Sally Snow

Jim Crow: Blow my old shoes, but dat's Miss Sarah. How you am, Miss Snow? I partik'lar wish to 'peak to you. 'Pose you guess de subject I wish to converse 'pon?

Sally Snow: Iss, Massa Crow, me know berry well you want to make lub to me. Not proper, Sir, in 'publican streets.

Jim Crow: Miss Sarah, I wish to 'splain de sediments of my heart— you know me hab infection for you. Now, look at me. I'm berry nice man—berry well made and make berry good chum chum.

Sally Snow: For shame talkee so in 'em 'publican streets. You am gay deceiver—you know dat berry well.

Jim Crow: Miss Sarah, Ma'am, if you 'lude to my 'fair wid de Lady in Wall Street, I 'sure you, I'm not to blame; as to de oder Lady who trew herself into de river, what de debil could I do? If ladies will be fond of us gemmen, how can we help it?

Sally Snow: Will you promise to be constantine for eber and eber?

Jim Crow: For eber and much longer dan dat. Here I am on my knees, in a kneaded poster, all same as at camp meeting.

Sally Snow: I shall 'sidder your compositions. Dere's one or two Gentlemen anxious for my hand.

Jim Crow: Where are 'em? Damned black niggers. I be de death a' 'em. Oh, Miss Sarah, if you no hab me, I commit suetside. From trumpery arrangement, I am little darker than you. What of that? Good men ob all colors. I'm berry good man. Belong to the first class, and berry much suspected in upper circles.[45]

Sally Snow: Well, Massa Crow, if your Boss hab no 'jection, dere's my hand.

Jim Crow: Oh Miss Sarah, you hab make me de happiest of colored gemmen.

Duet

Jim Crow:

Who so merry as you and I?
Trig and gay and brisk and spry!
Ladies, look at me and cry,
What a berry beautiful nigger

Sally Snow:

As I by de Five Points go,
Gemmen standing in a row
Smile and nod and go just so,
And each one fain would be my beau.

Both:

Holey, holey, bango thrum—Jango, bango, diddle-de-dum!
Strike de tambour, swig de rum, merry the maid and her nigger

Exeunt both

✦

Scene 2. Tavern. Enter Pirouette and Mrs. Marigold.

Pirouette: I never sall see such womans as you are. Pour quoi you talk to me? I sall go where I please. Madame Pirouette, are you not shameful of yourself?

Mrs. Marigold: Not a bit. I say your jigging at a nigger party is *un-*graceful, Mr. P.

Pirouette: You talk to me? You ugly old rascals; you are ron away; I forgive you; now we meet again; you are jealous, eh? Mais I ave more cause for to be jealous as you.

Mrs. Marigold: You, cause? Did I go to a nigger ball?

Pirouette: No, but you ave smile and talk wis de nigger man. Diable, I ave seen you smile and shew your tooths—so many as you ave left. I will not ave him.

Mrs. Marigold: Oh! very well. I believe I am pretty well known here—*de*preciated by my friends, *in*spected by my neighbors. This a land of freedom, Sir.

Pirouette: C'est vrai, every land is land of freedoms wis you.

Mrs. Marigold: I'm my own Missus. If you can't behave yourself, halley von song[46] to Paris and, if you come to talk of goings-on, Sir, who is the lady you came here running after?

Pirouette: Ah! mon Juliette, she is lost to me for ever. Some time ago, I vas make de love to dat charming girl. Now I have you, very differ-ent ting, indeed.

Mrs. Marigold: What does she do now with this Mr. Dalton?

Pirouette: Have you so little connoissance wis an affair de coeur to ask him? Dey are in love wis one anoder, same as you and I sall be, thirty year ago.

Mrs. Marigold: I don't care, I'll have no loving here.

Pirouette: I believe Madame vish for no love, but vat she make herself.

Mrs. Marigold: Now, Mr. Pirouette, one word's as good as a thousand.

Pirouette: For why you always speak a thousand, then?

Mrs. Marigold: I'm not going to be made a nigger slave of! I'll have my own way and in my own way of having it. I know there's some plot connocting[47] in this house. If the whole party shall turn out, the wretch gets more uglier, and more suspiciouser, than ever. *Exit Mrs. Marigold.*

Pirouette: Dere you are go. You are very vell gone. Plot! Vat is dat plot? Aha, she ave hear me ven I tell Sally Snow vat I have heard of to endanger ma chere Juliette. Ah! Dat Sally Snow is very handsome brown. She is charmant. Diable, dere is Madame talk wis dat black fellow, agains. Madame, Madame, I say! *Exit Pirouette.*

Enter Blinkinsopp and Juliette.

Blinkinsopp: Well, it's an extraordinary thing—whilst I've been running away from you, you've been doing the same by me.

Juliette: Precisely so.

Blinkinsopp: And is it possible that you really didn't wish to marry me?

Juliette: I neither wish'd nor meant it. You're a very interesting person for a friend, but as a husband—

Blinkinsopp: You had much rather not! Oh, never mind, out with it. You think me, in plain English, a very good now-and-then acquaintance, but won't do for a standing dish. No accounting for taste. Now, and as to you, when I first saw you chasseuing it and dos-a-dosing it, I was charmed. But now, though I like you very well, I like your friend a vast deal better. I can't help it, but I am so confounded susceptible.

Juliette: My precious guardian is now in New York and Sally Snow has told me of a scheme he has formed which we must frustrate.

Blinkinsopp: Your guardian? Why then that accounts. There has been a stranger here enquiring for you, a suspicious looking chap.

Juliette: Guardy's lawyer, no doubt. Was it a little man and bald at the top of his head?

Blinkinsopp: Bless you, no! A big one and howl'd at the top of his voice.

Juliette: Some enemy, no doubt. I think, Mr. B., now that I have lost you for a lover, you will befriend me.

Blinkinsopp: With all my heart—No, not that, that belongs to the other lady, but with all my power. First, as to your guardian, shall I break his rascally head?

Juliette: Oh! no, no, there's no occasion for breaking his rascally head or the public peace. I was to go tonight to the theatre in what they call a Go-chair.

Blinkinsopp: And don't mean to do so—it will be a No Go-chair.

Juliette: We have concerted a scheme to fool Guardy who had bribed the Negroes to take me again to the tyranny of Old Hickory.

Blinkinsopp: I've a scheme. Don't ask me anything about it. I say I mustn't be much with you—if I am I shall relapse, I am so confoundedly susceptible.

Exeunt

>‹

Scene 3. A Room. Hickory, Slapup, and Pawks discovered.

Pawks: A paction's a paction. You see I'm thirty years old now—I nat'rally reckon the balance of my life at forty years more. I'm no ways disagreeable to your proposition, but I calcilate living forty years with a woman I've never seen is worth £100 per annum, and sha'nt take no less.

Hickory: £4,000, well, I consent.

Pawks: Then there's her keep—at £150 a year.

Hickory: Zounds, that makes £6,000, in addition to the £4000—do you release all claim upon the estate?

Pawks: Yes, but I must have it down on the nail. I ain't going to commit matrimony on credit.

Hickory: But there are other difficulties. In the first place, the girl will be adverse to the match.

Pawks: Now, don't agonize about that. I'm the spryest chap in our

parts. I can make love better, and faster, than any six chaps in Old
Virginia.

Hickory: When she comes, do you see her alone—say she is once
more in my power, but offer generously to release her, for if she
thought you were my choice that alone would determine her
against me.

Pawks: I calcilate if she does but see me, it's enough; however, I ain't
no ways objectionable to do as you say.

Hickory: You'll be delighted. She's a fine grown girl. I can tell you,
fortunes like hers are not to be sneez'd at.

Pawks: No. I calcilate if fortunes could be got by sneezing there
wouldn't be a chap in the 'Nighted States without a cold in his
head.

Hickory: Well, then, [*to Slapup*] if you'll step with me, I'll put you in
possession of the papers; and [*to Pawks*] you will remain here and
receive the lady.

Exit Hickory and Slapup

Pawks: I realize that that old chap, my uncle, is as big a rogue as ever I
clapt eyes on. I wonder what the girl's fortune's really worth? My
uncle's uncommon 'cute, but I've a tarnation mind to try if I can't
roll up the pair on 'em and carry off the girl without no advance-
ment of money at all.

Enter Negroes bearing a Sedan

Oh! here she is, I reckon. Put her down gently and don't bump her.
Get out, you niggers. I'll orationize her into loving me. I guess,
Miss, you'd be glad to get out. [*opens sedan; Jim Crow rises in female
attire*] A fine grown girl, he calls her! She's tarnation tall: a poplar
in petticoats, I calcilate. I can never kiss her without a ladder. How
she do swiggle about, surely. You see, Miss, your guardian has you
once again. [*Crow affects to weep*] Don't go to cry. I'm very tender
inwards, myself. I shall weep a waterfall, if I once begin.

Jim Crow: Heigho!

Pawks: She *is* the longest acquaintance I ever had, and does step out
remarkable, surely. Don't be grieffull, Miss; I'll save you from Old
Hickory and carry you slick away to Virginny. I'm no palaverer—a

spry fellow as you see. Stand 5 feet 4 inches, cast iron sinews, and double-jointed all over; can lick a bushel of bears and don't valle copperheads or rattlesnakes no more than a flash o' lightning does a rusty conductor. So, give me your hand and say it's a paction.

Jim Crow: Heigho!

Pawks: Here's old Hick, I s'pose. [*To Crow:*] Pop back again for an instant, I'll soon be rid of him and then . . . [*puts Crow back*] Remarkable tall, surely, but a particular, fair woman, nevertheless.

Re-enter Slapup

Slapup: I say, young'un.

Pawks: Well?

Slapup: I'm an individual of nice feeling, and I've been thinking that it's an atrocious shame that this old fellow should cheat the poor girl of her fortin.

Pawks: Hush! [*pointing to sedan*]

Slapup: Oh! She is there, is she?

Pawks: I calcilate she is.

Slapup [*speaking low:*] Now, that money had much better be in our pockets than his'n.

Pawks: Well, did I ever—now who could imagine that? That's the very individual retrospection I've been a-taking myself.

Slapup: Now, if you was to . . .

Pawks: Run slick away with her—I designate doing so, most unquestionable.

Slapup: Her father died worth £15,000.

Jim Crow [*peeping over top of sedan, aside*]: Aha!

Slapup: Which has been accumulating ever since—besides some land. Here, I have all the papers about it.

Jim Crow: Damned old rogue!

Slapup: When you marry her, all is yours. And then, as an honorable man, I expect you to pay me the £10,000—instead of Old Hickory.

Pawks: Yes, aye, I see. Hush, here's Hick; let's go to him; he mustn't see the girl. You keep him in play, and I'll pop her off. He's a tarnation rogue, but I'm a tarnationer—and I realize that, in any roguery, you'd lick the pair on us. I don't flatter, really; I take you to be the biggest rascal that ever I saw. Beware, don't take the papers with you—he mustn't have 'em anymore. [*Pawks puts the papers in desk*] I'll turn the key on Miss. There you are, safe enough. I say, they must wake early that's a match for Old Virginny and London. [*Exit both*]

Jim Crow [*comes out:*] Dere, white rascals! What um say if dey catch nigger at such tricks? Where 'em papers? Ah! here. [*takes them*] Now, I get away. That little rascal, my boss—take me up as run away nigger!

Blinkinsopp [*intoxicated without:*] It won't do, old one. I say she *is* home.

Blinkinsopp enters followed by Dalton, Hickory, Slapup, and Pawks.

Jim Crow: There's t'oder boss. I must get back in. [*Crow goes in sedan*]

Dalton: I am not to be trifled with, Sir. I demand to know by what right you make any attempt on the liberty of Juliette.

Blinkinsopp: Yes, Sir, and I demand too, Sir.

Pawks: Leave me alone. [*crosses to Blinkinsopp*] Now you, Sir, I'm a reg'lar built, not to be denied Virginny lad. Hard as a block o' marble, fast as a flash o' lightning, sudden as an airthquake, certain as quarter-day. I calciate you don't know what gouging is.[48] Now, it's done in a moment, I can tell ye. I've entered on a contract of connubiality, and the lady ain't no ways inclinated to the contrary. And, if you interfere with me, I'll smash you into so many atoms that it'll about take eternity to pick up the pieces.

Blinkinsopp: You fight me? It's like a sentry box pitching into St. Paul's.[49] I'll put you into one end of a funnel and blow you out at t'oder. If you go to that, I'm a reg'lar Eastender. Finished my education at Offley's and the Rainbow, have got two bottles of wine under my waistcoat, care for nobody, and *I* calculate, if I hit you once, Green's balloon[50] won't be able to fetch your wind back for you.

Hickory: Oh! we'll put an end to this. Here, Constables, watch, I say.

Crow [*coming out of sedan:*] Knock 'em down, Massa Boss, down with 'em!

Pawks: Holloa! Why, if my oracular eyes don't deceive me, that's my run away nigger. You black varmint, I've got you once again, have I.

Jim Crow: No, you habn't. Here, Sambo, Brown, Charley, I say.

Enter Negroes and constables

Jim Crow: Fight for cause of bobolition!

Blinkinsopp: Well said, Snowball. I haven't had a row for many a day, so, if it is to be a skirmish, here goes.

General row between watch, Negroes, and party; they fight off. Blinkinsopp knocks Slapup in sedan, and scene closes.

→‹←

Scene 4 [the last]. Enter Juliette, Ellen, and Sally Snow.

Juliette: I am on thorns, my dear Ellen, until I hear of the result of Blinkensopp's project.

Ellen: Or rather, till you hail the return of Mr. Dalton. Is it not so? [*To Snow:*] All my fear is lest your representative, Mr. Crow, should make some blunder.

Sally Snow: Oh! no, Missee, Massa Crow, berry cleber man—he make no blunderbuss at all, I quite sure.

Juliette: If his talent keeps pace with his intentions, I am sure he will not. Sally, here, I am afraid, has a sort of sneaking kindness for Mr. Crow—

Sally Snow: Iss, Missee, and he hab a squeaking kindness for me. Him offer both him hands in marriage. And if you and him boss tink proper, me berry much like to be married, if you please.

Juliette: You have aided in defeating my guardian and deserve any return in your power—so, cheer up, Sally, I'll answer for Crow's "boss," as you call him, and you shall have a husband.

Sally Snow: Tank you, Missee, same to both of you, and many of them.

Enter Blinkinsopp

Blinkinsopp: The rascals, I'll Yankee rig'lar 'em. Come athwart me—me—a man of bulk and prowess. I let them know, I hadn't been at the Five's Court for nothing. Ha, ha, ha, I can't help laughing at that little Virginny scamp—standing before me, 'pon my soul, it was too absurd. Like a sentry box pitching into St. Paul's. Beg pardon, ladies—am rather *en dishabille,* as you see. Been in a row, all on your account.

Juliette and Ellen: Oh! do tell us.

Blinkinsopp: I'll give you a concise description. It was a sweet sight to see Dalton clear the Broadway. George Robins himself never knock'd down such lots as we have.[51]

Juliette: But who? Why? and where is Dalton?

Blinkinsopp: Practicing the art of self-defense at the Five Points. You must know your guardian and a little hop o' my thumb Virginny fellow captivated poor Jim Crow.

Sally Snow: Oh! poor Massa Crow—him am hurt!

Blinkinsopp: Yes—"him am hurt"—a good many. When I saw my nigger seized by little Virginny, I ran to the rescue; they pitched into me, and Dalton into them. Charlies came in. Everybody punch'd everybody's head, and that's a clear account of the matter.

Enter Dalton

Dalton: Oh, you are here already. Victorious, my dearest Juliette. We have put your foes to flight.

Blinkinsopp: And, my dearest Ellen, if you go to that, we have put *our* foes to flight.

Ellen: But why did this racket occur?

Sally Snow: Iss, and where am my Jimmy Crow; where my chum chum?

Blinkinsopp: Your chum chum's a trump and no mistake. There hasn't been such a black since Molyneux.[52] He's a prince of a fellow.

Sally Snow: Iss, I know dat. He am Prince in him own country.

Blinkinsopp: A Prince: don't doubt it. The Black Prince, as likely as not.

Enter Jim Crow and crowd

Jim Crow: Dere you am, what a debil of a mess I'm in. You am my boss—save me, save me from damn Virginny Planter. Hab me, when piccaninny, for him slave. Lick me four days a week and starve me t'oder tree.

Enter Pawks with constable

Pawks: I don't care. This is a land of liberty, and I claim my nigger.

Dalton: Such is the law here, and it would be futile to attempt opposing it.

Pawks: I calcilate you're as sensible a chap as I've met since I left Virginny. [*As Pawks turns to Crow, Dalton turns to speak, aside, with Blinkinsopp*] Now, you two and a half yards of hard stuff, you've given me more trouble than you're worth—a great, lanky, scrawling, ill-formed varmint, all in and out like an ill-made corkscrew. I wonder for my part how I ever came to keep such a fellow—slow as a 'possum and hungry as a wolf.

Blinkinsopp: Well, if I must deal in flesh and blood, it shall be as a *buyer*, at least. As you undervalue this poor fellow so much, what sum will you take for him?

Pawks: Why, when I come to look at him, as a seller, I make small bestowment of time and blemishes. He's a fine, tall nigger, uncommon well-made.

Jim Crow: Dat am berry true.

Pawks: Strong as a buffalo, willing as a watchdog, long in the reach, clean in the fetlocks and, altogether, a very desirable lot: say, 300 dollars.

Jim Crow: And berry cheap at de money.

Blinkinsopp: I won't refuse £60 to save him—there.

Jim Crow: Huzza! Oh! Miss Sally Snow, now I am free nigger [*crossing to Pawks*] You damn little Yankee bagabone. If eber you come where I am again, I show you what a free color'd gemman can do. And now, look ye here, here's de papers, Miss Julium, show your estates—what dat rascal, Virginny, and your guardian, want to rob you of. [*Dalton and Juliette go up, inspecting the papers*]

Pawks: I realize it's up with my Uncle. You Englisher, I wish you joy of your nigger. He sleeps sounder and lies longer a-bed than any chap in Virginny. He's too lazy to eat his own dinner—you'll be obliged to hire another chap to wag his jaws for him. The first word he ever spoke was a lie, and he's spoke nothing else ever since. His mother was right down ashamed of him, and he never had a father. In fact, for a thorough, good night, slick away fore-and-end undeniable and not-to-be-worsted varmint, he's your man. *Exit Pawks*

Jim Crow: Go along, you dirty white trash. Now, Sir, if you ab no objection, dis lady and myself wish to enter the holy state of hemlock.

Blinkinsopp: You must find a parson.

Jim Crow: No, Sar, in Virginny, boss always marry him niggers himself. We much wish to hab Virginny marriage.

Blinkinsopp: Very well then, married you shall be.

Enter Pirouette

Pirouette: Non, non, dere never sall be no more marriage. Oh, Madames and Messieurs, je vous demande pardon, mais, vat you sall tink—Madame Pirouette ave ron away again.

Dalton: No!

Pirouette: C'est vrai, ah! ma chere [*to Sally*] you sall not marry him. All dese Othello fellow make very bad husbands. My wife has ron away with nasty copper Charley.

Jim Crow: Sar, dis lady am my wife, as will be in a few minutes. Beg you speak with proper respect to de lady of a free colored gemman.

Two Negroes enter with broomstick

Blinkinsopp: Now then for my canonical duties à la Virginia. You, Jim Crow, are desirous to take Sally Snow as your wife, as long as you two live?

Jim Crow: No, Sar, long as she behave herself proper.

Sally Snow: Me always do, you know dat berry well.

Blinkinsopp: And you willingly take him?

Sally Snow: Iss 'um do.

Jim Crow: And berry glad to catch me.

Blinkinsopp: Now, I say, young fellow, cut all your tricks, you know. No larking in plantations, hide and seek after female ebony. And, for you, Sally, if he doesn't make you a good husband, complain to me. So, join hands, and over you go.

Jim Crow: Much obliged by your 'gratuations, I'm sure.

Juliette: We'll take you to Old England with us and, as a token of 'um good humour on this occasion, we'll even now dance at your wedding.

Dalton: Then I will be your partner.

Blinkinsopp: And now we will have a happy end of this day.

Chorus and dance at same time

Air—"Finale to Obi"

Fifth July Fifth July!
Eb'ry color'd soul be gay
Banish Care Banish Care
Strike de bango dance and play
Freedom reigns o'er the plains
Bobolition for de nigger
Beat big drum, tamborine thrum
On dis happy day.

Curtain

✑ THE PEACOCK AND ✐ THE CROW
A Farce in Two Acts[1]

Act 1

Scene 1. An Apartment in Hollybush Villa[2]

Enter Podge *&* Miss Podge *disputing, followed by a lad in a stable dress, bearing an old board upon which is still visible—"Steel Traps and Spring Guns[3] Set in These Grounds"*

Podge: Now don't talk to me, you're an old goose. Put that down, Jem, and go and give Box a helping hand in the garden. *Exit Jem*

Miss Podge: Mr. Podge I must say—

Podge: Yes I know you must, and you *will* say but allow me to ask you what the devil do you mean by clacking about things you don't understand?

Miss Podge: An old goose! Clacking! I don't understand!

Podge: That's exactly what I say and mean, too; you don't understand anything of the business—how the deuce should you?

Miss Podge: What, Sir? Do you pay no deference to my judgement, or experience?

Podge: I don't believe you have one or t'other—where the plague should you get them?

Miss Podge: Why, from my books, guided by a refined taste.

Podge: If you had Mrs. Glasse's Cookery book[4] and a refined taste I might perhaps get my dinners a little better dressed. But you are so full of your cursed romantic novels.

Miss Podge: But there is no romance about this dreadful affair. The unfeeling reality is too evident. How can you reconcile to your conscience the thought of mutilating and maiming the precious limbs of your fellow creatures? And for what? The preservation of a few apples and plums.

Podge: If you are not enough to make a man swear to murder all the old women in the country, may I be the first to be caught in my

[**264**]

own trap. Do you see that board? Do you see how that's "mutilated and maimed"! Not only its precious limbs but its precious head is battered—look at the *S.* knocked out in *Spring,* it has stood in my ground for three years, the object of derision to all the petty larceny rogues in the district. I wonder that it's not a petrifaction by this time, for it has been stoned often enough.

Miss Podge: I must say, that that was right.

Podge: And I say it was quite right—never threaten without performing. Why it was but last week that some Newgate Poet[5] chalked on the back of it

> We've come again old Governor Podge
> To give you once more the artful dodge.
> You threaten us with traps and fierce spring guns
> But, bless you, we knows it's only your fun.

Miss Podge: I have always heard that your authors are sad thieves!

Podge: But let them steal from one another, then it wouldn't matter much.

Miss Podge: But now that a fresh board is painted, and you have actually laid down the dreadful engines, steel traps and spring guns, suppose you were to slay some of those misguided creatures. What would be the feelings of your family? To see you incarcerated in a loathsome dungeon, stand your trial convicted of murder, led out to a sudden and disgraceful death?

Podge: Eh! what! You've a great knack of setting everything in a disagreeable light. I don't mean to go to such lengths. The trap is what they call "The Humane Man Trap." It doesn't hurt much. It merely holds fast, and as for the gun, I'll take care that it shall be charged only with powder.

Miss Podge: Only think now of going to the county jail just at the moment when you are about to come into such a pretty increase of property.

Podge: Ah!—you allude to the will of Cousin in the nineteenth degree, the late Nehemiah Peacock, eccentric old fellow. He separated from his wife upon a foolish quarrel within two years of his marriage. She quitted Europe with her infant, a boy, and went to the West Indies, and from that hour to his death, old Nehemiah never heard one syllable of mother or child. At his decease, he bequeathed his fortune to heirs male direct, if they could be found. Fifteen years were allowed for their recovery, with the proviso that advertisements should be inserted in the principal London papers, every New Year's day, calling upon such heirs, if any, to appear. In default the estate is to come to me, worthy old gentleman.

Miss Podge: And the fifteen years will expire on the first of March. Mrs. Peacock's death I know was clearly ascertained. But her son, after arriving at man's estate, left the West Indies, and went to South America where it was rumoured he married a woman of colour. I was relating the affair to Mr. Quickset the other morning and he is of the opinion that . . .

Podge: And what the devil made you do that? That Mr. Quickset appears to be a monstrous favourite of yours.

Miss Podge: Is he not a friend of the family?

Podge: He likes it well, that is my opinion—that he wishes to get into it. If he is after Araminta, he'll find himself out in his reckoning. I can give her money enough now to command a Baronet. In a few weeks she shall have a portion that an Earl would jump at.

Miss Podge: What should you do among Lords and Baronets? Money can never make you a gentleman! You forget that you were only a provision dealer, sold cheese and bacon, and that forty years ago you were educated at the Parish School of St. Anne's Limehouse. Suppose some needy Lord should marry Araminta. He'd slight the girl, and despise you! And you'd be laughed at by the very man that you were supporting. He might take your money, but he would never be able to swallow your eggs and bacon.

Podge: But I don't sell bacon and eggs now, and let me tell you, Miss Podge, that I think it's damned bad taste to allude to any person's origin. In this jumbling upsetting world you know not who may be affected by it. At the Charity school, I managed to learn the multiplication table, and I never forget it. I'm worth at this instant eighty thousand pounds: and if I get the Peacock estate I shall be worth double that sum. What do you say to that? My money's as good as any Duke's. It will go as far and smell as sweet. What do you say to that? And I won't have Mr. Quickset for a son in law. What do you say to that?

Miss Podge: Mr. Quickset is a *gentleman.* I can account therefore for your dislike.

Podge: And I know the reason why he stands so high in your good graces. He complimented you the other day upon the colour of your hair! He was a bold man to praise that which he never saw— for to my knowledge you have worn a wig these ten years.

Miss Podge: Really, Mr. Podge, your brutality is such that was it not for my niece, I would quit the house never to re-enter it. A wig! Laugh!

Podge: [*aside*] Come, I think I have match'd her "eggs and bacon."

Enter Araminta laughing.

Araminta: The drollest thing in life has just occurred, would you believe it? [*aside*] I don't think any drollery will be acceptable at the present moment.

Podge: Come Araminta and if possible be serious for five minutes. Look in my face

Araminta: I'm afraid, Sir.

Podge: Afraid of what?

Araminta: Why, Sir, you look so black, I'm afraid that if I gaze at you it will spoil my complexion.

Podge: No fooling, if you please, Miss. I want a little common sense.

Araminta: Supposing the want to be mutual, you can hardly blame it as a fault in me, knowing that you are my father.

Podge: There, there, confound it you are all alike, but I won't suffer it to put me out of the way. Hark ye, Miss, you may smile! But I'm in earnest. There is a person who has somehow or other laughed and joked himself into this house, and . . .

Araminta: Who can it possibly be?

Miss Podge: Why he means poor Mr. Quickset!

Podge: Exactly. You couldn't have described him better. *Poor* I suspect him to be. *Dear* I know him to be. He has never dined here without swallowing at least a couple of pounds worth of wine.

Araminta: Now really I do think he drinks too much wine. Why don't you tell him you can't afford it?

Miss Podge: Insufferable meanness.

Podge: Will you be quiet! I insist on being heard, attended to, and obeyed. I don't like Mr. Quickset.

Araminta: Nor I, much.

Miss Podge: What! why he doats on *you.*

Araminta: [*eagerly*] How do you know that?

Podge: Miss Podge! You will do me a favor by retiring to your own apartments.

Miss Podge: I shall do no such thing. I consider the honor of the family to be at stake and am prepared to vindicate it.

Podge: What has an old maid to do with honor? But you must be gabbing upon matters you know nothing about.

Miss Podge: But I do know he loves her sincerely and, after my experience, I should advise no young woman to slight an affectionate and a noble heart, more especially when that heart is enshrined to a manly and elegant form.

Podge: That woman will drive me mad! Miss Podge! You may think it your duty to encourage my daughter to disobedience. If so, perhaps you will be kind enough to give her a fortune. For if she marries without my consent she shan't have a sixpence from me, and to prove to you I am not to be trifled with, I shall give orders that when this "elegant Mr. Quickset" calls, I'm not at home. But I won't wait for that. I'll write to him at once and say that we can do without the honor of his visits. I mean it! What do you say to that?

Exit Podge

Araminta: Well, I never saw my Papa in such a passion.

Miss Podge: My dear it's dreadful. It is the gold that's turning his brain. He forgets that your grandfather was a carman and your great grandfather a journeyman tailor.

Araminta: Are we the worse for that? They were honest, I believe, and while my father infringed no social duty, it redounded to his honour, that he was able by unwearied industry to soar so far above his humble station.

Miss Podge: That's all very true, but don't let him forget the ground from which he soared. Why should he wish to wed you to some rakish man of quality? Why?

Araminta: Now my dear Aunt, I must interrupt you. I'm in no hurry to pledge the matrimonial vow.

Miss Podge: Take my advice, I speak from experience. When a fair opportunity offers, don't reject it. When young, I was proud and unbending. I slighted many honourable advances! Now! hem!

Araminta: You will allow me to steer a middle course, not too eager, nor too indifferent. At all events, I shall ever yield a deference to your good opinion and sound judgement.

Miss Podge: Ah, you're a sensible kind girl and it will delight me to find you some day the wife of the gay Quirk Quickset.

Araminta: Mr. Quickset is well enough as a man, but I think he's a little too volatile.

Miss Podge: A good fault which time will be sure to cool. A man who is serious as a lover, will be very likely to turn out morose as a husband.

Araminta: Really, Aunt, you are quite erudite on the subject. Who could have supposed that you . . .

Miss Podge: Ah, my love, I never communicated to you the adventure of my younger days. Ha! the gay Charles Fitzarslet! I broke his heart by my cruelty and am still Miss Podge. My feelings will not allow me to continue. Someday I may summon up fortitude to relate the details.

Exit Miss Podge

Araminta: Poor Aunt, your griefs are uttered in such a serio-comic strain that I can scarce refrain a smile. But are my own circumstances in a less tragic state? Is not my heart already yielded up to the gallant marauder, Mr. Quickset, and yet I dare not own it. Am I not playing the *arch* hypocrite by forcing my tongue to utter sounds of dispraise that my soul rejects. And why? That a too precipitate avowal of the trick should not be the cause of our entire separation—and yet that moment is at length arrived.

Song. Araminta

The violet in her green wood bower,
Where birchen boughs with hazel mingle,
May boast itself the fairest flower
In glen or copse or forest dingle.
But I've seen an eye of brighter hue,
More sweet than flowers when bathed in dew.

Enter Patience

Patience: A charming day, Miss.

Araminta: I thought I heard it raining.

Patience: Oh, yes! Miss, so it does. I meant to say a charming day of the sort.

Araminta: Exactly. But still it's not of a sort I should choose.

Patience: Do you think the milliner will bring home your new dress today, Ma'm?

Araminta: You are certainly bewitched, Patience; you must be aware that it arrived this morning, when you assisted me in trying it on.

Patience: Oh, true. So I did Ma'am. Do you know, I was thinking of something else when I asked the question.

Araminta: So I should imagine.

Patience: I was cogitating, Miss, just asking myself whether we should have much company this week at the Villa, and I said to myself, says I, now I shouldn't be at all surprised if Captain Pumpkin or Mr. Dwaddling came, or perhaps Mr. Quickset.

Araminta: Bless me, the rain comes down in torrents.

Patience: Young gentlemen don't mind a little rain when they've an object in view. Now, I think I know one who wouldn't mind riding from London to Hampstead, though it rained pitchforks.

Araminta: Ha! that's the gate bell! I dare say it's the postman.

Patience: There a'nt no occasion for him to come. Somebody else has done his business, Miss. Miss, now it wouldn't astonish me if I had got something for you under my apron. [*show letter in left hand*] Perhaps you will read the direction, for I can't very well read your fashionable masculine hands. There's such a lot of flourishing and such long tails to the Y's.

Araminta: [*aside*] Provoking! This girl suspects my secret. I must endeavour to deceive her. A very likely thing, indeed, that the letter should be for me. It belongs to my Aunt, from Mrs. Godfrey. She dropped it and [*she suddenly takes the note*] I'll return it to her. Oh dear me! One of the lashes has got into my eye. Run and fetch me a handkerchief.

Patience: Well, if that is not cool, may I never. I'm going, Miss. I'll make her speak out before many minutes are over. *Exit Patience*

Araminta: Love make me artful. Ha! 'Tis his hand. [*reads note with eagerness*] It is indeed a passionate delaration of attachment, with an offer of his hand.

Reenter Patience: Here is the handkerchief, Miss. Why the other eye must be bad also—they're both full of tears.

Araminta: I have got the hair out now. Patience, you are out of breath. It was very kind of you to make haste when I was in pain.

Patience: Yes, Miss. But that wasn't exactly the reason as I heard footsteps behind me and I really thought it was Mr. Quickset again.

Araminta: Mr. Quickset appears never to be out of your thoughts.

Patience: Why he is such a good natured gentleman that I can't help it. Do you know, Miss, we had a long bit of chat about you the other evening.

Araminta: About me?

Patience: Yes. He said that he had heard you were going to be married to Captain Pumpkin and we would have such a jolly day of it.

Araminta: Then the idea of my marriage did not appear to distress him?

Patience: Distress him, Ma'am? No, he was quite in ecstasies. Hoped the Captain would make you a good husband. Swore we should have a ball in the evening, that I should be his partner, called me Goddess, Beauty, Jupiter. Took me round the neck to salute me. It was like the firing of the Tower guns.

Araminta: Traitor! May I never more behold his false face.

Patience: Oh dear, what's the matter? You are ill! Why it would break Mr. Quickset's heart to see you in such . . .

Araminta: Mention not his hateful name.

Patience: I'm afraid, Miss, you misunderstand me.

Araminta: Do you not say he call'd you a Goddess. That he caught you round the neck and . . .

Patience: What, Mr. Quickset, Miss? No such thing. It was the gouty old Captain Pumpkin that saluted me. Mr. Quickset never attempted such a thing. He's too modest a gentleman. [aside] Heaven help me.

Araminta: Then I have been too hasty. I see your trick cruel girl. You have my secret. But if you regard me, pray be cautious.

Patience: I will be so, but you scarcely deserve it. Remember, I gained the secret by strategem. As the soldiers say, you surrendered at discretion and therefore are at the mercy of the conqueror. However, I know the truth, and therefore you may consider me as your ally. Let all young ladies learn that it is an impossibility to keep their attachments from their maids. In fact, love wouldn't be downright *love* in earnest without a confidential.

Song. Patience

In the world I have no pleasure.
Far away's my heart's own treasure.
Could I but speak to him, oh then
My heart were whole and well again.
Lady Nightingale, Lady Nightingale,
To greet my treasure never fail.
Greet him kindly, right prettily,
And bid him ever mine to be
Greet him kindly, etc.

Exeunt

➤◄

Scene 2. Quickset's Lodgings. Quickset discovered at breakfast L. H.

Quickset: 'Pon my life this is capital. I haven't been so much amused for many a day [examines shelf]. Here's ammunition for fun—wigs, helmets, turbans and togas—swords, shields, and sandals. The costume of almost every nation under the sun. Coats, old fashioned, original and oriental—capital. But let me read Charley Morden's letter again.

My dear Sir, you may remember about a twelve-month back during a visit to the North of England you encountered an actor called Morden. Your kindness and generosity he has not forgotten. A family dispute fanning the roving flame that had early heated his imagination, indeed drove me first to adopt the precarious profession of the stage. That cause is happily now removed, and the death of an uncle places him at once in the possession of a considerable estate. Though he has changed his name, and Morden is no more, he trusts that you will find him still the same. But as he does not wish you to be convinced of the fact upon mere assertion, he requests the honor of your early presence at Oakworth Park, where you may see your old acquaintance under the new appelation of

Your true and obediant Servant.

Charles St. Louis Frampton

P.S. Knowing you to be an enthusiast in the gay and noisy masquerade, I send you all his theatrical gear, which pray accept as a small mark of esteem from

C.S.F.

To be sure I will. I'll be with you, my boy, before the winter is over. I'll work your dogs, horses, and birds for you. I'll keep *alive* everything and damn it I'll kill everything. I expect some rare fun. Talking of fun puts me in mind of my melacholy situation. What hard hearts some fathers have. My father is flint-marble-adamant. I've only overdrawn my allowance a year and a half and yet he refuses me any further supplies. Well, I must do something, hang it. I've a stock in trade here. Suppose I try the stage. I think I could play Romeo if my charming Araminta were the Juliet. Araminta Podge! Hang it, I must get her to change that name as early as possible. I think I see her now at the balcony. To make love, I must look sentimenal. Damn it, I'm afraid I should make a hodgepodge of that. No, I must have something energetic, furious. Ha, Richard! A horse, a horse, my kingdom for a horse![6]

Enter Slide

Slide: Lord Sir, It an't of no use your calling for a *horse.* You know there is an execution in the stables and the officers won't let one out. You'll be obliged to walk today.

Quickset: I was in *tip top* spirits, and your infernal croaking voice has unhinged me. You're an excellent damper upon a glowing imagination.

Slide: You'll find a worse damper out of doors, Sir, for it does rain in style! And I took your silk umbrella last week, it's very awkward.

Quickset: Yes, so you seem to think. What's the reason, sir, that my coat was not brushed this morning? And I rang the bell three times for any shaving water.

Slide: I had stepp'd out on a little business, Sir.

Quickset: I was not aware that I gave you directions for going out so early.

Slide: No Sir. I don't think you did.

Quickset: Then let me tell you, Mr. Slide, that such neglect will not do. The toast at breakfast was burnt to a cinder and the eggs, I'm certain, were boil'd yesterday.

Slide: I'll tell you how that was, Sir. Mrs. Shark, the landlady, is precious queer to day, Sir. Master likes his eggs boiled just three minutes and quarter, says I. He's not so very exact himself, says she. The eggs is in along with my dumplings, and I can't let them go off the bile by taking off the cover. As as you didn't get up so very early to day, Sir, I think they was in about three hours and a quarter.

Quickset: Mercenary Jesabel! I'll give her notice to quit. [*knock heard*] Why the devil do people give these long single knocks for?

Slide: If you had not been in here so late this morning, Sir, you would have heard a good many more of them. That *one*, sir, means *dun*.

Quickset: I'm done for. Say I'm not at home. I'm out of town, gone abroad, anywhere.

Slide: I said so but they swore and threatened to pummel me. One chap said he had brought three weeks provisions with him and as long as they lasted he wouldn't budge till he had seen you.

Quickset: Insatiate locusts. Run down, Slide. Say to them that if they will be here on Thursday at two or half past, some arrangement shall be made.

Slide: I beg your pardon, Sir, but thinking under present circumstances that you would not want a servant any longer and that I might be burdensome, I have accepted another situation.

Quickset: [*aside*] Scoundrel! I believe, Mr. Slide, I owe you for wages nine pounds some odd shillings

Slide: Nine pounds, nineteen and sixpence, Sir.

Quickset: Well, there's a ten pound note for you. [*aside*] My last. And with the odd pence you may purchase a rope and rid the world of as ungrateful a scoundrel as ever tainted its atmosphere.

Slide: If I a'nt well out of the mess. I've got my tin, they may wait for theirs.
                                                                      Exit Slide

Quickset: I'm certainly much lighter than I was five minutes ago. No, I have got rid of that cur—nothing can annoy me.

Enter Letty

Letty: I beg your pardon, Sir.

Quickset: Curse that "beg your pardon, Sir"—what disagreeables do *you* bring?

Letty: Lawk, sir, I bring nothing but myself and a letter and I hope there's nothing disagreeable in that.

Quickset: A letter for me?

Letty: Yes, Sir. I thought it might come from somebody what you like —you knows what I mean—and so I would bring it up.

Quickset: Thanks little Letty, you are a Hebe.[7]

Letty: Yes, sir. There's several gentlemen below, waiting to see you. Shall I send them up, Sir?

Quickset: Oh, hang them, yes.

Letty: Yes, Sir.
                                                                      Exit Letty

Quickset: Who the deuce is this from? I suppose it begins in the old style "Sir, I am instructed to proceed." What matter of fact fellows these lawyers are. [*opening*] Sir—"beg pardon" There's mischief in the very sound of it—

Sir, I beg your pardon but circumstances require that I should take the liberty of informing you that all future visits on your part to Hollybush Villa can be dispensed with.

I am your obediant servant.

Jeremy Podge

Upon my soul this day is beginning very pleasantly. The doors to be shut in my face. Ha! ha! ha! Araminta must have informed him of my declaration and the result is Podge's letter. He ought to be dry-salted with his own hogs. [*A tap at door*] Come in.

Enter Kersey

Mr. Kersey, I'm very glad to see you. I haven't met you for some time—

Kersey: It hasn't been my fault. I've several times—

Quickset: Wished to come, but business wouldn't let you. Time must be very precious to persons in trade.

Kersey: Exactly, and therefore I'm sorry—

Quickset: That you can't oftener have the pleasure of waiting on your customers. Is trade brisk now?

Kersey: Why, I must say, pretty fairish, us tailors at the West End have plenty of work on hand, but money—

Quickset: Money, money is nothing in comparison of a good fit. You charge high, to be sure, still one half of the men of town are indebted to you. I mean *obliged* to you. You bolster the bad figures, stuff the stingy, and pare the puffy; in short, you make the man, if not the gentleman.

Kersey: Really that's very good of you, Mr. Q., but I came to ask you—

Quickset: Whether I wanted any thing new! Yes, make me a couple of dress coats and three or four waistcoats.

Kersey: Your orders have always been attended to but if you will please to recollect—

Quickset: Yet, but I had *forgot* it though, that last coat you built for me didn't sit easy. I'll call at your place in the course of the week. Make the coats and let me have your bill.

Kersey: It is about that, that I—

Quickset: I know you're too high-spirited a man to mention your bill. Bye the bye, how is Mrs. K. Make the Lappets broader? I understand you have a fine family. Good morning, Kersey. Mind the surtout is to be double-breasted [*he completely walks Kersey out of room*]. Well, I've dumbfounded the tailor. [*another rap door*] Here's another of them. I must endeavour to be grave. [*enter Logwood*] Ha! Logwood, is it you? Haven't seen you for a long time.

Logwood: Your most obedient—your servant told me that you were abroad.

Quickset: Yes. I am at this moment in Persia, but had I known that you were here.

Logwood: You are very good, I merely called to know if you can spare me a draught—

Quickset: Excuse my interrupting you, but have you received a letter from me?

Logwood: No.

Quickset: Then it's on the road. A friend of mine, Mr. St Louis Frampton, asked me to recommend him a wine merchant. Of course I could do no less than mention you.

Logwood: Thank you for your consideration, honoured by your friend's support—

Quickset: Yes, if we didn't *sup-port—you* would be in a bad way.

Logwood: Dear me! That's a *pun!* may I ask you—

Quickset: Decidedly not. When I am engaged upon scientific studies I never answer questions. In a day or two, you may calculate upon a three hundred pound order from Frampton. The money's as safe as the bank. Apropos, you can send me another half pipe of Port. [*aside*] Any port in a storm. You can send me at the same time, a case of the Partridge Champagne.

Logwood: Certainly. [*aside*] As he has recommended me a new customer, I suppose I can't ask him. [*a pause*] But I will—

Quickset: You know my taste well enough, I leave everything to you.

Logwood: I wish you a very good morning.   *Exit Logwood*

Quickset: He's off. I ought to be a Secretary of State for the ability I display in evading unpleasant enquiries. But why should I be pestered in this manner. Those fellows have fattened upon my extravagance and now that I am compelled to hold back the profuse hand that was ever stretched towards them, they hunt me down. [*Another tap at door*] Is this another of the pack? I shall no longer be able to support the *Suavita in Moda.*[8] [*enter Kidskin*] Well, who told you to enter?

Kidskin: Nobody. I can't wait any longer. I've been kicking my heels downstairs long enough.

Quickset: Now take care, Sir, the kicking doesn't confine itself to your *heels.* It may ascend. Who *are* you?

Kidskin: Mr. Kidskin. Managing man for Mr. Trotter, the Booter.

Quickset: The Booter! And a pretty booty he makes of it. Well, Sir, what's your business?

Kidskin: Payment of your bill. Forty-eight pounds thirteen shillings and five pence.

Quickset: Hear me. I've expended hundreds with your employer, and when he sends a ruffian like you to collect for him he degrades himself at the same time that he insults me. There is the door. Make a precipitate retreat or I presume you know the strength of your own boots. [*poising foot*]

Kidskin: Sir, I shall not—

Quickset: Say another word and you'll find the longitude of the stairs.

Kidskin: Oh, very well, there is such a thing as writs.

Quickset: "Hang a calfskin on those recreant limbs."[9]

Kidskin: Oh!   *Exit Kidskin*

Quickset: Am I to be baited and not shew my teeth, no, I'll astonish these merciless rascals. Woe be to the next villain who may have the temerity to ask me for money. [*another tap*] Enter, wretch, and meet your doom.

Enter Jim Crow

Jim Crow: Well, and how is you, Mister? Why what de debil am you staring at? Hab you neber seen a gentleman afore? If you am going to be polite and ax me sit down, you needn't hold de chair up de sky in dat manner.

Quickset: Why what in the name of Erebus[10] brought you here?

Jim Crow: It warnt a Hairybus nor a omnibus dat brought me. I war carried here upon my own legs.

Quickset: And a pretty pair you have, for the purpose.

Jim Crow: Yes, dem rather handsome.

Quickset: And who the devil are you?

Jim Crow: I'm Jim Crow. I thought ebry body know'd me about here.

Quickset: [*aside*] This *is* a character. May I ask to what I owe the pleasure of this visit?

Jim Crow: Sartinly, cos I come to request the gratificuratation of your settling my account.

Quickset: By what possibility can I owe you a sixpence?

Jim Crow: Sixpence! It am a few many times more dan dat. It am for brightening up de understanding.

Quickset: Will you have the kindness to speak a little plainer?

Jim Crow: Well, I tink I am plain enough. You owe me one pound and a half crown, all but two pair.

Quickset: I don't remember to have dealt in any thing *black*. You're not an agent for Day & Martin[11] are you?

Jim Crow: No, but I'm a great consumer. I takes a shilling bottle ebery four days.

Quickset: And so the doctors recommended you to take a bottle ebery four days. Perhaps they thought it would improve your complexion.

Jim Crow: Ya! ha! ha! Well, if you am not the stupidess chap I eber seed. Drink de blacking, ya, ha, ha. It am a pity you did not send your head at de same time with your boots. Cos I might have brush'd up dat a bit. If I had known you had been such a flat, I'm damn'd if I I wouldn't have charged sixpence a pair for cleaning de boots.

Quickset: Curse that fellow's laugh. Do you mean to say, Sir, that you ever cleaned my boots?

Jim Crow: Did I eber clean dem? Just look at dem pair what you hav got on. No gentleman ought to want more polish dan dat.

Quickset: Do you know, Mr. Rook?

Jim Crow: You're at your stupids again. My name an't Rook. It am Jim Crow.

Quickset: Are you aware that I paid a rascal thirty guineas a year for brushing coats and cleaning boots.

Jim Crow: Well you am de softest fellow I ever heard on. Massa Slide am no edification. He couldn't polish up de boots. So he handed dem ober to a gentleman and a man ob talent what did dem at de small charge of twopence de pair. So I'll trouble you to settle de account cos tomorrow I hav some berry heaby bills to meet.

Quickset: Hark ye, Mr. Blackbird!

Jim Crow: You don't appear to hab much more edicumcation dan oder man. My name, Sar, am Crow, no blackbird.

Quickset: Confound you and your name, too. Before I pay this demand I shall insist upon knowing how you make out such a sum. Let me have a bill of particulars.

Jim Crow: Dat am berry soon settled. I neber go out widout my books. You can hab your bill in no time. [*takes out tallies and selects one*] Dere, 'tis exactly one pound five.

Quickset: I suppose I must admit the validity of your claim. Therefore, we'll call it one pound five, though I must confess . . .

Jim Crow: I neber notched dis morning's work. Dat was two pair.

Quickset: Stop! I cannot afford such a heavy bill, Mr. Raven.

Jim Crow: What de debil do you mean by Raben? My name am Misser Jim Crow. It am considered damn'd insulting to call a gentleman out of his name.

Quickset: Yes. Yes. I recollect now you are a *Crow*.

Jim Crow: Yes, Jim Crow. It am berry simple. You am call me all de beastesses what flies. I wonder you didn't say I war a *howl* or a *Peacock*.

Quickset: [*aside*] Peacock! damme that's the name of the lost heir to the property old Podge holds in trust. I wish I could produce a claimant, if it were only to annoy that selfish old Midas.

Jim Crow: Come, I wish you would hab de civility to pay me dat one pound ten shillings. I'm using a great deal ob time here. I must put you down anoder pair.

Quickset: This rascal won't leave me till I pay him, and I haven't a shilling! Podge forbids me his house and I'm over head in ears with love with his daughter! Desperate diseases call for desperate remedies! Podge is an old fool and I'll be revenged for the insult he has put upon me.

Jim Crow: Now look here. My moments is waluable and I looks upon your conbersation as bery dear at a shilling an hour. And if you don't pay me at once I shall make up de six pair.

Quickset: Mr. Crow, little things must give place to great ones. The moment I beheld you, I thought you an extraordinary creature. The stamp of nobleness is upon you. Allow me to ask, were you ever in America?

Jim Crow: Why I habn't left above more dan six months. I came ober here to return thanks cos dey 'mancipated de Niggers—

Quickset: Was it *South* America?

Jim Crow: I was raised in Surinam.

Quickset: [*aside*] Patagonia I should think by your size.

Jim Crow: But I run away from dar and got to New Orleans.

Quickset: Were you ever located at Carolina?

Jim Crow: I don't know what you mean by *located* but I got *tumped* dar cos I was saucy to de observer. Oh, I despises dat Carolina.

Song. Jim Crow.[12]

One negro say one ting you take no offence.
Black and white be one color a hundred year hence.
And when massa death kick him into a grave,
He no spare negro, buckra, nor massa nor slave:
Then dance and then sing, and a banger,[13] thrum thrum.
He foolish to tink what tomorrow may come.
Lilly, laugh and be fat de best ting you can do,
Time enough to be sad when you kickaraboo.

Quickset: Wonderful vicissitude of fortune! Excuse my feelings! But my heart is ready to burst, when I reflect upon the miseries you have undergone. The noble heir of the still nobler 3,000 a year.

Jim Crow: I'm hang'd if that chap an't fooling me.[14] I say, Mister, dat am not de way to pay me my one pound *fourteen*.

Quickset: Ah, you may look upon me with incredulous eye, but I will maintain to the world that you are the lost son of a before lost father.

Jim Crow: What de debil should you know about my fader, when I never know'd him myself.

Quickset: That's it—he the last and bravest of his race, the last of the Peacocks, went to Surinam, was there trepanned, assassinated, leaving his ebony widow to deplore his loss, and you the sweet unconsious heir to encounter the rough buffets of an unfeeling world.

Jim Crow: Ya, ha, ha, what den? You knowed my *moder*, too? Perhaps you can give me some intelligence of the other part of the family.

Quickset: You should see them all before the day is over, happy day! For fifteen long years have they sought you, and accident throws you up.

Jim Crow: But am sure no damn accident will throw me down again. Am you quite sartin dat I am a gentleman of property?

Quickset: Sure there's a noble mansion with spacious parks, only waiting for you to take possession.

Jim Crow: Is dar? Den clear de way, ya, ya, ya. I won't clean anoder par ob boots for a month, and I'm damned if I don't keep an omnibus myself.

Quickset: Now, Podgy, I'll torment you. Frampton's wardrobe will furnish disguises and, hang it, not a moment to be lost. Action! Action!

[Rings bell violently]

Jim Crow: Dat's right! Make him call out 'til him throat's sore. Where will de cuss servants not come up and wait upon us.

Enter Letty

Letty: Lord, Sir! What has happened?

Quickset: Ask no questions, but run to the next coach stand and call a hack. Pick out a good pair of horses, as they will have to carry me to Hampstead. Don't stop, push on—Boo!

Letty: Lawk, I never seed such a gentleman as you are. You're always in a flusterification.

Exit Letty

Quickset: [*aside*] I shall be better able to impose upon Podge by something outrageously outré. Mr. Crow must be a native chieftain at least, and there's a Rolla's dress that will be the very thing for him.[15] Now, Jim, help me with this chest into the next room and I will equip you in style.

Jim Crow: No tank you. A gentleman wid parks in de mansion house nebber condescend to do porter's work.

Quickset: I beg ten thousand pardons. [*aside*] The rascal's purse proud already. I'll do it myself.

[*Quickset removes chest into room*]

Jim Crow: Ya, ya, ya, dis am capital! But what sall I do wid all de money? I muss hab ebery pocket made bigger! Dey is pretty full already, cos I always carry about me my stock in trade. [*takes brushes and blacking from pockets and looks at shoes*] I'm thinking I shall want a little polish myself, now I'm a man of fortune. Where am all de lazy white folks? [*pulls bell rope violently*]

Quickset [*from off*]: James Ezekiah Crow Peacock, Esq.

Jim Crow: Well dat's a fine name anyhow.

Quickset: Your toilet awaits you.

Jim Crow: Well let him sit down a minute. [*rings bell*] I'm going to blow up de whole ob de house.

Enter Letty

Letty: I'm sure I haven't been a minute. [*seeing Crow*] What! Was it *you* ringing the bell so violently?

Jim Crow: Why to be sure. Come here, you Missy servant.

Re-enter Quickset

Quickset: If you don't make haste—Eh? For shame, Mr. Peacock! What do you mean by getting little Letty into corners? Your father was a moral man.

Jim Crow: I hab nothing to say against dat, I war going to obserbe.

Quickset: Observe, Sir! We have not a moment to lose. Your dress, the native costume of your country, is there. Away with you and equip yourself. Run, run.

Jim Crow: Oh! I nebber run. If I'm a *Peacock*, in course I ought to keep up de consquences of de family.

Exit Crow

Letty: There are two or three persons waiting to see you, Sir.

Quickset: Then let them wait. You must assist me to escape by the side door, and next week I'll buy you a new dress.

Letty: You're sure you won't forget it.

Quickset: By this kiss, I will not.

as he is kissing her, Crow re-enters

Jim Crow: Hollo! Mister. Oh fie, for shame! I'm blushed all ober. Did your fader eber tell you to do dat?

Letty runs out. Quickset pelts Crow with brushes, etc., as the drop falls.

End of Act 1

⇥⇤

Act 2

Scene 1. Interior of Hollybush Villa. Enter Podge and Miss Podge

Miss Podge: I can't believe it possible that you have been such a savage —send to a gentleman and forbid him your house?

Podge: To be sure, I did. When I say anything, I mean it. If you doubt it, you can call upon Mr. Quickset and ask him!

Miss Podge: After your conduct I can never look upon that elegant youth again, without sinking into earth!

Podge: As long as you did but vanish, I don't think it would matter whether you sank into earth or evaporated in air.

Miss Podge: Thank heaven! All men do not profess your brutal way of thinking. There are yet some persons ready to appreciate and defend our sex.

Podge: Fiddlededee—you want no one to defend you. You can take your own part. I'll tell you what it is Miss P. You have been trying hard for the last twelve years to break my spirit, but I'm too tough for you. I mean now to turn the tables and break yours.

Miss Podge: Ridiculous malice!

Enter Box

Box: It's all beautifully laid down, Sir.

Miss Podge: What's laid down, Sir?

Box: Our new patent Human Man Trap.

Podge: *Humane* Man Trap.

Miss Podge: It's a pity, Mr. P., that you don't take out a patent for humanity.

Podge: The article wouldn't sell. There would be no buyers.

Box: Well, Sir, the patent humanity trap is beautifully set. It will catch hold of any man's leg quite delightful.

Podge: That's right. We'll see now whether the villains will dare to come and rob me, and then laugh at me.

Box: The spring gun, Sir, is among the summer cabbages, and the wires are charmingly hid. You couldn't see them a foot before you even in daylight.

Miss Podge: Oh! I haven't patience with you. I shouldn't be sorry to see you and your myrmidon there the first victims to your abominable contrivances.

Exit Miss Podge

Box: Old Missus, Sir, seems to be rather sour about the matter. If she was a gard'ner, she would not like to have her beds trod upon and her fruit stolen.

Podge: Never mind her. Only catch me a man, and I'll have him committed to the county jail.

Box: But I think under submission, Sir, that if you was to put a few swan shot[16] into the spring gun, you would save a great deal of trouble by shooting the rascals.

Podge: No, no, only powder—no shot. I am not quite satisfied as to the law on that subject. [*a ringing at the gate heard*] Bless my soul! What is the meaning of this alarm? Why there never can be a man in trap already, the sun's scarcely set.

Enter Patience

Is the villa on fire?

Patience: No, Sir, but there's a hackney coach just driven up to the gate and there's a gentleman who insists upon seeing you upon business and he has got the reddest head and whiskers I ever did see.

Podge: Dear me, this is very peculiar, just at nightfall, too. I say, Box, keep a sharp lookout, this may be incendiary.

Patience: His head's fiery enough to burn anything, Sir.

Box: I'm going down into the garden to see all's right there [*aside*] and if I mayn't charge the spring gun with shot, I'm hang'd if I don't ram in a handful of gravel just by way of luck. *Exit Box*

Podge: What sort of a person is this stranger, Patience? I hardly think it is proper I should see him.

Patience: Lawks, Sir, he seems to stick at nothing. He pushed by everybody with such a commanding air, as much as to say . . .

Enter Quickset

Quickset: Young woman! Get out of town! I have important matters to settle: woman improves pleasures, but mars business.

Podge: Really, Sir, I cannot understand.

Quickset: I know that you are not the first of the name who has been placed in the same difficulty. I say, young woman, you didn't take my hint just now.

Patience: No, I never take hints.

Quickset: I'm aware of that, nothing but half crowns! You're not bad looking—there's the door, retire.

Patience: Well, I'm sure, not bad looking, indeed!

Podge: You may go down, Patience. [*Aside to her*] Tell Jem and Box not to leave the house. There's something very suspicious about this man.

Patience: [*aside*] Suspicious! Odious! There's a head! Well, I never did see such carrots! *Exit Patience*

Podge: Now, Sir, I may ask—

Quickset: No Sir, I came here to talk, you must therefore be content with listening.

Podge: Sir, such rudeness to a man in his own house.

Quickset: Are you sure that it is your own house? Was no part of the purchase money furnished from the Peacock estate?

Podge: [*aside*] Bless me! How very odd. What can he know of the Peacock property? What do you mean, Sir, by asking me questions that impugn my honesty?

Quickset: [*aside*] I've terrified him already. Be seated, Sir, and you shall learn. [*They sit*] I believe, Sir, the late Mr. Nehemiah Peacock was an early patron of yours. That he enterain'd the highest opinion of your honour and probity.

Podge: Certainly, Sir—or he would never have delegated to me the important trust of carrying into effect his last will and testament.

Quickset: Then, Sir, I bring you intelligence that will surprise and delight you.

Podge: [*aside*] I'm very happy to hear it. I hope you will excuse any little coolness that you might have perceived upon your entrance. Not expecting—I

Quickset: I am perfectly satisfied. You know how anxious the old gentleman was for the discovery of his heir.

Podge: Yes. The poor fellow flatter'd himself to the last that someday a grandson would turn up, but after so long a period such an event cannot be expected.

Quickset: You are right, Sir. Such an event cannot now be expected.

Podge: I am very glad of the opportunity of making your acquaintance!

Quickset: I agree with you, Sir. An event cannot be *expected* when it has *already* happened!

Podge: What *do* you mean? Your manner is so very abrupt, that it agitates me. I am really at a loss.

Quickset: You *will* no doubt—for learn, Sir, to inexpressible satisfaction, I'm sure, that the long lost son and heir to the Peacock estate is well, is here.

Podge: I shall never get over it.

Quickset: You're right. There's no getting over it.

Podge: There must be some cheat.

Quickset: Cheat! This to the respectable heir of the house of Catchcosts and Seizeflats, attornies at law! We can prove beyond doubt that Peacock Junior went to Surinam, and married a woman of colour. The result of that union was a male infant who lays just claim to the restitution of the property and which, if you are rash enough to retain, twelve honest Englishmen will force you to yield —confounding illegal power and rescuing oppressed innocence! You shall behold the injured Peacock. *Exit Quickset*

Podge: That fellow's a lawyer. Should it really be Peacock's grandson? I don't care how soon they send me a coffin. I'll be calm if I can.

Re-enter Quickset

Quickset: I have sent for him, Sir, as I deem it advisable that you should see him.

Podge: You said nothing just now about an infant. Is he so very young?

Quickset: No, no, not exactly an infant, a fine promising youth. [*a laugh heard*] Damn it, they are queering[17] him already. Mr. Podge, he can only speak the Dutch language and I have not been able to persuade him to throw aside his native costume, but you'll find his manners very pleasing.

Enter Jim Crow

Jim Crow: I tell you what it am, Sar. Dis dress is too airy and breezy like for de time ob year.

Quickset: Never mind. Keep your tongue still. Didn't I tell you that you couldn't speak English.

Jim Crow: But what do you say that for?

Quickset: Mr. Podge, this is Mr. Ezekiah Peacock, grandson of Nehemiah Peacock, deceased.

Podge: Is *this* Nehemiah's Grandson?

Quickset: Yes, so providentially brought to light.

Podge: Brought to light! Why he's a blackamoor, and the ugliest one I ever beheld.

Jim Crow: It am all damn lie. What do you know about Beauty?

Podge: I thought you said he knew nothing but Dutch, that was plain English enough.

Quickset: How some peoples ears deceive them. Now that was as pure Dutch as ever I heard.

Podge: But how he looked at me—he appeared as if he was coming over to shake me.

Quickset: The very thing he intended to do—to shake you by the hand.

Jim Crow: You need to hab no more *speechyfumcation.* Gib me ma property at once, and I should like to hab a few pounds for liquor money to begin wid.

Quickset: Be quiet, you'll spoil all. This is the man that keeps you out of your property.

Jim Crow: What! Dat him, den I'll be whipped if I don't lick him fine as silk. Look you here now, you old bear.

Quickset: Don't be a fool! That's not the way to get it.

Podge: What am I to understand by this violence?

Jim Crow: I tell you what, Mister, you hab to understand. If you don't pay me, cuss me if I don't tump you into a dough cake.

Podge: Don't you call that English?

Quickset: You had better ask me whether I call it Greek.

Podge: Very well, I know what I begin to think.

Quickset: You begin to think how unpleasant it is to restore an estate you've looked upon as your own.

Jim Crow: Am you beginning to tink what a damn rogue you is for taking de estates from me.

Quickset: Confound you, can't you speak bad Dutch as well as bad English?

Podge: As you're a professional man, Sir, I shall only correspond thro' my attorney. I will bring him here to meet you.

Jim Crow: Spose now you send us a drop of whiskey toddy or rum punch.

Podge: [*aside*] If I could put a little arsenic in it, I should have no objection. I am convinced that they are both impostors.   *Exit Podge*

Quickset: You are ruining every thing, Mr. Jim Crow. Did I not tell you to keep silence?

Jim Crow: Dat am all berry well, but a gentleman ought to keep a little cold meat in the house. I'm hungry enough to eat a possum wid de skin on.

Quickset: I've put Podge upon the centre hooks. I must therefore make the most of my advantage, see Arminta and arrange some plan for the future. This way leads to the drawing room.

Jim Crow: Now look here, Mister, I put on dese wild Indian tings cos you told me I couldn't be a man of property widout 'em, but I'm empty in de stomack, and de pockets, so I'll tank you to hand over someting on account.

Quickset: Everything is in train, and if you dare murmur or act in opposition to my advice, I'll go over to the enemy, abandon you and your cause. You will be treated as an impostor and instead of parks and a mansion house, you will be conducted to a prison and the pillory.

Exit Quickset

Jim Crow: Ye, ye, ye, if de butcher boys of New York were to see me now. I'm hang'd if they wouldn't pelt me. I should like to get a few refreshments. Dat flighty chap what brought me he neber tink dat I hab no dinner.

Enter Servants

Footman: Now stand back all of you. If Master knows of this he'll be downright furious.

Cook: Well, but I want to have a peep at the great foreigner.

Coachman: If he can't talk English, how can we tell what he wants?

Jim Crow: Well, white folks, what de debil do you all want? Ladies, I am berry glad to see you. How is all your husbands? I can't exactly tell how it happen, but I do make all de folks laugh.

Foot: We have heard from our fellow servant, Patience, that you are the posterity of old Nehemiah Peacock and we all congratulate you upon your getting your fortune.

Jim Crow: I condescend to tank you all for dis berry flattering mark ob your contempt. But I shall tank you much more if you bring me some wittals.

Cook: That's my department. I'm happy to inform you there's a splendid round of beef, boiled ham, cold, just set out for our own dinner in the kitchen.

Jim Crow: De kitchen, dat's de place for me. I likes to be near de cookery. Look here, white folks, you should see me clar de kitchen in old Virginny.

Song
"Clar de Kitchen"[18]

Jemmy, once a slave, poor man—
Old Abdalla was my master,
Who, tho' we worked fast we can,
Whipped to makee work de faster.
Preacher preacher call me doggee.
Always work none to eat but much floggee.
Clar de Kitchen
Christian man buy Jemmy den,
And with slavery chain him partee.

And when Jem leave de man
It warm de cockles of him heartee.
Now Jemmy free, him skip like froggee.
Him lots to eat and nebber floggee.

Clar de Kitchen

Omnes: Bravo! Capital!

Housekeeper: He sings like a nightingale.

Foot: Or a blackbird.

Jim Crow: Well, and what situation dat you hab in dis here establishment?

Cook: Please your highness, I am cook.

Jim Crow: I'll stick by you anyhow, you am de gal for my money.

Foot: When your honor gets into your property if you should want a good footman, I shall be happy to serve you.

Omnes: And me too.

Jim Crow: Den my intention is to hire you all, you sall hab plenty to eat and drink, cos I like dat sort of work myself.

Foot: And you won't give us too much running up and down stairs.

Jim Crow: Nebber stop. When I gibs you my grand ball, after de fashion of dat I gave in New York, den dare was such a getting up stairs. Come now, I'll sing dat and you'll all join in chorus.

Song

"Sich a Gittin' Up Stairs"[19]

The merry dance, I dearly lub such revels.
Fun and frolic night and day,
Quick to old Nick, kick blue devils.
We dress so smart and look so gay,
Oh me, here we'll have a rare time.
Fun and frolic each step we go,
All de year round it is fair time,
Ebery where a raree show.
   Dance and song
   All night long
     Such a getting up stairs

Exeunt all. Servants following.
Enter Araminta and Quickset

Araminta: Indeed, Sir, you are too polite. [*aside*] It is Master Quirk sure enough. He must think me blind indeed not to discover him under those enormous whiskers.

Quickset: I assure you, Miss, my heart is not proof against the captivating charms of so fair a creature.

Araminta: I am a devotee to candour and though prudence ought to restrain me, yet there is something in your manner that induces me to confide. I must acknowledge I never beheld a gentleman in whose welfare and happiness I have felt a warmer interest at first sight than I do in yours.

Quickset: [*aside*] A thousand devils and their attendant imps! Is this the woman I have loved, caught by the fulsome adulation of a stranger?

Araminta: I dare scarcely trust myself in the expression of delight that this happy moment has occasioned, but let not my candour make you too bold. I know you can feel for my sanguine disposition. But tell me, is it possible that in so short a time you can love me?

Quickset: No Ma'am. Oh, yes! Oh Ma'am, I love you to distraction. [*aside*] Hang her.   *Quickset goes up*

Araminta: [*aside*] Now Mr. Quickset, I think I am even with your attempt at deceit.

Enter Miss Podge

Miss Podge: I'm sorry, I was out of the way to entertain you.

Quickset: Oh!

Miss Podge: What's the matter? I see how it is. Fie on you Araminta, you have been treating the gentleman with disdain. All girls in love are but poor company for any but the favor'd swain.

Araminta: But I'm not in love, Aunt.

Miss Podge: I'm shock'd at you, Araminta. You know I hate a fib. The coffee has been taken into the drawing room, may we hope to have the honor of your presence?

Quickset: Where *you* lead Ma'am, he must be a stoic indeed that will not follow, permit me to have the happiness of escorting you.

he hands Miss Podge out

Araminta: There's for you. The Turk! I don't know whether I ought not to be jealous of my Aunt—at any rate, I shall follow them. *Exit Araminta*

Enter Patience and Crow

Jim Crow: Stop you little debil. I want to have some chatty conbersation wid you.

Patience: What leave your glass to follow a woman?

Jim Crow: Yes, I hab lef de glass, but you see I hab bring de bottle. You am lubly as berry fine weather.

Patience: I declare you are quite poetical. Who is your favorite author?

Jim Crow: Oh! I hab got no author, but I feel a great partiality for plays. Dem is de tings to open de sensibilities of natur. Did you ebber read de works of Missa Shakespear, de gentleman who writes de plays upon ebberybody and all tings?

Patience: I idolizes him.

Jim Crow: Dan dars a symphony between us—what am your name?

Patience: Patience!

Jim Crow: Ya, ha, ha, I know'd I war right. Dars someting about dat, you am Patience, and I should berry much like to look up and see you sitting on a monument, and, and dar is someting else but I don't recollect him just now.

Patience: Which do you prefer, Tragedy or Comedy?

Jim Crow: Oh, Tragedy, in course. Dars Otello, dat berry pleasant play, ya, ha, ha, I should like to play Otello—and smoder de white gal.

Patience: Would you? Then you're a brute.

Jim Crow: No, no brute now—nebber since de passing ob de mancipation act.

Patience: [*aside*] He can never be the rightful claimant to this property. There must be some hoax. I'll find it out: I confess I have a very favorable opinion of gentlemen of color.

Jim Crow: To be sure you hab. I am a berry nice man. Sugar candy, what am white, is berry sweet, and so is Spanish liquorice, dough it black.

Patience: Now my tall stick of Spanish liquorice, I'll give you a keep-sake if you will tell me the truth.

Jim Crow: You gib me a kiss from dem lubly lips ob yours and I'll tell you a lie, which am much more easier.

Patience: No, no, I must have the truth and nothing but the truth.

Enter Podge

Podge: Folio will be here in a few minutes and [*seeing Crow*] Ha! there's that infernal black peacock mischief! I'll listen.

Jim Crow: Now, look you, go ahead, and for a kiss I'll answer ebery ting myself.

Patience: What were you doing this morning before you came here?

Jim Crow: Why I put de polish on thirty-nine boots.

Patience: Then you're only a shoe black?

Jim Crow: Boot cleaner am more polite—pronunshyashun. I went to a gentleman's house for settlement ob my account and, instead ob paying, he said I was a man of parts and property in de mansion houses. Den he said "You must wear dem clothes," cos they are more karytyristick, and den he said you come along wid me, and den I'll gib dem to you.

Patience: And that gentleman's name is?

Jim Crow: Oh, dat berry hard name—Quiddy Quixysigh.

Podge: Yes, to be sure it is—now the villainy's out.

Patience: Ha! Here's a catastrophe! [*aside*] this will be news for Araminta. *Exit Patience*

Jim Crow: What de debil am you meaning to frighten Patience in dat manner?

Podge: Why you impudent rubber of muddy leather, get out of my house, or—

Jim Crow: [*flourishing bottle*] If you come close to me, I'll crack a bottle wid you, ober your cauliflower head.

Podge: I shall be assassinated here? Help . . . Help John, Sister, thieves! Fire! Here, you, Box, unloose Towser and Clincher.

Jim Crow: Oh cuss de dogs! And I nebber wear boots. Am dere neber no pine tree dat I can get into? Here Mass Quiddy Quixysigh . . .

Exit follow'd by Podge

✦

Scene 2. An Extensive Garden

Enter Crow in terror, dashing through windows of library

Jim Crow: Dis am berry pleasant way of getting into property. If I war in a sugar plantation, dey should nebber catch me.

Podge [*without*]: Here this way, Towser! Towser!

Jim Crow: I must get out of de way of dem damn dogs, anyhow.

Enter Podge

Podge: Ha! here he is. Now you black villain surrender yourself and go quickly to the station house.

Jim Crow: Hap I get up into dat Tree, den I talk wid you and dem dogs.

Crow attempts to get up tree but is caught in a trap. Podge, following, is shot.

Podge: I am a dead man!

Jim Crow: And so I tink I am too!

Enter Box

Box: We have got the robbers. Thieves! Thieves!

Enter Araminta, Miss Podge, and Servants

Araminta: Good heavens! It is my father!

Box [*aside*]: What? Is master the thief, after all? I'm dash'd if there isn't some of the gravel sticking in his stockings.

Miss Podge: I thought that would be the end of this. He's speechless—somebody run for a surgeon.

Patience: He's more frightened than hurt, I can see. [*aside*] Here will be an excellent opportunity for Mr. Quickset to display his versatility.

Exit Patience

Servants help Podge into chair

Jim Crow: Am nobody coming to help me? If you don't let me out ob this, I'm damn if I don't bring de matter afore de House ob Commons.

Araminta: Are you wounded, Sir?

Podge: Severely. I am the victim of a dire conspiracy to rob me of all that's dearest, my property and life.

Jim Crow: Is you going to let this leg out? You look out for de consequences. I sall bring an action for false imprisonment, 'sides de doctor's bill.

Podge: Take away that black ruffian, but keep him secure till the arrival of the police.

Box: We'll lock him up in the store room at the top of the house. [*they release Crow*]

Jim Crow: If you go to touch me I'll hollow, I will now. I'm damn if I don't alarm de neighbors. Dis am berry handsome behaviour to a gentleman, anyhow. You may laugh wid your ugly mouths, but wait till you hear what de Goberment will say to this. Oh, I hab no wish to stay in such blackguard society. You can follow at a respectful distance.

Exit Crow and Servants. Enter Patience

Patience: Ma'm here's Mr. Tourniquet, the new surgeon come to see Master.

Enter Quickset disguised

Quickset: Ladies, your most obedient! Where is the unfortunate gentleman?

Podge: Here, Doctor, here. You must know—

Quickset: I do know, I heard the account of the accident from the servants that some person or persons with malicious intent discharged a gun loaded with Swan! [*aside*] hem! *Goose*-shot[20] which unfortunately took effect—

Podge: Upon my leg, pray don't waste valuable time, Doctor, but tell me at once what I am to expect.

Quickset: True, moments are precious! I've brought my instruments in case amputation should be necessary. Don't be alarmed, I beg. I shall put you to no pain—whip off your limb as quickly as I would a leg of a roast fowl.

Podge: Whip off my leg!

Quickset: Don't talk, it may increase the fever. Let me see the full amount of injury. Compoound fracture! Simple fracture, excessive hemorrhage, excruciating ossification and—consternation!

Podge: You alarm me, Doctor, surely there's no necessity for taking off the leg?

Quickset: None in the least. Let me feel your pulse. I thought so—it is too late.

Podge: What is too late? Do you mean to say my pulse is slow?

Quickset: No, that's going at the rate of 350, but—

Podge: He shakes his head. It's all over with me. Let me know the worst, what will be the result?

Quickset: Mortification! If you have any business of moment, be brief and settle it.

Podge: Yes. Yes, fetch me pen and ink. [*Patience goes*] I've drawn up an account of the Peacock estate, but it is not signed.

Re-enter Patience

Patience: Here's the ink and a bran' new pen.

Podge: The document is in my coat pocket.

Quickset: Let me assist you [*business with papers, which Quickset switches*] [*aside*] P.O.D.G.E., what a nice short name to sign in a hurry. [*handing paper to Miss Podge:*] Perhaps, Ma'am you'll be kind enough to add your name as a witness.

Podge: That's not requisite.

Quickset: You had better not say anything. You'll have enough to talk about bye and bye. Now, I'll subscribe for you, and in a couple of days you will be better than ever you were in your life.

Podge: *What?* Did you say this instant it would end in *mortification?*

Quickset: Yes, rapid, extensive, deadly mortification. [*throw off wig*] And when I tell you I am Quickset, that you have given your consent to my marriage with your daughter, I think you must allow that my prophecy will be fulfilled to the letter!

Podge: Oh, why wasn't I killed?

Enter Box

Box: Oh Lord! Here's another catastrophe; plenty of work for the coroner. The poor nigger, Sir—

Podge: I'm glad to hear it. Let somebody suffer besides me.

Box: I think his sufferings be all *over.* We lock'd him in at the top of the house, and he tried to make his escape out of the window, but his foot slipped and he has fallen slap through the new hot house that they're building at the next house—seventy feet at least.

Quickset: Poor devil! He must be injured, run to his assistance and bring him here.

Exit Box

Jim Crow: [*without*] Oh dat's de cuss place where do grow de dam big rat traps. They nebber catches me dere again.

Miss Podge: There, I foretold it all. I knew, Mr. P., that you would be foiled. You'll never get over this!

Podge: But I will though, if it's only to annoy you. You think that I'll not acknowledge their marriage, but I will. What do you say to that?

Quickset: I will answer for her. It is a very sensible resolution. And one for which she will forgive you. Have you anything to say on the subject? [*to Araminta*]

Araminta: Why I always say, As Papa says—when it pleases me.

Podge: Then take her hand Mr. Q, and you shan't want something handsome to keep the wolf from the door.

Quickset: Sir, I love your daughter sincerely, and I will endeavour to make her a worthy husband though I have the candour to confess it will give one great pleasure to find you a willing party to the contract. Whenever you sign your name it is in letters of gold.

Enter Crow, Box, and Footman

Jim Crow: You will hear of dis affair agen, I can tell you dat. If de British Parliament do not take it up, I'll send a letter to de President of dem United States, or it may 'casion a war.

Quickset: I fear you had a tumble, Mr. Crow. I hope you didn't hurt yourself.

Jim Crow: No, but I hurt de ground. I fell on de top ob my head and I'm sartin sure I made a hole large enough for a fish pond.

Quickset: Ha, ha, ha, you must have a powerful head.

Jim Crow: Look here, Mister Quiddy-quick, you am fine chap to make fun, but you mustn't hab de laugh at me—am I Misser Peacock or Misser Crow? Dough when I survey myself, I tink I am rader more ob de Magpie.

Quickset: I believe your affinity to the Peacock tribe must be confined to the feathers. Content yourself with being Jim Crow, the veritable Jim Crow.

Jim Crow: But am de property to persist in noting but steel traps and smokey lime?

Quickset: My good fellow, I must undeceive you. You have no more claim upon the property than I have. I set you up as a claimant to impose upon this worthy gentleman.

Jim Crow: What, make me a poster?[21] Damn your imperance.[22] If I had got my boots here I'd stick him up six oder more for dat.

Quickset: He has been kind enough to relent and forgive my impudence, and I'll take care that a handsome compensation shall be made to you for your trouble.

Jim Crow: Yes, pretty well, I tank you. When a gentleman's leg and two iron bars try which of 'em de strongest?

Quickset: I'm very sorry.

Jim Crow: So am I. I should be better if you'd pay me de Two pounds, fifteen you owe me.

Quickset: Hush! Don't expose me. That pretty little girl behind you is about to become my wife, and the father's very rich. Consider that I owe you Twenty pounds.

Jim Crow: Twenty pounds! How many pair will dat make. I must get anoder book for you.

Quickset: Many things have occurred this morning of which you, and I, and our friends opposite better keep secret from the family. Ladies and Gentlemen you have witnessed our pranks will you favor us by over looking the little irregularities of my self and dark friend?

Jim Crow: Stop, Mr. Quiddy Quick! Ebery one for himself. I hab noting to do with your regularities. Don't forget dat twenty pounds and de balance ob accounts. If de pretty ladies and good gentlemans what I see before me hab laugh'd at dem misfortunes what hab happened to Jim Crow, him am quite delighted. But wedder

him Peacock or Crow, when he do take wing, he hope him will eber
fly away wid your good opinion.

Finale

Applaud kind friends before you go
The Peacock and the Crow.
You dispense both weal and woe—
The sentence let us know.
We trust success will meet no foe,
But cheer the Peacock and the Crow.

Curtain

JIM CROW IN HIS NEW PLACE
A Burletta in One Act[1]

Scene 1. An Apartment. Enter Sir Solomon *and* Deborah

Sir Solomon: You are, then, the last of my servants, the only one I have now to wait upon me.

Deborah: I am, Sir Solomon, they're all gone; and I wouldn't for the world repeat what they said of you—but I dare not repeat the shocking expressions, for the world.

Sir Solomon: But I insist upon it that you do, Deborah.

Deborah: Oh, since your honor is determined to be horrified until the very hairs of your wig shall stand on end, as the poet says, "Like quills upon a fretful porcupine,"[2] I suppose I must comply. Well then, the butler said you were a drunken Old Brute, and would guzzle up all the wine in Christendom to your own share. Then Thomas the groom said you were an old Rogue. The footman asserted you were a most abominable Swindler, and Sally the chambermaid said she could prove you no better than a Vile Seducer.

Sir Solomon: She did? The baggage! And what did you answer, Deborah? Did you not heroically take my part?

Deborah: To be sure I did, Sir Solomon. I spoke my mind in pretty plain terms. Sally, says I, as to what you say about our worthy Master, being a Seducer of Innocence, that I deny, for myself am a living example of the contrary—he never seduced *me* from the paths of virtue, but always proved to me in moments of temptation a father and a friend. But I hope you'll soon get some more servants, for one pair of hands will never be able to do all the work of the house. I declare, I am so bewildered that I shouldn't at all wonder if seduction or some other terrible calamity was to happen to me. [*Knocking and Ringing*] Coming! Coming! I must run, for, if it should be Mr. Grub, the lawyer, 'twould be terribly expensive to keep him waiting—he'd be sure to charge six and eight pence for every knock. [*Knock*] Coming! Coming! [*Exit.*]

Sir Solomon: Now then for a legal consultation with my solicitor on a matter of the utmost importance to my happiness.

Enter Mr. Grub

Sir Solomon: Mr. Grub, pray be seated. I wish to consult you professionally on a most interesting subject. [*They sit*] You are aware, Sir, that I am the guardian to the only daughter of the late Alderman Goggleton, the young and beautiful Arabella. Now, you must know Miss Arabella has had the audacity to fall in love with a young man—a sort of a deputy music and dancing master. One of those nondescripts who carry all their recommendatory qualifications outside.

Mr. Grub: If I can clearly comprehend your somewhat dark and ambiguous phraseology, Sir Solomon, the young spark who has contrived to kindle a flame in the heart of your ward is of a prepossessing exterior, but empty within, both in pocket and brains. And, as you have some more worthy match for the young lady in view, some rich citizen like yourself, or mayhaps some sprig of nobility who expects to pop into a snug government situation, and that you want me to draw up the marriage contract—eh, ah! You're a sly old fox, up to a thing or two, I see.

Arabella *enters & listens*

Arabella: What can those two old foxes be laying their heads together about—I'll listen.

Sir Solomon: Here, Mr. Grub, is the rough draught of the contract, so get it engrossed in proper form, according to law.

Mr. Grub: It shall be done. Let me see, who are the contracting parties? [*reads*] Contract of marriage entered into between Arabella, daughter to the late Alderman Gobbleton, and Sir Solomon Slygo —Eh! What do I see, Eh! Impossible. Do then my eyes deceive me, and do you really intend to lead the charming Arabella to the altar?

Arabella: [*aside*] Here's a discovery! Oh! the unconscionable old Turk!

Sir Solomon: Now, Mr. Grub, having received your instructions, hasten home, get the contract drawn up and see that it be ready by this time tomorrow for the signatures of myself and—

Arabella: [*coming forward*] Arabella. Ha! ha! ha!

Sir Solomon: Why, you impertinent young hussy! So you've had the audacity to act the listener, eh?

Arabella: To be sure I had. Now, dear Sir Solomon, it shall have a new doll. I mean a new wife, to comfort it, that it shall, Ha! ha! ha!.

Sir Solomon: Odds[3] fire and fury, Miss Saucebox! Have you then lost all respect for the authority of a guardian?

Arabella: Have you lost all respect for the memory of your poor dear dead and gone wife? If she were alive now, she'd read you a most impressive lecture. I think I hear her now.

Sir Solomon: Where, where?

Arabella: And depend upon it, if she were present her lecture to you would be illustrated by some very striking arguments. You understand me?

Sir Solomon: To my sorrow, but happily the days are past and gone for ever. So I may as well pop the question at once, as the saying is. Will you consent to sign the marriage contract when drawn up and renounce the beggarly Henry Seymour, and become for life the second Lady Slygo!

Arabella: In plain English—will I make a most egregious fool of myself?—never!

Sir Solomon: Then you remain lock'd up in your chamber for the next twenty hours at least and have nothing but bread and water. So get along with you into your room, I say.

Arabella: I go, because I know I must obey you for a time—until I get married. But if you give me nothing but bread and water for the next month, I'll never sign the contract, that I won't.

Sir Solomon: To your room, I say, this moment.

Arabella: Oh, my dear Henry, if you knew what I suffered for your sake from the ugly cross, ill-natured, cantankerous old—

Sir Solomon: Damn it, get along, do. [*forces her into room*] Oh dear! Oh dear! If it wasn't for her fortune, she might marry Tom the Tinker, for aught I care.

Mr. Grub: Really, Sir Solomon, if you'd take my advice, you'd have nothing to do with this virago, who will very likely prove a second edition of your defunct wife, Lady Sligo, who as you must allow was—

Sir Solomon: The very devil. I fancy I hear her tremendous voice now ringing in my ears—

Deborah enters

Deborah: I said, Sir Solomon, one pair of hands could never do the work of this house. You must get some more servants, or you'll have me laid up, and then what will you do? Bless me, don't I smell a smell—I must run and look. I'm really afraid the chimney is on fire. [*Exit*]

Sir Solomon: Do you happen to know any one, Mr. Grub, whom you can recommend to me?

Mr. Grub: Why, yes, I certainly do know one, a sort of a Jack of all trades—a fellow who can turn his hand to anything, and one who will obey his employer's instructions to the very letter; so much so, that he often commits the most ludicrous blunders. He occasionally goes on messages for me and I expect him to meet me here with my letters from the Post Office. Apropos you've no objection to his being a man of color—the individual I speak of being an emancipated Negro from New York?

Sir Solomon: Not in the least. I care not a straw what color he is, black, white, or brown, so he does but obey my orders to the very letter, I am satisfied.

Mr. Grub: On that, Sir Solomon, you may rely.

Jumbo Jum [*without:*] Master Lawyer Grub upstairs, you say? Bery well, Madam, him step up and speak wid him.

Jumbo Jum enters

Mr. Grub: Well, Jumbo, is the mail arrived? Any letters for me?

Jumbo Jum: Don't know, Massa. Him tell Jumbo to go and see if de mail come in. But him not tell Jumbo to ax for him letters, Master—

Mr. Grub: Jumbo, I've got an excellent situation for you here in the family of my worthy friend Sir Solomon, so mind you are attentive, in order that you may fully justify my recommendations.

Jumbo Jum: Tank you, Master, Jumbo always do exactly what him bid. 'Pend upon it.

Mr. Grub: Sir Solomon, I must step to the post office myself. A very good day to you, Sir Solomon. [*Exit*]

Sir Solomon: Hark ye, my good man, pray what's your name?

Jumbo Jum: Him name Jumbo Jum, Master.

Sir Solomon: Jumbo Jum, I shall take you into my service and give you good wages, provided you do exactly what I order you. Now, in the first place, as my house and the surrounding country is sadly infested with disorderly characters, I desire you to have an eye upon them. So, mind you, have your eyes on all disorderly characters who may be seen lurking about my house. And as I am a man of the strictest morality and decorum I will not suffer any loose women on my premises on any account—mind that, Jumbo Jum.

Jumbo Jum: Him sure to look after de loose women, Master.

Sir Solomon: And hark ye, Jumbo, as the season is advancing, I wish you to hire a few more hands to work in the park and finish digging the fish pond I began last autumn.

Jumbo Jum: How many hands, Master?

Sir Solomon: Why, let me see, five good hands will be sufficient, stout good laborers, d'ye hear? And if, as they proceeds with the execution, they should happen to meet with any rare geological specimens—mind you preserve them for my museum. And now, as business calls me from home for a short period, I leave you to follow my directions. [*aside*] Thank goodness I have a servant at last who will implicitly obey his master's orders.

Exit Sir Solomon

Jumbo Jum: Jumbo hab got plenty to do, anyhow, and, as him always like to hab ebery ting in black and white, him write down all master's orders, dat him no forget. [*sits at table and writes*] Dat all right, him make no mistake now at any rate. Jumbo quite in luck's way, got new master, plenty ob work, and when him work done, him get plenty money, ha! ha! ha!

Song—Jumbo

"Sich a Gittin' Up Stairs"

Sich a gittin' up stairs and play pon de fiddle,

Sich a gittin' up stairs, I neber did see.

etc.

Exit Jumbo

Enter Deborah *and* Henry Seymour

Henry: Well, but my sweet, interesting Deborah, procure me a few moments interview with my adored Arabella, and I ask no more.

Deborah: Well, well, I sympathise with poor distressed lovers, having myself a heart susceptible of the tender passion. I will therefore procure for you an interview, though if Sir Solomon were to know of it, he'd discharge me on the spot.

Henry: Well then, where is she, my dear Arabella?

Arabella *without sings*

I'd be a butterfly born in a bower

Where roses and lilies and violets meet

etc.

Henry: Ah, that's her voice. Come forth, beloved, 'tis thy Henry calls.

Arabella: I can't get out, I'm locked in.

Henry: I'll break open the door, I'll—

Deborah: Hold, Sir! If you proceed to violence, I shall scream out. I hate all kind of violence. No man should kiss me, no, not if he were as big as Goliah.*

Henry: Well, then, my amiable Deborah, what is to be done?

Deborah: Be calm, and I'll assist you, my master has entrusted me in my official capacity as housekeeper with this master key. A five minutes interview, d'ye hear, and no longer. [*opens door*]

Arabella *comes out.*

Arabella: Thank goodness the bird has flown at last.

Henry: Now, if my dear Arabella has no objection to a fond and doting husband, she will not hesitate to follow him at once to joy and happiness.

Arabella: With all my heart, come my dear Henry.

Deborah: But what in the world will become of my reputation with Sir Solomon?

Arabella: Never fear, Deborah, if my guardian should discharge you, come to my house, when I am Mrs. Henry Seymour, and I'll provide for you, won't we Harry?

Henry: To be sure, we will. The poor old soul shall never want a crust as long as she's got a tooth to nibble it. So, come my angel! Let us fly to church.

Exit with Arabella

Deborah: What's to be done. I must alarm the house, the neighborhood! What ho! help! robbery! abduction! seduction! Help!

Runs off

➤◄

Scene 2. A park. Enter Jumbo Jum *with a pail, scrubbing brush, etc.*

Jumbo Jum: Him done part of him work already, and now for de rest. De five extra hands come presently to work in de park. Ah! Who comes here? A woman in great fright. Him no like her look, so him step behind dat tree and hab both his eyes on her as Master order. [*retires*]

Deborah *enters*

Deborah: They're gone off as clean as a whistle, what will Sir Solomon say when he comes to hear of it?

Jumbo Jum [*coming forward:*] What your business here? Him no like your looks.

Deborah: Not like my looks? My looks are as good as yours, at any rate, I should suppose.

Jumbo Jum: No matter for dat, you be loose woman, at any rate.

Deborah: What? I? A loose woman? Oh, you good for nothing fellow to dare to traduce my character.

Jumbo Jum: Him no seduce your character. Him say you're loose woman and Massa order him to tie up all loose women so him take de liberty to tie you up. [*ties her to tree*]

Sir Solomon enters

Sir Solomon: Why, what in the world is the meaning of all this?

Jumbo Jum: Dere be loose woman, Master, running bout de park, so him tie her up as you order him. Jumbo Jum always do as him bid.

Sir Solomon: Why, that's my housekeeper, Deborah. Jumbo, this is a mistake—let poor Deborah loose by all means [Jumbo *lets her loose*] Here, Deborah, you must overlook this little blunder of honest Jumbo Jum.

Deborah: Jumbo Jum, indeed, and nicely Mr. Jumbo Jum has jumbed me, I think.

Jumbo Jum: No, Missee Deborah, dat false, Jumbo Jum neber jumble[5] nobody and ticklar[6] not de ladies. Him dreadful deal too modest. De bery thought of such a ting make him ready to blush all ober.

Deborah: Yes, like a japanned[7] Tea Pot.

Sir Solomon: There now, no more about it. Go indoors, Deborah, and in consideration of the flurry and agitation you have been thrown into by this untoward accident, I allow you before dinner to take two glasses of cherry brandy, but no more, you keep the keys, you know.

Deborah: Many thanks, Sir Solomon for your kindness. [*aside*] what a dreadful explosion there will be when he finds his ward is gone. [*Exit.*]

Sir Solomon [*to Jumbo:*] Why, what the Devil are you about?

Jumbo Jum: Him scour de country, as you order him, but him soon wear out all de scrubbing brushes.

Sir Solomon: I didn't mean scrubbing the country. I only wish'd you to look after the poachers. Will you stay where you are and leave the scrubbing brushes alone. Tell me, Jumbo Jum, have you hired the laborers I ordered you?

Jumbo Jum: Yes, Master, all right, and here dey come.

Three laborers enter, one with one hand

Sir Solomon: Yes, these will do very well, they seem good stout workmen. But, Jumbo, this one has got but one hand.

Jumbo Jum: Him know dat bery well, Master, and great deal ob trouble him hab to find him. Master ordered Jumbo to order five extra hands and a hard job him find it to get dem. So him went to de hospital and ax'd Doctor to recommend him some man wid only one hand, what want a job, and so him pick out dis poor fellow, at last.

Two and two make four and one make five. Jumbo always do as him bid, Master.

Sir Solomon: My patience is exhausted with this fellow's literal obedience. Hark ye, Mr. Jumbo, if you go on jumbling and blundering so—

Jumbo Jum: Beg pardon, Master, him do exactly what him bid. You order five hands and here dey are.

Sir Solomon: Zounds, you blockhead, five hands signify five men all the world over. But I see it is in vain to argue with such a numbskull, so I must settle the point at once. There, these two able bodied men may go to work, and as for this cripple, this one-handed fellow, he may be off about his business.

One-handed laborer: And who is to pay me for my loss of time in coming here?

Sir Solomon: Not I [*retires up*]

Jumbo Jum: Poor fellow! Perhaps him got nothing for dinner or supper for him poor wife and children. Jumbo got half a crown here, and him no want money, now him got in good situation. Here, poor man, buy someting for him children. Jumbo Jum gib it him wid all him heart.

Laborer: God bless you. God bless you. [*Exit*]

Sir Solomon: I am determined to lead this life no longer and as my ward Arabella refuses to become Lady Sligo the Second, Egad, I'll e'en make a choice elsewhere, and keep her out of her fortune by way of chastisement for her impertinence. Egad! It's a droll idea, and now at once to put it into execution. Hark ye, Jumbo!

Jumbo [comes forward]: Yes, master.

Sir Solomon: Have you any taste for beauty, Jumbo?

Jumbo Jum: Oh, bery great, Master, him eat the red herrings for him breakfast dis morning and em taste bery nice, Master.

Sir Solomon: I mean female beauty, you blockhead.

Jumbo Jum: And Jumbo Jum, too, all three be female herrings. Jumbo Jum know dem by de hard roes—oh, so nice.

Sir Solomon: Female herrings? I mean females of a far more noble species than red herrings: ladies, girls, women.

Jumbo Jum: What *loose* women, Master!

Sir Solomon: No, women tied up and be hanged to you. Now listen to me, and presume not to utter a syllable until I have given you my positive. My late wife being dead, I am resolved to marry again, but as the most prudent generally make the worst choice in the grand bazaar of matrimony, I intend to leave the choice of my future better half entirely to you, Jumbo. Go therefore and among the fair Ladies you may happen to meet, select and conduct to my expecting arms my future bride. Speak, Sable Ambassador of Cupid, what hast thou to say to my proposal?

Jumbo Jum: Him do him best, but what kind of a lady you like for your wife, Master?

Sir Solomon: A very prudent question, Jumbo. I see we shall agree admirably well, after all. The lady must be interesting and above all things have a bright, sparkling eye, and a handsome leg and foot. And now having given you your instructions, I shall wait the result in my study. Hark ye, Jumbo, a bright sparkling eye. No, hang it, *two* bright sparkling eyes and *two* handsome legs and feet. So, mind Jumbo what I order you, for on your judgment and good taste depends my future happiness, and if you succeed to my wish, I'll give you a hundred pound note for your reward.

Jumbo Jum: Jumbo always lub ebery ting in black and white, if you please, Master.

Sir Solomon: With all my heart. There, Jumbo, and now to your task without delay. Recollect, two bright eyes and all the sweet etceteras of love. Adieu, Jumbo Jum and success attend you. [*Exit*]

Jumbo Jum: Well, now before I go and find the lady dat Master wants, I'll just amuse myself wid jumping Jim Crow.

Song

Jim Crow

Here's the old Virginian, and he wants to let you know
That he'll wheel about and turn about and jump Jim Crow
etc.

Exit

Jumbo Jum *re-enters with band box*

Jumbo Jum: Jumbo got to take dese tings to get mangled[8] for de housekeeper, him to go to Mrs. Jenkins, 24 Crooked Lane, and him to get for him reward a sop in de pan. Well here goes, then. [*Exit*]

✦

Scene 3. A Street. Enter Lady in White *and* Sally Snowball

Lady: The reason, Sally, why I conceal my features is best known to myself, you know well who I am and will allow I have more cause than ordinary for such mystery.

Enter Jumbo Jum

Jumbo Jum: Oh! Eh, why what him see before him eyes! Him own dear darling, lubly little Sally Snowball. Why, how in de world you come all de way from New York, Sally?

Sally: Sally come wid dat Lady.

Jumbo Jum: And dat Lady be? [*she whispers to him*] Eh! what, oh, dat capital! Glorious news. Madam, will you allow me to hab the honor to exhort you to your hotel? Dis way, dis way. Him got wonders to tell you as you walk along. Dis way, dis way.

Exeunt

✦

Scene the Last. *Sir Solomon's Study.*

Sir Solomon: Ah! I hear footsteps. It is, it must be Jumbo, and with him no doubt this divinity, this Goddess, who

Jumbo *enters*

Jumbo Jum: All right, Master, Jumbo bring you home such beautiful Lady, she got two eberyting, Massa, and here she come.

Lady in White *enters,*
followed by all the Characters, Lady is veil'd

Sir Solomon: Why conceal thy beauty beneath this envious veil, lovely fair one, as my second spouse? Therefore unveil, and let thy enraptured bridegroom gaze upon thy heavenly charms.

The Lady unveils

Omnes: Lady Sligo!

Lady: Yes, it is indeed the much deeply-injured Lady Sligo, whose life was providentially spared to return to England and take most exemplary vengeance on that old driveller yonder. So you meant to marry again, eh? You hypocrite, there is only one condition on which I'll forgive you and that is that you consent to your ward, Arabella, marrying young Henry Seymour.

Sir Solomon: Oh! by all means, Lovey! Go and let Arabella out, d'ye hear.

Deborah: The bird has already flown, Sir Solomon.

Henry: Yes, to the fond arms of a doting husband.

Sir Solomon: What? married already? Here's treachery.

Lady: Now, restore to the young woman her fortune this moment, or tremble for your ears.

Sir Solomon: By all means, my Sugar Plum. Now do you really think I could ever have dreamt of marrying a second wife, my angelical Lady Sligo?

Jumbo Jum: Please gib Jumbo Jum him hundred pound note. Here is de written promise. Jumbo always lub to hab ebery ting in black and white, you know.

Sir Solomon: Go to the Devil!

Mr. Grub: Nay, justice compels me to interfere. If you demur, Jumbo can sue for damages.

Sir Solomon: Here's the reward.

Jumbo Jum: Now him make him dear little Sally Missus Jumbo Jum, tonight before tomorrow.

Deborah: And as I, of course, wish to appear to the best advantage at the wedding, and above all on the return of my worthy Lady, now, Jumbo, where are all my things you took to Mrs. Jenkins? Are they well mangled by her?

Jumbo Jum [*giving box:*] Now Jumbo mangle 'em all himself, Missy Deborah. Here de gown and here de petticoat and here [*business*]

Deborah: Mercy on me! What do I see! My best gown and petticoat. Oh! I shall faint! Go into hysterics on the spot.

Jumbo Jum: Well, look in the dictionary. Dere's de word. Mangle. To tear tings to pieces. And Jumbo to make amends for him mistake buy Deborah another new. No matter.

Sir Solomon: Don't mention a word on that topic. I'm sick of the very thought of it.

Jumbo Jum: Don't be angry, Massa, him always obey your orders. And him hope he shall have a great many calls from de friends him see before him.

Curtain.

❧ THE FOREIGN PRINCE ❧
A Burletta in One Act[1]

Characters in order of appearance:

Jim Crow	
Dabble	An acquaintance of Jim's, a con artist
Letty	Maid to Miss Emily
Barney	Servant
Emily	Dawkins's daughter
Ebenezer	Acquaintance of Dawkins, in league with Dabble
Dawkins	Emily's father
Mrs. Mouldem	Dawkins's sister, Emily's aunt. Widow.
Milkman	Policeman
Stagem	
Mrs. Crow and children	

Scene 1. St. James's Park by Spring Gardens. Jim Crow *discovered sitting on a bench.*

Jim Crow: Berry pretty situation for Gemman sich as me—money all gone, clothes in a consumption, shoes out at em elbows. And I out ob luck. That cow munch, munch all day and neber say hab you a mouth? When I was piccaninny my moder used to say—my fader great Prince in Africa. Golly! tink ob dat, a son of a Prince in St. James Park widout a penny in his pocket. Wid my person and 'compliments, I ought to make a conquest. But de white trash gals go by and neber look at me. I'd cry myself if I had but a bell: "Oh yes, oh yes, Who'll marry a Foreign Prince? Six feet three long, two feet six broad. A good standing color and warranted to wash."

Dabble enters

Dabble: What's all this noise about, you nigger?

Jim Crow: Nigger! Who you am call "nigger"? [*recognizing him*] What, am dat you, Massa Dabble?

Dabble: What? Jimmy! My length of ebony, how are you?

Jim Crow: How am I? Ha! ha! How am yourself?

Dabble: So so. When I last saw you in New York matters were going on swimmingly but your precious Yankees couldn't see the beauty of my schemes—so I was popped into prison. But mum as to that.

Jim Crow: Mum in Yankee prison. I know that berry well. Dey put you on what my wife would neber consent to—de silent system. But I've left her now. She bother me wid her relations; her fader came to 'monstrate wid me about his daughter's jealousy. Ben I say, look you here, your daughter hab berry handsome husband, she must 'spect oder ladies will fall in lub wid my person and figure. Besides, I say, I spring from royalty.

Dabble: I remember you told me your father was an African Prince,

Jim Crow: Yes Sar! And I am now come over here to captivate English lady.

Dabble: And a very good figure you are for the part. But now, Jimmy, I have a scheme that will make your fortune, my boy. I'll introduce you as a Prince in disguise.

Jim Crow: But I neber can go to Court in this dress.

Dabble: There'll be no going to Court in the matter—except going to court a very pretty girl, daughter to a man who wishes her to be nobly married. I'll say you're travelling *incog.*

Jim Crow: Cog—who's he?

Dabble: Psha! You come hither to observe the customs of England by the desire of your Father, King of—. I have a friend deep in the old man's confidence who can make him swallow anything.

Jim Crow: Massa Dabble, introduce me to your friend. P'rhaps he'd make me swallow something for I am had no breakfast.

Dabble: Join me in my scheme—you shall. Is it a bargain?

Jim Crow: It am.

Dabble: Well, then! There's a sovereign to bind it. Don't be frightened, it's a good one.

Jim Crow: Ebery body know dat de *English* sovereign is a good one.

Dabble: Well, then, enquire for me at the Castle and Ball[2] in an hour, adieu! [Exit R.H.]

Jim Crow: Lookèe, now let me see, if I commit polly-bigamy? Leave Mrs. Crow and my little mahogany piccaninnies? I must, I must. I hab disgrace my family, but dat low marriage. I was born for a great man and I shouldn't wonder but England 'preciate my talents, make me first Lord of de Treasury and Chancery of de Chequer into de bargain.

Song—Jim Crow's Budget

It's very true, in state affairs I haven't had much practice.
Yet I've a pretty knack, you'll find, at large on the taxes.
I'll lay a tax on slanderous words and those who heard
    and spoke 'em.
I'll lay a tax on light cigars and little boys that smoke 'em.
    etc.

Exit R.H.

➔◄

Scene 2. An Apartment

Enter Letty and Barney

Letty: Don't pester me. I tell you, I look higher, Sir. You know your master has long since said that Miss Emily shall marry a Lord.

Barney: Aye. Lord knows who, I reckon.

Letty: Then I shall be my Lady's Lady! Do you think I can have anything to say to one who sprang from the plough tail?

Barney: I wish I'd stuck at plough tail 'stead of dangling arter your'n. Now I work hard and never sleep. I keep awake all night like a lunacy chap athinking of you.

Letty: How romantic!

Barney: I don't know about 'mantics, but I know it's very uncomfortable. But, now Letty, wean't you say you'll ha'e me? I be a steady lad.

Letty: Very.

Barney: And lasses down in our parts do say I'm main pratty.

Letty: Oh! very.

Barney: Well, I'm sure thee's turn'd crazy. There's thee and young missus gets reading and crying like a couple of watering pots all day.

Letty: Well, I love elegant recreations. My taste is Miss Emily's. Oh! it's melting to hear her warble the songs of LaBlache and Grisi.[3]

Barney: Why the greasy[4] melodies come natural to her. Her feyther were a tallow chandler, and now he's retired and lives genteel as he calls it. He wants to make me genteel, but I defies 'em.

Letty: Uncultivated agriculturist. Alas you have no soul for music and the graces.

Barney: I don't know about graces—but I'm main fond of music. I shall never forget the first song I heard you sing.

Letty: Shall you not, my Barnaby? And what song of mine would shake you so forcibly.

Barney: Why, 'twere "All Round My Hat"[5] a pretty cutting sort o' thing.

Letty: Leave me Barney, leave me, and when next you speak of my warbling, don't mention "All Round My Hat."

[*Barney exits singing "All Round My Hat"*]

Letty: The brute to recollect it. I believe I did sing it, but that was before Miss Emily came home for good and taught me una voce pokee far and de tante papillottes—I doat on music and love.

Song

Oh! 'tis love, tis love.
That makes the world go round
Every day beneath its sway
Fools old and young abound
etc.

Emily *enters*

Emily: Oh, Letitia, I'm so happy and so's Papa. Such an event has happened. I've got a new lover, one I never saw but he has seen me. He's a great-great-great man. Guess who he is.

Letty: It's the Adelphi Giant.[6]

Emily: Psha! I don't mean a great long man but a man of title and fortune.

Letty: Gemini! Is he a Lord?

Emily: More than that.

Letty: A Duke?

Emily: More than that!

Letty: Is he a King?

Emily: No, unfortunately he's only a Prince—

Letty: Prince of where?

Emily: That we don't know. He's a foreign Prince. He saw me at the window and he's been mad ever since. I'll fly to the window, he *may* pass.

Letty: He will. Call me if his Lord is waiting with him.

Emily: I will, I will. [*Exit*]

Letty: A Prince in love with her, ha! ha! if he does but come and has a soul of sensibility, he's mine as sure as eggs are eggs.

Dawkins and Ebenezer enter

Dawkins: I don't know what she'll say to that there

Ebenezer: She'll be surprised at first. That'll wear away, and she'll fall in love with him—I'm your friend and say it.

Dawkins: You see Emily's had a boarding school edication, and in course she's a little, what do you call it?

Ebenezer: Romantic! I know it's a boarding school disorder. First hooping cough, then measles, small pox, and then romance. All young and interesting persons are given that way. I've a turn for it myself. Strike the iron while it's hot. Let Letty break it to her.

Dawkins: That never struck me. Oh, here is Letty—you're a good girl and a werry nice one too. You are not aware, Letty—

Letty: Yes Sir, I am perfectly, but is he really a Prince?

Dawkins: I believe so, but to some there might be an objection, and he happens to be—

Letty: What, what?

Dawkins: A black man . . . a sort of a . . .

Ebenezer: Blue black, now you must break this to her.

Letty: I break a black husband to her—I couldn't do it.

Dawkins: Yes, you can. Don't blab it all at once, let it out by little and little. Say he's rayther dark.

Letty: But who is he? What's his name?

Ebenezer: You'll learn all in good time.

Letty: Who can it be? It flashes across my mind. It's Edward the Black Prince. [*Exits*]

Dawkins: What will they say in Tooley Street, really, old friend, I don't know what to say for your kindness.

Ebenezer: Do you know what to do? Give your consent to my wedding your sister. Dawkins, don't sever loving souls.

Dawkins: Well, I mind I never see a Prince in my life, and in course I should like to have him for a son in law. Does he talk English?

Ebenezer: Yes, yes, that is a sort of African English.

Dawkins: But I can't talk African English. What shall I do?

Ebenezer: I'll be beside you and explain.

Dawkins: Thank ye, thank ye. A Prince for a Son in Law. Did I ever think my long dips would come to this?

Exit RH

Ebenezer: I must keep up the deception of this Sable Prince or else all the fat's in the fire. So, here are my confederates.

[*Enter* Jim *and* Dabble]

Jim Crow: Ha! Ha! My legs don't know one anoder in dese silks. I shall ride about in three hackney coaches—one for my cane, 'toder for my hat, and the third for myself.

Dabble: Guard against discovery—if he asks any awkward question break into the gibberish I taught you.

Jim Crow: Lordy! Leave me alone—I'll boder his old rig. I'll talk what I don't understand myself and no one else can understand, but how am I do to if de lady fall violently in lub wid me?

Dabble: Don't alarm yourself. To *that* complexion she'll come at last. Now, for it, they come.

[*Enter* Dawkins, Emily, Ebenezer, Mrs. Mouldem, *and* Letty]

Dawkins: Most noble Prince. I feels on this occasion that the obligation is such that—

Jim Crow: De honor all on my side. How am you, old fellow? What a lubly creature. [*laughs and whistles*]

Dawkins: What does he mean by that?

Ebenezer: An African Prince always makes that noise when he falls in love.

Jim Crow: Berry delighted man to be happy to see you. Oh! Ladies, if you were to wander in my lubly country—not like dis London, bere you am run ober ten times a day by dose omnibusters, dere am de beautiful walks wid de lion and de tigers and de hippopotamus frisking before you. So I be come to lay all my beasts—serpents and crocodiles, at your lubly feet.

Letty: She'll be able to set up a new theological garden.

Jim Crow: Allow me to hab de inexpressable felicity.

[*taking* Emily's *hand*]

Ebenezer: And permit me the exquisite sensation [*taking the hand of* Mrs. Mouldem]

Dabble: And me the inconceivable delight [taking the hand of Dawkins]. [They exeunt with great ceremony]

Letty: What a charming man the Prince is—quite out of the common way. [*Jim heard singing*] That's his charming voice. He comes this way! What an elegant gait he has, swinging from one side to the other. As Captain Macheath says in *The Beggar's Opera,* "This way and that way, and which way you will."[7] [*Retires*]

[*Enter* Jim Crow]

Jim Crow: Berry agreeable family I'm got into. I hab frightened old womans. Golly, I do feel so odd—wine always rouse de tender sediment. Dat was berry pretty girl I see as I come in, she's de young woman for me.

Letty: Oh! my palpitating perri-*cranium*—Sable and sentimental Prince. I am your devoted servant.

Jim Crow: Ha! ha! you lubly creature. I 'dore you. Say can you lub me.

Letty: Oh! Consider my situation—your revered and elaborate Papa may object to de match.

Jim Crow: Object! I lick old fader any day in de week. Lookye, here. I throw myself on my knees and offer you my love.

Letty: Connubially, great Potentate?

Jim Crow: I offer you connubial hemlock.

[Dawkins, Emily, Ebenezer, Mrs. Mouldem, Dabble, *and* Barney *enter*]

Dawkins: The Prince on his knees!

Emily: Well, I never!

Dabble: Explain, Sir.

Dawkins: Oh, there needs no explanation. I'll give you a month's wages and a moment's warning. Get out.

Letty: I can't go.

Dawkins: Can't go? You shall go.

Letty: Dear Prince,

Jim Crow: I nebber interfere in family matters.

All: Oh! Away with her.

[Jim Crow *and* Ladies *Exit* RH, Dawkins *and* Letty LH]

Dabble: Hang me, if I don't think Emily has made up her mind to a black husband and a whitey brown family.

[Jim Crow *heard without laughing*]

Dabble: Here he is, and the pair of 'em hanging on his arm.

Ebenezer: Then do you go and keep the old man in tow whilst I watch here. I'm your friend and will take care of you. [Dabble *exits*] There's the widow and that long baboon grinning in her face. Suppose he prefers the widow and her ten thousand. Oh! as the man says in the play, that we sho'd call these creatures ours and not their jointures. I'll watch them at all events. [*Retires*]

[Jim Crow *enters, laughing*]

Jim Crow: It's no matter, go where I will, de lubly creatues neber can resist me. [*Sees* Ebenezer] Oh, you am dere, am you?

Ebenezer: Yes, I am. You seem very happy with those two ladies.

Jim Crow: Yes, berry.

Ebenezer: I suppose you don't mean to marry 'em both.

Jim Crow: Oh! Just as it may happen.

Ebenezer: Well, it so happens that one of the ladies is to be mine. In one word, if you will marry the youngest and leave me her aunt, I will still countenance your imposture. If not, I'll explain all to Mr. Dawkins. [*Aside:*] and now, Mr. Dabble, I've followed your example and taken care of myself. [*to Jim:*] I'm your friend and you ought to do it. [*Exit*]

Jim Crow: Ha! ha! ha! Well, before I do make up my mind about the ladies, I'll have a little getting upstairs.

Song

"Such a Gettin' Up Stairs"

[Dawkins *and* Dabble *enter after song*]

Dawkins: Werry good, but I don't understand this here.

Dabble: I say, Sir, that gentleman is making love to your daughter and her aunt at the same time.

Jim Crow [*aside to Dabble:*] What am you about? I want the old woman's and leave lilly gal for you.

Dabble: Then why didn't you explain that before?

Jim Crow: Cos of Mr. Ebenezer. [*they go up*]

[Ebenezer *enters*]

Ebenezer: The more I talk to Mrs. Mouldem, the more I doubt—if I thought you were playing false . . .

Jim Crow: 'Pon my honor.

Ebenezer: Oh, Sir. [Emily *enters*]

Dawkins: Oh, here you are. There seems to be in this here affair—a queer sort of—hey—and if your Royal Highness would just answer one or two questions?

Jim Crow: Of course him hab no 'jection.

Dawkins: Then first and foremost—are you in love with my daughter?

Dabble: I say, Mr. Dawkins, he's an imposter, and you, Mr. Ebenezer, know it as well as I—

Dawkins [*to Dabble:*] You're drunk, young fellow.

Dabble: Drunk?

Jim Crow: Oh, berry.

Ebenezer: Oh, horrid—

Dawkins [*to Dabble:*] Leave my house! Coming here and insulting his Royal Highness!

Jim Crow: I am berry great mind to scalp de vagabond.

[Dabble *exits followed by all but* Jim Crow *and* Emily]

Emily: I wish you had. I never saw a man scalped. But your Highness seems disturbed?

Jim Crow: Permit me, lubly Princess, to imprint one kiss on your ruby lips. [*Kisses her*]

[Mrs. Mouldem *enters*. Emily, *seeing her, runs off*]

Mrs. Mouldem: Delusive false one.

Jim Crow: Look'ee here. I am lub you and nobody else. Say de word and we run away dis berry night.

Mrs. Mouldem: Would you persuade me to an elopement?

Jim Crow: Yes. At ten o'clock all am ready.

Mrs. Mouldem: Impossible. My brother don't retire until eleven.

Jim Crow: Berry well. At eleven den in de hall. Good-bye, good-bye.

Mrs. Mouldem: Farewell. [*Exit*]

Jim Crow: De sooner I am out of dis place de better. So I'd better run away wid old gal at once, for I shall be found out before I can marry the young'un.

[*Exit*]

✦

Scene 3. Outside of House. Letty discovered sitting on bandbox.

Letty: Well, I suppose I must go. I'll see if there's a cab upon the stand. Perhaps, in the driver, I may find one who pities my affections, [*A milkman enters*] one with some . . .

Milkman: Milk! What, Miss Letty, whatever are you doing here?

Letty: I'll confide in you, you are a young man, but an ancient Briton. Can you procure me a lodging at about two and nine pence per week?

Milkman: Oh, yes, there's Stagem, the policeman, he'll be glad to take you. Indeed, he has asked many questions about this house. He ask'd if you had not here a black gentleman?

Letty: A black gentleman? A blackguard!

Milkman: So he said. Look you—he is after him, indeed.

Letty: Where is dear Stagem on duty?

Milkman: Three or four streets off. Shall I call you a cab?

Letty: No. I will walk. Give me that box. Come along Milk. He'll make a fool of me, will he? We'll soon see who's made the fool of.

[*Exeunt*]

✦

Scene Last. An Apartment. Jim Enters with a lantern.

Jim Crow: It am all right. Old woman's ready and we shall run away from eberybody.

[Mrs. Mouldem *enters*]

Mrs. Mouldem: H-u-sh!

Jim Crow: Dat am you, eh! Come along—

Mrs. Mouldem: Will your Highness condescend to take care of these things whilst I prepare? [*retires*]

Jim Crow: Golly! I'll take care of dem tings directly. [*going*]

[Dawkins *enters*]

Dawkins: Crikey! What, are you robbing the house? Here, Emily! Barney! [*Enter Barney*] Call a policeman, Barney.

Barney: There beant no need to call, Sir. Here be one, has called himself—

[Emily *enters*]

Emily: Dear Papa. Whatever is the matter? Prince, explain.

Jim Crow: Madiboo—how—kow—row—kow

[Mrs. Mouldem *enters*]

Mrs. Mouldem: Now—then for flight. Ah!

[*Enter* Ebenezer, Dabble, Letty, *and* Policeman]

Emily: Wretch! You was to wed me a Wednesday.

Mrs. Mouldem: And to run away with me tonight.

Police: That's the hidentical wagabond I want! You're a werry nice man to go a committing bigamy—Come in Mrs. Crow.

[Mrs. Crow *enters*]

Mrs. Crow: Oh, you false deceiving feller. Why don't you embrace your wife?

Jim Crow: Keep your mahogany hands to yourself. I neber see you in all my life—'pon my honor.

Mrs. Crow: Oh, you villain. Can you deny dese little piccaninnies? [*fetches children*]

Jim Crow: Damn'd child ob mine—dey not mine piccaninny.

Mrs. Crow: Not? Berry 'orrid dispersion ob my character!

[children *sing*]
We wer born in de Kentucky
And across de sea we go
Like Daddy we can wheel about
And jump Jim Crow

Jim Crow: Golly! Dem *am* my childs!

Dawkins: This is very pleasant. We shall be laughed at by all on Tooley Street.

Ebenezer: No, you won't. The ladies and our friends have mutually explained—forget and forgive, eh Dabble? Consent and mum—I'm your friend and advise it.

Dawkins: Well, anything for a quiet life.

Jim Crow: Quiet life! [*to the audience:*] Well, I hope the past will be forgiven and my tricks overlooked. I'm no longer a Prince. What ob dat? I'm a family man, though not a man ob family. Tink of dese beautiful babies—only smile on dem and me. And when I set up a carriage de motto shall be: While I live, I Crow.

[*Curtain*]

❦ YANKEE NOTES FOR ❧ ENGLISH CIRCULATION

A Farce in One Act[1]

Scene 1. A vestibule or hall in an American hotel at Saratoga. Bar R.H., practicable window, doors R & L leading to several rooms, names over each: "Liberty," "Eagle," "Lamb," "Tiger," etc. Bells hung against wall. A statue of Washington in a cocked hat and military coat stands in the garden at back. A sofa with cushions on. Bells all ringing when the scene opens and voices calling for "Mint Julep," "Cobbler Sherry," "Sangaree," "Gin Sling," etc. A number of persons *discovered drinking at the bar served by* Miss Zip Coon, *a mulatto girl.*

Chorus.

"Calais Packet"[2]

Now, now, why are you pausing so?
Quick, quick, you keep us too late.
Why, why! On our friends are you dawdling so?

[*large bell rings*]
Hark! The bell rings we shall all be too late.

All run off R., L., and C. Bells ring. All the doors open at once and Dorothy, Emma, Pippin, *and* Bilberry *show their heads after each other.*

Dorothy [*her hair in papers*]: Hiccory Dick,[3] some hot water [*withdraws*].

Pippin [*looking out in a red nightcap*]: That's her voice. Sweet as sugar, soft as butter, it melts in my mouth. Hiccory Dick, you nigger, my boots [*retires*].

Emma [*appears*]: My shoes, Hiccory.

Bilberry [*rushing out in his dressing gown, half shaved, face lathered, razor in hand, dragging a chair*]: You black spider, where's the news? Nice house, this, I guess. Never quiet, night or day. Bells like ring-tailed monkeys. Knockers like rattlesnakes, cats on the tiles all night, cats in the kitchen all day: won't do for me. I shall pack up and go back to New York. When I say a thing, I mean it. It won't

[326]

do at no fix. Too much go ahead work. If Sprawl had come for my gal I'd have gone before. Recommended here for health and comfort. Never had a taste of it since I put my foot inside the door. Curse boarding houses, they're all bores. So's my daughter. So's her maid. The house beats the devil. And that ugly nigger beats the house. [*Re-enters "Lamb," banging door and calling:*] Hiccory Dick!

Hiccory Dick [*heard singing without, R.H.*]:

> Yankee doodle, doodle dandy,
> Corn stalks rum and Gin Sling brandy,
> An Indine pudden and a green peach pie
> Golly, how we make de British fly.

Hiccory Dick *enters carrying boots, shoes, hot water, and a newspaper.*

Hiccory [*throwing Boots at the "Lion" door*]: Dere's de boots for de Lion, shoes for de Lamb, water for de Tiger, and news for ma self [*sits on chair*]. What a debil ob a ouse dis is, nebber satscumfied. I'll look out for anoder place, too much work for me. Heaps ob white trash boarders. Eight in de Lion, six in de Lamb, den dere's ten in one attic, ten in anoder. I'm poked up in de cock loft, where all de rats and mice come when dere biggerest—and bite de harderest.

Pippin [*taking in Boots*]: Hiccory you're a trump. [*retires*]

Hiccory: Tankee, Sar. Nice boss, dat. Plenty ob dollars. Not keep'em long I think, though one or two for ma'self, ah hope. Am berry fond ob English—dem all gentlemen like ma'self, not so proud as 'Merican white niggers—'em no respect for *us* color'd genlemen. Massa Pe-pin in lub. [*sighs*] So am I, wid berry fine gal, but berry sassy. [*Puffs his cheeks out. Reads paper. Bells ring.*] Cuss'em bells.

Bilberry [*within*]: Who the devil's been at my razors?

Hiccory [*laughs*]: By gosh! I only opened a few eyesters wid 'em last night, tenderly. Ya, ya!

Dorothy [*opening door*]: I want the hot water.

Hiccory: To *shabe* wid Missee, him afraid 'em too cold.

Dorothy: Shave! Brute. [*slams door*]

Hiccory: Sassy ooman, dat.

Emma: Am I to have my shoes today?

Hiccory: I shall hab de honor to bring 'em . . . when I hab finish'd de news, Missee. [*reads*]

Emma: This is independence with a vengeance. [*retires*]

Hiccory: Nice piccaninny dat 'em spose, she'll fall in lub wid me, like all de oder gals. [*laughs*] Golly! Yaw! Yaw! De poor tings can't help demselves, dese legs win dere hearts. [*reads*] By Gor! Anoder Ball. Almacks, Five Points, next Monday. Quality assembly, admission fifty cents. Ugh! It's too cheap and make a common niggers too familly-li-ar wid us perlite swash ci-e-ty! Vulgar critters! 'Em go, though. Gor! How 'em will dance if 'em take Miss Zip Coon, yaw, yah! Clear de kitchen! [*dances and sings*]

Song *"Clare de Kitchen"*

Pippin enters from room, and Dick stumbles against him

Pippin: Ulloa!

Hiccory: Nebber mind, don't a pol-i-cum-gize, you couldn't help it, Sar.

Pippin: Rather cool. What are you doing?

Hiccory: Practizing de Tag-li-o-ni⁴ for de next Ball.⁵ Appy to hab de onor of seeing you dere, Sar. Lubly gals dere, Sar, berry!⁶

Pippin: Free and easy, 'pon my word. How long have you served here?

Hiccory: 'Em nebber sarve, Sar, 'em only help for amoosement. No *common* nigger, 'em a prince in 'em own country.

Pippin [*laughing*]: A Prince, eh! It must be a *black* Prince then.

Hiccory: No, Sar, whitey brown. 'Em modder white and fadder brown.

Pippin: Capital, Blackee!

Hiccory: What 'em mean by Blackee, Sar? Read history. Dere you see Adam wab a colored gentleman, an' all de family till 'em catch de yellow fever and turn 'em white, yaw, yah!

Pippin: This is a regular black diamond. Harkee, Dick, do you like a dollar?

Hiccory: Issa, Massa, but 'em like two betterer.

Pippin [*gives one*]: I hope you are honest.

Hiccory: I hope yore de same, Sar.

Pippin [*pointing*]: Who's in the Tiger now?

Hiccory: A sassy ooman!

Pippin: She is a fine woman, [Hiccory *nods*] good figure, bright eyes, white teeth, clear complexion, eh?

Hiccory: Yes, Sar, just like mine.

Pippin: Yours! You dog, ha! ha! Why she's a divinity, I'm sure, by the tones of her voice. I must contrive to see her. Give this note to her unobserved and wait for an answer.

Hiccory [*laughs*]: Yagh! 'Em see, Massa, that imperent young nigger coopid as stirred up your heart wid his bow and arrow. You're in lub. 'Em know wab dat is. My heart like soft soap. [*sighs*]

Pippin: How long has *she* been here? [*points to Tiger*]

Hiccory: A week. She come wid Massa Bilberry and Missy Emma.

Pippin: And her name is?

Hiccory: Worth anoder dollar, 'em tinks, Sar. [*grins*]

Pippin: I think so, too. There, [*gives it*] now.

Hiccory: Him go and ask her! Den it will be worth anoder, 'praps.

Pippin: Stop! Stop [*holds him*]. You don't slip off so. The name—is?

Bilberry [*calling from door*]: You black rascal, am I to have the news today?

Hiccory [*laughs*]: 'Em hab de onor, Sar, ob coming up. [*sees* Miss Zip Coon *at the Bar*] Ah, Miss Looize, how you do? Pon 'em soul you more lublier den eber, dis time.

Miss Zip Coon: Massa Hiccory, you make em blush all ober like 'em Rose.

Hiccory: De color becomes your fine cum-plex-shun berry much.

Bilberry [*at door*]: Are you coming, Sir?

Hiccory: Hoosh, hoosh! Don't you see 'em busy wid de fair sexes? [*throws paper*] Take 'em, I done wid em now. Dese white trash nebber no manners.

Pippin [*laughs*]: Ha! ha!

Bilberry [*rushing out*]: I'll have you cow-skinned tarnationally for this, I will, as I am a true born American. How dare you look me in the face, eh?

Hiccory: Golly, Mister, 'em can look a wild cat in de face, and grin 'em to death after. [*grins*]

Bilberry: I'll call your master, the colonel.

Hiccory: 'Em can't come, as he up a top ob de ouse mending de chimbly and I hab tuk away de ladder. [*laughs*]

Bilberry: Pick up that paper, and fetch the breakfast things or I'll send you flying. [*threatens*]

Hiccory [*laughing, picking up paper*]: Yaw, Yah! Gor, my life! How 'em nigger a-flying widout wings would make 'em laugh! Ha, ha! [*runs into room "Liberty" followed by* Bilberry]

Pippin: And this is a specimen of the land of liberty, eh? Where every body takes liberties with every body, and all do as they please. *I* shall study to please myself, do a little trading, I calculate, and speculate on a good constitution, tolerable appearance, and a decent share of brass.⁷ My last spec in England turned out a bad one —matrimony. Caught a Tartar. Mrs. Pippin was not an angel. We differed before marriage, quarrell'd on the wedding day, and ran away from each other during the honeymoon. She walked out at the front door, I ran out of the back, and thank the stars we've never met since. With a light heart—ditto pockets—I crossed the Atlantic and have scarcely landed when a woman's sweet voice (forgetting their bitter tongues) finds its way to my heart. Ah, man's a gregarious animal and can't help it. [*whistles "Oh, 'tis Love." Sees* Miss Zip Coon] By George, that's a pretty bit of brown holland.⁸ I'll try another Julep of her mixing. Oh, Pippin, Pippin! Black, brown, or white. A petticoat has the same influence in spite of color or climate. [*Exits into bar whistling* "Oh 'Tis Love"]

Dorothy Enters from "Tiger," Hiccory with tea things from the "Liberty"

Hiccory [*calling to Dorothy*]: Missee, Missee, 'em want you. [*chuckles*]

Dorothy: Want me. Mr. Hiccory?

Hiccory: Iss, 'em got lubly lub letter for you, all sugar stick and kisses.

Dorothy: For me? Who is it from?

Hiccory: Great man, berry. Twice as big as me—English nobleman. Dat him, [*gives letter*] some white Ladies gib me two dollars for lilly one, not hab so big—

Dorothy: Do they? There's a cent. [*offers it*]

Hiccory: Nebber take coppers, Marm, nebber.

Dorothy: And I seldom give them. [*pockets money*] A letter from a nobleman to me! Goodness gracious, what does he want?

Hiccory: To make you his chum chum.

Dorothy: La, Mr. Hiccory do you think so? What a nice man you are.

Hiccory: Specially in 'em Sunday go to meeting clothes.

Dorothy: I mean you are a *fine* man.

Hiccory [*grins*]: You tink so? 'Em was too dootiful a piccaninny to be a bery fine man.

Dorothy: How so?

Hiccory: Why, you see, when 'em wab twelve years ole, Fader put him hand on 'em head and said "stop there Jul-li-cum-Caesar," den he ranned away and 'em neber see 'em since so a didn't tink it right to grow no biggerer. Any answer to dat? [*pointing to letter*]

Dorothy: I'll read it and see. Now I think of it, I have a little silver, as you dislike coppers. [*gives silver*] I'll return in a few minutes—[*exits reading letter*]

Hiccory: Wid much pleasure. Silver, [*looks at it*] 'em to't so, only tickle de ooman's fancy, and you soon tickle dere pockets, Yah! Yah! [*turns and sees Pippin endeavoring to kiss Miss Zip Coon at the bar —violently agitated*] Twenty tousand debils, wab dat? Dat white nigger kissing Miss Coon, by gor! 'Em shall go mad. I feel a steam engine a-bursting under em waistcoat. Ma head, a railroad, all fire and smoke. [*They laugh*] Oh, de 'possum down de gum tree. War shall 'em go? Wab shall 'em do? I'll hab revenge. [*Pippin kisses her*] Agin! Him take dat—[*throws tea things towards bar. Bilberry enters from room in time to receive them. Dorothy re-enters and runs to Hiccory*] Golly! I'm mad, don't you see 'em white in de face! [*stamps on floor, throws himself on sofa. Pippin comes from the bar—* Dorothy *sees him*]

Dorothy: Pippin! [*screams and runs off*]

Pippin: The devil! [*runs off L.H.*]

Bilberry: The house is going mad, they're all bitten.

   Miss Coon screams, bells ring, and the scene is closed in.

→←

Scene 2. A corridor in the hotel. Door in Flat leading to a passage. Several pictures on scene: General Washington, ships, and an old woman in a white wig. Bells ringing still. Emma *enters followed by* Bilberry.

Bilberry: It's no use. Back, back to New York you go tonight, unless Sprawl arrives. This fix won't do for me no ways, it may suit *you* but it don't suit *me*. I hate the house and hate the people. They're none of my raising. I'm the wrong sort of man for 'em, *I* am! I'm from Missisippi, I calculate. Go to your room, and prepare for our journey. [*Emma exits R.H.*] These gals are all tarnation plagued, and she's one of 'em. I opine she aint over fond of the match I've made for her with Sprawl, Junior. What odds? *I* am—and that's sufficient for both. Sprawl, Senior, and I are old friends and traders, and tho' I've never seen his son, I'm sure he's a saleable article, as we say on change, and Emma shall be duly consigned to him when he arrives, as per invoice and agreement with Sprawl, Senior and Co., of Mud River, old Kentucky. [*Miss Zip Coon enters crying.*] Another plague. This location swarms with 'em like mosquitoes. Well, what are you crying for?

Miss Zip Coon: Julius Caesar Washington Jackson Dick, La, he mak a ma heart so full ob water dat it run ober out ob my eyes, and drown ma face . . . [*wipes eyes*]

Bilberry: More fool you, wipe your eyes and forget the rascal. [*aside*] Rather a pretty bit of mahogany, this. Hem! What has the nigger done to you?

Miss Zip Coon: 'Em jealous, mad, and roll de whites ob 'em eyes about so berry much.

Bilberry: Jealousy? Bah! you're too pretty for him, Gal. Give him up.

Miss Zip Coon [*sighing*]: 'Em would if 'em could, but a can't, him have grow sich berry fine hair.

Bilberry: Hair! *Wool*, you mean. Come here, I'll soon fix you. I have taken a liking to you. I *have* my little ice crusher, and when I *do* take, it *is* a liking, I guess.

Miss Zip Coon: Lore a massy, Sa, what 'em mean?

Bilberry: Mean! Eh, why hang me if I know, but I can't help it. I can't. [*Offers to kiss her. Hiccory enters from passage.*]

Hiccory [*seeing them*]: Tunder, rattlesnakes, and brimstone wab 'em see agin! [*Stamps feet. Bilberry, disturbed, exits. Miss Zip Coon covers her face with apron.*]

Hiccory: De ole warld is a-knocking to pieces and every body is a-jumping upon eberybody's heads. [*comes down*] Oh, you white debil, I hab cotched you two times, hab I, wid de white trash. Golly, ma life! 'Em hab a mind like Massa Otello in da trashedy to gib you a slockdologer. [*raises arm*] But no, 'em too proud, got too big heart, ebber to touch a sassy ooman. I'll whistle you, I— [*blows*] dere now, you blown quite out, 'em hab done wid you for ebber. [*struts*]

Miss Zip Coon: Massa Bilberry would talk a me.

Hiccory: Why you listen for? When you hab sich a man as me to talk to? [*drags her to wing, points*] Look on dat ugly picter, den look at dis. [*puts out his head*] After all I hab done for your amoosement, too. Haben't I played all de fancy toons on da fiddle and guved up Yallar Fan, who you jealous ob, besides loads of dullars a spent in fancy balls, pepper pot, jangolango tea, dog's foot pie, and sassengas?

Miss Zip Coon: Am beg your pardon, ten hundred times ober.

Hiccory: It am no good, ma heart am turned green wid jalousy. Julicum Caesar occipation's gone[9] [*sighs*] an am nebber catch him again, nebber.

Miss Zip Coon: Let 'em expla-an-shun to you, Sa.

Hiccory: No, Miss Coon, 'em quires no ex-pla-ni-cum-na-shums. It is too much bad. [*she follows him*] Stand ob, ooman, don't come near ma. I am all red hot, biting red hot, and shall burn your fingers. Kiss 'em *white* Boss—oh, I shall as-washinate maself. [*she approaches*] Keep ob, cock-a-dil. Da Queen ma moder, killed twenty five niggers, wid her rifle, one fine morning, and I was born soon after. 'Em chock, full up ob gun powder, and may blowup. I will hab revenge. [*Hiccory strikes about his arm and breaks the picture of old Lady.* Miss Zip Coon *screams and runs off. Hiccory stands aghast then bursts into laugh.*] Gar a ma life, de ole ooman's head tumble out. Yah, Yaw! [*looks at it*] Wab I do wid 'em now? My Massa, de Conol, give me cowskin for knocking ole ooman's head off.

Dorothy [*without*]: Don't fret, I'll soon settle it for you, dear.

Hiccory [*laughs*]: Ha! ha! [*door L.H. partly opens*] Dat Lion hab a creeping out ob 'em den agin. I'll hab ma revenge now—run up against, and squeeze 'em flat in de passage! [*retires into passage, half closing door*]

Dorothy *enters R.H.*, Pippin *L.H. at same time*

Dorothy [*receding*]: Sir!

Pippin: Mrs. Pippin again, by jingo! [*turning away*]

Dorothy: What business have you here, Sir? But I can easily guess.

Pippin: Then you take more trouble than I do.

Dorothy: You are come after me, fellow.

Pippin: Just so, you came three days before I arrived. I thought you were snug in London.

Dorothy: It cannot possibly concern you where I am—just so that I never see your ugly face.

Pippin: Exactly! We are neither of us beauties.

Dorothy: Monster!

Pippin: Vixen!

Dorothy: I should have imagined after the ten months we have been separated—

Pippin: Ten! Eight, my love.

Dorothy: I say ten, Sir. Heaven knows I have reason to remember them.

Pippin: So have I, for the happiest of my life.

Dorothy: Then I trust you will immediately leave this place.

Pippin: Can't—I've only just come.

Dorothy: But I was here before you.

Pippin: Then it's your turn to go first.

Dorothy: Give way to you? Never—I'd sooner die. Yet to be obliged to live under the same roof?

Pippin: Well, the roof is large enough. Let us make the best of it. No one need know that you are my wife.

Hiccory [*aside*]: His chum-chum, golly!

Pippin: And I'm sure *I* shall be too glad to forget it. Can't leave. Capital reasons, spent all my cash and must live on my wits and I fancy this is a good spot to try them. Besides, it wouldn't be respectable to vanish so suddenly.

Dorothy: Don't talk about your respectability, Mr. Pippin, I beg you, that was brought up in a parish work house and christened at a parish pump.

Hiccory: Dat berry good! Da Pump stick in 'em t'roat.

Pippin [*laughs*]: And no child ever worked his Godfather more, or liked him less, but since you allude to my family connections, look to your own. Didn't your mother keep a mangle[10] and wasn't your father a retired smuggler, a sort of Sea Norse, with three wives in the West Indies, four in Morocco, besides bushels of children all over the world?

Dorothy [*locking door in passage*]: All the house will hear your vile falsehoods. Viper! I hate you.

Pippin: And I love you, at a distance.

Hiccory [*thrusting his head through picture*]: Da shooved ma out, so I hab shooved maself in.

Dorothy: Won't you go, Blue Beard?

Pippin: Can't afford it, Fatima.[11]

Dorothy: What shall I do? If he remains, he may discover and ruin our plans. [*aloud:*] Mr. Pippin, I know you are a man of taste.

Pippin: Doubtful, I married you.

Hiccory [*laughs*]: Yaw, Yah!

Pippin: Did you laugh?

Dorothy: No.

Pippin: I thought you did, on the wrong side of your mouth.

Dorothy: I must trust him to prevent mistakes. I know that you have talent in spite of your imperfections, also that you have been on the stage and possess powers of imitation.

Pippin: You're right, I can imitate everything from a penny trumpet to an elephant [*imitates*]

Hiccory [*aside*]: Dere's a roar for a lion.

Dorothy: Since we have jumbled[12] together, I think we can mutually assist each other before we part. Listen.

Hiccory [*aside*]: Blow'd if I don't.

Dorothy: My young Mistress, the daughter of Mr. Bilberry, is in love.

Pippin: Poor devil!

Dorothy: With a Major in the American Army. Now her father wishes her to marry a Mr. Solomon Sprawl, a silly Kentuckian booby, whom he has never seen. We are here, for the purpose of meeting him, and unless the lovely youth arrives tonight, back to New York we go.

Hiccory [*aside*]: Joy go wid you and nine pence.

Dorothy: Now if you would assist us, you shall be well paid.

Pippin: Ready money, no credit.

Dorothy: Never fear. I want you to personate this Sprawl and amuse the old Gentleman, while the . . .

Pippin: Young gentleman runs off with the girl, eh?

Hiccory [*aside*]: Dat him, Massa.

Dorothy: You hit it. The Major will be waiting in the garden at dusk to carry us off. If you should meet him, take no notice. He's in uniform—a cocked hat and military cloak.

Pippin: I see. And the rhino, I mean the pewter, the tin, for aiding and abetting . . .

Dorothy: A hundred dollars.

Pippin: Make it two, and I'm your man—just imported from old Kentucky, half horse, half alligator, and a bit of the steam boat, a regular screamer [*imitates*] I guess, oh yes!

Hiccory [*aside*]: Dat good.

Dorothy: Come with me to Miss Emma at once for the money and instructions. The clothes you can purchase at the store, over the way. Not a moment is to be lost. Come.

Pippin: I fly on the wings of love—dollars, I mean. [*going*] You ain't poking fun at me, Dolly, eh?

Dorothy: Can't you trust me?

Pippin: I did once. [*sighs*] You're sure it's all right?

Dorothy: Yes, certain.

Pippin: Honor?

Dorothy: Bright, and no . . .

Pippin: Gammon.[13]

Pippin and Dorothy run off R.H.

Hiccory <i>laughs, puts arm through picture and turns key then enters</i></div>

Hiccory: Here's a kettle ob fish! Nice boss dat Britisher, berry! I'll go and tell ole man and get de dullars maself. [*going*] No, 'em won't— 'em'll hab biggerer revenge. A'l ranned away wid de gal, Miss Embily, maself, and break Miss Coon's heart, by gosh, a will. Den dey all go mad and bite dere own heads off. [*laughs*] I'll borrow ma Massa de Colonel's militia-going cloak and cap. De Major to be in de garden at dusk. She say berry well when I am dere, it'll be quite dark. And, gor a ma life, when a git the money an de gal how a will drink, an play upon de fiddle! Such a turn about, wheel about!

Song: "Jim Crow"

End of Scene

➤◄

Scene 3. The courtyard of the hotel. House R.H., windows and door practicable, wall running from it to the L.H. An outbuilding R.H., an ice house L.H. In the centre of stage, a statue of General Washington in a military coat and cocked hat and leather. A large triangle hangs near the house with an iron to strike it.

Bilberry and Miss Zip Coon enter from house

Miss Zip Coon: Oh, goody gracey, Massa, 'em couldn't for all de world.

Bilberry: Stuff, moonshine. You be at the General's. [*gives dollar*] There's a dollar to keep your memory from going.

Miss Zip Coon: Em take 'em dullar, and tell Massa Dick.

Bilberry: I want . . . [*takes her hand*]

Pippin [heard without]: In the Garden is he? I'll be with him in the sprinkle of an earthquake. I'll go right ahead like a ring-tailed roarer and a screamer.

Pippin enters dressed as a Kentuckian. He smacks his whip.

Miss Zip Coon runs off

Bilberry: What wild horse is this?

Pippin: I calculate you're old Bilberry and my gal's father. I'm Silas Solomon Sprawl, Junior, a spry, slick, upright and down-straight, no-mistake Kentuckian, full of right stuff, and no outside. I can climb when no man can follow and my arm is entire iron grates, I guess—nothing but a vice made double-strong on purpose can make me leave go, when I lay hold. [*seizes Bilberry's hand and shakes it heartily*] Oh no!

Bilberry [*withdrawing his hand*]: I'm glad to see you, Solomon. Your father's well, I hope? [*Pippin nods*] and your mother?

Pippin: Oh, yes—and the pigs, tho' the critters have a dash of the measles just now.

Bilberry: I calculated you'd have been here before now to see Emma.

Pippin: I guess I should, Father, but for the tarnation ugly fogs down East[14] They're so plaguey thick, you can't get thro' 'em no ways, unless you cut your way with a knife. Why, I lost my dog in a fog, on the banks of the Muddy, he was hacking away at it, but I calculate he was rather too slow in his movements, for afore he'd time to squeeze thro', it closed agin and crushed his two sides as flat as a pancake. But how's your Gal? Is she ready to jine matrimony, eh? All the gals in our part ere teetotally in love with me. I'm con-sider'd so amasin hansum. The women run to the windows as I pass by and cry out "Oh, there he goes a perfect picter of a man, bean't he lovely? Ain't he a Sneezer?"

Bilberry: I'm thinking, my daughter's heart is not so easily touched, but come in and try.

Pippin: People talk an everlasting sight of nonsense about woman's hearts. Now, as far as my experience goes, it's just like a new India rubber shoe. You may pull and pull at it, 'til it stretches out a yard long, and then let it go, and it'll fly back to its old shape. Their hearts are all made of stout leather and there's a plaguey sight of wear in 'em. Oh, yes? [*exits with Bilberry*]

Hiccory *enters in a military cloak and cocked hat with drooping feather*

Hiccory: Em all right. Miss Embily a-comin up. Got 'em Colonel's clothes on and 'em tink a look like da army, one ob da light Infantry. [*struts*] For al men, 'em just like de ole General stuck up dere, [*points to figure*] Praps 'em his broder an don't know it.

Emma *enters cautiously*

Emma [*seeing him*]: He is waiting there. [*whispers*] Are you there, dear?

Hiccory [*aside*]: Iss, as large as life.

Emma [*approaching him*]: Don't you think we are doing very wrong to *steal* away?

Hiccory [*in his natural voice*]: Debbil a bit, I always steals whatever I can catch, Missee.

Emma, *alarmed, screams and runs off*

Hiccory: Wab a fool I is, to tread on da cat's tail. She won't jump into da bag agin.

Dowbiggen [*heard without*]: Answer no questions, and keep the horses near the gate, boy.

Hiccory: Dat's de oder gentleman comed after her. A mustn't be cotched in des clothes. What 'em do? If I go back, Massa'll whip ma. An if I stops here dee Soger'll shoot me. [*pauses*] I got 'em.

Runs to statue. Dowbiggen *seen scaling wall.*

Hiccory [*throwing statue down*]: Dat chap a–climbing up, dis chap must go down. Giner al Washington must gib way to Giner al Necessity.

Hiccory *mounts on pedestal.* Dowbiggen *descends wall*

Hiccory: Dis is rising up rapidly in the army.

Dowbiggen [crossing to house, looks in]: Not there.

Hiccory: No, but 'ems here.

Emma *and* Dorothy *enter from house*

Dorothy: Impossible, Miss, you must have been mistaken.

Dowbiggen [*runs to* Emma]: Dearest.

Emma: Stop—don't come near me! Look at his face, Dorothy.

Dorothy: La, Miss! The fact is, Sir, she fancied she saw you with a dark face just now in the garden, but it must be a joke.

Dowbiggen: Silly girl! We haven't a moment to lose. The horses are waiting, all is ready and . . .

Dorothy: Willing. I have secured the key of the gate. Here it is, Sir. [*holds it up—Hiccory takes it and grasps her hand*]

Hiccory [*aside*]: Da key's poked in de wrong hole now.

Dowbiggen: You are our Guardian Angel, Dorothy! Give me the key.

Dorothy: I gave it to you, Sir.

Dowbiggen: Gave it to me? You are dreaming, girl.

Dorothy: Oh, no, I'm not in love. But, as you are, in your agitation, you may have swallowed the key.

Hiccory: Den he hab a *lock*jaw, poor ting.

Dowbiggen: You are jesting with us. Pray unlock the gate for us at once.

Dorothy: Sir, I really placed it in your hand. Perhaps you have dropped it, [*stoops to search*]

Emma: How unfortunate.

Dowbiggen: We shall be ruined.

Dorothy: What is to be done?

Hiccory: Nutting! [*holds up key. Bilberry seen coming from house*]

Bilberry: This is the time that little puss promised to meet me here. I guess I had some difficulty to part from my son-in-law, the young wild horse.

Dorothy: Hush! [*listens*] There's somebody in the garden, for Heaven's sake be careful.

Dowbiggen: Pray don't be alarm'd. Let us conceal ourselves a few minutes.

Dorothy: This way, step light.

They retire to door, R.H., Pippin and Miss Coon appear at door in flat

Pippin: The old buffer made love to you, did he?

Miss Zip Coon: Iss, Sar, and 'em waiting to meet ma dere.

Hiccory: Golly! Dat Miss Coon's lubly voice! Wab up now?

Pippin: I calculate, I shall send him into immortal smash, oh yes!

Hiccory: Anoder—dere are more peas in de pod den.

Bilberry: I wish she'd come.

Pippin: Keep close behind me, and answer when he speaks. Hist! Hist!

Bilberry: Hush!

Miss Zip Coon: Hush!

Hiccory: What am all hooshing at?

Bilberry: Is that you, my dear?

Miss Zip Coon: Issa, Massa. 'Em come to see you.

Hiccory: False agin, a blow me.

Hiccory *in a violent passion knocks* Bilberry's *hat over his eyes*

Bilberry: Murder! [*staggers*]

Dorothy: Oh! Criminy! That's master's voice.

Bilberry [*raising hat*]: What the devil was that? [*catches* Pippin's *hand*]

Miss Zip Coon: My hand, Massa.

Bilberry: Then it's a tarnation heavy one, Gal!

Hiccory: I'll hab revenge and 'spose 'em all! [*runs to triangle*]

Bilberry [*recovering*]: Sprawl! Solomon!

Pippin: Oh, yes!

Solomon Sprawl *runs on*

Sprawl: Oh *no!* I am Solomon Sprawl, I calculate, jist come from the Muddy in a steamer.

Bilberry: Two Solomons! I'm in a fix! Who are you then, stranger? [*to Pippin*]

Pippin: An Englishman, down brown!

Bilberry: My Daughter, too! And pray, who is that?

Dowbiggen: An American, Sir, and an officer in the . . .

Dorothy: United States. If you'll let him, Sir.

Bilberry: Impossible! She's engaged to marry Sprawl Junior.

Sprawl: Oh, no! Can't do it, no ways. Gineral! I'm already wedlocked to a gal down East, a roarer unknown to Father, and I've come to ax you to beg forgiveness for us.

Bilberry: I calculate we're all in a pretty considerable confusion here. The least said about it now, the better. [*to Dowbiggen:*] Sir, as my girl seems inclined, I'll think of your pretensions, and if found worthy, why perhaps I may give her to you. [*in a whisper*] A word of caution to all—keep this night's affair quiet or I guess we shall soon have her Yankee Notes[15] in print.

Hiccory: Dat you shall! Dere's one up here look down dere. 'Em print you all in de news.

Omnes: Dick! Hiccory! [*astonished*]

Hiccory [*descending*]: No, Julicum Caesar, white trash! A Prince in 'em own country, I'll hab ma revenge on you now. Go now Grand Tower, make a book, and publish you all like Missee Trollope and Massa Boz[16] an circulate da notes ma self—dat is, if dey will pass current wid our kind friends, here. It remains wid you Ladies and Genlmen [*to audience*]—your wishes must decide whether de Yankee Notes shall or shall not be duly honored and whether generally circulated in dis country.

Curtain

✒ OTELLO ✒
A Burlesque Opera[1]

Act 1

Scene 1. Stage ¼ dark. Front Street, House in L. H. Flat:
Window and Door used: knocker on door. Enter Roderigo *and* Iago, R.H.

    Roderigo

Pshaw that's all gammon,[2] and what makes it worse,
You know you always could command my purse
As if the strings were thine—[*aside*] when it was empty—
Yet would not that to honest friendship tempt ye?

    Iago

Well, how you talk. Say, did I ever spare him?

    Roderigo

Didn't you tell me that you couldn't bear him?

    Iago

Well, no more; I can't and I've good cause to hate.
I'll tell you how he "sarved me out" of late.
Three great men of the City—aye and wise men—
To make me one of Venice's Excisemen
Tried all their interest and walked some miles
From one to t'other, even doffed their tiles
To this same nigger—who said he do his best
But in dat department he hab no interest;
He did not like in piping times of peace
To urge upon de Town a "new police."
But if the common council next election "hatch,"
He'd make me Captain of the City Watch—
You go de ticket, de council dey will pay
And raise de salary, quarter dollar a day.[3]
The Aldermen did all their pledges fill
But curse the Mayor—he vetoed the bill.
He saw my friends were hurt and so, says he,
If he'll serve in de army under me,
I'll make him Ensign. So the post I've got—
But twixt ourselves, I don't like being shot.

[**343**]

Roderigo

Then why d'ye follow him?

Iago

                       You just lay low.

I'll some day kick up such a precious row.

I'll seem to be his most particular friend

And thus more easily will gain my end.

I've plenty of stout friends about the Man—

We'll kick him—if we can but git him down.

The gal . . .

Roderigo

 A lucky nigger is this thick-lip chap.

Iago

Let's call her Daddy who's taking his first nap.

Roderigo

[Crosses to left] I'll call him up. *[knocks]*

Iago

                   Don't knock so loud

Or else about the house you'll get a crowd.

            Music—"Merry Swiss Boy"[4]

Roderigo

Come arouse thee; arouse thee, Brabantio arise!

And look to your daughter and your bags.

Iago

What ho, there Brabantio, Old Signor arise!

Or you'll not have a stiver[5] or a rag.

There's thieves on the premises, so look to your life—

Your daughter's squatulated[6] and become a nigger's wife.

Both

Come arouse thee, arouse thee, Brabantio arise

And look to your daughter and your bags.

       Brabantio appears at window with blunderbuss

Brabantio

What's the reason of this rumpus,

And this knocking at my door,

When honest folks should all be in bed?

Iago

You are robbed, Sir—oh, your daughter
With the Moor has run away.

Roderigo

It's a fact, Sir, indeed what we've said.

Brabantio

I know thee, Roderigo.
And I've told thee off before:
Never let me catch you loafing
Round about my door.

Roderigo and Iago

We beseech you—we beseech you,
Straight satisfy yourself,
If she be in her chamber
Or her house.

Brabantio

Get me lights and get me tapers
Till I satisfy myself
If she be in her chamber
Or the house.

[Dialogue]

Brabantio

Holla there, who is making such a clatter?
Who are you? What the devil is the matter?

Roderigo

Why, you've been robbed—oh! Could I have caught her!
A nigger's just now bolted with your daughter.

Brabantio

The trick won't do—I know it's all my eye.
I don't believe a word on't. It's a lie.
You think to have her for yourself—but won't.
You want my daughter.

Roderigo

                    On my life, I don't.

Brabantio
Should there be truth in this—I'm in a fright.
I'll get the tinder box and strike a light.

exit from window

Iago [sings]
Farewell, friend Roddy, I'll now cut my stick.[7]
Rather than meet Brabantio, I'd meet Old Nick.[8]
Who knows but what he'd take it in his noddle,
And straight before the Duke to make me toddle—
There to confront and give my testimony
Against Otello and fair Desdemona.
The state, I know, cannot do without him,
So I rather guess I'll not say much about him,
And though I hate him as I hate the devil,
I'd cut his throat but wouldn't be uncivil.[9]

Exit R. H.

[Lights up] Enter Brabantio and all the servants from door in flat
Brabantio
There's no mistake, the nigger's back I'll fleece.[10]
Give notice, do, good Sir—to the Police.
Roderigo
Notice alone will but the case retard,
Unless you offer, too, a good reward.
Brabantio
D'ye think they're married? Where were they seen?
Roderigo
Last on their road, he told, to Gretna Green.[11]
Brabantio
Rascals bestir ye! Try to overtake her
Before this nigger chap his wife can make her.

The two go off L. H. *(Music until off)*[12]

Sirrahs, go: some of you, call up my brother,
Some one way—some the other.
On, good Roderigo, I'll deserve your pains
When we do catch her, then count your gains.

Exeunt L. H.

➤✦

Scene 2. Another Street. (Lights up) Enter Iago *and* Otello, R. H.

    Iago

Though often in a row I've knocked down men
And, had I causes, would do the same again,
But, cut a throat? I rather guess I'm nervous—
For I lack villains to do me service.
Nine or ten times my passion so high rose
I thought to have given him a bloody nose . . .

    Otello

All better as it is—

    Iago

                  But his tongue went

    Otello

Let him do his spite,
De sarbices dat I hab done, will set me right.
You know, Iago, as you my crony,
I dearly lub de gentle Desdemony.
But see what lights am dem what's coming yonder?

    Iago

It is her daddy, looking black as thunder!
It's true your courage never had a doubt,
He's in a rage—you'd better, Sir, put out.

    Otello

What? Cut my stick? Dat, you mean to say?
Dis child's Otello—sogers don't run away.

  Enter Brabantio *and* four attendants *with lights*, Roderigo *and* two
                        policemen

    Brabantio (dress disordered)

There, that's the nigger—Seize him I command.

    Iago

You, Roderigo, come, Sir—hand to hand.

                  They draw swords; policemen seize Otello

    Otello

You want my purse?

    1st Policeman

                  Oh, certainly for that . . .

    2nd Policeman

Don't hold the gentlemen so hard, you Pat . . .

Roderigo

You're summoned to the Council of the Nation.

Brabantio

Pshaw, nonsense, off with him to the station.

He's ruined my daughter. He shall rue it.

Otello gives purse to policeman[13]

1st Policeman

We can't take him—cause we didn't see him do it.

Enter Cassio L. H.

Cassio

Faith, you're a nice man, ain't you? By the powers,

You've kept the Senate waiting [*looking at watch*] just two hours.

Otello

Twasn't my fault, I would not, Sir, hab tarried,

But for my farder-in-law.

Brabantio

　　　　Damn 'em, then they are married.

Take him in custody. Gentlemen, I insist.

Down with the nigger, if he do resist.

As attendants approach to seize Otello

Music (Three chords)

Otello

Recitative

Hold your hands, all you ob my opinion and de oder ones. Whar it my cue to raise a row, I should hab know it widout your telling me. And old Massa Signor, you should more command with years den with your swordesses. What is you want me for to go to answer dis are charges? Nay—to prison.

All exclaim

Aye to prison. [*pointing off*]

Solo and Chorus

What if I do obey you, Sar,
And go along with you?
De duke may be offended
And dis conduct you may rue.

His messengers are here upon
Some business of de state
    And he may be damn angry
      For troubling him so late. [*repeat two last lines*]
           Brabantio [*Second Verse*]
The Duke I hear's in Council now
And will be all the night;
And if a white man's justice
The Duke will set me right.
Mine's not a soaplock[14] rowdy spree
That I do want relief.
    But I have lost my daughter, Sir,
      And this chap is the thief. [*repeat two last lines*]
           Third Grand Chorus
Come march, Sir, to the Senate
And perhaps you'll there find bail.
Your black looks and your blustering
Will be of no avail.
For if a black shall wed a white,
And afterwards go free,
    In a very pretty pickle then
      Our daughters soon will be. [*repeat two last lines*][15]
               Exeunt R. H.

⇥⇤

Scene 3. The Senate Chamber. Duke and Senators discovered sitting.
        Music "Sitting on a Rail"[16]
           Chorus
For council we have met to night,
Like men, to do the thing that's right
And beat the foe that's now in sight.
For Venice shall be free,
Venice shall be free,
Venice shall be free.
We'll beat the foe that's now in sight,
For Venice shall be free.

Music while Brabantio, Otello, Cassio, Iago *and* Roderigo *enter*
  Duke

Valiant Otello, we're very glad you've come,
For in this war we fear we'll suffer some.
Would you believe, Sirs—the galley slaves[17]
Are kicking up a dust upon the waves.
Here's one good gentleman, defend us Heaven,
Says there's a hundred and twenty seven.
And, this, my letter, says the slaves that naughty
Amount to full one hundred forty.
The other gentleman has got a letter
Which says two hundred and something better.
What's to be done? Otello: try and lick 'em.
Take all our soldiers and you're sure to nick 'em
Haste them away and do just as you oughter.
  Brabantio, rising

Stop, good Sir Duke—he's stole away my daughter.
He is a buzzard.[18] Sir, a very Elf.
I do believe he is the Devil himself.
He has dissolved my daughter into air
Or else has mesmerized her, Heaven knows where.
A rogue—a vagabond—I could his claret spill:[19]
Commit him, I beseech you, to the treading mill.[20]
Oh, that I had him out in Carolino,
I'd tie him up and give him thirty-nino.[21]
  Duke

There must be some mistake. Come speak, Otello.
What say you to the charge, my noble fellow?
  Otello

[*Recitative*[22]] Most potent, grabe, and reberand Signiors, my bery noble and approbed good Massas: Dat I hab tuck away dis old man's
darter—is true and no mistake.[23] True, I's married her. De bery
head and tail ob my offence hab dis extent, no more: rude am I in
talk. I cannot chat like some folks for, since a piccanniny two years
old, I'b always been in rows and spreezes. Yet, by your gracious patience, I'll tell you how I won his darter.

All

Hear him! Hear him! Hear him!

Duke

Silence. Say it, Otello.

Music—Air: "Ginger Blue"[24]

Her farder lub'd me well

And he say to me one day,

Otello, Won't you come wid me and dine?

As I whar rader sharp set,

Why, bery well, I say,

I'll be up to de trough, Sar, in time.

We had terrapins, chicken stew,

and nice punking pie,

And a dish filled with nice macaroni,

And last, not least, come de fried sassengers,

All cooked by de fair Desdemona.

2nd Verse

When de dinner it was ober,

And de whiskey flew about,

And de old Man was high in his glory,

He axed me to sing a song,

Fore the company put out.

Or else, would I tell again my story

Ob de sprees dat I get in

And de scrapes dat I get out

And how often run away when leff loose

And how dat I got free

From de Southern Slabery[25]

And how often was I in de Calaboose.[26]

3rd Verse

Now, dese tings to hear,

Desdemona cocked her ear

And wish Heaben hab made

Her sich a nigger.

But den de house affairs

Would call her down stairs

War she'd sit in de corner,

Cry, and snigger.

My story being done,

She only wished I had a son,[27]

And to tell this story

I would undo her.

Den she wink and blink at me—

And I did de same to she.

And upon dis suit, Sar, I won her.

    Brabantio

Tis all a lie, told to defraud the bench.

Please you, order some one fetch the wench

That she may here confront him face to face.

    Otello

Ancient, conduct her, bring her—you best know de place.

                       Exeunt Iago and Roderigo L. H.

    Brabantio

And if she do confess she first began

To throw sheep eyes and ogle at the man;

If, as he says, she took these means to woo him—

Then blow me tight if I don't give her to him.

                  Enter Desdemona and Ladies, Iago and Roderigo

Oh here she is—my child—my darling child,

Your poor old father has been almost wild.

But tell me—since you lost your poor dear mother,

Don't you love me dear more than any other?

    Desdemona

Why, my dear father—if I must be candid,

You've loved your child as much as ever man did.

And, as in duty bound, I loved or, rather,

Worshipped my parent. But then you're my father.

I've followed the example of my mother,

Who loved her father but left him for another.

    Brabantio

Madam, your mother never left her home.

    Desdemona

Pshaw, pshaw—confess the case now, do, Sir, do.

Did she not give up all the world for you?

And of her peculation ne'er did rue.
I've only done as folks have done before.
I've cut you all for this—my Blackamoor. [*crosses to Otello*]
He is my husband. What's done can't be undone.
 Otello
Dat am a fact: one and one make one.

Air—"Down Fly Market"[28]

Desdemona
I'll tell you why I loved the Black.

Chorus
Tell us freely—tell us freely!

Desdemona
Every night I had a knack

Chorus
Speak sincerely—speak sincerely!

Desdemona
Of listening to his tales bewitching.

Chorus
Drive us frantic—drive us frantic!

Desdemona
My hair while curling in the kitchen,

Chorus
How romantic—how romantic . . .

2nd Verse

Desdemona
Once while darning father's stocking,

Chorus
Recreation—recreation . . .

Desdemona
Oh, he told a tale so shocking,

Chorus
Execration—execration!

Desdemona
So romantic, yet so tender,

Chorus
Shrewd and witty—shrewd and witty . . .

Desdemona

That I fell across the fender.

Chorus

What a pity, what a pity . . .

3rd Verse

Desdemona

When I came about—ah, me!

Chorus

Rather supple—rather supple . . .

Desdemona

I was sitting on his knee—

Chorus

Loving couple—loving couple!

Desdemona

Greatful for the scrape I'd missed.[29]

Chorus

Tender touches—tender touches!

The Moral

Desdemona

Listen, ladies, if you please,

Chorus

All attention—all attention . . .

Desdemona, rather slower

Never sit on young men's knees,

Chorus

Pray don't mention—pray don't mention!

Desdemona

For though I got a husband by it,

Chorus

Lucky creature—lucky creature!

Desdemona

The plan's not good—so pray don't try it [*goes to Otello*]

Chorus

We beseech you—we beseech you.

Brabantio [spoken]
A white man's daughter and a black man's son
Well, Heaven be with you both—for I have done.
A word, Otello: watch her, mind you do—
She cheated me, you know, and may cheat you. *[goes up and sits]*
    Otello
My life, upon her faith, dar's no mistake.
She only cheated you for her Otello's sake.
    Duke
Now then, Otello, that affair's all right—
And you must lumber off this very night.
    Otello
Tonight? good Massa, Duke—me[30] just now married.
    Duke
I can't help it—go you must—too long you've tarried.
I shall be robbed and murdered by these chaps
If you don't go and whip em for me, p'haps.
    Otello
Whar shall I leave my wife?
    Desdemona

                    Did you say—leave me?
Do you begin already to deceive me?
    Duke
Go to your father, dear.
    Desdemona

        I sha'nt.
    Duke

          O, fie.
    Otello
I won't hab it so.
    Brabantio

        Nor I.
    Desdemona
I won't go anywhere but with Otello.
That's what I want.
    Brabantio

        Well, don't begin to bellow.

Desdemona
I will—I'll cry for ever—all my life.
What was the use of being made a wife?
    Otello
Your voices, fellow citizens, I pray.
    Duke
That's a brave lass, and so you shall, I say.
    Otello
Honest Iago—you am a cleber fellow.
My wife I leab wid you—Missus Otello.
If she catch cold and gits the cough and sneezes,
Gib her some candy, what you buy at Pease's.
And when she hab packed up her trunks, my man,
Den bring her arter me best way you can.
I'be but an hour, or someting dar about,
To pass wid dee before I do put out.
    Duke
Signor, your son, though black as Fancy Rooks,
Is like a singed cat—better than he looks.[31]

        Air—"Lucy Long"[32]
        Otello
    Dont weep, sweet Desdemona,
    Kase we must part tonight.
    I am a sodger, honey,
    And my trade it am to fight.
    But when de wars am ober,
    I'll return to thee, lub, soon,
    As a hero and a lubber,
    To keep up our honeymoon.
        Chorus
    Bravo Otello, He's a clever fellow.
    One so glorious, will be victorious.
        Otello
    Don't cry, sweet Desdemony.
        Desdemona
    Oh, oh, oh, oh, oh, oh, oh!

Otello

Don't fret, sweet Desdemona,

Chorus

Bravo, Bravo Bravissimo,

Otello [*second verse*]

Black folks from sheer vexation
Will grumble at me a few;
And call dis 'malgamation[33]
Well, I don't care *damn* if they do. [*pause*]
If I hab no objection,
What de debil's dat to dem?
You can't help your complexion;
Nature made you as well as dem.

Chorus

Bravo Otello: he's a clever fellow;
One so glorious, will be victorious.

Otello

Don't fret sweet Desdemony

Desdemona

Oh, oh, oh, oh, oh, oh,

Otello

Don't fret, sweet Desdemony.

Chorus

Bravo, Bravo, Bravissimo.

Desdemona [*third verse*]

Where's the use of getting married
If our husbands have to roam?
Far better to have tarried
A single life at home.
For, if this is a beginning,
I plain 'gin to see,
This thing called matrimony
Is not the thing crack'd up to be.

Chorus

Bravo Otello: he's a clever fellow
One so glorious, will be victorious.

Otello

Don't fret, sweet Desdemony.

Desdemona

Oh, oh, oh, oh, oh, oh,

Otello

Don't fret sweet Desdemony.

Chorus

Bravo, Bravo, Bravissimo

Exit Otello, Desdemona; Duke *and* attendants, Brabantio *and* Policemen, L. H.

Business of tossing with Duke and Brabantio

Roderigo

Iago,

Iago

What's the matter with the chap?

Roderigo

I'll drown myself.

Iago

Oh, git out, you silly chap.

Roderigo

Silly, indeed; answer me this query,

Why should I live when done out of my deary?

Iago

Oh, hush! Shut up your trap—she loves you still.

Or, if she does not, I rather guess she will.

No matter how—it's the fashion nowadays;

If you would win her, sport the rhino.[34] Come,

Put money in your purse—she's yours, by gum.

Drown yourself, eh? Why, what a silly body!

Hark you, go drown care and take an apple toddy.

Roderigo

It must be so—I'm really tired of thinking,

And blow me tight, if I don't take to drinking.

Iago

That's the ticket, meet me again tonight—

I'll sarve this black chap out, else I'm not white.

Duet—"Polly will you now"[35]

Iago and Roderigo

Iago

I have told you oft,
And I tell you again,
How worse than pisen[36]
I hate the Moor.
For, to my wife,
Upon my life,
He's been making love
To her, I'm sure.
Now, if his wife you once can count,
You'll make him jealous and me a sport.
Put money in your purse.
Put money in your purse,
And that's the way we'll have revenge.
Put money in your purse

Roderigo [*Second Verse*]

Will you, indeed,
If I succeed
To get the wife
From this black Chap,
Should it come to blows
And a bloody nose,
Stand from behind me,
At my back?
For, by the mass,
Should this pretty lass
Just get a glimpse at me, my boy,
From the highest window
No doubt she'll throw
Herself in the arms of Roderigo!

Iago

Put money in your purse!
Put money in your purse,

And that's the way we'll have revenge.
Put money in your purse.

Exeunt L. H.

✦

Scene 4. Cyprus. Enter Cassio R. H.
    Cassio
Faith, then I wish Otello, safe and sound,
Was treading once again upon the ground.
For while on terra firma all seems level
The sea beyon't is rolling like the devil [*gun fire*]
Sure that's the signal, then he's come at last

                Enter Montano L. H.

    Montano
A ship—a ship—has just her anchor cast
And one Iago's come
    Cassio

          Iago said ye
Then, by the powers, he's brought the Captain's lady.
    Montano
What? Is Otello married? Why, how is this?
    Cassio
And to as fine a gal as one could kiss.
Mistress Iago's come too—for 'tis said,
She's to the bride, a sort of Lady's maid . . . [*laugh* L. H.]
By the hokey's and here they are
        Enter Desdemona, Emilia, ladies, child[37] *and* Iago, L. H.
    Cassio
Madam, I wish you joy.
Blood an' zouns and whiskey, what a bouncing boy!
Mistress Iago, I'm glad to see you, too.
Mister Iago, Sir, the same to you. [*crosses to* L. C.]
For old acquaintance sake; give us a buss.
Don't mind your husband—he'll not raise a fuss. [*kisses Emilia*]
    Iago
Oh, pile on a load or two; don't mind me, pray,
'Stead of her lip—would she'd give her tongue away.
She often blows me up—

Emilia

You tell a lie.

I never blow you up, you fool, not I.

Except when you get into brawls and fights,

And come home reeling every hour of the night.

You've killed my peace and almost broke my heart.

Oh, if I had some friend to take my part. [*falls on Cassio's neck*]

Wait 'til I get home! You say I scold you?

I'll make the house, you wretch, too hot to hold you.

Desdemona

I never hear her scold, nor think she can;

So don't you be so cross, you naughty man.

What would you say of woman, if you could

Find one amongst us that was very good?

Air—"Yankee Doodle"[38]

Iago

I'll tell you. [*cue for orchestra*]

Now, she that's fair and never proud,

A gal so nice and cozy,

A smartish tongue—but never loud—

And lips so red and rosy,

With lots of cash—but none too gay—

Just neat and not too dashy,

With locks just the flowers of May,

and bonnet not too splashy.

Second Verse

The gal that being in a rage

And could keep down her dander;

One who in scandal won't enquire

Nor go ahead on slander;

One who could think without a word—

Where do you think I'll find her?

One who a young man's footstep heard

And would not look behind her.

[*Spoken*] She'd be the critter that I see very clear.

Desdemona

For what—

   Iago

  To pickle tripe and bottle ginger beer!

   Desdemona

Your wit and spleen are both surcharged in vapour.
You shan't write puffs for me in Bennett's paper.[39]

   Cassio

Oh, don't you mind or care a fig about him.
Faith, he's a ladies man; the devil doubt him.

Takes her hand, both retire up

   Iago

He takes her by the hand and slaps her shoulder,
I'll have you stranger,[40] yet, ere you're much older.

Otello sneezes without

The Moor! I swan, I know him by his sneeze.

   Desdemona

Come then we'll go and meet him, if you please.

Music and crash of Symbols [sic][41]
Enter Otello *and* attendants, *L. H.*

   Otello

Oh, my fair warrioress, I embrace dee thus!
Welcome, Honey, to de town of Cyprus.

   Desdemona

Behold this pledge—your image here is seen.
Not this side love, the other side I mean [*points to child's face*].[42]

Otello *takes the boy and kisses him*

   Otello [*to Cassio*]

How do our old acquaintance of the Isle?
Honey, you shall be well-desired de while.

Music—"The Girl I Left Behind Me"[43]

Otello

My wonder's great as my content
To see you here before me,
Because you said, before I went,
You bery much adore me.
If arter tempest comes sich calm,

De winds may blow and find me,
I don't care damn—when in dese arms
De gal I leff behind me.

Second Verse

To die would be most happy now.
I'd kick de bucket freely—
But leab you, lub, a widow now
Would grieb me too sincerely.
May dis our greatest discord be [*embrace*]
And lub still deeper bind me,
Nor grief nor sorrow eber cross
De gal I leff behind me.

Third Verse

I've libed on land; I've libed on sea,
In ebery clime and station.
And dere no station in all de world
Like de state of annexation.
Kase if you like me, and I like you,
And our lubs are in communion,
De longer den de family grows,
More stronger am de Union.

Iago

You're well tuned now. I'll give you sich a kick
I will bring you down a peg and stop your music.

Otello

Now for our honey moon. Our deeds are crowned,
De wars am ended, and de Turks am drowned.
Come, dear, let us in to dinner—
Welcome, once more, to Cyprus or I'm a sinner.

Air—"Nix my Dolly"[44]

Otello

Oh, de wars and de scrapes
And de sprees am done—sprees am done
De foe am beat.
De Turks am drowned—Turks am drowned.
All safe and sound
To our wives we come

Wid de sprigs of laurel
In battle we won.

    Den drink, my boys,
    Dar's notin' to pay. [*repeat*]
    Drink deep, drink deep, 'tis a holly day.

Second Verse

Otello

Once more well met in Cyprus here,
My duck, my lub, my charming dear.
Iago, my coffers you disembark,
And bring de Captain to hab a lark.

    Den drink, my boys,
    Dar's notin' to pay [*repeat*]
    Drink deep, drink deep,
    Dar's notin' to pay. [*Music*]

Chorus and dance: exit Otello, Desdemona, Emilia *and* child, R. H.

Iago

Come here, Roderigo, [*Enter* Roderigo L. H.] I've just now seen 'em;
I swan, there's pretty goings on between 'em.

Roderigo

Between 'em—between who?

Iago

                  Hush, man, lay low.
Just put your finger thus [*to nose*] and you shall know,
I tell you: Cassio's now her fancy man.
The Black was all a whim. D'ye think she can
Care that [*snaps fingers*] for him, while you or I
Would cast sheep's eyes at her—or heave a sigh?
Wouldn't she take your squeezing notion civil,
Rather than cuddles from the very devil.

Roderigo

I can't believe it, bless her. She's so good!

Iago

Bless'd apple sarce—Ain't sawdust made of wood?
Isn't she, flesh and blood, her mother's darter?
Ain't pancakes made of eggs and flour?

Roderigo

and water?

Iago

A bless'd huckleberry pudding then! Hearken to me:
Cassio keeps watch this very night, d'ye see?
Go you and tease him, blow him up or, damn him,
If that won't do, with brandy toddy cram him.

Roderigo

I'll do it. Dear Iago, where shall we meet?

Iago

This evening, on the corner of this street.

Roderigo

I will, adieu. [*exits* L. H.]

Iago

The same to you.

Air—"Rosin the Bow"[45]

That Cassio loves her, I believe it.
And she loves this Cassio, no doubt,
But if I once catch 'em together,
I'll be darned if I don't blab it out.
Like brimstone, her husband I hate,
And I'll worry him out of his life,
For I see by the papers, of late,
He's been making love, too, to my wife.

Second Verse

I'll give Michael Cassio tarnation,
But not till I first get him drunk.
And as no law protects reputation,
I'll swear he's been stealing a trunk.
This vengeance I'll not let it slip,
And to morrow I'll at it right slap,
I'll have Mr. Mike on the hip,
Cause he's also had on my night cap.

Third Verse

I'll make this Otello so jealous,
This pudding he'll eat without sass.
Whilst he calls me the best of good fellows,

Most egregiously he'll be an ass.
He'll pull the wool out of his head
When about his wife all's understood—
For I'll swear black is white[46]—'fore they married,
She jilted the whole neighborhood.

Exeunt, R. H.

➤←

Scene 5. Stage ¾ dark. Enter Otello, Cassio, *and* attendants, R. H.
    Otello
You, Massa Michael, who am always right,
While I go roost, you keep the watch tonight.
And don't you wake me morrow morning soon—
I shan't get up much 'fore the arternoon.

Exit C. D. *with attendants*
Iago *enters* L. H. *as* Otello *exits*

    Cassio
By my soul, Iago, I must to my post.
    Iago
Why, how you talk, 'tisn't ten, at most.
Otello's early: Well, and so he oughter,
For Desdemona. She's a regular snorter.
    Cassio
She's a charming eye—
    Iago
                    Oh, Cassio, fie—
And yet, you're right: Scissors, what an eye!
    Cassio
Faith, she's right modest though—
    Iago
                                    I think no less.
Let's go and liquor and drink their happiness!
    Cassio
Sir, not to night—I've already had a toddy.
Another one would soon capsize the body.
    Iago
Pooh, nonsense, man—we'll find here at the lunch
Plenty who'll join us in a whiskey punch.

Cassio

Well, just one glass—Devil the more I'll take.

Enter Montano *and* Ludovico[47]

   Cassio

Here's health to Desdemona and Otello—

Although he's black, he's a devilish good fellow.

Come, Iago, as I can't stop here long,

Suppose you tip us just a little song.

   Iago

With all my heart

Air—"Corn Cobs"[48]

Come fill the Can

And I'm the man

Will challenge anybody

To sing all night

Till broad daylight

And drink fine apple toddy.

Then let the can go clink, clink, clink!

We'll never think of shrinking.

While there's a drop we'll never stop,

But go ahead on drinking.

   Cassio

A capital song! [*sings*]

A very good song and very well sung,

Jolly companions, every one.

I say, Iago, where did you learn that strain?

   Iago

In Massachusetts, next to the State of Maine.[49]

They're the chaps for drinking, what a swallow,

They beat New York and Philadelphy Boys all hollow.

   Cassio

Faith, it's right good stuff—it makes me frisky.

No doubt it's "Cuter Cousin" to good old whiskey.

Iago

Air—"Gabby Glum"[50]

To cheer the spirits up,

There's nothing like a good whiskey.

Jist you take a sip,
It makes you feel so frisky.
It gladdens up the heart
Jist to whet the throttle;
And never more will part—
Your mouth and this sweet bottle.

Both join in Chorus

Cassio

That's a more exquisite song, Sir, than the first.
'Tis strange how drinking does improve one's thirst.
Iago, I'll thank you for another swig.
If we'd the lasses here, wouldn't we have a jig?
Well, Saint Patrick help us! We must drink, you see.
The Captain, he must drink as well as we.
There are some folks, to be sure, can't drink;
And there are some that can—I'm one, I think.

Iago

Guess I am, too. [*about to drink*]

Cassio

Not before me, Sir, if you please.
I'm senior officer—in my own right I seize.

Enter Roderigo, R. H.

Roderigo

He's getting drunk.

Cassio

Drunk! That word again dare speak,
I'll knock you in the middle of next week.
Drunk? And it's me that's drunk, you said?
Isn't this your fist and isn't that my head?

Takes off coat and prepares for a fight

Roderigo

He smells of whiskey worse than any skunk.
Why, what a shame to get so horrid drunk.

Cassio

Ah, ha! That's twice I'm drunk! You just wait awhile
And maybe I won't polish you off in style.

Iago

Stick to him only for a round or so,
And I'll put out and let Otello know. [*exit* c.d.]

[*Music*. Roderigo *and* Cassio *fight. Enter* Iago *and knocks Roderigo down from behind. Enter four* supers *with torches.* Otello *enters and beats the whole party. Roderigo's face is covered with blood. Cassio has a black eye: Otello has a stuffed stick*]

Otello

[*Recitative*] Hold for your lives. Why, how is this? Am we turned
Turks to scratch and fight and to ourselves do dat which am forbid
de common loafer? He dat strikes anoder blow I'll butt him all to
pieces. Dat noisy bell, stop him[51] clatter.

Air—"French"

Otello

Iago, who began dis spice?
Dis instant tell me who's to blame—
And 'dough de chap was twin'd wid me
Dat moment he lose all de claim.

Second Verse

Montano, is you drunk or mad?
Your conduct used to be so civil,
But now you so damn bad—
You're worser den de bery Devil.

Third Verse

How comes it, Michael, you mistake
To get so drunk and leff your passion loose?
I had a good notion for to take
And put you in de calaboose.

Montano
Oh! What a blow in the ribs—that was a poser.
Roderigo
Pshaw! What's a blow in the ribs? Look at my nose, sir!
[*exit* L.H.]
Otello
Come speak, Iago, none of dis here nonsense.
Tell me de truth, at once, and ease your conscience.

Air—"My Long Tail Blue"[52]

Iago

I had rather my tongue was cut slick out
Than speak ought to offend this youth.

But if you insist to know what 'tis about,
Why, I guess then I'll best tell the truth.
[*chorus*] I guess then I'd best tell the truth [*repeat four times*]

Second Verse

Thus it is: we were taking a glass of Stone Fence[53]
Good Montano, myself, and a friend.
And, when once in the liquor we 'gan to commence,
Why, we thought we'll just drink to the end.
[*chorus*] I guess then I'd best tell the truth [*repeat four times*]

Third Verse

Now Cassio, you see, had swallowed all down.
And by this time had got rather blue.
When a fellow comes crying, "There's a fire downtown—
Turn out, turn out, twenty two."[54]
[*chorus*] I guess then I'd best tell the truth [*repeat four times*]

Fourth Verse

In returning, I saw that young gentleman there
Give Cassio a blow in the eye.
I did all in my power to stop the affair,
But their fury my aid did defy.
[*chorus*] I guess then I'd best tell the truth [*repeat four times*]

Fifth Verse

Then to it they went. But, my friend do forgive.
For you know, Sir, that men are but men.
And, if you'll excuse him, my word I will give
That he never will do so again.
[*chorus*] I guess then I'd best tell the truth [*repeat four times*]
      Otello

Cassio [*crosses to him*] to you, Iago bery partial.
So I discharge you widout de court martial.
      Iago
Oh, good Otello, put on him a fine.
      Otello
Cassio neber more be ossifer ob mine.

                              exit Otello and attendants

      Iago
Come, come, friend Cassio, where's the use—tarnation.

Cassio

My reputation lost, my reputation.
I'm bothered, Sir. I'm bothered, quite, with thinking
I've lost my reputation, Sir, with drinking.
I, who in punch ne'er flinched to any body,
Drunk and bewildered with an apple toddy.
Was ever man in such a situation?
Oh, blood an' 'ouns, I've lost my reputation. [*crosses* R. H.]

    Iago

Why, how you talk! Guess we can mend your reputation—
Your stomach was a leetle out of calculation.

    Cassio

Oh, that the devil thus should dwell in toddy,
To steal men's brains and then capsize the body.
What shall I do to ease my mind of pain?

    Iago

Suppose you ask him for your place again?
I have it! Go and make some pretty speeches
To Mrs. O. You know she wears the breeches.
Come the soft sodder.[55] And if you find she freezes,
Don't be afraid, give her a few sly squeezes
Until her bosom thaws. Then she will plead;
And, if she does, the place is yours, indeed.

                Cassio [*crosses,* L. H.]

Tis a glorious scheme. I'll do it! Thank ye.
A plan that's really worthy of a Yankee.
By the powers, it is the way. You're right.
I thank you much, my friend, and so good night.

                  Shakes hands and exits L. H.

        As Cassio exits, Roderigo *enter,* R. H.

    Iago

How do ye do?

    Roderigo

About so so, how get you on?

    Iago

A little longer and the thing is done.
Listen!

Air—"Oats, Beans and Barley oh"

Iago

I guess at last I've found a plan
Where in you'll say that I'm the man
Can do just what no other can
In female speculation.
Otello shall his wife divorce,
Kase Cassio's held with her discourse,
And then, my boy, she's your's, of course,
Beyond all calculation.

Second Verse

While Cassio kneels with all his grace
To Desdemona for his place,
Otello shall meet him face to face
And the fat will be in the fire.
Then they'll be in a pretty fix—
With their broken hearts, with their thumping sticks.
As long as there'll be plenty of kicks,
It's all that we desire.

Exeunt L. H.

⇥⇤

Scene 6. Room in castle. Sofa R. H.

Enter Desdemona, Emilia *and* Cassio R. H.

Desdemona

I'll ask him when he's had a glass or two.
There's no one, I'd do more for, Sir, than you.

Emilia

That's a good soul. She'll bring the thing about.
Oh, Sir, my poor dear husband's much put out.

Desdemona

You're a good chap. The Moor'll be home to sup.
I'll tease him, 'til he says he'll make it up.

Cassio

But stress my place. If we're not sure today,
The chances are he'll give my place away.

Desdemona

Don't fret yourself. Here, before her face,
I promise you that you shall have your place.
I'll tease him so, he ne'er shall hear the last, Sir,
So don't you stew.

 Emilia

Madam, here comes my master.

 Cassio

Oh, then I'm off . . . [*crosses* R.]

 Desdemona

Don't be a fool, pray stop.

 Cassio

I can't—I tremble so that I shall drop.

exits R. H.

Enter Otello *and* Iago L. H.

Otello reading newspaper

 Iago

He here! I don't half like that.

 Otello

What's dat you say—

 Iago

Nothing, I spoke to the cat.

 Otello

Was not dat Cassio, parted from my wife?

 Iago

I do not think 'twas him, upon my life.
What reason, Sir, should he, or any one,
Seeing you, cut stick, clear out and run?

 Otello

I do belibe 'twas him, for see . . .

 Iago

Perhaps your wife has axed him home to tea?

 Otello

Missus Otello, who is dat to whom you speak?
And why—when I come in—away he sneak?

 Desdomona

The fact is, Ducky, bless your snowball face,[56]
'Twas Cassio pleading to get back his place.

If you refuse me—then the news that next is
Cassio's off and making tracks for Texas.
Shall I run after him and say you will?

>Otello

No, not tonight. I feel so rader queerish ill.

>Desdemona

Well, then tomorrow morning, or at noon,
Or else tomorrow night, or sometime soon.
Say Wednesday morning then—or noon—or night.
I'll take compassion on the luckless night.
Well, Thursday? Friday? Saturday or Sunday?
At most you'll not defer it after Monday.
Why how is this, Otello? Speak Sir, pray.

>Otello

Why, leff him come and all will be O.K.

>Exeunt Desdemona *and* Emilia R. H.

>Otello

De way I lub her really is a sin
And, when I doesn't, chaos comed again[57] [*crosses L*]

>Iago

General, did Cassio know you really lov'd her so?

>Otello

Yes, be sure he did, what for you wish to know?

>Iago

Indeed. [*winks*]

>Otello

Indeed! What for you wink your eye?
And cry, indeed, and look so bery shy—
Am he not honest?

>Iago

Honest, my lord? [*looking up*]

>Otello

Yes, honest.

>Iago

As well as this world kin afford.

>Otello

What do you tink?

Iago

                  Think, my dear Otello?
Why, then, I think, Cassio an honest fellow.

Otello

I tink so too. But dat's no news to tell.
You don't tink so, I know bery well.
You tink him tief!

Iago

               I think him something worse.

Otello

Aye! You tink he pick your pocket or your purse.

Iago

Who steals my purse steals trash.[58] Look here a minute:
There once was something; now there's nothing in it.
Twas his, 'tis mine, and been in all disasters.
But never hold again, I fear shinplasters:[59]
Cassio, I guess, would aim at higher game;
He'd sign a check in any man's good name
To take my all. Oh, how my heart doth bleed!
I would make him rich but leave me poor indeed.

Otello

Iago, you mean someting 'pon my life.
I tink, you tink Cassio lub my wife.
No, Massa Iago, I prove before I doubt;
And when I prove, why den I sarbe her out.
If she lubs Cassio and not me, I find,
I'll whistle her off and leff her down the wind.[60] *[crosses L]*

Iago

You're right. Wear your eyes open; look to your wife.
I wouldn't have you jealous for my life,
But she's a critter, here in Venice bred;[61]
Her father she deceived in marrying you—'nuf sed.

Otello

Why, so she did.

Iago

            —You seem a little dashed or so.

Otello

[crosses R. H.] No, I assure you, not a jot. No, no.

Iago

I now must leave you, Gineral, and what's going on
You'll hear from me, you may depend upon.

[*Exits L., crosses L.*]

Otello

Why did I marry? More could Iago chat,
If he'd but let de bag out of de cat.

[*plays with tassel*]

Re-enter Iago *L. to R.*

Iago

Gineral, I've just stepped back to beg that you'll incline
To scan this thing no further. Leave it all to time.
Don't let what I have said put you in a flurry;
And don't fill Cassio's place up in a hurry.
If much your wife in Cassio's interest takes
It's my opinion, then, she's no "great shakes."

Otello

I'll watch her close.

Iago

Once more, adieu [*going*]

Otello

Iago, I am much obliged to you. [*exit Iago L. H.*]

Enter Desdemona *with towel*, R. H.

Desdemona

Come, come, Otello. Recollect, I pray.
You asked some folks to take pot luck today;
They're all arrived and only wait for you.
Come and receive you guests, Otello do.

Otello

I'm not quite well. My head hab got a pain.

Desdemona

Why that's with watching; 'twill be well again.
Here, let me bind this towel round it tight
And you shall take some Brandreth's Pills tonight.

Otello

De towel am too little [*puts it away*] dat neber mine,
Let it alone. Come, I'll go in to dine.

Exeunt

Emilia *enters as they exit*

Emilia

I'm glad I've found this towel on the floor.

This was her first remembrance from the Moor.

My husband wants it—I can't tell why or wherefore;

This is not stealing. What did he throw it there for?

Enter Iago, L. H.

Iago

What on earth are you hovering here about?

Emilia

What's that to you? You may go find out.

Iago

You're a nice one.

Emilia

        Oh am I, very well,

Then what I've got for you I shall not tell.

Iago

For me? What can you have for me?

Emilia

If you speak prettily you shall see.

Iago

Why, how you talk.

Emilia

        Well, a towel then.

Iago

What towel?

Emilia

        Desdemona's—don't you ken?

Iago

Oh Scissors![62] The one Otello gave her, let me see.

That's a good critter [*snatches it*] give it to me.

Now travel!

Emilia

    Oh, let me put it in its place:

She's got no other towel to wipe her face.

Iago

Clear out!

Exit Emilia, R. H.

Iago

I'll just put this towel in Mr. Cassio's room,
And, when discovered, she'll be a gone coon.
Enter Otello, *his wool all on end.*[63] *Seizes Iago and butts him.*

Otello

False, false to me, villain, be sure you prove what you hab said,
Or else, Iago, much better you be dead.

Iago

If this fact ain't enough, then call me dunce.
Did you not give your wife a towel once?

Otello

Yes, I did. What you hab me understand?

Iago

This morning, with it, Cassio wiped his hand.

Otello

Enough! I'll tear her all to pieces, Sar, like dis,
Dow she'd as many lives as de tom cat.
Don't let dis ar matter go no furder:
Us two, 'dem two, will murder.
You kill Cassio, you hab him place;
And Desdemona, I'll spoil her face.

Air—"Dandy Jim"[64]

A Gypsy woman, whose name was Cowell
To my poor moder gib'd dat towel.[65]
And, if she lose or gib it away,
Wid my father, she would fight all day.

　chorus De Gypsy woman tell me so,
I was born to be a General, oh.
I looked in the glass and find it so,
Jist what de Gypsy told me, oh.

Second Verse

De towel was made of raccoon hide
And in de bakehouse often dried,
'Twas washed and bleached wid coconut milk,
And sewed and hemmed with hot cornsilk.
　chorus

Third Verse

I did not care if all de camp,
De Gineral, province, and rank,
De fifer and de drummer, oh,
Hab kissed her—so I did not know.
   chorus

Fourth Verse

To lub a wife dat don't lub me,
I'd rather be a toad, you see;
And den de face to lib upon
De wassous ob a demijohn.
   chorus

"Air." Otello kneels

Farewell to de banjo and de cymbals,
De drum, fife, and trumpet loud swell;
Farewell to de jaw bone and jingles,
De fiddle and jew's harp, farewell.
Farewell to de mind dat was quiet
And de big wars whar laurels am won.
Farewell joy, pride, pomp and come riot:
Otello's occupation am gone.

"Air"

Come now Iago, go wid me
And put some pisen in shoushong tea
And gib to Desdemony
And make her drink it up.
And for her Irish crony
He too shall hab a sup.

Iago

If you will pisen her, we're sure to swing.
I'll just propose another thing:
We'll say the cat had bit her.
She went mad and broke our heads;
And so we took the critter
And we smother'd her 'tween two beds.

Otello

Iago, I'm oblige to you
Dat's de bery ting I'll do.
We'll smoder her like fury,
And I shall git divorce,
And den de judge and jury
We will not pay, in course.
    Exeunt L. H.

>←

Scene 7. Bed in C: Desdemona asleep. Cradle and child[66] *in it,* L. H. *Soft Music.*[67] *Enter* Otello *with candle,* L.

 Otello

It am de cause,   *caw—caw—caw*[68]
It am de cause.   *caw—caw—caw*
Let me not tell you ob it, oh you lubly stars,
It am de cause.   *caw—caw—caw*
Yes, she must die, dat is plain,
Else more niggers she'll betray again.
Put out dy light, why den dow ain't candle, still,
And I can light dee up, jist at my will.
Put out dy light, sweet Desdemony.
Why den, indeed, it all day wid dee, Honey.
But wives, you see, should neber do amiss.
And now me gib de last, de last fond kiss.
   Approaches to kiss, when she kicks him over[69]

 Desdemona

Who's there? Oh, dear me, is it you, Otello?

 Otello

You're right. It am indeed dat much-abused poor fellow.
Tell me, Desdemona, and tell me right,
Hab you, Honey, said your prayers to night?
And since dat kick jist now from you I tuck it,
You now, my lub, hab got to kick de bucket.

 Desdemona

Talk you of killing? Oh, for mercy's sake!

 Otello

It are a fact—and no mistake.[70]

Desdemona

Otello, you are jealous—that's the truth—
Of Michael Cassio, the poor dear youth.

Otello

Dear youth! Dear debil! Why you call him dear,
Here, to my face, my eye, my ear?
Dat towel you gib to Cassio—well I know it.

Desdemona

Upon my life and soul, I didn't do it.
Now ain't you quizzing?

Otello

True, as here I sit.

Why, damn you, I seed de towel, seed Cassio using it.[71]

Desdemona

Some towel like it, p'raps. How should you know?

Otello

Kase, in de corner, dars de 'nitial O.

Desdemona

Send for Michael Cassio.

Otello

Send for Michael Debil O—He can't come at all,
Kase he hab put him spoon into de wall.[72]

Desdemona

Dead, ah, I can't help crying for the lad.

Otello

What, cry before my face? [*rises*] Dat's too damn bad.
[*seizes the bed: child cries*] Hush you damn jaw.

Desdemona

Kill me tomorrow: let me live to night.
If you come near me, I'll scratch and bite. [*knock* L. H.]

Emilia [*outside*]

Oh, my good lord, I'd speak a word with you:
There's been foul murder done! What shall we do?

Otello

Here's some one coming, dar's no use of kicking.
You must be smuddered 'tween dese ar bed ticking.

Desdemona

Give me but half an hour

Otello

—not as you knows on.

Desdemona

A minute while I pray.

Otello

Take care den, dis goes on

Smothers her with bed. Enter all the characters except Roderigo.

Music—"Dan Tucker"[73]

Emilia

Oh, good, my lord, in town this night,
There has been such a desperate fight:
Michael Cassio with a blow
Has laid poor Roderigo low.

   Chorus   Bring them along before Otello,
Cassio, Rod and the other fellow.
Bring them along before Otello,
Cassio, Rod and the other fellow.

Otello

Roderigo dead and Cassio libing,
To desperation I am driben,
For what I've done, dar's no forgiben.
Eh, eh, eh! Good bye, wife.

   Chorus

Chorus

Oh you hateful, ugly fellow:
After killing Mrs. Otello,
You may cry and moan and bellow,
With your "Eh, eh, eh! Good bye, wife."

   Chorus

Otello   *Alma Opera*[74]

One word before you go:
I hab you for to know
I done de state some sarbice,
And de foe hab laid her low.

   And, when you dis relate,
   Noten extenuate,
But merely say, Good lack,

If his wife hab but been black,
Instead of white, all had been right
And she wouldn't hab got de sack.
 So, now, if it please your will,
 I'll go to de Treaden Mill. ⌈*Gong*⌉
  Desdemona comes to life and pops up

   Chorus—"Fifth July"[75]
Oh, look here; Oh, look there!
Desdemona's come to life:
See her rise and ope her eyes.
Otello's once more got his wife.
Then dance and sing
'Till the whole house ring,
And never more his wife he'll smother.
And, if all right tomorrow night,
We'll have this wedding over.
     Repeat
   Dance by all the Characters
    Curtain[76]

Street Prose

This section presents two biographies that purport to give histories of Jim Crow. Perhaps a more exact, relational term for this genre, however, might be *secular colportage*. These texts address and inform the people who have become fans of Jim Crow the way common people in earlier eras followed saints and martyrs. The first of these "lives" is an American pretended autobiography, sold or handed out at the Walnut Street Theatre in Philadelphia in 1835 and again in 1837, with slight variations. Its voice imitates Jim Crow dialect and spirit but yields no certain evidence that T. D. Rice wrote it—there are no signature phrasings or coinages indubitably his, and some of the events appear nowhere else in his songs or plays. If Rice did not write this autobiography, he probably did not object to it, for it accompanied some of his performances. As I have insisted throughout, "Jim Crow" was a cultural collage.

The second biography is English, five years later. Its third person narration pretends to authoritative objectivity, but is as far-fetched as everything else connected to the topic. This aptly sub-titled "erratic life" appeared at the end of a Jim Crow songster published in London to capitalize on the Jim Crow boom. It has no direct stylistic connection to T. D. Rice, who probably neither knew it was coming nor gained from it. This life announces that Jim Crow is not only black but also Indian (i.e., native American). The author is thus able to attribute noble-savage attitudes to Jim Crow, and to deploy him in vernacular critique of European mores.

LIFE
OF
JIM CROW,
showing
HOW HE GOT HIS INSPIRATION AS A
POET;
THE NUMBER OF FATHERS WHO CLAIMED HIM WHEN HE GOT
UP IN THE WORLD, THOUGH NONE WOULD OWN
HIM BEFORE;
THE MAGIC SPRING
"WAY IN DE WOODS OB OLE KAINTUCK, WHERE DE LITTLE
FAIRY TOLD HIM OF HIS FUTUR GREATNESS AND
CONSEQUENCE IN DE WORLD;"
HIS
INTERVIEW WITH GINERAL JACKSON
WITH
A WHOLE BASKET FULL OF INCIDENTS WHICH BEFEL HIM
BEFORE HE MADE HIS GRAND JUMP ON THE
STAGE!

WRITTEN BY HIMSELF

PHILADELPHIA:
For sale, wholesale and retail, at No. 96 North Seventh
street, and No. 44 Strawberry st.

1835.[1]

✦✦

Entered according to the Act of Congress in the year 1835 by James
M'Minn in the clerk's office of the District Court of the Eastern District
of Pennsylvania.[2]

✦✦

To my Feller Citizens de Public.

Ben I inspirate dis manscrip, I no think I ebber pit him in massa print-
ers hand; but some how or toder, tis fernal hard for a gemmen like me to
know my thoughts fore I born; but den again someting tell me tro' de

milk ob my mudder's kindess dat I mus some day or todder come to be
great liderary character, so now you see de folks in de city Philumdelfy
make me vocalificize my histry so often toder night, I make my infernal
sensibilifications yieldify to de "Fox poplar," as I tinks dey call de people's breath at de Walnut street Te-atre—bere I do say dey git along
from Six to Six. I am gwaing in short time to do like oder great hactors,
publish my account ob men and manners in dese blessed States, an I trus
I shall be inable to do dem as much justice as dey desarve, on account ob
my debilty to use falsificationority as de foreignificated deatrical ladies
do.[3] Ib I do not howebber beat some dem up a gum tree, den I trus my
dear little Jimmy may fall off de chimbly top and—pop safe and sound
into de arms ob ole moder Public.

JIM CROW,
dis time de year 1835

❧ THE LIFE OF JIM CROW. ☙

Be reader Tom, or Dick, or Dolly,
I make dem crack deir sides by jolly.

Doe de niggers us'd to tell me, ben I was no higher den chaw tobacco, dat
I cum into dis world a crying, de good buckra[4] folks mus allow I send
good many ob dem out ob it wid laughing, and, as I hab been told by several mighty larned Doctors, hab cured eb'ry gal dat ebber see me jump
ob dat cruel incease de insumption ob de bones, dats de reason dem ugly
ole maids what make belly bands for de ladies, dont courage my informances, caze I make deir cusomers swell out so wid my pretty looking
face dat dey buss de trings, right straight, dereby gibbing de bowels
plenty room for de food ob mirth to injest in. But stop nigger! guess de
folks tink I gwan to do like ole Dan Webster, when he spit him great
speech 'bout de Bank,—begin to talk 'bout one ting and end wid anoder,
for all de world like de sea sarpint, de head or tail ob which nebber found
yet, nor ebber will be, 'cording to my notion of noseology, or whigology,
its all de same to a rale Kaintuck 'bacco nigger.[5]

I war born one cold frosty morning, I recollect him well, and I was so little dat mudder made me a cloak out ob a possum skin, and send me up to de planter's house in a little basket. Gor a marcy[6] how de young ladies did laff ben aunt Susabella held me up for deir 'spection. Why he's no bigger den a hop-toad, said one ob de gals; "he will raise to fortune by hopping," said a voice from de ceiling—It's de child of a witch, cried dey all, running out of de room as quick as dere drumsticks would let dem. Aunt dropp me on de floor an ran too, ben a big tom-cat tinking I war a possum for sartain picked me up in he teet an ran out to de barn wid me, but jis as he war 'bout to make a dinner ob me an ole woman cum into de barn on crutches and hit him sich a rap cross de back dat he jumped out ob de window; and putting me in a bag she carried me to my mudder's, who war right jollificated at seeing me, as she heard dat de cat had caught me an thought I was a gone nigger, for Kaintuck cats often do eat young darkies, dats sartain. De ole white woman, (and she war right funny looking,) blow'd in my mouth, as she said, to send all melancholy breath out of my ribs, and taking a bottle out ob her bosom she poured some ob de contents down my troat, saying dat was ginsprashun from de fountain ob de nine muses what sing on de Pellicon mountain.[7] Bidding my mudder take good care ob me she sung something and den went down through de floor in a big blaze ob smoke. By jolly, de ole log cabin shook like de ole debbil in a gale ob wind, and mudder war so frightened she covered me and herself so tight under de clothes dat I like to smother for sartain. Bel it soon get 'ported all ober de country dat de debbil had widout joke something or oder to do wid me on 'count ob de ole woman wid de crutches, mudder being sich a fool as to empty de story out her mout to ebbery body. Whites, blacks, mulattoes kangarees, and cream colour faces flocked round de cabin ebbery day to see de wonderful imp ob de ole boy as dey use to call me, but mudder did'nt care much what de fools say as dey bring her plenty ob good tings to fill her tomach and make milk for poor little me. Some tell her she better feed me on sulphur gruel, as dat all I git to eat bine by; and one tarnal he nigger put me in he coat pocket to carry me home for a pattern for him wife, but I gib de darkee such a nip in he sitting part wid my squirrel teet, dat he sing out glory halhimlugee and take me out as quick as no time, for you see I been born wid sharp set grinders jis like dey say in de play King Dick hab.[8] Ole mistress frightened half to death 'bout de incircumtance ob de voice dat cum from her kitchen chimbly ben I wrapped up in possum skin, so she writes for her husban to cum home from Congress quick as lightnin caze she tell him ole mudder brought to bed wid a young debbil, doe she 'low'd I hab no tail nor claws. Ben I be six week old, Massa cum home in a debbil ob a way, and dey say war a gwan to hab me burnt right straight, but ben he saw me, by gosh if he did'nt roar out like ole Davy Crocket; he laff so harty dat he shook him watch out de pocket, but catch him by de chain, an he swore I be de blackest nigger him ebber see—so he christened me Jim Crow, right off de reel. But guess him git a mighty big fright for him ugly name, for jis as him sprinkle de cole water in my innocent face a whapping big clap of thunder make him start, as he know berry well dat he war taking a job out ob de parson's hands, and by jingoes ib de ole woman on de crutch did'nt pop her head right in at de door, all burning like wid fire. Massa shake like alligator on a snow bank, but him could'nt git out ob de cabin no hows he could 'magine. "Keep dis slave," says de ole woman, "till he be twenty years of age, an by using him well you shall hab eberry kind of good luck, you family all lib and you grow rich; ben he be twenty, you mus set him free or all your good luck go to de ole Harry." Den she make him berry low bow and fly up de chimbly jis like screech owl;—gor bless me tis long while to 'member from time I six week ole, but I tink I see massa's face turn blue as him shot out ob de door like a ball out ob rail Kaintuck rifle. Nex day he hab us moved to more comfortable quarters, bere mudder was kept busy doing noting but taking care ob me; as massa be fraid he lose him fortune ib anyting should happen me. I suck de ole woman dry in 'bout six months, so dey fed me on mush an milk till I grow big 'nough to run 'bout, den dey gib me hoe cake an 'lasses which be one great cause ob my sweet an musical voice, which de fair sex say beats dere panny forty's[9] all hollow. One day as I war playing in de road, a tin pedlar cum along in a waggon an tinking he could teal me right handy he jumped out and picking me up, he pit into a tin bucket an drove off like ole scratch, but guess him got played yankee trick heself dat time, caze he soon smell brimstone, an on looking round saw de ole lame woman carrying off bucket and all in a cloud ob smoke. By gorry how him make him horses fly den—massa Reeside's flying coaches[10] bere no touch to dem, I swan, for de poor pedlar thought he'd pick'd up Ole Sam's youngest son, so he cut him stick fas as possible. De ole woman set me down at mudder's door who I dare say has got de berry same water bucket to dis day ob de year 1835. After dis I grow'd pretty big and massa he grow'd berry rich an had me larnt to read and write, an I nebber work'd only ben I pleased, which war'nt berry often I tells you, for I used to ride upon a stick most de time which make my legs quite suple, an 'nables me to jump so much to de sasfaction of de buckra folks at de presen time o'day. Bel tings all go on smooth an nice, my young missus all get married to rich men, and I git on to be sixteen year ole, ben one day as I be strolling through de woods, way back in ole Kaintuck, I gwan to feel dry and set my pretty sef down on an ole stump, wishing I had drink water—I nebber drink rum dem days, caze it war'nt thought genteel. Bel, what you tink—dont tink about any ting to eat doe,—jis as I was wishing for something to drink away rolls de arth from before me an up spouts a beautiful spring of water, an out ob de centre of it a little fairy popped her pretty little sef all dressed in gold an green, an handing me a silver cup, jis like de one de Bostonians gwan to present me wid nex time I jump dat way,—she tell me to drink till my tomach burse, but nebber to come to her premises again, or she would take my pretty voice from me. Gor a marcy, I gwan to git frightened mysef—but I took good drink an started for home, but lor bless you, if I did'nt git sich a belly ache as no nigger ebber git den my name's not Jim Crow. Twitch, twitch, went de small gut:—waugh, waugh, went de big ones, ben jis as I got over a fence up come de intents of my tomach into de road:—guy, I to't it war a gone case wid me, but when I look'd down it war a big roll of music dat I had heaved up. I looked at him, an all at once de tune pat as sugar on de end oh my tongue and I rhymed to it from dat dey to dis, for twar nothing more or less den de fashionable air ob your humble sarvant to command. Jim Crow. Short time arter dis, as I war swinging on de gate, who should cum along but ole Gineral Jackson. I trows up my hat as he cum'd up, and singing,

> If I war president ob
> Dese United State

"what would you do?" said a gemmen in he comp'ny. I said, why

> I'd eat molasses all de day
> An swing upon de gate.
> > An wheel about and turn about
> > And do jis so,
> > And eb'ry time I wheel about
> > I jump Jim Crow.

"Well done darkee," said de gemmen; de ole Gineral laff'd and throwing me half a dollar, tole me if I ebber come to Washington I mus gib him a call. By gum, if dat did'nt set wool on an end, den I nebber poked de eye out ob green lizard. What, git a half dollar from de great Jackson! why it made my head wheel about all de day, and cocking up my ears jis like de ole gray jackass, I roar'd out him praises like a mad bull; I could'nt bear to speek to one ob my own colour for a whole month, an dat night ben I war eating supper, I got so tickled about de gills tinking ob de high honour I git, dat I swallowed de tea cup instead ob de tea, an I 'bliged to hit myself two, tree confounded hard pokes on the 'tomach fore I could break him china sides to let him out, for doe like de kind public, I hab a large swallow, I did'nt know dat my internal tubes were quite so spacious.

One day as I war looking in de bushes for birds nest, I hear something go hiss, hiss, hiss; den him go rack-a-de, rack-a-de rack; ben out popped snake, two tree times bigger den de sea-sarpint, and made right at me. I cut dirt no ways slow and he cut grass arter me, poking out ob he mout two stings big as scyd[11] blades—I bellowed, he hissed and rattled, ben jist as de infernal chap was about, as I thought, to run his stings through de marrow ob my back bone, de ole woman make her imperance, and de

Snake chasing Jim Crow.

sarpint put he tail into he mout and swallowed himsef. By gosh, dey did'nt catch me gwan arter birds nest in de bushes agin, no hows.

De berry day I be twenty-year ole, massa gib me fine new suit clothes, an a riproarous drink ob wine an told me I war now free an might either stay wid him or go seek my fortun elsewhere, so tells him I did'nt zactly know yet what I would do, though thought I war'nt born in de woods to spend my days mong owls doe I war named Crow. He laff'd right hearty and gibbing me little change, said I'd been de making ob him, so he hoped I'd be streemely lucky myself.

Den massa help himself and me,
To nudder glass ob wine,
Which soon make my pretty eyes
Wid liveliness to shine.
An I wheel about—

An go swing on de ole gate to show de travellers dat be passing, my spic an span "long tail blue" which you all recollect de fernal circus folks stole from me some time ago, but him no fit de nigger who wear it no hows he can fix him. Bine by a strolling company of play-actors came past, and hearing me sing so charmingly, one ob dem cum up an took off him hat to me, in de mos civil way you can 'magine; tinks I my eyes mus be los dere right way ob seeing or I been a greater feller den I tink I be—so I puts on a long face, an keep my hat on, jis like General Jackson did, ben I trow'd my hat off to him. "What be your name," says the hactor to me. "Jim Crow," says I—"Crow," says he, "why bless my soul Mr. Crow, if you will come along with us to Insinnatti, you'll make a fortune in no time." "By hoe cake," says I, "den I'll go; but I got no hoss."—"Oh! it aint far," says he, "come along an you can ride on mine ebbry now an den." I tank'd him berry kindly but said I'd soon find one for myself, so I jis run to de cabin bid mudder good-bye, and taking a long bean pole, I mounted him an by gorry if I did'nt keep ahead ob de show folks bone setters all de way to 'Hio! doe now since I hab time reflec and keep a first rate horse myself, I tink I might jis as well walked, for I rather guess, as our yankee overseer used to say, de bean pole war more in de road den oderwise, doe conceit be great ting in dis world,—specially wid de half-cut gentry and half bred (who sometimes lack bread) lawyers,—so jis as long as I tought I war a horse-back, I gallopped on no ways slow. Ben we got into Insinatti I throw'd my thin horse ober a fence an walked on de pavement, but I soon had a mob arter me for I unluckily in passing de market, jis sing one varse bout it, an gib a jump or two, ben de farmers dropped dere butter, de butchers dropped dere knives and de hucksters[12] broke dere eggs, all in dere hurry to see Jim Crow, for dey had heard all about me from ole massa. Den dey all want to know who wur my fader;[13] one ob de butchers said if he know him he gib him fifty dollars, and an ole cow wid two calves, a merino ram, an ole sow wid eleben young pigs, for me. I tole him I was my own fader now, caze massa know bery well dat cording to de 'structions he get from de ole lady on de crutch, dat I mus be my own massa when I be twenty year ole. I tole him I did not 'member now zacly which wur my fus fader, caze ebery he niggar on massa's plantation, said I wur his lubly boy—doe ebery one at fust disown me, an keep out sight an hearin. Near as I member now, de fus who wur willing to be my fader, (caze he undertan I wur to be free when twenty year ole—he tought he be too) wur long-leg Joe: de nex, Ben; den Tim; den Jimy; den Ned; den

Harry; den big Bill; den little Bill; den Tom; den Ike; den lean Jack; den Dick; an last little Dave. Gosh my namesakes nebber flocked so thick round a dead horse as de Insinatti folks did round poor me, an ben I got to de hotel bere de players put up, I hab to go out on de balcony and make dem a speech, jis like Mr. Binney did to the bank folks in Baltimore, only I got ten times more plause, doe I did'nt say half as much as him did, doe I spec mine war more to de parpose.[14] "Ladies and gemmen," said I—(de manager ob de show folk said I mus begin so)—"de insincere inspect wid which you conceive de parson ob Jim Crow, make de stream ob ingratitude run ober de brim of my tinder heart, jis like buttermilk out ob a churn in a hot day, an as I hab make gagement wid Mr. Diddler,[15] to muse you on de stage wid a specimen ob my liric ginspirashun which war poured down my troat ben I war no bigger dan a goose egg, I hopes I shall hab de honor ob displeasing you all, as I can grin like a wild cat, roar like a bull, and jump jis like de little hop-toad dat cuts him shines mong de grass in ole Kaintuck,—

> So come and see de play
> To-morrow night,
> An I fill each merry heart
> Wid laughter an delight.
>> An I wheel about an turn about,
>> An do jis so—
>> An ebery time I wheel about
>> I—

Fell right plump though de rotten roof ob de piazza, landed on de Judge's head, and pitched right straight head foremost into a big basket ob eggs;—gorry, how my wool look all over white an yellow. De people huzzaed, de judge shook him cane,—I ginn'd; de huckster cursed bout her eggs, de landlord swore I mus mend him roof an twenty or thirty oder folks handed me swallows as fast as could swallow dem, an I got sniped before dinner—doe I soon jumped de liquor out ob my head to de tune ob Jim Crow. After dinner I gwan to de theatre,—by gum but it seemed a quare place, de woods an de houses looked jis as natural as life, an de gold dat shined all about made my eyes glisten like de black snake. Bine by de fiddlers come in;—gor a marcy ib one ob de fiddles warn't as big as de ole log cabin I be born in—dey tell me I must larn dem my favorite hair,—but I tole dem dat be impossible, caze I got noting but wool. Den dey laff,—I grin,—dey laff louder,—den I jump,—an dey all hole dere sides, caze dey say I be the funniest feller ebber darkened de boards. But dey den tell me dey mus hab de music for my song, so I gib de roll dat popped out my mout arter drinkin ob de water ob de spring, way in de woods ob ole Kaintuck, an dey struck up the tune at once an I sing bout de times jis as fas as dey culd scratch de gut, an de manager and show folks low'd I be an improdigy at rhyming, but bless your sole what in mus come out, an as de ole wich blow'd my belly full ob varses I spec I wont want to eat any more for long time to come; not till de chip ob de ole block, young massa Dyonisius Julius Caesar Fenny Kimble Sylvester Daggerwood Richard Third Coriolinus Bobby Trott Sammy Dobbs Jim Crow, Jr., is big enough to take my place any hows;[16] so de public may res sattisfied ob my bilities to displease dem for some years yet, ben I will happy to introduce my little youngster wid he big names to dere kind discountenance and favour, an ib he only jumps de rhino in he pocket fas as him fadder do, by Dinah an I can lib live game chicken an de gold I got in my rattlesnake skin puss,[17] which be hardly big enuff to hole de shiners I make by my delicate heels an red lips, for I sartainly blieve de white folks will nebber git a belly full ob Jim Crow, till he git all dere spare change. Bel next night I make my fus impearance before pub-lic, an dey bere so much pleased wid me, dat dey anchored[18] an make me sing twice as much as I promise, but gitting tired ob dis fun, one night I gib dem ginteel hint in de following manner, which make dem more marciful on my libber an lights for de rest de time:

> O! white folks, white folks,
>   For nigger never feel,
> You tink my belly nebber ache
>   While toeing de big heel.
>   But I wheel about an jump about,
>   An do jis so—
>   When twice I sing, of breath I'm out,
>   I am, Jim Crow.

Dey gib me three cheers an nebber inquest me to sing more den twice ob an evening agin. I make pockets full ob money in 'Hio, den I takes off my stage coat and puts on my long tail blue and hoe'd it right parpendiclar to Baltimore, and pits up at Massa Barnum's.[19]

First day I pit up at Massa Barnum's, I buy a handsome quizzing glass, caze I hear dey be all de go; but I forgot to ask de man I buy it from how to use de quare ting.[20] First I try to look troo it wid both eyes, but I could'nt see a bit;—den I try one eye, but him looked quite cloudy so as I war coming down stairs I hold him up and shut both eyes, ben I catch my foot in de carpet, pitch head foremost into a turreen of turtle soup de waiter war carrying up,—spoilt my new coat and silk hat and broke de chinee into smashes; so nex day I take de fernal glass out ob de frame and den I could see all de way to Boston wid de 'spensive article.

Dandy peering through a monocle.

I den goes to de theatre an makes engagement for six night at a hundred dollars a night and free benefit, which was a rail smasher,—pit, boxes, and gallery jam full ob de pretty Baltimore gals an dere stiff looking beaux, a tousand dollars went smack into my pocket, slick as possum fat. Bel tinks I dis beats ole 'Hio for sartain. Ben I gits up next morning arter my benefit de waiter gib me a letter. Now who dat from tinks I—by Venus twar a right down lub letter signed Dinah Rumpfizz Quashdiddle, cake baker, Gay street. Hollo! nigger, tinks I my happiness an fortune come right plump down togedder.

So you see de tarnal quizzin glass spile my new coat, de fust ting I do is, go rite off to de tailor and git a new one; den as I hab such bad luck wid de glass, tink best go git bigger one, caze 'spect toder so small dat mus be de reason ob all de trubble; soon as de new cloas cum from de tailor, arter eatin two bowls coffee, a twis loaf, six saft crabs and a dozzen eggs for breakfast I goes an paid my inspecs to de lubly Dinah—who tole me she wur up to her middle in lub for me, and said if I'd only marry her and jump Jim Crow to her ebbery night, she'd sell her cakes all day and keep me like a gentleman. I tank'd her, but tole her guess she could'nt make cakes jump to de tune ob a tousand shiners in one night like I could Jim Crow. She blushed quite sprized at dat, and began to cry, saying she sposed she mus break her little heart bout me and die and go to de debble widout my tinder infections. My delicate tomach, you see could'nt iszactly bear dis, specially as him had'nt much to eat dat morn-

Dandy looking in a mirror.

ing, so I hugged her in my arms an tole her she should'nt die an ole maid dis time so she dress herself an we went to de parsons an get made Mr. an Mrs. Crow for de small sum of five dollars; cheapest piece ob flesh ebber I bought. I makes re-gagement for nudder six nights to de tune ob seventeen hundred dollars, so I sells Dinah's cake shop out an starts off for Washington, bere I din'ed wid de Gineral's Kitchen Cabinet[21]— supped wid Davy Crockett—sang ole Webster into hireogliphics, tickled Gen. Green[22] in de palm ob de hane for a puff—made de duel fighting Pointdexer[23] laugh tree times—git traduced to de star Fanny,[24]—an jump de congress folks an Washingtonians out of nine hundred dollars, ben I cut stick to Philadelphy to see dat great musicianer, Frank John- son,[25] and make de quaker folks grin de dust out of dere rusty[26] pockets, which by gosh I done no ways slow, for I clipsed all de stars dat ebber shot dis way from ole England, bere I soon spec to go for de parpose of jumping de gout out of Johnny Bull's big toe, an handling a few of de king's pretty golden pictures. Gor bless you I'd sooner hab a pocket full of dem jingling tings den wear de crown of de original. Arter making successful hit among de quakers I lef Dinah at boarding, caze it be bout de time she feel queamish, and I soon 'rive in de mighty city of ships, steeples and dandies, called New York, bere as soon as my rival war known, I war waited on by de great bolitician ole Noah,[27] some 'lation I bound to de man who went a sailing in de flood and landed some where dis side de moon;—pity he had'nt thrown de snakes he hab overboard, doe guess de sea sarpint mus hab fell out of de window and grow good bit since dem days.

Bel I gwan wid de man of types,[28] to de Park Theatre, bere I make gagement for twelve nights at pretty high rate for sartain, but Lor bless you, instead of twelve I hab to sing twenty nights—and sich houses,— good Lor I spec sometimes to see de sides burst out an de roof come down an put a stinguisher on some de folks, but he ribs be strong nuff I find to bear all de weight dey could put in him. Ben I make my gagement wid de manager, ole Noah said 'twar 11 o'clock, an we might as well wash it down with a little punch an turtle.[29] So away he takes me to an infectory, bere he guzzle two bowls to my one and tip two tree glasses Ice punch to cool he internals. Den he took out his pencil an write a long puff bout Mr. Crow, which said should shine in large caps in de Ebening Star. What kine ob caps says I do you wear in de Star office—he laffed right merrily at my ignorance of de black art, and said he meant capital letters—bel den I was as wise as before caze I always insider all letters *capitals* dat contain a good gagement for me.—Before we leave de table he call de landlord for de reckning, which he tole me was nine shillings and sixpence York,[30] which I had to pay, as he said he gave his last fip[31] dat mornin to buy lollypop for his young son Mordica Noses Dnablidie (or some other die) Noah, den telling me dey cooked excellent suppers where I put up, an sold excellent chapaign, promised to introduce me to some jolly dogs arter de play was over, he den took him leave, but if he drink any champaigne dat night, guess some body else pay for it besides Jim Crow, for I slipt out of de theatre and got home an into bed before him tought I hab time to undress. I like puffs berry well, but champaign ones be too dazzling for de white ob my eye, specially ben dey poked into de tail of a Star.

I nex pay my devotions to de folks ob de lidderary henporium, bere I sung and jumped to a petty fine tune. Here I git traduced to all de puff makers, blue stockings, &c. an after spending a pretty ingreeable month, took steamboat for Albany, where I made de sour crout eaters laugh till dere faces were as round as their cabbages, and getting hole ob plenty of dere rusty[32] dollars, I slipped back again to Filladelphia, bere I jump

berry successfully again, an hab done so stremely often since my dear
Dinah presented me wid an inzact minature of myself, in de parson of my
little son who I tend to raise as gently as a monthly rose dat de sweetness
of him skin, (gor, him no much smell like rose dis warm day doe) shall
pour its indelicate flavour among de fashionable roses dat visit Chesnut
st. house, bere de stars dat shine wid foreign light and injure the peoples
eyes, as bel as dere pockets,[33] will all twinkle and turn pale beneat de brilliant rays of my comet, Dionysius[34] &c. &c. Jimmy Crow de younger, who
wid he young broder dat I spec come in de world next week, if Dinah hab
luck, will stonish de natives much as I hab done. But some oder spare
time I let de public know how dey cum on, an gib like Miss Fanny, my
journal ob de manners an customs of de peoples,[35] which like her I larnt
by looking at dem from de stage or stage-coach window, pretty much as
just the same;

> So I bid adieu unto dis life,—
> Bless you dont you cry,
> Dis paper life I only mean,
> So haste de book to buy:
>> An I turn about an wheel about
>> An do jis so,
>> An ebbery time I turn about
>> I jump Jim Crow.

A FAITHFUL ACCOUNT OF THE LIFE OF JIM CROW THE AMERICAN NEGRO POET[1]

No collection of songs ever gained more popularity than those sung by MR. RICE, in the character of JIM CROW. In the fashionable colonnade, in the filthiest street, in the naked damp cellar, and the luxuriantly carpeted drawing-room, the words and the tune of Jim Crow are constantly to be heard, and the humourous imitations of the eccentric being is the prevailing theme of conversation. Having become so well known, in regard of his poetic abilities, it is but just to give a faithful account of the life of this "AMERICAN NIGGER IMPROVISTORY."[2]

In this memoir we are spared the tedious and dry enquiries of genealogical branches, roots or trees—the fooleries of descent—of marriages and intermarriages—or any application to the herald's office. We shall not go further back than the parents of the subject of these pages.

Oulamou, the Indian name of Jim's father, in his youth was celebrated as a hunter and a warrior, and as he grew older he became a councillor among his black[3] countrymen. In the celebrated treaty of Lancaster, in Pennsylvania, in 1774, between the government of Virginia and the Six Nations,[4] he was selected to deliver the strange and amusing answer to the commissioners who had made an offer to take some of their children and educate them, it should be noted that oratory is a favourite study with the Indians: we cannot refrain from translating a portion of the address:—"Our opinion of your manners and habits is such that we should wish our children to avoid them, they are base and slavish—base because you labour to support part of your people in idleness, and submit to others who possess neither age or oratory—slavish because you continually labour. What would you return to us as our sons? Men who have neither activity or vigour—men who could not run down their game—suffer cold and hunger—build their huts or kill their various enemies. But we heartily thank you; and offer in return to take any of your sons and make men of them." On another occasion he was selected to answer the Swedish minister, who after labouring hard to make them acquainted with our sacred truths was thus replied to:—"What you have told us is all very good. It was most assuredly wrong for the woman to eat a raw apple. It is better to make them all into cider. We are much obliged by your kindness in coming so far to tell us those things which you have heard from your mothers. We practice all we believe. We have no prisons—no officers to compel obedience or inflict punishment—we have no hypocrisy from fears of loss or gain—we boast not of wealth, nor are we disgusted at poverty. Shall we come and teach you."

His mother, like other Indian women, tilled the ground, and dressed the food,—attended the public councils that her memory might preserve and hand down to posterity the public transactions. She was very handsome in person, and the following beautiful and poetic answer is attributed to her: meeting a man in the woods who implored her to look upon him and love him, "Oulamou," said she, "my husband, is ever before my eyes and hinders me from seeing you."

Shortly after the treaty of 1774, Jim's father died; and his mother going to Albany to exchange beavers' skins caught an epidemic, which it will be recollected raged there about that period, and it proved fatal to her.[5] The hero of our story, then a mere boy, was taken in charge by a merchant, who changed his Indian name into that of JIM CROW.

Jim was sent to this gentleman's country-house, where he was soon taught many domestic duties which he would be expected to perform. An indolence of disposition and an ardent love of mischief were his most conspicuous qualifications; he was constantly ill when any work was to be done, and after having been dogged and driven to a job he was sure to find something else to do. Yet give him a game to play with his master's children and he was the most active, good natured, little fellow ever seen. Jim in incessant acts of mischief, and in receipt of daily thrashings was retained in this service until the following performance in his darling delight. One day as he was attending the orders of his mistress in the drawing-room, she had occasion to go into another room and leave him by himself, first of all he caught all the flies and impaled them upon long pins, which he sought for and hoarded with miser care for the purpose, and then left them sticking in the window frames; next turning his attention to his master's favourite pointer, and his lady's two tortoise-shell cats, that were laying basking on the hearth-rug, he most industriously set to work and tied all their tails together. The dog rising felt his tail confined whilst the cats, terrified, sprang forward in an opposite direction. A complete hurly-burly ensued, the dog howled, the cats yelled, the dog jumped about the room, upsetting chairs, tables, glasses, and ornaments. Jim chased and shouted at the dog, his mistress screamed, the servants rushed in, at last the terror-stricken dog dashed through the window, and away through the town with the cats lifeless at his heels.

In his next situation he had to attend upon the servants and be a complete drudge. Here he was the pest and amusement of the whole kitchen. The servants would often have him to sing, tumble, and play upon a penny whistle, at all of which polite accomplishments he was particularly expert. An Irish footman was the peculiar delight of his torment. On one occasion seeing this man's coat hanging up he took out the pocket handkerchief and in its stead placed a cap belonging to one of the maids and a red garter. It happened as the lady was descending from her carriage she perceived some dust on her shoes, and requested John to knock it off, John put his hand into his pocket, and with all alacrity possible, brought forth the girl's night-cap with the red garter dangling from it; he gazed with astonishment at it and then hurried it back again; his lady's countenance flushed with vexation. On returning home he was told he knew the reason why he had to state what was due to him, and that he and another had to leave instantly. It was with the greatest difficulty, and most solemn protestations of innocence that he was allowed to retain his situation. He immediately went to the kitchen, and without any preliminary discourse belaboured poor Jim's back. Jim while yet in tears went up to the innocent man, and laying his hand on his shoulder said, "Massa Patty you forgib poor Jim, him no one take him part." "Well and sure," said the good natured Irishman, "if you be a good boy I'll be your father." But whilst this short dialogue was going on, Jim who had bent a large pin, hooked one of the tails of his coat up to his epaulette, and the bell ringing at that moment off ran the man, in this ridiculous plight, to attend upon his mistress and her company. John was told to hand some wine when on turning round he presented in appearance an indication of feeling inexpressible contempt for the ladies. Poor John, in perfect innocence, was rudely ordered out of the room, and not to be seen there again.

In this situation Jim might have been comfortable, but like many other extraordinary characters in history, with a trifling *shade* of difference, a failing pursued his footsteps and occasioned his ruin, and that failing was a restless and unceasing love of the *black* sex. Here as he said:

> One night upon an afternoon,
> To a fine gal—'tis just so
> I did play a pretty tune,
> Dey did call *Young* Jim Crow.[6]

For this accident he was ordered a slight punishment, but as he sung:—

> I jump aboard de boat, ah, urly in de mornin,
> An I lebe Orleans, jist as de day was dawnin,
> I hide under wood, war de niggas jist hab toss em.[7]

The next place where we have any trace of this eccentric man, is at Washington, where in company with another nigger,

> Jim beat de drum, an big Bill's de fifer.

With these harmonious instruments these two sons of Apollo attended all the merry-makings of the black people about Washington, and from Jim's humour and songs he was always a welcome guest. Whilst here, although he preferred going in dirty, slovenly, ragged dresses, combining all fashions, costumes, and colours, he was selected by the rich niggars to be an orator, at a public meeting—

> 'bout de colonization,
> An dere I spoke a speech 'bout amalgamation.[8]

Having thus enjoyed the delight of addressing a multitude who listen with respect, and applaud with fervour, at the same time finding there was really no difficulty in the matter, the thought struck him of commencing business as a preacher, he afterwards sung:—

> O I is dat boy dat knows to preach a sermin,
> 'Bout temperance and "seven up," and all dat kind of varmin.

His sermons abound in humour and are ridiculous in the extreme, as he frequently would preach nearly the whole in rhyme: a volume of them was published in New York; they highly delighted the black people. He might have lived here comfortably and even respected under the ample and hackenied cloak of sanctity, but—

Den I meet Miss Fillacy, corna ob de lane,
* * * * * *
Den in six months time, oh, Fillacy get bigga,
An in three months ater dat, den then comes a little nigga,
Den de wite man come for to take away my wife,
Den I up an I stick him wid a big Jack knife.[9]

He fled from Washington for this offence, and for some time led a rambling life, working for farmers and in villages, until thinking his offence would be forgotten, and loving society, he ventured to New York. He worked during several years as a porter: nothing in this period of his life is worth recording until we find him engaged in a matrimonial affair. Returning home one night, attempting to preserve an equilibrium, he stumbled over something and in utter helplessness and senselessness he lay and fell asleep. In the morning he was awakened by a woman's screams, and starting up he found himself in a strange room, on a pallet of straw, with a woman who had taken their single covering to hide her nakedness whilst she exposed his. To a person coming in she declared, in tears, that Jim must have made her drunk and then taken advantage of her hitherto spotlessnesss. Jim declared on his part, with much gravity, that he believed it was a scheme of hers to deprive him of his innocence. After many more words, Jim said as their tastes appeared to agree in one respect, perhaps they did in others, and he appeased the wrath of the imagined sullied woman, by proffering marriage. The fact of the case was, that the patrol finding two black people laying together took them to be man and wife, carried them into the nearest hovel, and undressing them, placed them side by side, and left them snoring in harmonious concert. Like almost all hasty marriages it proved unfortunate, for by a reference to the Police Office reports, of May 7th, we find Jim applying for a divorce, his wife having gone to live with another man. Jim stated, "he had been to Parson Arly, the black preechee, for a divorce, who say— look to God in my troubles—Den me ax Parson if wife no for bedience to him husband—den, my good massa, Parson say, wen my wife quarrel and so lazy, I must call upon God—Den me ax Parson if God will boil me pot, and make me shirt—Me ax him, wat him preechee good for, so him no nyam, so him naked, so him see him own lawful wife in noder man bed." The case was dismissed, with a recommendation.

To avoid this termagant he visited England and France; the only particulars known are what he relates in his songs. It was whilst on his voyage to England, a sailor of the name of Charles Miller, of Hull, learnt him to play upon the violin, an accomplishment that proved exceedingly useful to him in after life; hearing Paganini perform he used to give the most grotesque imitation of that odd looking being ever witnessed. Jim soon returned to his native country, when he fixed his residence at New York, occasionally visiting Philadelphia, where his humourous vagaries, and ready wit in recording public events, or describing nigger tricks and cunning in rhyme, always ensured him a hearty welcome.

Thus he lived for years, his presence giving always uncontrollable delight to children, of whom he was very fond, and pleasure to the aged. He had no enemies, excepting, always, that unnatural, selfish, repulsive thing, that stalks about the world, and terms itself "an evangelical." If he had an enemy, he a was solitary, but may be a powerful one, and that was himself.

As he grew old some slight compunctions of mind, for acts of his early life, although he did not then know them to be so heinous, affected his thoughts, and the moment being seized by some earthly saints, they soon blackened his moral errors with such a deep dye, as to outstrip that of his own skin, and with a worn out frame, a feeble mind, and a terrified imagination, he sunk to the peaceful grave, in 1830.

No sooner was this odd being known to be at his eternal resting place, than all his humour was brought into the recollections of young and old, and the remains of his poetic genius, that could be recollected, given to posterity by means of the printing press. The wealthy, intelligent, and comic Mr. Rice, did not think him unworthy of being the subject of his inimitable mimicry on the stage, which was hailed with enthusiastic delight by his countrymen, and lately received with thunders of applause in happy England.

Notes
Acknowledgments
Index

Notes

INTRODUCTION

1. See W. T. Lhamon, Jr., *Raising Cain: Blackface Performance from Jim Crow to Hip Hop* (Cambridge, Mass.: Harvard University Press, 1998), 180–185.

2. Carroll Smith-Rosenberg, "Bourgeois Discourse and the Age of Jackson: An Introduction," in *Disorderly Conduct: Visions of Gender in Victorian America* (New York: Knopf, 1985), 79.

3. Karl Marx, "The Eighteenth Brumaire of Louis Bonaparte," in *The Marx-Engels Reader,* ed. Robert C. Tucker (New York: Norton, 1972), 516.

4. For the theory of fetishes dependent on "cross-cultural spaces" see William Pietz, "The Problem of the Fetish, I," *Res* 9 (Spring 1985): 5–17. Pietz convinces me that a fetishized performance, like Jim Crow dancing, is a "'composite fabrication' . . . of articulated relations between certain heterogenous things" (5, 7–8). In fetishes, which are embodied things, one finds "the site of both the formation and revelation of ideology and value-consciousness" (13).

5. Beyond my account of Jim Crow as trickster in *Raising Cain*, pp. 180–185, cited above, see Bessie Jones and Bess Lomax Hawes, *Step It Down: Games, Plays, Songs, and Stories from the African-American Heritage* (New York: Harper & Row, 1972), 55 ff.

6. According to clippings in his file at the Harvard Theatre Collection, Charles White was born in New York City 4 June 1821 and died there 4 January 1891. He performed with the Christy Minstrels, organized the Kitchen Minstrels in 1844, and was with many companies until he opened the Melodean Theatre at 53 Bowery in New York, which was twice burned and rebuilt before White closed it on 22 April 1854 and moved to 49 Bowery. When this location burned, White relocated at 585, then 598 Broadway. He was still connected to Edward Harrigan's minstrel company when he died.

The edition of *Bone Squash* that Frederic A. Brady published in New York, "as adapted by Charles White," is characteristic. It has no date, but Brady bound its forty pages of text with ten pages of ads for other plays and books that his house issued from about 1859 onwards.

7. A partial exception: Julian Mates correctly reported that Rice's *Otello* manuscript was in the Theatre Collection of the New York Public Library, Lincoln Center (Julian Mates, *America's Musical Stage: Two Hundred Years of Musical Theatre* [Westport, Conn.: Greenwood Press, 1985; reprint, New York: Praeger, 1987], 211, n. 6). But Mates may not have read the MS or followed the production history because he misspells the title, seems unaware of the play's astounding features, and incorrectly states that men played the female parts in drag.

8. Thanks to Michael Belanger, of Merriam Webster, for confirming these usage details in a message to the author, 20 May 1999.

9. Adams noted his early concern with Desdemona's cross-racial attraction in his di-

ary on 5 November 1831, calling Desdemona's "sensual passions . . . over-ardent, so as to reconcile her to a passion for a black man" (John Quincy Adams, *Diary of John Quincy Adams: 1794–1845*, ed. Allan Nevins [New York: Longmans, Green and Co., 1929], 424). Then he published his essay, "The Character of Desdemona," in *The American Monthly Magazine* (March 1836, quotation on p. 210). This essay circulated widely; for instance, it also appeared in *The Spirit of the Times*, 27 February 1836.

10. The two actors sometimes played together, as at London's Adelphi, the week of 30 September 1839, when Rice played the servant Caesar in Hackett's frontier chestnut, *The Kentuckian*, adapted for him by William Bayle Bernard from James Kirke Paulding's *The Lion of the West*.

11. James Henry Hackett, *Notes and Comments Upon Certain Plays and Actors of Shakespeare, with Criticism and Correspondence* (New York: Carleton, 1863), 224.

12. Abigail Adams, wife of the second President and mother of the sixth, wrote to a friend that "disgust and horror . . . filled my mind every time I saw [Othello] touch the gentle Desdemona" (Abigail Adams, *Letters of Mrs. Adams, the Wife of John Adams*, ed. C. F. Adams [Boston: C. C. Little and J. Brown, 1840], 125).

13. Lhamon, *Raising Cain*, pp. 16–19, and further in the first chapter, summarizes the case for these assertions. See also Shane White, *Somewhat More Independent: The End of Slavery in New York City, 1770–1810* (Athens, Ga.: University of Georgia Press, 1991), 153–155, 186, and Peter Linebaugh and Marcus Rediker, *The Many-Headed Hydra: Sailors, Slaves, Commoners, and the Hidden History of the Revolutionary Atlantic* (Boston: Beacon, 2000), esp. Chapters 6 and 7.

14. John Quincy Adams, *Diary of John Quincy Adams: 1794–1845*, 499.

15. William Miller calls this phenomenon "upward contempt": William Ian Miller, *The Anatomy of Disgust* (Cambridge, Mass.: Harvard University Press, 1998), 235.

16. James C. Scott, *Domination and the Arts of Resistance: Hidden Transcripts* (New Haven: Yale University Press, 1990), 19.

17. Eric Lott, *Love and Theft: Blackface Minstrelsy and the American Working Class* (New York: Oxford University Press, 1993), 95.

18. New York *Courier & Enquirer*, Monday, 2 September 1833. Shane White generously sent me this citation. The emphasis is mine. Here, and when I give the full passage later, I have silently corrected spelling errors and typos, and modernized some punctuation, in the newsprint. The announcement was for the second performance of *Life in Philadelphia, or, How They Do Go On*, the opening night having been the previous Friday. *Life in Philadelphia* became *Bone Squash Diavolo*, one of Rice's most enduring plays.

19. See E. P. Thompson, "The Moral Economy of the English Crowd in the Eighteenth Century" and "The Moral Economy Reviewed," both reprinted in his *Customs in Common* (New York: New Press, 1991; reprint, London: Penguin, 1993), 185–351.

20. The quoted phrase is E. P. Thompson's, "The Moral Economy Reviewed," 344.

21. The best work on Melville's indebtedness to popular theatre remains Ray B. Browne, *"Popular Theater in Moby-Dick,"* in *New Voices in American Studies*, eds. Don-

ald M. Winkelman, Ray B. Browne, and Allen Hayman ([West Lafayette, Ind.]: Purdue University Studies, 1966), 89–101. For more canonical theatre, and the claim that Melville approves social hierarchies, see also Alan L. Ackerman, Jr., *The Portable Theater: American Literature & the Nineteenth-Century Stage* (Baltimore: Johns Hopkins University Press, 1999), 88–135, and Joel Porte, *In Respect to Egoism: Studies in American Romantic Writing* (Cambridge: Cambridge University Press, 1991), 198–208.

22. Theodore Parker, *Sermon of The Dangerous Classes in Society* (Boston: C & J. M. Spear, 1847); Marx, "The Eighteenth Brumaire of Louis Bonaparte," 479; and Herman Melville, *The Confidence-Man: His Masquerade*, ed. Elizabeth S. Foster (New York: Dix, Edwards, 1857; reprint, New York: Hendricks House, 1954), 6.

23. In the later Adelphi script, which was cut to one act and thus represented the spine of the play, Rice pared the lyrics to this essential verse sung with plural pronouns as the curtain rose: "We de Niggers dat do de whitewashing."

24. From the Dan Emmett papers at the Ohio State Historical Archives, I have recovered and edited the holograph script for "German Farmer, or, Barber's Shop in an Uproar." This skit is forthcoming in *Benito Cereno*, ed. Jay Fliegelman (New York: Bedford Books, 2003). Eph Horn was a linking figure in these theatrical worlds. He was in the Emmett skit; then he was scheduled to play several blackface and lowlife characters (Gloworm, the barman at the oyster cellar, Dusty Robert of the Dead Vault's motley crew) in the aborted play of *The Quaker City* in 1844 in Philadelphia (playbill surviving at Pennsylvania Historical Society). Then he was in Emmett's Virginia Minstrels when Emmett wrote and originally performed "In Dixie's Land." "The Doll," which appeared in *The Crisis* (3:6, April 1912, pp. 248–251) has been republished in *The Short Fiction of Charles W. Chesnutt*, ed. Sylvia Lyons Render (Cambridge, Mass.: Harvard University Press, 1981), pp. 405–412. Thanks to Joe McElrath for this reference.

25. The New York *Mirror,* 5 October 1833, p. 110.

26. See Leonard L. Richards, *"Gentlemen of Property and Standing: Anti-Abolition Mobs in Jacksonian America* (New York: Oxford, 1970).

27. Rice had played Farmer Ashfield in Thomas Morton's comedy *Speed the Plough* as early as 8 December 1828, the night Noah Ludlow's troupe opened in Mobile, Alabama (advertisement in *Mobile Register,* day of performance).

28. Theodore Sedgwick Fay and Nathaniel Parker Willis, the other two editors of the *Mirror,* were living abroad to report on European matters. Rice underlines the contradiction of encouraging American native culture from Europe.

29. Colonel Pluck, with whom Rice elides Morris, was a figure of ridicule in lower-class and black parades mocking the draft and the military. Colonel Pluck also appears as a graphic caricature in numerous broadsides of the period: a small man with a slack face, huge sword curving up from his groin, strutting in boots he cannot fill. See Susan G. Davis, "The Career of Colonel Pluck: Folk Drama and Popular Protest in Early Nineteenth-Century Philadelphia," *The Pennyslvania Magazine of History and Biography* 109, 2 (April 1985): 179–202.

30. In *Oh! Hush!*, Rice's character Gumbo Cuff mocks a dandiacal poseur reading a newspaper upside down. The paper is unspecified. *Bone Squash*, staged a few years later, returns to this slight and specifically spurns the New York *Mirror* in favor of the Seventh Ward's own organ of street credibility, the *Hawk and Buzzard* (Act I, scene 1).

31. Playing on the "native talent" that Morris says he befriends, Rice belittles his competition. Morris himself had written "Brier Cliff," never published. It ran in the summer of 1826 at the Chatham Garden and was revived at the Bowery in the spring of 1828. Militia Musters were the sort of spectacles that the Colonel might have acted in, given his last paragraph urging the tarring and feathering of Jim Crow and Gumbo Cuff; Colonel Pluck was a stock figure in such behavior. And *The Kentuckian* was an American play written at James Henry Hackett's behest by James Kirke Paulding and rewritten for Hackett by William Bayle Bernard, an American living in London, where this "native" play was first produced at the Theatre Royal Covent Garden in 1833, this same year. Its prompt scripts are at the Enthoven; see also James Kirke Paulding, *The Lion of the West, Retitled to: The Kentuckian, or, A Trip to New York*, revised by John Augustus Stone and William Bayle Bernard, ed. James N. Tidwell (Stanford: Stanford University Press, 1954).

32. William Thomas Moncrieff (1794–1857) created the (London) Adelphi theatre's first great hit when, in 1821, he adapted *Tom and Jerry, or, Life in London* from Pierce Egan's sporting novel, *Life in London or The Day and Night Scenes of Jerry Hawthorn, Esq. and his elegant friend, Corinthian Tom in their Rambles and Sprees through the Metropolis* (London: Sherwood, Neely & Jones, 1821).

33. Perry Miller reminds us that this phrase had scatological undertones, especially in Morris's circle in these years. See Perry Miller, *The Raven and the Whale: The War of Words and Wits in the Era of Poe and Melville* (New York: Harcourt, Brace & World, 1956), 17.

34. Meredith is a character in *Brier Cliff.*

35. Slang for biting bugs of various sizes from no-see-ums to flies.

36. James Townley's English play *High Life below Stairs* (1804) was in Sam Drake's provincial repertoire while Rice was with Drake's company; Rice played one of its below-stairs characters in Louisville, 27 December 1830 (Louisville *Public Advertiser* on date); and even after he left Drake's troupe, Rice had acted the play at his benefit as recently as 26 January 1833, in Washington, D.C. (Washington *Daily Intelligencer* on date). The phrase "high life below stairs" predated Townley's play. As Philip D. Morgan has pointed out, in "William Humphrey's 1772 print, *High Life below Stairs*, the black butler pets the white maid, who responds warmly to his affections" ("British Encounters with Africans and African-Americans, circa 1600–1780," in *Strangers within the Realm: Cultural Margins of the First British Empire* [Chapel Hill: Institute of Early American History and Culture, 1991], 166).

37. In its first number "the editor [of the *Mirror*] wrote: 'To the LADIES, in particular, we look' . . . emphasizing the ladyward look by the periodical's subtitle, 'Ladies Literary Gazette.' From one end of the file to the other this attention to women's in-

terest is noticeable. Fashions, toilet hints, 'female characters,' and articles on the education of young girls are frequent . . . Sentiment is a prominent characteristic." Frank Luther Mott, *A History of American Magazines, 1741–1850* (New York: Appleton, 1930), 322–323. By 1833, the time of this interchange, Morris had changed the subtitle to "A Weekly Journal Devoted to Literature and the Fine Arts."

38. In the drastically truncated, one-act version of *Bone Squash Diavolo* that Rice performed in London, September 1839, he cut most of the extended business that alluded to these attitudes, but he kept the reference to the *Mirror*'s appeal to women, even though it then made no sense at all out of context and across the Atlantic. This argument had etched itself in Rice's mind so deeply that it had become an ineradicable part of the play's emotional core.

39. Lines from Rice's song, "Jim Crow."

40. There can be few words with more compound meaning in these years than "goose." To be associated with a goose was to be called a fool with ridiculously excessive overtones. "Goose quill" in Rice's riposte is to be understood as oppositional to the "Crow quill"—the one orthodox, the other heterodox, both in the extreme. Elizabeth Johns has made an initial foray into goose matters in *American Genre Painting* (New Haven: Yale University Press, 1991), 216, n. 26.

41. Tilden G. Edelstein, "*Othello* in America: The Drama of Racial Intermarriage," in *Region, Race, and Reconstruction: Essays in Honor of C. Vann Woodward*, eds. J. Morgan Kousser and James M. McPherson (New York: Oxford University Press, 1982), 179–197.

42. Peter H. Wood, "'Gimme de Kneebone Bent': African Body Language and the Evolution of American Dance Forms," in *The Black Tradition in American Modern Dance*, ed. Gerald E. Myers (American Dance Festival, 1988).

43. Ralph Ellison, "Change the Joke and Slip the Yoke," in *The Collected Essays of Ralph Ellison*, ed. John F. Callahan (1958; reprint, New York: Modern Library, 1995), 100–113.

44. Louisville *Public Advertiser*, 23 May 1832. Two days later, the newspaper's anonymous reviewer confirmed the popularity of these links.

45. "Gumbo Chaff as Sung at the different Theatres" (Baltimore: G. Willig, Jr. [1834]), verses 3 and 4.
    To understand the depth of disdain coded in the vocation of wood-sawyer, one should read Chapter 2 in Linebaugh and Rediker, *The Many-Headed Hydra*, 36–70. For confirmation that wood-sawyer was code for black slave, particularly when the person was nominally free, see Richard Weston, *A Visit to the United States and Canada in 1833* (Edinburgh: Richard Weston & Sons, 1836), 69. In making Massa into the Devil's wood-sawyer, Gumbo is practicing world-upside-down inversion.

46. The British trips were 1) from the summer of 1836 and returning to New York at the end of the summer of 1837; 2) from December 1838 through the first week of February 1840; 3) from Boxing Day 1842 through the next April.

47. Rice's will is indexed in room 402, City Hall, Chambers Street, New York City.

48. Joe Cowell, *Thirty Years Among the Players in England and America* (New York: Harper & Brothers, 1844), 86–87.

49. See Lhamon, *Raising Cain*, 192–194.

50. John Baldwin Buckstone, *The Lottery Ticket and the Lawyer's Clerk* (London: C. Chapple, 1827), 8. I have modernized spelling and capitalization. See also Lhamon, *Raising Cain*, 165–166.

51. Advertisement in Mobile *Register*, 29 December 1828; this paper has not been filmed; it is at the Alabama state archives, Montgomery.

52. Dian Lee Shelley, "Tivoli Theatre of Pensacola," *Florida Historical Quarterly* 50, 4 (1972): 341–351; Jack L. Bilbo, Jr., "Economy and Culture: The Boom-And-Bust Theatres of Pensacola, Florida, 1821–1917" (Ph.D. diss., Texas Tech University, 1982); and John J. Weisert, "Golden Days at Drake's City Theatre, 1830–1833," *The Filson Club History Quarterly* 43 (1969): 252. Verified in Louisville *Public Advertiser*, 21 May 1830.

53. Richard Lalor Shiel (also spelled Sheil) revised and altered the version of *Damon and Pythias* often attributed to John Banim. The italics are Lope Tocho's own emphasis, in Louisville *Public Advertiser*, 29 September 1830. Lope Tocho was also a role in G. Coleman's musical play *The Mountaineers*, which the troupe had performed when Sol Smith joined the company a week and a half earlier. Rice played Kilmallock and Smith played the Moor, Sadi.

54. Louisville *Public Advertiser*, 7 October 1830.

55. Peter A. Tasch, *The Dramatic Cobbler: The Life and Works of Isaac Bickerstaff* (Lewisburg: Bucknell University Press, 1971), 157. Lewis Hallam, the younger, played Mungo first in the States, at the John Street Theatre in New York, 29 May 1769.

56. Louisville *Public Advertiser*, 21 May 1830. Dale Cockrell pointed the way here. His newspaper combings led him to suspect Rice "first jumped 'Jim Crow' sometime in 1830 between late spring and 22 September, most likely in Louisville on the latter date" (Dale Cockrell, *Demons of Disorder: Early Blackface Minstrels and Their World* [Cambridge: Cambridge University Press, 1997], 64). I have found Rice's earlier jumpings advertised in the *Public Advertiser* also on (counting backward from Cockrell's date) 7 August, 12 June, and on the 24th and 22nd of May.

57. Ad in Louisville *Public Advertiser*, 10 June 1830.

58. Ad in Washington *Daily Intelligencer*, 22 January 1833; and playbill for 1 February 1833 (now in the Washington Theatre folder, Harvard Theatre Collection).

59. See the lyrics for "Jim Crow Still Alive" and "Dinah Crow" reprinted in this collection.

60. Gary S. Gregg, *Self-Representation: Life Narrative Studies in Identity and Ideology* (New York: Greenwood, 1991), 47.

61. The dates of these productions, all in Louisville, are confirmed in the Louisville *Public Advertiser* on the day of production: *Julius Caesar*, 1 October 1830; *King Lear and His Three Daughters*, 30 March 1831; *Romeo and Juliet*, 6 June 1831; scene from

The Merchant of Venice, 30 May 1832; *Macbeth*, 4 March 1831; *As You Like It*, 21 March 1831; *Catherine and Petruchio*, 21 March 1830. In anomalous casting, Rice played the Lord Mayor in *Richard III*, 23 March 1831.

62. For Sam Cowell, see Nelle Smither, "A History of the English Theatre at New Orleans, 1806–1842" (Ph.D. diss. (partial), University of Pennsylvania, 1944), p. 39. For Nichols, see Colonel T. Allston Brown, "The Origin of Negro Minstrelsy," in *Fun in Black: Or, Sketches of Minstrel Life*, by Charles H. Day (New York: De Witt, 1874), 5; and Carl Wittke, *Tambo and Bones: A History of the American Minstrel Stage* (Durham, N.C.: Duke University Press, 1930; reprint Westport, Conn.: Greenwood Press, 1968), 17, 18.

63. Henry A. Kmen, "Old Corn Meal: A Forgotten Urban Negro Folksinger," *Journal of American Folklore* 75, 295 (January–March 1962): 29–34.

64. John J. Weisert, "Beginnings of the Kentucky Theatre Circuit," *The Filson Club History Quarterly* 34 (1960): 258.

65. New Orleans *Bee* for 23 and 27 March 1835; 23 February 1836; New Orleans *Picayune*, 4 March 1838.

66. New Orleans *Bee*, 23 February 1836.

67. Kmen, "Old Corn Meal," 31.

68. Quoted in ibid.

69. Henry A. Kmen, *Music in New Orleans, 1791–1841* (Baton Rouge: Louisiana State University Press, 1966), 29.

70. 23 August 1838.

71. Frances Anne Kemble, *Journal of a Residence on a Georgian Plantation in 1838–1839*, ed. and with an introduction by John A. Scott (New York: Harper, 1863; reprint, Athens, Ga.: University of Georgia Press, Brown Thrasher Books, 1984), 131. Kemble adds evidence for the existence of a Gullah Jim Crow independent of Rice's theatrical transformation.

72. Ibid., 163. For a fascinating discussion of related issues, see Chadwick Hansen, "Jenny's Toe Revisited: White Responses to Afro-American Shaking Dances," *American Music* (Spring 1987): 1–19.

73. *Spirit of the Times*, 13 May 1837, p. 99 (italics added); reprinted from the *Cork Herald*.

74. Baltimore *Patriot*, 19 October 1832.

75. 14 December 1832, as attested in theatre bill at Harvard Theatre Collection, Warren Theatre folder; I have corrected some printer's errors in this item.

76. A bill at the Harvard Theatre Collection, Warren Theatre folder, shows that Rice did *Love in a Cloud* in Boston, 17 December 1832. This play had the same character list as *Long Island Juba* at New York's Bowery on 9 January 1833 (reported by George C. D. Odell, *Annals of the New York Stage, Volume III [1821–1834]* [New York: Columbia University Press, 1928], 635, except that Rice's character is named Gumbo Chaff in *Love in a Cloud* and Guffee in *Long Island Juba*. Performance of *Long Island Juba* is confirmed in New York *Evening Post*, day of performance. For eels, see

Lhamon, *Raising Cain*, 1–55. For oyster cellars, see Shane White, "The Death of James Johnson," *American Quarterly* 51 (December 1999): 753–796.

77. Ad in the Philadelphia *National Gazette*, day of performance. An ad in the *National Gazette* the previous day stated that *Oh! Hush!* had been "performed in New York and Boston with bursts of laughter and applause," but I have only found references in those cities to the same subject under the other titles I have named. Rice's role is now listed as "Gumba Cuffee."

78. The earliest bill for this sketch I have seen is for Monday evening, 19 October 1829; the cast was: Sambo, Mr. Dixon; Rose, Mr. Madden; Cuffee, Mr. Orson (Harvard Theatre Collection, Chatham folder). But Dixon may have been doing the play in the summer of 1828; see S. Foster Damon, "The Negro in Early American Songsters," *The Papers of the Bibliographical Society of America* 28 (1934): 148. The best scholarship on Dixon and blackface is Cockrell, *Demons of Disorder*.

79. An exception that proves the rule here is the revenge that Rice exacted on Madame Vestris in October 1838, during her bitterly abbreviated tour of the States. In retaliation for the way Vestris had mocked Jim Crow while Rice was on his first English visit, he similarly travestied her persona deriding him. Blackfaced all the while, Rice dressed himself in a short-skirted, low-bodiced dress and minced through one of her medleys. He was not wenching Vestris so much as attacking her coarsening of his act. In any case, cross-dressing was for him an exceptional tool. The fullest account of this *contretemps* is in Charles Durang, "History of the Philadelphia Stage," Articles from the Philadelphia *Sunday Dispatch*, begun 7 May 1854, bound in 4 volumes at the Library Company of Philadelphia, 401.

80. Theatre bill for 28 October 1829, Harvard Theatre Collection, Chatham folder.

81. Durang, "Philadelphia Stage," III, 55.

82. Louisville *Public Advertiser*, on date.

83. P[hilip]. S. White, and H. R. Pleasants, *The War of Four Thousand Years* (Philadelphia: Griffith & Simon, 1846). The Philadelphia-based minstrel Sam Sanford says in his memoirs that White wrote *Oh! Hush!* for Rice in Pittsburgh, before Rice came east. See Sam Sanford, *Personal Reminiscences of Himself Together with the History of Minstrelsy from the Origan [Sic] 1843 to 1893 with a Sketch of All the Celebrities of the Past and Present*, unpublished holograph MS, 2. (Sanford's memoir is at the Henry Ransom Humanites Research Center, Austin, Texas.)

84. Jonathan B. Blewitt's arrangement of "Jim Crow": "as sung by Mr. T. D. Rice at the Theatre Royal Adelphi in the popular Drama of a *Flight to America* . . . by permission of Mr. Rice." This is dated 1836, the 34th edition, and its shelfmark is h.1601.m.(56.) at the British Library.

85. The date is inked faintly on the MS (Add. MSS 42940, ff. 822–867) in the British Library; a bill in the Mobile *Commercial Register*, on the day, confirms the MS date.

86. A playbill at the Library Company of Philadelphia, for Sanford's Opera House, 10 December 1864, advertises "T. D. Rice's Farce of the Virginia Mummy." For Aldridge, see Herbert and Mildred Stock Marshall, *Ira Aldridge: The Negro Tragedian*

(London: Rockliff, 1958; reprint, Carbondale, Ill.: Southern Illinois University Press, 1968). For Christy's version, see their prompt script at the Historical Society of Pennsylvania. White's two different arrangements of *Virginia Mummy* were published by Dick and Fitzgerald, New York, no date; and by Happy Hours, New York, no date.

87. See *Morning Courier and New York Examiner* on 12 November 1832. These ads are frequent in this period and appear on the same pages as the theatre ads in the daily newspapers. Here is a similar ad from the *Louisville Focus*, 5 June 1827:

MUSEUM Main Street
THE EGYPTIAN MUMMY
with its Sarcophagus!
Upwards of 3000 years old!

Taken from the King's Tomb at the City of Thebes, in Upper Egypt, together with other CURIOSITIES, found with her and imported into New York by Captain Larkin T. Lee, and has been exhumed by Samuel L. Mitchell, Valentine Mott, and a number of other physicians, and pronounced by them to be a genuine embalmed mummy.
Also two life size Paintings, one representing
A MANIAC,
An original painting from the pencil of Mr. Street, an American Artist. The other representing
THE ANACONDA
Destroying a Horse and his Rider.
... The mummy, &c. will continue until the 12th, when they will be removed to Cincinnati.

88. Carol Andrews, *Egyptian Mummies* (London: British Museum Press, 1984), 11.

89. Ibid., 7–8.

90. Ibid., 23.

91. Ibid., 5.

92. The condition of the Christy Minstrels' prompt script objectifies this sputter. It is a collage of printed and hand-scripted lines that finally deliquesce into illegibility.

93. I have only found two productions of *Where's My Head*, at the Bowery on 23 and 24 May 1834. From this material, both *Virginia Mummy* and *Bone Squash Diavolo* would soon deviate. The two advertised characters in *Where's My Head* were named "Squash" (Rice's character, which became Bone Squash), and "Major Cataract" (played by Thomas Flynn, became Captain Rifle in *Virginia Mummy*).

Rice's *Discoveries in the Moon, or Herschel out Herscheled*, which played at Philadelphia's Walnut Street Theatre from 5 to 10 September 1835, was a thorough debunking of the tabloid articles the English journalist Richard Locke wrote for the New York *Sun*, 21 through 28 August 1835, fantasizing lunar man-bats who had all the usual stereotypical characteristics of blacks. Locke pretended he based these sci-fi fantasies on John F. W. Herschel's *A Treatise on Astronomy* (London: 1833; Philadelphia: 1834).

94. The first production of *Oh! Hush!* was at the Walnut Street Theatre, which Wemyss was then running, on 20 July 1833. After playing *Virginia Mummy* once at Ludlow's benefit in Mobile, the next production I have found was at Wemyss's Walnut Street Theatre, 30 June 1835 (playbill at Harvard Theatre Collection, Walnut Street Theatre folder).

95. Nearly everyone, including T. D. Rice, misspelled Wemyss's surname.

96. Playbill at Library Company of Philadelphia.

97. Playbill and holograph letter both at Harvard Theatre Collection. Wemyss noted in his memoir: "'Bone Squash Diablo,' for which [John] Clemens had written the music, and Landers prepared the machinery, was transfered to the Bowery Theatre, New York. Thus we lost the credit of its original production" (Francis Courtney Wemyss, *Theatrical Biography; or, The life of an actor and manager* [Glasgow: R. Griffin & Co., 1848], II, 264).

98. A bill on 24 September announced "A new Opera is in Rehearsal—tomorrow (Friday), for the Benefit of Mr. Rice" (Warren Theatre box in the Harvard Theatre Collection; the Warren Theatre became Boston's National Theatre the next year, 15 August 1836).

99. For the Bowery Theatre, see George C. D. Odell, *Annals of the New York Stage, Volume IV [1834–43]* (New York: Columbia University Press, 1928), 74; for the Walnut Theatre, see Arthur A. Wilson, *A History of the Philadelphia Theatre, 1835–1855* (Philadelphia: University of Pennsylvania Press, 1935), 140; and Durang, "Philadelphia Stage," III, 372.

100. According to an ad for the play in the New Orleans *Bee*, 27 March 1835, *Life in Philadelphia* was "written by Dr. Burns, of Philadelphia, expressly for Mr. Rice." Philadelphia directories list a Dr. William Burns only in 1824 and 1833–35. The National Union Catalogue records a volume in his name, published in 1851, *Life in New York, Indoor and Out*—it is a domestic description, with no apparent relation to *Life in Philadelphia.*

101. Clay is also the lithographer for the most famous version of the dancing Jim Crow image, reproduced in the Endicott printing of "Jump Jim Crow" (see Figure 1). See Lester S. Levy, *Picture the Songs: Lithographs from the Sheet Music of Nineteenth-Century America* (Baltimore: Johns Hopkins University Press, 1976), 20–22.

102. "Life in Philadelphia," in *The New Comic Annual* (London: Hurst, Chance, and Co., 1830), 223–237.

103. Jerrold spurred Rice continually. The American had played Jerrold's *Drunkard's Fate* while he was in Drake's troupe in Louisville (20 December 1830) during his first phase. Then Rice had headlined as Silver Jack in Jerrold's *The Rent Day* 7 and 8 February 1833 at Washington, D.C. during his second career phase.

104. Letter in Rice folder, Harvard Theatre Collection. W. B. Bernard had written *The Mummy* and adapted Hackett's play *The Kentuckian.*

105. Douglas Jerrold, *Beau Nash, the King of Bath*, Dicks' Standard Plays (London: John Dicks, 1835), p. 6.

106. *Figaro in London*, 17 September 1836, reprinted in *The Spirit of the Times*, 12 November 1836, p. 307.

107. Greil Marcus first showed me this functional parallel between American blackface and English Punch and Judy.

108. Quoted in Elaine Freedgood, "Groundless Optimism: Regression in the Service of Egos, England and Empire in Victorian Ballooning Memoirs," *Nineteenth-Century Contexts* 20 (1997): 61.

109. In his comments on the later play, *Otello*, Julian Mates realized that Rice was altering ballad operas; see Mates, *America's Musical Stage*, p. 79. These earlier plays in Rice's career demonstrate that he was pushing against ballad opera all along.

110. William Empson, *Some Versions of Pastoral* (London: Chatto and Windus, 1950), 3–26 and 195–252; Michael Denning, "Beggars and Thieves," *Literature and History* 8, 1 (Spring 1982): 41–55.

111. For comments on a later version of this cultural shape, see W. T. Lhamon, Jr., "Break and Enter to Breakaway: Scotching Modernism in the Social Novel of the American Sixties," *boundary 2* 3, 2 (Winter 1975): 289–306.

112. Playbill at British Library.

113. *Evening Star* 22 and 26 August 1836 (this last, dated on 26 July in Liverpool); *The Spirit of the Times*, 27 August 1836, p. 220.

114. 22 October 1836, p. 284.

115. Playbill in Enthoven Collection, Theatre Museum, Covent Garden, Surrey folder for 1836.

116. The London *Times* reviewed *Black God of Love* on 13 September 1836, the morning after its opening. For the *Times* to notice the Surrey was extremely unusual, but they now began reviewing Rice's acts. Rice's remark is in *The Spirit of the Times*, 22 October 1836, p. 284.

117. London *Times* on 26 and 29 September 1836. The full bill for *Mr. Midshipman Easy*, with cast list and plot description, is in the Enthoven Collection, Covent Garden, Surrey folder for 1836.

118. 27 August 1837, p. 217.

119. Clipping in the Surrey Folder, Enthoven Collection.

120. 26 August 1837, p. 217.

121. *The Observer*, 30 December 1838, clipping in Enthoven Collection, T. D. Rice folder.

122. Appearance listed in London *Times*, 7 November 1836; reviewed in *Times* on next day; the first bill is at the Enthoven Collection, Covent Garden, Adelphi folder for 1836.

123. Playbills in the British Library Playbills Collection, catalogue 313, attest to performances at the Surrey on 12 and 13 December 1836. Advertisements in the

London *Times* on these days, and playbills in the British Library Playbill Collection, catalogue 367, warrant the appearances at the Adelphi on the same night. For Jim Crow's horseback abolitionist speeches, see scene 5 of *Flight to America* in this volume.

124. See bills at the Enthoven Collection and in theatre casebook 313 at the British Library. I have written more about the yoking of London's neighborhood and class audiences in Chapter 4 of *Raising Cain*.

125. Here, listed chronologically, are the twenty-two plays of Rice's fourth phase about which I am certain, because multiple contemporary sources confirm them. I list subsequent and alternate names along with the playwright and original titles.

1. *Bone Squash Diavolo* (Rice; sometimes *Bone Squash Diablo*).
2. *Virginia Mummy* (Rice; also *Sarcophagus*, and *Mummy*).
3. *The Black God of Love* (Joseph Graves; Graves claims authorship of *Black God of Love* on the title page to his *The Wife: Tale of a Mantua Maker* and *Cupid: A Burlesque Burletta* [London: W. Strange, 1837]. Also *The Black Cupid*).
4. *Mr. Midshipman Easy* (adapted by W. H. Oxberry and J. Gann from Captain Frederick Marryatt's 1836 novel).
5. *Oh! Hush!, or, Life in New York* (Rice; sometimes subtitled, sometimes titled, *The Werginny* [or *Virginny*] *Cupids*).
6. *Flight to America* (William Leman Rede; the MS is titled *Life in America, The flight, the pursuit, the Voyage*).
7. *The Peacock and the Crow* (Thomas Parry).
8. *The Peregrinations of Pickwick* (William Leman Rede adapted Dickens's 1836–37 novel; although Rice repeatedly performed in this play, there is no part for him in extant copies).
9. *The Court Jester* (Frederick Fox Cooper; also *Jim Crow in London, Jim Crow at Court*, and *The Black Ambassador*. I have found neither a MS nor a printed version of this play.
10. *Jim Crow in His New Place* (Thomas Proclus Taylor; also *Jumbo Jum, The Humours of Jumbo Jum, Black and White, Literal Interpretation, Jim Crow in Foreign Service*).
11. *The Eighth of January, or, Hurrah for the Boys of the West*.
12. *The Pet of the Petticoats* (J. B. Buckstone).
13. *La Masque* (also The Masquerade).
14. *Hamlet* (Shakespeare).
15. *The Kentuckian* (John Augustus Stone; revised by William Bayle Bernard as The Lion of the West in response to a call for a play for James Hackett; it became The Kentuckian, or, A Trip to New York).
16. *Uncle Pop.*
17. *Black Hercules, King of Clubs* (probably by Frederick Fox Cooper, who wrote *Hercules, King of Clubs*).
18. *Whew! Here's a Go!* ("written by a gentleman of this city" and performed first at Thorne's New Chatham in New York City on 19 October 1840).

19. *Sign of the Times* (advertised to be by Rice, and performed first at the New Chatham on 26 October 1840).

20. *Unwelcome Visitor* (adapted from a French source by John Poole; also known as *Black Pompey*).

21. *Yankee Notes for English Circulation* (Edward Stirling; opened at London's Adelphi on 16 January 1843).

22. *Otello* (Rice, radically adapting Maurice Dowling's *Othello Travestie*).

126. 13 February 1837 was the play's "fifth time" (bill in Enthoven Collection, Theatre Museum, Covent Garden).

127. The hits at Trollope are attested in the Baltimore *Patriot*, 19 October 1832; Washington *Daily Intelligencer*, 5 and 6 February 1833. Odell, *Annals of the New York Stage, Volume III [1821–1834]*, 685. For the "foreignificated . . . ladies," see *Life of Jim Crow* in "Street Prose," below. Prompt scripts and bills for *The Kentuckian* are at the Enthoven Collection, Adelphi folder for 1839.

128. Philadelphia *Daily Chronicle* and the *Pennsylvanian* on 12 and 17 June 1833.

129. On 23 June 1840, Rice wrote Wemyss that he had suffered "a very *bad Weariness* brought on by hard work at Liverpool" (letter now at Harvard Theatre Collection in Joseph N. Ireland, *Records of the New York Stage from 1750 to 1860, Extended and Extra-Illustrated for Augustin Daly by Augustus Toedeberg*, vol 2, pt. 2 [New York: T. H. Morrell, 1867]). This "weariness," which would have been during early February 1840, seems to have been his first bout with the debilitating illness every contemporary biographical comment termed, vaguely, "paralysis."

130. Stanley Wells, *Nineteenth Century Burlesques*, vol. 2 (Wilmington, Del.: Michael Glazer, 1978), xii. In this volume, Wells reprints Dowling's play.

131. England had ended its slavery in August 1833. Dowling's production opened in Liverpool—the slave-trade port—seven months later.

132. See "Dancing for Eels at Catherine Market," Chapter 1 of Lhamon, *Raising Cain*, especially the images on pages 23, 26, and 27. Chanfrau always credited Rice as his mentor and tried hard to hire him in later years to arrest his decline.

133. Prompt script TS 3258.51, Harvard Theatre Collection, p. 29. Benjamin A. Baker, then the prompter at the Olympic, wrote the script for his own benefit performance; he recruited Chanfrau to play the role.

134. This expression was evidently a familiar reversal of the proverb—Rice used it earlier in a letter to Francis Wemyss, written from London on 13 March 1839; letter now in Harvard Theatre Collection.

135. See E. A. J. Honigmann, "'Othello', Chappuys and Cinthio," *Notes and Queries* 211 (April 1966): 136–137; Geoffrey Bullough, *Narrative and Dramatic Sources of Shakespeare* (New York: Columbia University Press, 1973), 193–238; and Kenneth Muir, *The Sources of Shakespeare's Plays* (London: Methuen, 1977), 182–195.

136. Thanks to June Piscitelli and Sean Christian, then my students, who applied the term "problem child" in class.

137. See Wesley Brown, *Darktown Strutters* (New York: Cane Hill Press, 1994; re-

print, Amherst, Mass.: University of Massachusetts Press, 2000), 174—my afterword to that novel extends these remarks. Colescott's "Knowledge of the Past Is the Key to the Future (St. Sebastian)" (1986) and Bruce Nugent's drawings are both reprinted in Susan Gubar, *Racechanges: White Skin, Black Face in American Culture* (New York: Oxford University Press, 1997), facing page 137, and on pages 108–111, respectively. Stivenson Magloire's Haitian Voudou canvas, "Divided Spirit" (1989) appears in Karen McCarthy Brown, *Tracing the Spirit: Ethnographic Essays on Haitian Art* (Davenport, Iowa: Davenport Museum of Art, University of Washington Press, 1995), 67. The Pende masks are illustrated and interpreted in Z. S. Strother, *Inventing Masks: Agency and History in the Art of the Central Pende* (Chicago: University Press of Chicago, 1998), 139–152.

138. In Henry Louis Gates, Jr. and Nellie Y. McKay, eds., *The Norton Anthology of African American Literature* (New York: Norton, 1997), 615, my emphasis.

139. Philadelphia *Public Ledger,* 28 October 1844 to 7 November 1844; 11 December 1844 to 17 December 1844. Rice's play particularly attracted blacks. While he was playing *Otello* at the Chesnut, where seats cost 25 cents in the "Gallery for Colored Persons Only," William Burton was playing Dowling's *Othello Travestie* at the Arch Street Theatre, where both the pit and the black gallery seats sold for 12½ cents.

During Rice's *Otello* at the National Theatre in New York, according to a playbill for 9 May 1846, the seating was as follows:

> Prices of Admission:
> Private Boxes . . . $1.00
> Dress Circles and Second Tier . . . 75
> Pit . . . 35
> *Boxes for Persons of Color . . . 50*
> Gallery . . . 25

Blacks came not only to *Otello* but to all his plays. The theatres that Rice played all during his career, from Louisville to New Orleans to Philadelphia and New York, advertised seats for "Colored People," or some other synonym. Not all theatre bills include these seatings, and not every theatre in each city advertised them continually, but they are more usual than not. Even in the deep South, blacks came to see Rice perform. On 12 April 1836, a free black man named William Johnson, a barber in Natchez, Mississippi, went with his best friend Robert McCary to their local theatre to sit in the gallery and watch T. D. Rice perform. It was Rice's benefit performance, Johnson wrote in his diary; Rice "had a very good House [but] I made up my mind not to go up there any more untill there was some Regulations made up stairs." See William Johnson, *William Johnson's Natchez: The Ante-Bellum Diary of a Free Negro,* eds William Ransom Hogan and Edwin Adams Davis (Baton Rouge: Louisiana State University Press, 1951), 114. William Johnson was no casual fan. This Mississippi black man also owned a copy of *The life of Gim Crow* (1 July 1842), and he went to great trouble to get it back when one of his servants stole it to give to her lover. This surely was the pamphlet I have reprinted here as *The Life of Jim Crow.* Thanks to Dale Cockrell for sending me this reference to Johnson's diary.

140. Playbills for the Walnut Street Theatre in the Philadelphia *National Gazette* and the *Pennsylvanian*, 20 February 1833. Jackson's rejoinder to the South Carolina Legislature is in the Washington, D.C. *National Intelligencer*, in full, on Friday 18 January 1833, special supplement to the paper.

141. Edward L. Widmer, *Young America: The Flowering of Democracy in New York City* (New York: Oxford University Press, 1999), 47.

142. Dowling's one-act *Othello, According to Act of Parliament*, licensed 11 May 1836, is in the British Library, Add MSS 42936 ff. 289–306.

143. See Walter Benjamin, "Some Remarks on Folk Art," in *Selected Writings*, vol. 2. p. 278.

144. The coupling of *The Moor of Orange Street* and *Jack Sheppard* is confirmed in a playbill for 26 May 1849 surviving in the National folder at the Harvard Theatre Collection.

The coupling of *Otello* and *Uncle Tom's Cabin* is recorded in a playbill for Purdy's National that is graphically documented online at: http://jefferson.village.virginia.edu/UTC/onstage/bills/tsbills24f.html, and confirmed in a clipping in the T. D. Rice folder at the Harvard Theatre Collection.

The *New York Tribune* reviewed Rice's 16 January 1854 performance of Uncle Tom on the next day; I quote it below.

145. Harry Birdoff, *The World's Greatest Hit: Uncle Tom's Cabin* (New York: S. F. Vanni, 1947), 101.

146. *Spirit of the Times*, 21 January 1854; *New York Tribune*, 17 January 1854 (my emphases).

SONGS

1. George Washington Dixon seems to have originated this song, perhaps as early as 1827, says S. Foster Damon in his headnote to the song in *Series of Old American Songs*. Dixon expanded the song into his elaborate interlude, *Love in a Cloud*. It also became the core of T. D. Rice's much simpler *Oh! Hush!* in about 1833. This version, said to be "Sung by Mr. T. D. Rice," was published in London by D'Almaine & Co, Soho, likely in 1836.

2. The legendary New York constable.

3. "The Original Jim Crow" as published by E. Riley in New York at 29 Chatham Street, probably 1832.

4. There are many Tuckahoe place names. Perhaps the most famous, and patent for many others, is the plantation where Thomas Jefferson grew up because his father managed the estate. It is still preserved, on the banks of the Tuckahoe Creek, a tributary of the James River ten miles west of Richmond, Virginia. See Jessie Thompson Krusen, "Tuckahoe Plantation," in *Winterthur Portfolio 11*, edited by Ian M. G. Quimby (Charlottesville: University Press of Virginia, Published for The Henry Francis du Pont Winterthur Museum, 1976), 103–122.

5. Nicolo Paganini (1788–1840), Italian violin virtuoso, was the proverbial model of excellence.

6. Major General Edward Pakenham commanded the British forces invading New Orleans in the culminating battle of the War of 1812. General Andrew Jackson massacred Pakenham and more than 2,000 of his troops on 8 January 1814. Until the Civil War, most American theatres mounted special celebratory events on the anniversary of the Battle of New Orleans.

7. Viper.

8. Unleavened cornmeal batter, baked on a hoe before a fire.

9. In other words, if white workers worked honest days, like slaves, then Constable Hays would have no one to arrest.

10. Daniel Lambert (1770–1809), born in Leicester, exhibited himself in London and elsewhere in England during the last three years of his life when he weighed over 700 lbs. His weight at his death was 739 lbs. For an image, see Richard D. Altick, *The Shows of London* (Cambridge, Mass.: The Belknap Press of Harvard University Press, 1978), 254.

11. I have transcribed this complex song from a double broadside (now at The Library Company of Philadelphia). It prints "Jim Crow, Still Alive!!!" on one side and "Dinah Crow" facing and perhaps answering it on the other, both "Sold by B. Brammel, No. 572, North Second street; and by Johnson Scarlett, 8, Market street Philadelphia." This statement of responsibility is printed twice, once beneath each song. Dinah Crow was fast becoming a specialty of Dan Gardner, who was appearing in Philadelpia neighborhoods (the Northern Liberties) in J. B. Green's Menagerie and Circus in the fall of 1835, singing "The Extravaganza of Dinah Crow" (see playbill at the Historical Society of Pennsylvania). Dan Gardner went on to specialize in "wench" parts in New York and Philadelphia.

This broadside illustrates the fundamental vexation on which lumpen popular culture has often thrived. It presents two styles of storytelling and versemaking. Rice's Jim Crow verses generally present an action contained and completely told in one verse. When his topics extend to successive verses, each one presents a discrete action. Gardner's Dinah Crow verses narrate part of a story that will go on for several stanzas before the topic alters, and separate actions spread across verses. The broadside presents an argument between two street characters, much as if—in our time—they were enacting the dozens.

12. Edwin Williams, ed., *New-York as It Is in 1833; and Citizens Advertising Directory* (New York: J. Disturnell, 1833), 143.

13. See note 2.

14. New York's city government was known as the "Corporation."

15. Champagne.

16. Reverend Ephraim K. Avery. This Methodist minister in Bristol, Rhode Island was accused of murdering Sarah M. Cornell, a factory worker, near Fall River, Massachusetts, 22 December 1832. He was tried in 6 May 1833 and news of his acquittal

hit the newspapers one month later, 5 June 1833 (as in the *American Sentinel*, col. 1, p. 2). See Thomas M. McDade, comp., *The Annals of Murder: A Bibliography of Books and Pamphlets on American Murders from Colonial Times to 1900* (Norman, Okla.: University of Oklahoma Press, 1961), 13–18.

17. Catharine Market, where T. D. Rice was born and raised in New York City's Seventh Ward, was built on a swamp; tuberculosis and yellow fever raged through the Ward many summers.

18. Address of the publisher: B. Brammell, Philadelphia.

19. See note 10.

20. Patch was an early daredevil and falls jumper. He jumped the Passaic Falls on 30 September 1827, then jumped Niagara Falls several times, saying "Some things can be done as well as others," which became a cant phrase. He died in a jump on Friday the 13th of November, 1829 at the 99-foot Upper Falls at Rochester, New York. Friends and small crowds had seen him jump these falls more than once successfully, but this time he was inebriated from preliminary festivity; he dislocated both shoulders on impact and could not swim to safety; he was found dead in the ice the next spring.

21. Drinking cup.

22. "Stone Fence" was one of the earliest American mixed drinks: brandy and cider.

23. A "sham bishop" is a bustle.

24. "Old Hays" refers to an actual New York constable, here becoming metonymic in Philadelphia.

25. A block below South Street, the southern boundary of Philadelphia proper, Shippen was a fringe neighborhood where free blacks could buy property in the early nineteenth century; W. E. B. Du Bois lived there at the end of the century while writing *The Philadelphia Negro*.

26. Perhaps a reference to the band leader Frank Johnson's popularity in Philadelphia.

27. This revealed disjunction, or pretense of gentlemanliness, is complicated by its source: a wenched-up man, a white man cross-dressed in blackface. So it turns and turns inside out, irresolvable. A good contemporary painting of blacks sawing wood in Philadelphia, by Pavel Petrovich Svinin, is titled *Negroes in Front of the Bank of Pennsylvania, Philadelphia* (1814); it is in the Metropolitan Museum, New York City.

28. Jonathan B. Blewitt's arrangement "as sung by Mr. T. D. Rice at the Theatre Royal Adelphi in the popular Drama of a *Flight to America* . . . by permission of Mr. Rice." This is the 34th edition, dated 1836.

29. "Massa Davidge" refers to William Davidge, manager of the Surrey Theatre in London.

30. *The Negro Forget-Me-Not Songster; the Only Work Published, Containing All the Negro Songs That Have Ever Appeared* (Philadelphia: Turner & Fisher, 1844), 247–249; said there to be "Sung by the celebrated Tom Rice."

31. See note 22.

32. This reference dates this verse, if not the song, to 1836, the year Van Buren was elected and Rice went to London.

33. Leonard Deming was a prolific publisher of Jim Crow lyrics in Boston. The American Antiquarian Society, in particular, holds several different sheets of Jim Crow lyrics Deming printed as broadsides. This one dates to 1837–1840, when Deming was at 61 Hanover Street, Boston.

34. Long Island Juba.

35. I have only found this song printed once, in *Christy's Negro Serenaders* (New York [No. 82 Nassau-Street]: Elton & Vinten. n.d.), 187–188, where it is asserted to have been "Sung by Mr. T. D. Rice."

36. Timbuktu, or Tombouctou, is a town in West Africa, now in Mali, near the Niger River.

37. The *Dictionary of American Regional English*, vol. 2, ed. Frederic G. Cassidy (Cambridge, Mass.: Harvard University Press, 1991) defines "gill" as "a fool, dupe, rube." "Gillflirted" or "jillflirted" is used of a woman or female animal whose vulva is lacerated in delivery. It gives an example of a "Jilly-flirt . . . a mare with no membrane between anus and vagina."

38. Although the lyrics did not proliferate as wildly as they did in "Jim Crow," many versions of "Clare de Kitchen" entered print. This early example, published in Baltimore by John Cole, was transcribed from a copy in the DeVincent Collection at the Smithsonian.

39. Soldiers' clothes.

40. One of the most persistent stereotypes of wench characters in blackface is their grotesque flatfootedness, here going beyond flat to a convex stump.

41. Cucumber.

42. There were many printings of "Gumbo Chaff." This one by George Willig, Jr. in Baltimore is early. The variants I have seen retain the stanzas in order as here, although there are frequent changes in spelling, pronoun number (we for I), small details, and lines.

43. This version is "Sold by L. Deming . . . Boston" and must date between 1832–1837.

44. There were many versions of this popular minstrel song. This one is attributed to Dan Emmett's group, The Virginia Minstrels, and was published by F. D. Benteen, Baltimore, 1846.

45. "A celebrated Comic Extravaganza as Sung at the Theatres," published by J. A. L. Hewitt & Co., 239 Broadway, New York.

PLAYS

Oh! Hush!

1. The earliest production of *Oh! Hush!* for which I have found a record was Rice's benefit on 20 July 1833 at Philadelphia's Walnut Street Theatre. Frank Wemyss billed it as *Oh! Hush! or, The Wirginny Cupids*. The principal roles were Gumba (sic)

Cuffee, Rice; Sambo Johnstone, Mr. Hadaway; Diana, Mr. Eberle. Although he took this play with him to London in 1836, Rice must not have performed it north of the Thames, for the Lord Chamberlain did not deposit it in the British Library. Thus, there is no manuscript for *Oh! Hush!* The text here is the one that Charles White arranged for the Happy Hours Company, probably in 1873, when that publishing house was at 1 Chambers Street in New York. White's increasing indentation carefully preserves differences among spoken, recitative, and sung parts. Low blackface characters performing recitative furthered the burlesque on so-called Italian opera that high audiences favored.

2. Boot polish.

3. Much of the humor depends on our noticing that from here until the end of the play, despite all the capers and interruptions, nearly all the dialogue is now sung.

4. "Ad libidum" is a pun on *ad lib*, which conventionally refers to and shortens "ad libitum." "Libitum" is a medieval word probably formed from the verb "libet," "it pleases"; thus "ad libitum" means "in accordance with desire." "Ad libidum" as it appears in this stage direction, therefore, is a pun playing partly on Johnson's desire and lust, partly on such stage directions in Italian opera.

5. T. D. Rice was of course playing Cuff.

6. This and the next five interchanges are spoken.

Virginia Mummy

1. Rice's prompt script for *Virginia Mummy* exists in a scribe's hand as British Library Add MSS 42940, ff. 822–867. The script dates the the first performance as 22 April 1835 in Mobile, Alabama, and the Mobile *Commercial Register* confirms that Noah Ludlow's benefit took place that night: the play was "Written especially for the occasion, by Mr. Rice." The MS lists this original cast:

Ginger Blue	Mr. Rice
Galen	Mr. Marks
Rifle	Mr. Ruddell
[Ch]arles	Mr. Thompson
[O']Leary	Mr. Johnson
Paitent (sic)	Mr. Barclay
Schoolmaster	Mr. La Rue
Servant	Mr. Bacon
Porter	Mr. Hartman
Lucy	Minnick
Susan	Graham

Rice also played *Virginia Mummy* at least in Philadelphia, Boston, and New Orleans before he took it to England, where he opened it at the Royal Surrey on 1 August 1836. Plays for theatres south of the Thames, such as the Surrey, did not have to pass the censor. Thus it was not until Rice wanted to play *Virginia Mummy* at Covent Garden, north of the river, that he submitted it to the Lord Chamberlain. Rice submitted the play to the censor and performed it at Covent Garden on the same day, 13 March 1837; the Lord Chamberlain did not approve it until after the production, on the 15th. *Virginia Mummy* became a staple of the blackface Christy Minstrels as well as the expatriate black actor Ira Aldridge.

Much later, Charles White published two different adaptations of the play, neither dated. White's Happy Hours text is closer to the MS than is the Dick & Fitzgerald text. The latter begins with a different speech by Rifle, omits the first two scene changes, and sets all the early business in front of the hotel. The prompt script MS at the British Library is the best text of the play: it is full of Rice's business, his attitudes, his jokes. Unfortunately, a tear has obliterated its very ending. Thus I have completed the play by following the last few lines of the Happy Hours text. In the Historical Society of Pennsylvania, there is also a manuscript for the version of the play that the Christy Minstrels performed; its events are much the same, with some of the names and business changed. I have used this Christy *Mummy* to help determine the performed core of the play.

2. Patent leather; but perhaps this is a description of style, too, for "patent" also meant "open." This is the first play on "patent," meaning "licensed," in a script that regularly pokes fun at legitimacy.

3. A nineteenth-century plastic, caoutchouc was derived from the *Hevea brasiliensis* tree of South America and vulcanized with sulfur. An early example of a consumer technology become all the rage, it indicated Rifle's metropolitan manners.

4. Note the pun on exit/ax't.

5. Love letter.

6. In the British Library manuscript, a pencil has slashed the speech from this dash to its end.

7. See *Bone Squash Diavolo*, where Junietta tells Bone "de warm wedder hab so opened de paws of my system dat de perspiration flows just as copiously as de lasses from de hogshead" (1.2).

8. The Roman physician Galen (A.D. 130–200) made important contributions in several medical fields. His was an early voice in scientific racism, stating that "blacks inherited defective brains" and cataloguing stereotypes that became the classic delineators of black difference. See S. C. Drake, *Black Folk Here and There: An Essay in History and Anthropology*, vol. 2 (Los Angeles: Center for Afro-American Studies, University of California, 1987), p. 56; David Brion Davis, *Slavery and Human Progress* (New York: Oxford University Press, 1984), p. 42; and W. Michael Byrd and Linda A. Clayton, *An American Health Dilemma, Volume One, A Medical History of African Americans and the Problem of Race: Beginnings to 1900* (New York: Routledge, 2000), pp. 70–73. Rice and Ginger Blue targeted Dr. Galen for their sharpest ridicule.

9. Monkey (Jack) from Naples—an ethnic slur.

10. The settlement at Stonington was claimed both by Massachusetts and Connecticut in the mid-seventeenth century; it suffered naval attacks by the British during the Revolutionary War (1775) and again in 1814, during the War of 1812. Galen's chronology is as confused as his royal history. The various editions of the play substitute other battles.

11. Charles White gives, for Rice's "perplexing": *perfect stupid*.

12. Good will, aid.

13. Rice is playing on the often-repeated scene of slaves believing books talk to their readers. Ginger Blue hides within an image of blacks that Ginger knows Rifle will find credible.

14. The devil.

15. This conceit of mixing paint ingredients to represent race remains in play in the performance of American race at least up through Ralph Ellison's *Invisible Man* (1952) and its scene at the Liberty Paint factory (ch. 10). The mixture had more colors in the early nineteenth century than in the middle of the twentieth.

16. In the British Library manuscript, the stage manager has inked in here "Song Mr. Rice before change" and someone else has blocked in "Jim Crow" in pencil. Both of Charles White's adaptations indicate a "song" before the scene changes. But it is clear the song was not scripted in the original production; Ginger's remark, and the song he sang, register the entrepreneurial expectations that built up around Rice's performances, as around the representation of blackness at every level.

17. Holding out the boa.

18. Pointing to Charles's painting.

19. In 1773, J. Hawkesworth compiled the journals of James Cook's three principal journeys into *An Account of a Voyage Round the World, 1768–1771*.

20. In what may be Rice's hand, the MS has "ham" crossed out and replaced with "hog." "Hoggler" or "hogler" was an old word for a field worker of the lowest class; blacks were often said to be "smoked."

21. As in London and other cities, Philadelphia police had boxes at corners to protect them from the weather. They were sites of legendary pranks for streetwise youths, who would try to knock the cubicles over, especially with a policeman in them, preferably door-side down.

22. The joke in Rice's blackface theatre was that the black effect was produced by shoe polish. This is one of many references to the artificiality of the representation in Rice's performances that co-exist with simultaneous insistence on his authentic mimesis.

23. This last phrase in the stage directions is inserted in Rice's hand and double-underlined.

24. From the end of this line, for almost three and a half MS pages, until O'Leary announces the arrival of Patent and the new mummy, a pencil line has crossed out the text. The edition of the play that Charles White published in the 1880s omitted this passage, as crossed out. But much of the business in the deleted passage was clearly set up earlier, and several of the remarks that follow the omitted passage make no sense without it, so I am re-inserting it again—on the grounds that the original play, performed in Mobile, included this material.

25. Galen is expressing the same prejudice toward the Irish as was conventionally expressed toward blacks, and which Ginger Blue has just fulfilled.

26. *Laid in the mighty hetacombs:* in his excitement, Galen is compounding "catacomb" (underground tomb) with "hetaera" (a concubine).

27. Dead or sold south.

28. Amalgamation was the contemporary term for interracial mixing.

29. This is the end of the excised passage.

30. Woodchuck.

31. A hollow tree in which bees make their hives; often it was a black gum tree.

32. Dubious.

33. Someone has penciled over "before de She nigga," with "before Queen Shebera"; and White gives "before de Queen Sherbera."

Bone Squash

1. This composite text combines the manuscript of the 1839 one-act version Rice performed in London, *Bone Squash: A Burletta* (British Library Add MSS 42953, ff. 312–319), with Charles White's thrice-published editions, which he called *Bone Squash: A Comic Opera* (New York: Fredric A. Brady, n.d.; New York: Happy Hours Company, n.d.; New York: Samuel French, n.d.). In choosing among these variants, three factors determined my solutions. First, I wanted to give as full a text as possible. Thus, if there was no reason to doubt that Rice performed a scene in the adaptation by White, I included it. Second, when the short version conflicted with the longer printed texts, I preferred the one-act version because that was certainly the bare spine of the play, beyond which Rice would not cut; after all, the prompt script was in his own hand. And finally, I could check these four texts against long scene descriptions from early playbills in the United States and in London, and I had a letter from Rice to Francis Wemyss (11 September 1835, at the Harvard Theatre Collection) explaining the play's internal difficulties that prohibited its timely opening in Philadelphia. These early descriptions and their attendant cast lists indicate slippages, as well as continuity, among Rice's productions and White's.

2. "Duck legs" referred to a known posture in contemporary Philadelphia slang: "With a thick piece of cord reaching from one calf to another, [one character's duck legs] would have described the letter A; as they rubbed together at the knees, and were separated by the space of a foot between the boots" (George Lippard, *The Quaker City, or, The Monks of Monk Hall*, edited by David S. Reynolds, reprint, 1845 [Amherst: University of Massachusetts Press, 1995], p. 427).

3. In his Adelphi script, Rice cut the song to this single verse, made the pronouns plural, and gave it as the initial chorus, sung as the curtain rose.

4. The Park Theatre was New York's society theatre in the 1830s, at which no bootblack, sweep, or whitewasher—and few members of Rice's public—would have felt welcome.

5. Nicolo Paganini (1788–1840), the Italian violin virtuoso, was the gold standard for genius in Atlantic popular culture during these decades.

6. Rice early billed this song as "I Am the Paganini" (Surrey playbill, 15 July 1836, British Library Playbills, vol. 313). By 19 June 1840, he was listing it on playbills

as "I Am de Child ob Genus" (Bowery Folder, Harvard Theatre Collection). Another version of this frequent blackface song appears at the end of E. P. Christy, *Christy's Plantation Melodies (Book No. 3)* (Philadelphia: Fisher & Brother, 1853) as "Jim Brown's Address to His Sogers."

7. Charles White's texts give "log" here, but Rice's MS clearly reads "lag." The lag is the calm interval between tidal rushes, when optimal crossings occurred. Here, Bone is doubtless referring to the ferry between Catherine Market and Brooklyn. Rice grew up at Catherine Market, later lived in Brooklyn, and was buried in its Greenwood Cemetery.

8. *Ely's Hawk and Buzzard, or, New-York, Saturday Courier and Enquirer By Johannes Vanderdecken* began in 1832. Their slogan: "Our Gossip Birds Shall Keep a Bright Look Out And Show The World What Folly Is About." Their lead editorial on the occasion of their return to publication on 1 September 1832:

> It is well known by all unprejudiced persons, that the paper had a tendency to keep a certain class of beings under subjection through fear of having their deeds exposed by our *vigilant* BIRDS. The *spreeing blades* whose midnight revels so oft have disturbed the quiet slumbers of our peaceful citizens, were selected out as food for our *Buzzard*. We were ever on the watch—faithful and fearless —with a full determination to ferret out the secret movements of our city authorities, that we might lay their proceedings before our readers on each Saturday ... It shall be our duty to seek out every sink of infamy; that on each Saturday we may give the character of the inmates of these modern *hells* to our readers.
>
> We shall pay particular attention to the streets, see that all nuisances are removed, as we intend to make a St[reet]. Inspector of the Buzzard, who will remove every infected carcass from the city. . . . The HAWK will explore every part of Gotham, seeking out intelligence; and woe be to the *wretch* who falls within the grasp of his *talons!*

One cannot read too far in the *Hawk and Buzzard* (the best run is at the American Antiquarian Society) without realizing that it is a much more politically chocked forerunner to *Mad Magazine*. The *Hawk and Buzzard* is written in code, making itself up as it goes. It revolves around the lower East Side between Coenties Slip and Pearl Street (pretty much the circle Bone describes in his first speech). It is no accident that the paper is full of references to Jim Crow, for its readership is the literate portion of Rice's public. Like the Jim Crow plays, the *Hawk and Buzzard* maps the Catherine Market mentality.

9. The New York *Mirror*, a middlebrow literary magazine, had as its original subtitle, "Ladies Literary Gazette"; Rice had feuded with the *Mirror* since they published an attack on *Oh! Hush!* on 5 October 1833; for more on this conflict, see the Introduction, under the heading "Gumbo Cuff and the New York Desdemonas."

10. "Rhino" was street slang for money.

11. The protocols of "treating" were obligatory and paramount in working class culture; when Rice shortened this duet for his one-act version, he began with this verse, followed only by the Devil's last four lines at the end of the song.

12. Pest imagery clusters around the Jim Crow characters; they fight the war of the flea.

13. See Figure 2.

14. An equivalent to "Say, calf rope" or, "Say, Uncle"—except that it refers to the primary fight between brothers, Cain and Abel.

15. Joseph L. Hays was a legendary police officer in New York City, and the youth culture's bugaboo. His resignation from his position of police marshall in early 1833 was noticed in newspapers at least as distant as Philadelphia (*Pennyslvanian* 8 February 1833, p. 2, bottom col. 2). And a long, empty biography of him is in the New York *Sun*, 12 June 1834, calling him the "terror of evil-doers and little boys."

16. Charles White's adaptation omits this scene, but Rice retained it in his one-act version, and the accounts in playbills confirm that Rice opened Act Two of his full version with it.

17. The one-act prompt script for 1839 specifies "business" here, but does not say what it is. Actors might have kissed, danced, hugged, sung—and all would have been appropriate.

18. Touring actors played benefits before they left town to continue their circuit. On benefit nights they received a higher percentage of the gate. So, Bone is saying he wants to have his benefit before he goes with the Devil. But the saying is a pun, and Bone also hopes to consummate his marriage.

19. This is an early instance among a chain anticipating Rice's performance of Otello's "Farewell, joy, pride, pomp and come riot / Otello's occupation am gone" nearly a decade later. In 1842, at the Adelphi in Edward Stirling's *Yankee Notes for English Circulation*, Rice's character Hickory Dick will misquote Othello: "Julicum Caesar occipation's gone . . . an am neber catch him again—neber." All the up-market critics had been comparing Jim Crow to Othello, but Rice resisted the connection before he bitterly took it on in 1844.

20. The only evidence for this scene is that it exists in the Charles White variants.

Flight to America

1. William Leman Rede wrote this play for Rice to perform at the Adelphi Theatre, where it opened on 7 November 1836. Its original title, as submitted to the Lord Chamberlain, licensed by him on 3 November 1836, and deposited in the British Library as ADD 42939, ff. 444–479, was "*Life in America, The flight, the pursuit, the Voyage.*" However, the title in all playbills and reviews I have found was *Flight to America* and the title remained stable.

I have constructed a composite text based on the script in the British Library, plus the two quite different printed variants: William Leman Rede, *The Flight to America; or, Ten Hours in New York!* reprint, 1837, Duncombe's Edition (London: J. Duncombe, n.d.); and William Leman Rede, *The Flight to America: Or, Ten Hours in New York! A Drama, in three acts* (Philadelphia: Frederick Turner [of Turner & Fisher, 11 North Sixth Street], n.d.). The most significant problem with the printed texts is that they omit the important scene present in the manuscript, and mentioned in the reviews of the live performances, in which Jim Crow rides his white horse across the stage and makes an abolitionist speech. The printed texts also irrationally change the order of scenes. In reconstructing a text as full and as close to Rice's performance as possible, I have been instructed by the playbills and reviews. I welcome and use the evidence, included in the printed texts, of business Rice inserted as he inhabited the role, but I also honor the bills' and reviews' verification of scenes that the printed versions ignore. Since the printed versions differ in order of scenes, dialect transcription, and other matters, they do not legitimate each other. I have therefore privileged the manuscript.

The cast list for the original performance:

Benjamin Blinkinsopp, Esquire	Mr. J. Reeve
Antoine Pirouette, a Dancing Master	Mr. Yates
Sam Slapup, A Bailiff	Mr. Sanders
Mr. Hickory, uncle to Juliette	Mr. Cullenford
Peterkin Pawks, a riglar Yankee, his nephew	Mr. Buckstone
Major Mohawk, an American	Mr. S. Smith
Copper Charley	Mr. King
Julius Caesar	Mr. Gibson
Jim Crow, A Negro Porter and Ostler	Mr. T. Rice
Juliette la Belle, a Danseuse	Miss Daly
Ellen Freegrave, her friend	Miss Shaw
Mrs. Mohawk	Miss Harvey
Miss Sarah Snow, a Creole	Mrs. Stirling
Mrs. Marigold, Keeper of Hotel, New York	Mrs. Daly
Visitors to the Ball, Porters, Passengers, &c.	

2. This tune was a standard at the end of the eighteenth century and remained in print into the twentieth.

3. Rede's MS, unlike both printed variants, gives this American spelling.

4. French: "shame to him who thinks evil of it," or, "evil to him who evil thinks." A picturesque legend maintains the saying commemorates a 1348 incident in which Edward III was dancing with Joan of Kent, countess of Salisbury (later the wife of his son, the Black Prince). One of her blue garters dropped to the floor; as bystanders snickered, Edward gallantly picked up and put the garter on his own leg, admonishing the courtiers in French. His phrase remains as the motto of the Order of the Garter, considered to be the highest British civil and military honor. The saying is the last line of "Sir Gawain and the Green Knight."

5. "The Dusty Miller" was a popular song through the nineteenth century. The lyrics, by Robert Burns, began "Hey, the Dusty Miller."

6. Unlike the low characters who, in this play, invoke the devil in several argots, this middle-class woman, even cross-dressed as a man, can imply the devil (which rhymes with *revel* two lines above), but she will not say it.

7. As many jokes as possible are to be made about outsiders in this play.

8. As much discomfort as plausible is to be attributed to insiders during this play.

9. incognito: anonymous.

10. Marie Taglioni (1809–1884) was the most prominent *danseuse* of the century. Most famous for her buoyancy and bounding strength, she debuted in Vienna in 1822, appearing first in London in 1829.

11. This pun is a chestnut of the illegitimate stage in London. Richard Brinsley Peake wrote it into *The Hundred Pound Note*, licensed by the Lord Chamberlain in 1827, soon and often performed by Rice in the United States. He used this same pun, too, in his Jim Crow lyrics.

12. Wolfgang Amadeus Mozart's rousing finale to Act I of *The Marriage of Figaro* (1786)—played first in London in 1812, New York in 1824.

13. This song is from Gioachino Antonio Rossini's opera, *Il Barbiere di Siviglia* (1816, Rome; 1818, London; 1819, New York). An 1830 arrangement by C. Cummins, "adapted to the English Stage . . . the favorite buffa song" has these lyrics:

> Lo, the factotum of this gay place, I come!
> When in my shop I exhibit my face all come
> All say I'm the dandy, clever and handy.

14. Male singer of comic parts in operas.

15. These four singers starred in *I puritani (1835)* by Vincenzo Bellini (1801–1835), and became renowned as the "Puritani Quartet." Singing teacher in 1836 and 1837 to Princess Victoria, Luigi Lablache (1794–1858) was the most famous bass of his generation. In *I puritani*, Lablache played Sir George Walton. Antonio Tamburini (1800–1876), baritone, created the role Sir Richard Forth. Giulia Grisi (1811–1869), soprano, sang Elvira. Giovanni Battista Rubini (1794–1854), with his extraordinary high range, was Bellini's favorite tenor; Arturo was created for him.

16. The warlike melody in the second act finale of *I puritani* (1835).

17. Elvira's song in the first part of Bellini's *I puritani*.

18. Bully.

19. "Touch'd the cole" is "pocketed the money"; "rhino" is "money."

20. Traditional Scottish song, appearing in print as early as 1807, and often associated with storms at sea.

21. Benedict, after Shakespeare's Benedick, in *Much Ado About Nothing*, refers to a married man acting like a bachelor.

22. Sword.

23. By John Barnett, in print by 1826.

24. Daniel Steibelt (1765–1823), born in Germany, resident for a while in Paris, moved to London in 1797 and in March of 1798 first played his celebrated Third Concerto, the finale of which was a rondo pastoral imitating a storm. It achieved enormous popularity, remaining in print well into the twentieth century.

25. Roughly, furl up the lead sail.

26. Neither the MS nor the printed versions specifies the tune for this song. The lyric's rhythm, and spirit of the moment, make it possible that it was "Dan Tucker."

27. To explain the joke here is to smother it, but we may have to smother the pun to save it: in the dropping or adding of the "h" both class and regional markers are flagged. Americans pronounce the initial letter. Educated speakers in England drop it when referring to grooms, include it when referring to the owner of a hotel or hostel. That Crow is including it, when he can only be a groom, is funny to Blinkinsopp and Rede. They are also playing on the legend of Jim Crow as a hostler that turns on the way Rice is supposed to have appropriated the song and dance "Jump Jim Crow"; see my discussion of this issue in *Raising Cain*, pp. 180–186.

28. Here the printed texts add a significant scene that was not in the MS. I am retaining it because it was doubtless performed, and because its content is characteristic of the contemporaneous English picture of black-white attraction. An 1842 Adelphi farce written for Rice, *Yankee Notes for English Circulation*, by Edward Stirling, the husband of the actress originally playing Sarah Snow, centers on such transracial attraction.

29. Hyson is a Chinese green tea.

30. Well before Harriet Beecher Stowe's Adolph in *Uncle Tom's Cabin* (1851–52), Mark Twain's Tom/Chambers switches in *Pudd'nhead Wilson* (1894), and Zora Neale Hurston's retelling of the black folk stories sometimes known as "Phillymeyork" in *Mules and Men* (1935), T. D. Rice and William Leman Rede were exploiting this vernacular motif. Like the other stereotypes in play here, it must have been conventional even in the mid-1830s. Class-based (but not racial) variants of it were stamped out in the English farce tradition. See James Townley's *High Life below Stairs* (1804), which Rice played in Louisville and Washington, D.C. (and doubtless other cities) before he impersonated Jim Crow.

31. The MS gave no surname for Ellen Freegrave here. That the printed texts have Blinkinsopp specify her name incorrectly shows how Reeves developed the part's blundering aspects in production.

32. Hamlet does not say this.

33. This song was written for "The pantomime entertainment of Robinson Crusoe." It was in print as early as 1781 and often republished in the early nineteenth century.

34. Americans smoking and devouring newspapers, heels on tables, was a conventional English view of American public spaces. It appalled Mrs. Trollope, and that alone incited Americans to tease the English with the image, as did Hackett in *The Kentuckian*, and David Claypoole Johnston in his cartoons of the period. Here, the English author, Rede, has collaborated with Rice in the mutual cartoooning.

35. This speech is not in the MS and both printed texts specify that he was raised in Old Virginny; I have changed this to Kentucky here for consistency's sake: Sally Snow has already specified that Crow is from Kentucky; and additional lyrics to the song, cited in the next note, have Crow himself specifying Kentucky as his birth. All the texts of Jim Crow oscillate on this originary site. Most recently, he has escaped from Pawks's plantation in Virginia.

36. These lyrics were even more unstable than the text of the plays. Rice improvised new lyrics daily. For this slippage integral to his performance, see other "Jim Crow" lyrics among the songs, especially those published in London by J. B. Blewitt "as sung by Mr. T. D. Rice at the Theatre Royal Adelphi in the popular Drama of a Flight to America . . . by permission of Mr. Rice."

37. See E. P. Thompson, "Sale of Wives" in *Customs in Common* (New York: New Press, 1991; reprint, London: Penguin, 1993), pp. 404–466.

38. Frederick Henry Yates (1797–1842) was a fine character actor and important manager of the Adelphi Theatre, partnering in succession with Daniel Terry, Charles Mathews, and Thomas Gladstane until 1841. In the first production of *Flight to America*, Yates played Pirouette.

39. Horses.

40. "Tun" is keg; thus, a "one tun" would be a small pub.

41. *Obi, or, Three-finger'd Jack* was a "grand pantomimical drama" by John Fawcett (1768–1837), first performed at the Haymarket, 2 July 1800. Set in Jamaica, it concerned Obeah legends that were current around the Atlantic world since about 1780, in which loyal slaves kill Obi, a maroon priest who personified Obeah rites. The music was by Samuel Arnold (1740–1802). But by 1837 any allusion to Obi would be as complex as the story itself, which slides unstably across revolution and counterrevolution. By 1830, in Bristol, England, the American-born black actor Ira Aldridge was playing a dramatic version of *Obi* (Herbert and Mildred Stock Marshall, *Ira Aldridge: The Negro Tragedian* [London: Rockliff, 1958; reprint, Carbondale, Ill.: Southern Illinois University Press, 1968], p. 89) that was written by William H. Murray (*not* J. Murray, as the Stocks mistakenly claim). As the Stocks point out, Aldridge was enlivening rudiments of the story that are traceable back to the African Theatre in New York City. Michael Warner connects the Obi story to James Hewlett (Michael Warner [with students], "A Soliloquy 'Lately Spoken at the African Theatre': Race and the Public Sphere in New York City, 1821," *American Literature* 73, 1 [March 2001]: 1–46). Aldridge would have been introduced to the story there. For background and bibliography also see Charles J. Rzepka, "Thomas De Quincey's 'Three-Fingered Jack': The West Indian Origins of the 'Dark Interpreter,'" *European Romantic Review* 8, 2 (Spring 1997): 117–139.

42. The Fifth of July as a celebratory day in black New York City is best covered in Shane White, "'It Was a Proud Day': African Americans, Festivals, and Parades in the North, 1741–1834" in *Journal of American History* (June 1994): 13–50, esp. pp. 39–44. He details primary documents about the initial celebration on the fifth of July in 1827, in which three or four thousand African New Yorkers marched through the principal streets led by their own marshal on a "milk-white steed" (p. 44).

43. Policeman.

44. Nicolo Paganini (1788–1840), the Italian virtuoso violinist.

45. A theatrical pun—part of his core audience was in the "Gods," the cheap seats in the theatrical upper reaches, but of course the highest social circles deeply suspected Jim Crow's antics.

46. Street English pronunciation of French for, in this case, "scram": *Allez-vous en.*

47. Mrs. Marigold is perhaps crossing *concocting* with *connecting*—an inadvertent portmanteau word.

48. Gouging was the practice of popping or raking out an opponent's eyeball. Almanacs that circulated stories of western fighters often pictured men with thumbnails grown long especially for this practice. But these manners were attributed to Davy Crockett and other "gamecock" figures of the West, not with Virginia planters. This instance is the most obvious example, also evident in Pawks's speech and metaphors throughout the play, that Rede is mixing types that an American playwright would have separated.

49. The cathedral, by Christopher Wren, that then dominated the Thames and London skyline.

50. The Vauxhall attraction Dickens pictured on the frontispiece and described in *Sketches by Boz* (1836), his first book.

51. The pun is on "lots." George Henry Robins (1778–1841) was a noted auctioneer of the time in Covent Garden; he was active in theatrical sales, and friends with actors and *literati.*

52. Tom Molyneux (1784–1818) was an American freed slave, some say originally from Georgetown, West Indies, who had won his freedom as a reward for his boxing skills. Molyneux twice challenged the British boxing champion, Tom Cribb, in bare-knuckled prize fights, 10 December 1810 and 28 September 1811. Cribb won both fights. The best source is Pierce Egan's *Boxiana* (1812).

The Peacock and the Crow

1. The English actor and playwright Tom Parry (1806–62) wrote *The Peacock and the Crow* for Rice to perform at the Adelphi in London. I have transcribed and reconstructed the play from British Library Add MSS 42940, ff. 371–397, which the Lord Chamberlain received on 2 February 1837 and immediately licensed on 3 February 1837. The earliest bill I have found for the play is on 13 February, when the Adelphi was advertising the "fifth time" of its performance (bill at both British Library and Enthoven Collection).

2. Hollybush is at the top of Hampstead, a hilltop village then on the northern outskirts of London, now incorporated.

3. Charles Chesnutt's "The Goophered Grapevine" uses the same plot conceit: Mars Dugal's "en de oberseah sot spring guns en steel traps" to deter marauding neighbors from poaching the scuppernongs (Charles W. Chesnutt, *The Conjure Woman and Other Conjure Tales*, with an introduction by Richard H. Brodhead [Durham, N.C.: Duke University Press, 1993], p. 36).

4. Mrs. Hannah Glasse's *The Art of Cookery Made Plain and Easy* (London, 1763 [DNB says 1747]) had been through many editions by the early nineteenth century.

5. Newgate was London's infamous prison for capital cases, where inmates whiled away time with graffiti.

6. The famous last cry of Richard III, dismounted in Shakespeare's *Richard III* (5.4), before he is slain.

7. The daughter of Zeus and Hera; goddess of youth and spring; the original cup-bearer for Olympus; thus a young woman.

8. High life.

9. From Shakespeare's *King John* (3.1.129); calfskins were worn by licensed fools.

10. A purportedly dark zone between Earth and Hades.

11. Day & Martin manufactured shoe polish; today the firm is Carr & Day & Martin.

12. The character Jim Crow sings Charles Dibdin's "Kickeraboo." The manuscript has a line reading "Carolina Boys" at this point but also crosses it out. The indispensable S. Foster Damon notes that Charles Dibdin composed and printed this song for his *Christmas Gambols* (1795). It is an early instance of the slave's meditation on the master's death, and its meaning. This song came to be known as "Kickaraboo" and appeared many times in Atlantic songsters (see S. Foster Damon, "The Negro in Early American Songsters," *The Papers of the Bibliographical Society of America* 28 (1934): 136).

13. Banjo.

14. Indeed, author Tom Parry is packing in several levels of irony and parody that oscillate radically between sympathy, even celebration, and scornful dismissal. Quickset's adventitious scheming plays against Crow's direct earnestness. We see here how blackness is set and embedded differently during these years on different sides of the Atlantic.

15. Rolla is the Peruvian lead character in Richard Sheridan's *Pizarro* (adapted from Kotzebue and first produced in 1799), a tragedy about the Spanish conquest. The play was a regular part of Rice's frontier apprenticeship in Louisville and Cincinnati. Intending it or not, Parry thus touches on colonial issues beneath the surface ice that he sets Quickset skating. Aligning Jim Crow with Peruvian Indians is akin to the usual English genealogy of Jim Crow (see "A Faithful Account of the Life of Jim Crow, the American Negro Poet" in Street Prose, below). Parry and Quickset transmute the pain of empire into "something outrageously outré" in order to jolt the aspirants of Hampstead.

16. Extra large pellets.

17. Spoiling, putting out of order.

18. This anomalous lyric was evidently sung to the tune of "Clar de Kitchen" and used its chorus.

19. Again, as with "Clar de Kitchen," Thomas Parry has applied anomalous lyrics to the song and tune long associated with Rice.

20. See note 40 in the Introduction.

21. The play is on *poster*, as in bill-poster or sign; and *impostor*.

22. This pun is on impertinence and imperiousness.

Jim Crow in His New Place

1. Playbills and newspaper advertisements attribute this play to two different authors and Rice performed it under several titles, including *Jumbo Jum, Literal Interpretation*, and *Jim Crow in Foreign Service*. This last title was sometimes attributed to C. A. Somerset (who also wrote *A Day after the Fair*, which Rice often performed during his apprenticeship, before blacking up). When the Lord Chamberlain licensed the play at the end of 1838, however, the title was *Jim Crow in His New Place* and Thomas Proclus Taylor was the author. It is this manuscript now in the British Library that I have transcribed and edited here (Add. MS 42950, ff. 593–602b). Allardyce Nicoll lists nineteen plays by T. P. Taylor (*Early Nineteenth Century Drama, 1800–1850* in *A History of English Drama 1660–1900*, vol. 4 [Cambridge: Cambridge University Press, 1955], p. 411). T. D. Rice first performed *Jim Crow in His New Place* at the Adelphi on New Year's Eve, 1838. Copies in both the British Library and the Enthoven Collection of the playbill for that first night give this cast: "Sir Solomon Slygo, Mr. F. Matthews; Mr. Grub, Mr. Cullenford; Jim Crow, Mr. Rice, who will sing his two popular songs of 'Sich a Gettin' Up Stairs' and 'Jump Jim Crow'; Deborah, Mrs. Fosbroke; Arabella, Miss Reynolds; Lady in White, Miss Gower; Sally Snowball, Miss George." After opening night the men in the cast other than Rice changed parts (Sir Solomon Slygo, Mr. Cullenford; Mr. Grub, Mr George; Henry Seymour, Mr. Saville).

Unlike other plays attributed to Adelphi playwrights, however, this one had a short American history before Rice played it in London. Whether Rice wrote the play during his 1838 round of stateside theatres or T. P. Taylor sent him a copy of the play in New York before he sailed to England we may never know. But in New York, at the Franklin Theatre in Chatham Square, at the edge of Rice's root neighborhood, he performed *Jumbo Jum* on 17 September 1838 (Franklin Theatre Folder, Harvard Theatre Collection); the cast list on the bill specifies Jumbo, Rice; Sir Solomon Slygo, Mr. W. Jones; Squire Grub, Phillips; Seymour, J. Jones; Labourer, Burns; Arabella, Miss Mathews; Deborah, Mrs. De Grouche; Sally Snowdrop, Monell; Lady in White, Miss Wilson. Before going to London, Rice also performed this play in Boston (five successive nights beginning 24 September 1838—Harvard Theatre Collection, Warren Box) and at the Walnut Street Theatre in Philadelphia (10 October 1838, confirmed in Philadelphia *Public Ledger*, on day). Therefore, well before T. P. Taylor or C. A. Somerset put their names to it in England, and gave it names that did not stick, Rice was performing *The Humours of Jumbo Jum*.

Thence to London's Adelphi, where he opened with his old success at that theatre, *Flight to America*, but switched to what he or the Adelphi management called *Jim Crow in His New Place* on New Year's Eve 1838 (noted in the British Library Playbills Collection, catalogue 367). Almost always after this run of the play at the Adelphi, Rice reverted to the original American title, *Jumbo Jum*, or, sometimes, *Literal Interpretation*.

On at least two occasions in the stateside prototypes of *Jim Crow in His New Place*, the role of Deborah seems to have been cast in drag—at the Franklin in New York, when the gruffly named "Mrs. De Grouche" played Deborah, and more certainly at Philadelphia's Walnut when Mr. La Forest played her role. But I have found no other drag stagings of the part after the London performances.

Rice played *Jumbo Jum* continually throughout the 1840s and periodically during the 1850s, at least as late as 7 August 1858 (George C. D. Odell, *Annals of the New York Stage, Volume VII* [New York: Columbia University Press, 1931], p. 284.)

2. The ghost of Hamlet's father coins this phrase in *Hamlet*, 1.5.21; Shakespeare used *porpentine* for our porcupine. This image may be the source for the "fright wig" that minstrel shows used to illustrate stereotypical black fear of ghosts; the fear was not originally racially linked.

3. God's.

4. Goliath.

5. To jumble, the Oxford English Dictionary notes, has meant since the sixteenth century "to have carnal intercourse" and "to know carnally."

6. Particularly.

7. Lacquered with a hard black gloss.

8. Pressed.

The Foreign Prince

1. The popular Adelphi playwright William Leman Rede, author also of the 1836 hit *Flight to America*, composed *The Foreign Prince* for Rice during the early weeks of the American actor's second English stay. The top of the MS notes that the Lord Chamberlain licensed the play on 16 February 1839, and the first production was 18 February. The cast at the opening was:

Old Dawkins	Mr. Cullenford
Dick Dabble	Mr. Saville
Ebenezer	Mr. O. Smith
Jim Crow	Mr. Rice
Barney	Mr. H. Beverley
Milkman	Mr. Lansdowne
Dog-all (a Policeman)	Mr. Saunders
Letty (with a song)	Mrs. Keeley
Emily	Miss Shaw
Mrs. Mouldem	Mrs. Fosbrooke
Mrs. Crow	Mrs. Gower
Crow's four children	Misses Isaacs, Cooke, Appleyard, and Collins

Rice was listed to "sing his popular songs of 'Sich a Gettin' Up Stairs' and 'Jump Jim Crow.'" *The Foreign Prince* played the theatre continually until the end of the season, 23 March, sharing the bill with *Oliver Twist* and *Nicholas Nickleby*, in which Mrs. Keeley was playing the breeches part of Smike. Mrs. Keeley, the Mary Martin of her era, would have enormous success in late October at the Adelphi with her role of Jack Sheppard in J. B. Buckstone's adaptation of Harrison Ainsworth's novel.

2. A pub.

3. Opera singers: Luigi Lablache (1794–1858) was the most famous bass of his generation; Giulia Grisi (1811–1869) was a famous soprano.

4. Ethnic joke—punning on Grisi, and the ethnic slur that Italians are greasy.

5. A traditional Gloucestershire folk song, in print in England by 1834, and often reprinted.

6. The Adelphi Theatre was displaying "The Palestine Giant" on the same nights as *The Foreign Prince*—playbill at British Library for 25 February 1839.

7. Letty misquotes only slightly. In Air 53, 3.11, Captain Macheath sings:

> Which way shall I turn me? How can I decide?
> Wives, the day of our death, are as fond as a bride.
> One wife is too much for most husbands to hear,
> But two at a time there's no mortal can bear.
> *This way, and that way, and which way I will,*
> What would comfort the one, t'other would take ill.

Yankee Notes for English Circulation

1. Edward Stirling, then the Stage Manager of the Adelphi and married to the Mrs. Stirling who played Sally Snowball in *Flight to America* and Letty in *The Peacock and the Crow*, wrote *Yankee Notes for English Circulation* for T. D. Rice. He submitted his play to the Lord Chamberlain on 19 December 1842 and it was licensed two days later, 21 December. The first production was on 26 December 1842—scarcely preceding the moment that Dan Emmett and the Virginia Minstrels first performed their quite different blackface sendups at the Chatham Theatre in New York City and supposedly started the minstrel show. I have transcribed and edited Stirling's manuscript, now in the British Library (Add. MSS 42965, ff. 724–735). For information on the Stirlings, see Percy Allen, *The Stage Life of Mrs. Stirling* (London: T. Fisher Unwin, 1922), and Edward Stirling, *Old Drury Lane: Fifty Years' Recollections of Author, Actor, and Manager*, 2 vols. (London: Chatto and Windus, 1881).

This play's multiple maskings in its final scene call conscious attention to the blackface mask as an extension of farcical convention; the last scene also clearly associates Jim Crow with abolitionism and its tradition of outside agitators. That Jim Crow fancies himself George Washington's brother and even displaces him on the pedestal in order to judge the mad capers of whites establishes a remarkable imagery for playgoers to recollect later.

2. Although this is an incongruous tune to sing at an inland American resort—the first of Stirling's many such English connections and misunderstandings of the American scene—the intention seems to be an association with the rush at dockside when a packet comes in, and the pressure on porters at such moments.

3. The punning condensed in "Hiccory Dick" is broad. The name associates this character with Andrew Jackson, who was "Old Hickory." The spelling of Hiccory, a standard variant in the early nineteenth century, sustains a connection to the conjurer's phrase *hiccius doccius*, which the Oxford English Dictionary glosses as per-

haps "a corruption of the Lat. phrase hicce est doctus 'this or here is the learned man.'" In conjuring, the phrase was uttered to effect an exchange or pass, as we today say *hocus pocus*. And, *hiccius doccius*, Hiccory Dick's function in this play is to effect exchanges. Although the dictionaries do not cite the phallic meaning for "Dick" this early in the nineteenth century, I suspect that meaning was rising. If so, "Hiccory Dick" had its surprises there, too. In addition to the obvious connotation of hardness, one wonderfully contrary meaning for "hiccory" refers to a sliding or lapsed sectarian; for instance, the hiccory Amish go to movies. Hiccory Dick, therefore, is related to Bone Squash, hard and soft; he also lapses from his career's earlier opposition to Mrs. Trollope, appealing at the very end to propagate her take on America, her note.

4. Marie Taglioni (1809–1884), the most prominent *danseuse* of the century. Most famous for her buoyancy and bounding strength, she debuted in Vienna in 1822, appearing first in London in 1829.

5. For the social importance of dance and balls as meeting places in black American urban life during this period, see Shane White, "The Death of James Johnson," *American Quarterly* 51 (December 1999): 753–796.

6. Here is a fine example of how English playwrights were rendering black dialect as an amalgam. Perceived black English (de and hab) mingled with the cockney dropped H (appy and onor) and with a pidgin lumpen dialect ('em for I and my).

7. Money, coinage.

8. Unbleached linen.

9. Although it is Othello, not Julius Caesar, who laments that his occupation is gone, Hiccory is not mixing up his Shakespeare so much as he is identifying his position with Othello's—his full name, as Miss Zip Coon tells us, is Julius Caesar Washington Jackson Dick—and his father called him Julicum Caesar.

10. That is, take in ironing.

11. Bluebeard and Fatima are characters in *Bluebeard, or, Female Curiosity* (1798), by George Colman, the Younger (1762–1836).

12. To jumble, the Oxford English Dictionary notes, has meant since the sixteenth century "to have carnal intercourse" and "to know carnally."

13. Humbug, nonsense, rubbish.

14. This Kentuckian, or his English author, confuses American "Down East" Maine with Kentucky.

15. Charles Dickens published his *American Notes* in 1842, the year of this play's first production. It followed in the tradition, controversial in America, of Frances Trollope's *Domestic Manners of the Americans* (1832), Fanny Kemble's *Journal of America* (1835), and Harriet Martineau's *Society in America* (1837). All these books ardently supported abolition.

16. Charles Dickens's early pseudonym.

Otello

1. *Otello* has never been published. I transcribed and edited the manuscript in the New York Public Library, Billy Rose Collection, call number NCOF +. Dated April

1853, the manuscript says at its top: "Property of John B. Wright copied by permission from the Manuscript of His Friend T. D. Rice, Esq." Born in Newburyport, Massachusetts, 1 October 1814, Wright worked his way up at the Tremont Theatre, beginning as a call boy in 1833 to become its stage manager (Allston T. Brown, *History of the American Stage* [New York: Dick & Fitzgerald, 1870], p. 407). The manuscript also specifies the "Music arranged by Mr. Tyte."

Rice wrote this play. Its text includes remarkable supplements to the Othello story. It is based on the structure of Maurice Dowling's burlesque (Maurice Dowling, *Othello Travestie*, vol. 2 of *Shakespeare Burlesques*, Stanley Wells, 1834 [reprint, Wilmington, Del.: Michael Glazier, 1978]). But the language, the ending, and the progeny differ radically from Dowling's and all other versions of the story that I know.

The first production was at the Philadelphia Chesnut Street Theatre when Francis Wemyss was managing it, 28 October 1844; the cast (according to the Philadelphia *Public Ledger* on the day): Otello, Mr. Rice; Iago, Mr. Jordan; Brabantio, Mr. W. Chapman; Duke of Venice, Mr. Sullivan; Roderigo, Mr. Brunton; Desdemona, Miss H. Mathews; Emilia, Mrs. Hautonville.

2. Nonsense.

3. The dialect here indicates that Iago is summarizing Otello's talk.

4. Mrs. Rowbotham, playing Ninette in *The Bold Dragoons*, sang "Merry Swiss Boy" at the Chesnut Street Theatre in Philadelphia, 12 June 1833.

5. A small coin, as a penny.

6. "Squatulate" is a short form of "absquatulate," or "decamp," "run off."

7. Leave, be off.

8. The devil.

9. This formula for polite racism is Dowling's coinage. Shakespeare has at this point: "Though I do hate him as I do hell's pains, / Yet for necessity of present life, I must show out a flag and sign of love" (1.1.154–156). Dowling has Iago sing it to the air of "Bow, wow, wow": "And though I hate the black blackguard, as I do hate the devil, / I'd cut his throat with pleasure—but I wouldn't be uncivil" (9).

10. Cut, strip, whip.

11. *Gretna Green*, by Lawrence Dromcolloher, was a popular Scottish ballad opera about elopement.

12. Dowling specifies the music as "Follow, Follow." Wright's transcription of Rice's play does not specify the music.

13. This bribe, and the next line confirming its effectiveness, is a touch Rice continues from Dowling; it is one of the many nineteenth-century moves to make the Othello character less the Noble Moor and more a champion among streetwise sparrows.

14. Soaplocks were forelocks that youths created by soaping their hair. They were popular among Bowery b'hoys, one of the first youth cultures that middle-class commentators noticed spawning along the Lower East Side of Manhattan.

15. At the end of his 1.3, Shakespeare gives this racist remark to Brabantio, who says

"if such actions may have passage free, / Bondslaves and pagans shall our statesmen be." The idea is not uttered clearly in Dowling's variant; Rice revives it, making it the common sentiment given in chorus.

16. A generally reliable source reports Rice wrote verses to the tune of "'Sitting on a Rail' and dedicated them to Queen Victoria," doubtless at her coronation, when Rice was performing in London (Isaac J. Greenwood, *The Circus* [New York: William Abbatt, 1909], p. 127). By the 1840s, the song was infrequent in Rice's repertoire but "Sitting on a Rail" was popular with other performers. The underlying tune of the council's song is its chorus:

> As I walk out by de light ob de moon
> So merrily singing dis same tune
> I cum across a big raccoon,
> A sittin' on a rail,
> Sittin' on a rail,
> Sittin' on a rail
> I come across a big raccoon,
> A sleepin' wery sound.

In fact, in most of the variants, the song is about the escape of the coon—just as Otello will escape in this scene, and Desdemona will escape later. What does not escape in this song, nor in the play, is ultimate authority. The song figures this authority as the singer's master:

> My ole Massa dead and gone
> A dose ob poison help him on
> De Debil say he funeral song.

The play figures authority as the Duke, Brabantio, and the class that is trying to judge Otello in this scene. They are bumblers who need the dark hero to do their business.

17. Shakespeare says "galleys" (1.3); Dowling added the (perhaps redundant) "slaves." Rice followed Dowling. This addition emphasizes that the Senate has sent Otello—a former slave—to quell revolutionary slaves. The shift in attitudes toward slavery in the intervening two and a half centuries made the nineteenth century players feature this problem.

18. For Shakespeare's "mountebank" and Dowling's "wizard," Rice used "buzzard." This change is complex and coded. Brabantio clearly means it grossly negatively; buzzard is worse than crow, a grotesque bird. However, in the argot of New York's Seventh Ward—where Rice was born and grew up—a buzzard was a social cleanser that pounced on the society's rotten matter and bore it away. For instance, at the time Rice was establishing himself as Jim Crow, a scandal sheet printed in the neighborhood proudly named itself *The Hawk and Buzzard*. Its mast-head slogan: "Our Gossip Bird Shall Keep a Bright Look Out And Show the World What Folly Is About." Their statement of purpose: "We intend to make a St[ate or street?] inspector of the Buzzard, who will remove every infected carcass from the City" (*Ely's Hawk and Buz-*

zard, 1 September 1832). *The Hawk and Buzzard* is Bone Squash's paper of choice in *Bone Squash Diavolo.* Thus for some in the audience, to be called a buzzard would be a perverse, if inadvert, compliment. There is much inversive irony in the language the authoritative characters speak in *Otello.*

19. Or, "I'd like to cut his throat."

20. English civil engineer William Cubitt invented the tread mill in 1817 as a machine to punish prisoners.

21. Lashes.

22. Dowling has this speech sung to the tune of "Yankee Doodle." The Wright MS, however, stipulates "recitative" and the speech that Rice gives Otello no longer scans to "Yankee Doodle." By 1844, even "Yankee Doodle" was in some sense inappropriately marked: by then the English had too often applied "Yankee Doodle" as an essentially *national* air. Rice is opposing that unity by switching a few lines later to "Ginger Blue," the song named after his insouciant character in *The Virginia Mummy.* In scene 4, Rice specifies "Yankee Doodle" as the air behind Iago's sarcastic account of the ideal woman—emphasizing Iago's inappropriate clichés.

23. "And no mistake" is a vernacular tic of Bowery b'hoys. Four years later, in his Mose plays, Frank Chanfrau will use it to mark off his knowing characters from the innocents they guide.

24. Ginger Blue was the lead character in Rice's play *The Virginia Mummy,* which he began performing as early as 22 April 1835. But the earliest copyright I have found on the song "Ginger Blue" was 1841, by Richard Pelham, who would become one of the four original members of the Virginia Minstrels in the winter of 1842–1843. How these verses, each a different length, fitted the music is a mystery.

25. All of the black characters that Rice played enjoyed freedom. They were either runaways, like Otello and Jim Crow in *Flight to America,* or were wage servants like Bone Squash in *Bone Squash Diavolo* or Gumbo Chaff in *Oh! Hush!* Dowling's Othello was "an independent Nigger, from the Republic of Hayti."

26. Jail.

27. This is the first mention of what will be a cardinal feature of Rice's variant of the Othello story: Desdemona and Otello have a son that does not appear in Cinthio, Shakespeare, or Dowling. This son is the story's problem child—an objective correlative that flames for the first time the smoldering emotional issues at the story's core.

This moment in which Desdemona reveals her desire and leads on the Othello character is also the spot that most offended elite contemporary commentators on *Otello.* John Quincy Adams attacked Desdemona's forwardness in the *American Monthly Magazine* (March 1836, pp. 209–217), complaining in classic racist terms of a well-bred girl attracted to "the sooty bosom, the thick lips, and the wooly head" of a "blackamoor." James Henry Hackett, who was a star contemporary with Rice and often played in the same theatres with him, wrote in *Notes, Criticisms and Correspondence upon Shakespeare's Plays and Actors* ([1863] New York: Benjamin Blom, 1968), p. 224:

[Desdemona] falls in love and makes a runaway match with a blackamoor, for no better reason than that he has told her a braggart story of his hair-breadth escapes in war. For this, she not only violates her duties to her father, her family, her sex, and her country, but she makes the first advances . . . The blood must circulate briskly in the veins of a young woman, so fascinated, and so coming to the tale of a rude, unbleached African soldier. The great moral lesson of the tragedy of *Othello* is, that black and white blood cannot be intermingled in marriage without a gross outrage upon the laws of Nature; and that, in such violations, Nature will vindicate her laws.

Every aspect of Rice's *Otello* is heightened to call attention to and trouble this racism. For instance, in nearly every instance Dowling's white characters referred to Othello as "rascal" or "wight," Rice changed the epithet to "nigger."

28. Fly Market was at the foot of Maiden Lane in Lower Manhattan; there, New Yorkers sold and bought slaves in the eighteenth century. This part of Desdemona's story was added to Shakespeare's telling by Dowling, to be sung to "Bonnie Laddie." Rice compounds the addition by putting Desdemona's song into its camp call-and-response staging against the slave-market background of the tune. Desdemona's song in Dowling is a solo; the polyphony in Rice's variant multiplies the irony and emphasizes that her attraction to Otello was shared, hardly aberrant. Rice shows a cohort staging an emergent cultural option.

29. This may be the moment of conception, a possible play on immaculate, or unknown, conception. There is good wordplay here with *Great-full* and *(sc)rape*. Rice or his copyist changed the conventionally spelled "grateful" in Dowling to this "greatful." If Rice and Dowling are implying a sexual union, and impregnation, they are also admitting a motive for the lovers' hasty, secret elopement. "Scrape" may also refer to abortion.

30. This *"me* just now married," a Dowling coinage, is a vestigial remnant in Rice's text of English Black Stage Dialect, which Rice has generally scrubbed and replaced.

31. Rice used this line also in *Bone Squash Diavolo* (1.1), referring to the devil.

32. Billy Whitlock copyrighted "Miss Lucy Long" in 1842. It is a courting song with overt sexual overtones:

> Take your time, Miss Lucy,
> Take your time, Miss Lucy Long;
> Rock de cradle, Lucy;
> Take your time my dear.

33. Amalgamation was the contemporary term for miscegenation. As John Quincy Adams's and James Henry Hackett's remarks (quoted in note 25) indicate, middle-class conventions abhorred racial mixing. But the practice was, in fact, commonplace in New York's Seventh Ward, where T. D. Rice grew up (see Lhamon, *Raising Cain*, pp. 18–19). Particularly in the way Otello is *singing* the term in a burlesque of a canonical text and inverting conventional expectations of the meaning in the next few lines, Rice indicates his self-conscious reference to the radical form of his play.

34. Money.

35. "Polly Will You Now" was perhaps derived from Gay's *Beggar's Opera*, and its sequel, *Polly*. There is also this intriguing tidbit: "George Rice," wrote Charles White, "a brother of T. D. Rice, was singing a negro song called 'Sing Song, Polly, Won't You Kiss Me, Oh!' in 1837" (clipping from *The World*, titled "Old-Time Minstrels," dated Sunday 20 June 1880, in Rice file at Henry Ransom Humanities Research Center, Austin, Texas). Blues scholar Tony Russell has suggested to me that perhaps this song is the forerunner of the song that some hillbilly singers in the 1920s and 1930s recorded, usually under a title more or less like "King Kong Kitchie Kitchie Ki Me O." The lyrics and cadence match, and the parable hidden in the subject matter is not alien. One can hear a pleasant version of this song, sung by Chubby Parker, on the Harry Smith (ed.) anthology, *American Folk Music, Volume One: Ballads* (Folkways FP 251).

For more information on George Rice, see Dale Cockrell, *Demons of Disorder* (Cambridge: Cambridge University Press, 1997), pp. 69–70.

36. Poison.

37. An objective correlative for the sexual passion between Desdemona and Otello, this "problem child" (as my then student June Piscitelli wonderfully called him) makes explicit the theme of transracial and cross-class desire that had smoldered, but never been oxygenated, in all the previous variants of the Othello story. "Young Otello," as this child is called in the playbills, was enacted by "Mast. J. Murray" in August 1852, on the same bill with the first New York dramatization of *Uncle Tom's Cabin*, by Charles W. Taylor, at Purdy's National Theatre (Harvard Theatre Collection, National Theatre Folder). Purdy's was the same theatrical space that abolitionists contested with the youth culture of the 1830s—see Lhamon, *Raising Cain*, pp. 29–32, and the Introduction, under the heading "Phase Five. Passings and Afterlife."

38. This famous tune was first printed in the western Atlantic in 1794 by Benjamin Carr, in Philadelphia (Irving Lowens, *Music and Musicians in Early America* [New York: Norton, 1964], pp. 89–91). Especially early on, it had many folk variants.

39. James Gordon Bennett, one of the leading newspaper entrepreneurs of nineteenth-century New York, was friendly with T. D. Rice and, usually, a fan. His paper was the *New York Herald*, later the *Herald*.

40. Or, *I'll estrange you*.

41. Perhaps inadvertent for "clash of cymbals," perhaps intended, especially given the details immediately to be disclosed.

42. These lines indicate that the child actor was blacked up only on one side of his face; the other side favored Desdemona.

43. This song had been in oral circulation in the United States since the Revolution and appeared in several printed collections throughout the nineteenth century. It was apparently a colonial fife song, probably of Irish origin and perhaps via the English variant, "Brighton Camp" (c. 1715). Commencement ceremonies at West Point Academy featured it in the 1960s. The core of the song as usually performed is the *loss* of a lover that one had once hoped would faithfully wait for a return. (Charles

Hamm, *Yesterdays: Popular Song in America* [New York: Norton, 1979], p. 250; David Ewen, *American Popular Songs: From the Revolutionary War to the Present* [New York: Random House, 1966], p. 121; G. Malcolm Laws, Jr., *American Balladry from British Broadsides* [Philadelphia: The American Folklore Society, 1957], pp. 248–249).

Rice's incorporation of this song reverses its mood. Otello has overcome the song's dilemma: he has Desdemona back in his arms. He is as much a hero of renewal and connections as Elvis Presley was a century later when he changed earlier (both black and white) versions of "Mystery Train" so that the final stanza brought his girl back instead of taking her away forever. The whole previous history of that song, like "The Girl I Left Behind Me," was about irrevocable loss of one's love, full stop. (For "Mystery Train," see Greil Marcus, *Mystery Train: Images of America in Rock 'N' Roll Music* [New York: Dutton, 1975], pp. 201–203.)

44. Mrs. Keeley (as Jack Sheppard) and Paul Bedford (as Blueskin) sang the duet "Nix My Dolly Palls Fake Away" in J. B. Buckstone's *Jack Sheppard* at London's Adelphi Theatre in 1839. There were at least four other versions of this very popular play on London stages alone at the same time.

Herbert Rodwell wrote the music and Harrison Ainsworth the lyrics for *Jack Sheppard*. Their song went through at least fifteen printings by D. Almaine & Co., Soho Square—as attested on its title page in the Enthoven Collection's Adelphi folder for 1839. From the beginning, they published the song with footnotes that translated its patois. In the example below, I have rendered the original footnotes in brackets. That even the contemporaneous public required translations indicates the social distance that the song and performance were designed to cross. Bridging that gap was what such plays as *Jack Sheppard* and *Otello* were about—for they provided a special bonus value, a release of energy when the connection was made, that cemented the cross-class filiations these plays established. Here, then, is part of "Nix My Dolly Palls Fake Away":

Jack

In a box of the Stone-Jug I was born [in a cell in Newgate],
of a hempen widow [one whose husband has been hanged], the kid forlorn.

Blueskin

Fake away

Jack

My noble father, as I've heard say,
was a famous merchant of capers gay [a dancing master]

Blueskin

Nix my dolly palls fake away [Nothing comrades, on! on!] repeat

Chorus

Repeat 4 times . . .

Jack

But I slipp'd my darbies [fetters] one morn in May.
And I gave to the dubs [turnkey] a holiday

Blueskin

Fake away

Jack

And here I am palls merry and free,
A regular rolicking romany

Blueskin

Nix my dolly palls fake away,
nix my dolly palls fake away

Chorus

4 times

Since there is nothing comparable in Shakespeare or in Dowling that Rice was drawing on—the whole song is his addition—he clearly meant to make a point with this beautiful tune. It may be that Rice has Otello sing his "notin' to pay" lyrics at this point to emphasize his likeness to Jack Sheppard's Romany or "gypsy" mood. According to the legends and play, Jack Sheppard was hanged at Tyburn; there is plenty to pay.

45. "Rosin the Bow," or "Rosin the Beau," has mysterious origins. As they did with "Jim Crow," black and white singers swapped "Rosin" back and forth within an American transracial repertoire. Its lyrics are a palimpsest of its many performers. This song was the greatest hit of Old Corn Meal, a black street singer in New Orleans during the 1830s. Moreover, Rice performed a skit based on Old Corn Meal on 23 February 1836 at the American Theatre in New Orleans; perhaps he learned the song directly from the street performer (Henry Kmen, "Old Corn Meal: A Forgotten Urban Negro Folksinger," *Journal of American Folklore* 75, 295 [Jan.–March, 1962]: 31, 33). By the end of the decade, "Old Rosin the Bow" had been published in New Orleans and Boston (Henry Kmen, *Music in New Orleans: The Formative Years, 1791–1841* [Baton Rouge: Louisiana State University Press, 1966], p. 242; S. Foster Damon, *Series of Old American Songs* [Providence: Brown University Library, 1936]). But oral transmission continued to carry the song: Appalachian singer Dick Tillett performed "Old Rosin the Beau" for Frank and Anne Warner in 1972 and 1978. The Warners also suggest an older source in a printed "stall ballad by Ryles of Seven Dials" in London that may trace the song back to the seventeenth century (Anne Warner, *Traditional American Folk Songs* [Syracuse: Syracuse University Press, 1984], p. 361).

David Ewen reports that the tune propelled presidential campaign songs repeatedly between 1840 and 1875. In 1844, the year Rice first performed *Otello*, the Whigs twice used the tune to rhapsodize Henry Clay, their losing candidate. Among Democrats, therefore, the tune would have been immediately associated with the sort of hypocrisy that Iago expresses while singing it here.

46. This explicit reference to black/white substitution is neither in Shakespeare nor Dowling. In assigning Iago the "black is white" line during a song in which he declares his hypocrisy, Rice reemphasizes the phony binary of race. The whole point of

such performance is to show that race and other genealogical issues are never divisible into either/or options. The blackface mask, the problem child, and this hypocritical reference by Iago all show—singly and even more together—that black and white hybridization is a persistent fact that the audience must face just as the performers do.

47. Dowling changed Lodovico to Ludovico; Rice followed.

48. "Corn Cobs" was a folk variant on the early strains of "Yankee Doodle," with a mad refrain:

> Corn Cobs twist your hair
> Cart wheel run round you
> Fiery dragons take you off
> And mortar pestle pound you.

Its lyrics were printed in 1834 and the sheet music in 1836 by Endicott in New York (Damon, *Series of Old American Songs*; Constance Rourke, *American Humor*, ed. W. T. Lhamon, Jr. [Tallahassee: Florida State University Press, 1985], pp. 8, 93, 308). During the 1830s the song became associated with the actor George Handel Hill, who played Down East Yankees—often on the same bills with Rice jumping Jim Crow. But Rice had sung the song as an entr'acte, himself, as early as 2 November 1829 in Cincinnati, at about the same time he was starting to black up (but had not yet fixed his stage persona as black). To have Iago sing this song nails the Ensign as a Yankee rationalist. The lyrics here are an amalgam from Shakespeare, Dowling, and Rice; they have nothing of the Tom o' Bedlam refrain of the folk song—*that* is borne by the tune.

49. Dowling's Iago was Irish; Rice's Iago is a Yankee.

50. At what was probably his first benefit performance ever, on 12 June 1830, Rice sang this song in Louisville.

51. Another vestigial remain of Dowling's English Black Stage English.

52. Dowling had Iago make his explanation to the trite "Believe Me, If All those Endearing Young Charms." Rice instead specified "Long Tail'd Blue," one of the oldest and most popular blackface songs. George Washington Dixon was performing it as early as 1827 in New York City. The title refers to the formal morning coat affected by dandiacal flaneurs. It is particularly appropriate at this juncture in *Otello* because it is about an interracial love triangle in which two lovers, at least one black, court a "white gal":

> And yaller folks call her Sue
> I guess she backed a nigger out
> And swung my long-tail blue.

53. Once again Rice connects Iago to Yankee imagery—Stone Fence alludes to a distinctive feature of New England agriculture. Stone Fence was also one of the earliest American mixed drinks, made from brandy and cider, and mentioned as early as 1809 by Washington Irving. See William Grimes, *Straight Up or on the Rocks: A Cul-*

tural History of American Drink (New York: Simon & Schuster, 1993), pp. 65 and 63. Dowling's *Othello Travestie* had them drinking ale.

54. The social life of Bowery youths often revolved around the volunteer fire companies that marshaled young men to emergency actions, after which carousing and treating would take place.

55. "Soft sodder" appears also in Dan Emmett's "Bressed Am Dem Dat 'Spects Nuttin'" (Hans Nathan, *Dan Emmett and the Rise of Early Negro Minstrelsy* [Norman: University of Oklahoma Press, 1962], p. 411). Soft solder would seem to be the result of very "hot air" or inauthentic language.

56. This gratuitous slur is not in Dowling. But does it indicate Rice's racism or, perhaps, Desdemona's carelessness? Is it designed to elicit audience sympathy for Otello's growing anger?

57. Rice is paraphrasing Shakespeare's *Othello* (3.3.9); Dowling omitted the passage.

58. The reference is to Shakespeare's *Othello*, 3.3.157.

59. Slang. During the depression of 1837, many small banks issued poorly secured notes of small value. Iago is saying that his purse is worthless, but Cassio was after something more valuable.

60. This metaphor, from falconry, is extended in Shakespeare's text as part of Othello's soliloquy at 3.3.260–279: it refers to releasing a disobedient falcon downwind, thus discouraging its return. Rice has resuscitated this line, which Dowling omits.

61. They are, of course, still on Cyprus; Iago characteristically emphasizes animal sexuality.

62. Slang exclamation of disgust or impatience.

63. The joke that hysterical people's hair stands out had become so conventional in the minstrel show by the mid-1840s that there were "fright wigs" for actors to wear. That they have proved of lasting significance is shown in John Lydon (formerly Johnny Rotten, when he sang in the 1970s punk group, the Sex Pistols) wearing such a neon anti-conk wig in his publicity photos for his late 1990s tour of North America in a frank commodity, called "Filthy Lucre."

64. "Dandy Jim from Caroline" is an old blackface song attributed to several composers, including Old Bull Myers, Silas S. Steele, Cool White (John Hodges), Barney Williams, Dan Emmett, and T. D. Rice. William Mahar has argued that the song may refer to the scandalous behavior and extreme politics of James Henry Hammond, the "Dandy Jim" of South Carolina government in the 1830s and 1840s ("Black English in Early Blackface Minstrelsy: A New Interpretation of the Sources of Minstrel Show Dialect" *American Quarterly* 37 [Summer 1985]: 283). For more on Hammond, see Drew Gilpin Faust, *James Henry Hammond and the Old South: A Design for Mastery* (Baton Rouge: Louisiana State University Press, 1982).

65. In Shakespeare this towel was a napkin and handkerchief dyed in mummy and embroidered by a two-hundred-year-old Egyptian sibyl. Dowling's parody broadened the handkerchief to a towel and naturalized the Egyptian sibyl as a gypsy

named Powell. Rice changed Powell to Cowell, probably as an in-joke alluding to his friends Joe and Sam Cowell, father and son, with whom Rice had acted from Cincinnati to New York. Sam Cowell went on to a further career in the English music hall, mutating from blackface to cockney.

66. Second appearance of the problem child.

67. Dowling specifies "King of the Cannibal Islands" for this music. Rice's stage directions do not indicate which music he wanted.

68. These crow sounds were not in Shakespeare, not in Dowling. They are an association with Rice as Jim Crow, and they are characteristic of the way Rice registered his characters' tense madness at plays' ends; see the conclusion of *Bone Squash*.

69. Desdemona's waking spasm is Rice's addition; it is neither in Shakespeare nor Dowling.

70. More b'hoy jargon.

71. Actually, he did not see the towel; Iago told him about it. This remark is vestigial, from Shakespeare's *Othello*, 4.1.

72. Another of Rice's additions: this brilliant street expression, meaning "he's dead," has no antecedent in earlier variants of the Othello story.

73. "Old Dan Tucker" was probably written by Dan Emmett early in the career of the Virginia Minstrels, which is to say in the winter of 1842.

74. In the spirit of opera.

75. When Rice positions this song, with different words, also at the end of *Flight to America*, he and the play's author, William Leman Rede, specify that its tune was Samuel Arnold's "Finale to Obi."

Information about the parallel but separate celebrations blacks instituted to celebrate independence in the early Republic is admirably developed in David Waldstreicher, *In the Midst of Perpetual Fêtes* (Chapel Hill, University of North Carolina Press for the Omohundro Institute, 1997), pp. 325–337, and in Shane White, "'It Was a Proud Day': African Americans, Festivals, and Parades in the North, 1741–1834," *Journal of American History* (June 1994): 13–50. Also relevant is Frederick Douglass's famous speech "What to the Slave is the Fourth of July?" (Rochester, 5 July 1852), which comments on and instantiates the same tradition.

76. John Wright's manuscript here notes that the performance lasted "1 hour and 20 minutes / Boston Mass / April 1853."

STREET PROSE

"The Life of Jim Crow"

1. The two editions of "Life of Jim Crow," in 1835 and 1837, were both published by James M'Minn. Philadelphia directories list M'Minn as owning a "shoe finding store" at 96 N. 7th St. all through the 1830s, except for 1837, when he is also listed as making band boxes. No other M'Minn publications have appeared. The author of this "Life of Jim Crow" said to be "written by himself" remains just as uncertain as M'Minn's relationship with Rice and Jim Crow. Whoever the author, his account of

Rice's performances is not in accord with my reconctruction of it through other re-covered documents. For instance, he says later that the first public performance of Jim Crow is in Cincinnati, although the earliest jumping I have been able to docu-ment was in Louisville, 21 May 1830. Nevertheless, it is true that T. D. Rice was per-forming in Cincinnati more than a year before this date, and I may simply not have found a complete newspaper record.

I transcribe the first edition here; its clearer printing is held now at the Library of Congress. A second edition, to be found today at the Schomburg Library, made ram-pant small changes in dialect and spelling. It celebrates Rice's return from his initial trip to England by including songs whose lyrics refer to "Jim Crow in London" and France, as well as references to Martin Van Buren, whose presidential term began in 1837. The 1835 publication accompanied Rice's performance at the Walnut Street Theatre in Philadelphia on 3 July 1835, which was announced as featuring the per-formance of "Jump Jim Crow" "in which he will discuss in his lyric style, the *Event-ful History of His Life*, with various observations on the manners and customs of the Age" (playbill at Harvard Theatre Collection, Walnut Street Theatre folder). And the 1837 edition likely accompanied Philadelphia performances, 23–28 October 1837.

2. This paragraph was on a page facing the title page.

3. Jim Crow refers here to Fanny Kemble and Madame Vestris, whom he mentions later.

4. The *Oxford English Dictionary* traces *buckra* to black patois of Surinam: *bakra*, meaning "master"; it also cites language of the Calabar coast that would mean "demon, powerful and superior being."

5. A central feature of Jacksonian ideology was that the central bank, run in Phila-delphia by Nicholas Biddle, was monopolistic and favored elite interests. Jackson de-termined to break this control and spread banks to local interests. A large banker and debtor himself, Daniel Webster was one of Biddle's great defenders. A main re-sult of breaking down the Philadelphia bank was the consolidation of financial inter-ests in New York's Wall Street. The quarrel over the Bank lasted through both of Andrew Jackson's terms, with various strategies to dismantle it, and then occupied Van Buren's next term as he tried to find a substitute for the Bank of the United States. It was not until the Federal Reserve system was established in 1913 that this quarrel calmed.

Noseology, like phrenology—and, for that matter, raciology—was one of those nineteenth-century sciences devoted to ordering and ranking difference. Rice quickly connects these sortings to Whigology, the ideology of Whigs, the party op-posing Jacksonian Democrats and supporting the Bank.

6. Mercy of God.

7. Mount Pelion, on the Aegean coast in northern Greece, was the mythical home of Chiron and other centaurs; Chiron raised Jason there.

8. "That dog, that had his teeth before his eyes / To worry lambs and lap their gen-tle blood" (*Richard III*, 4.4.49–50).

9. Piano fortes, or pianos.

10. James Reeside was partner in a stagecoach firm with Amos and Henry Slaymaker. Their route ran from Philadelphia to Pittsburgh.

11. Scythe.

12. Provisioner.

13. The genealogy of blackface remains one of its most repeated motifs, right up through Spike Lee's film *Bamboozled* (2000), in which the two minstrels grotesquely parse their kin connections.

14. Horace Binney, a Philadelphia lawyer, and briefly congressman, delivered along with Daniel Webster a thumping speech against President Jackson's bank policy in Baltimore on 20 April 1834 (Charles C. Binney, *The Life of Horace C. Binney with Selections from his Letters* [Philadelphia: J. B. Lippincott, 1903], p. 120). Thanks to Phil Lapsansky for this reference.

15. One character in James Kenney's play *Raising the Wind* tells another that the central figure, Jeremy Diddler, "gets into people's houses by his songs and his bon-mots" (New York: William Taylor, 1821, p. 5). Rice often played Diddler in his early career.

16. Dionysius was a Greek God of ecstasy and theater. Julius Caesar was the Roman ruler and subsequent subject of Shakespeare's tragedy. "Fenny Kimble" was Fanny Kemble, the popular English actress of Rice's era, who toured American theatres before an unhappy marriage and divorce in the United States, and before commenting in print on American mores, including slavery. Sylvester Daggerwood was a character in the first play by George Colman, the Younger; Rice played Daggerwood often early in his career in *The Mad Actor, or, The Humours of Sylvester Daggerwood*. Richard III and Coriolanus were English and Roman rulers who became subjects of Shakespearean plays. I have not recovered Bobby Trott and Sammy Dobbs. These contrasting roles register the democratic ambition that Jim Crow bequeaths to those who would follow him.

17. Purse.

18. Encored.

19. Major hotel in Baltimore, where Horace Binney also stayed (Binney, *Life*, p. 120).

20. Figure 6 illustrates the "quizzing glass" and Jim Crow's deployment of it at a distance from his face.

21. Amos Kendall, Major William B. Lewis, Isaac Hill: all intimates of Jackson, and whose counsel he trusted.

22. Perhaps this is a reference to Duff Green, editor of the Washington *Telegraph*.

23. George Poindexter, senator from Mississippi, formerly Jackson's friend and political lieutenant, had turned against him in a patronage squall of 1830; he fought and killed an opponent in a duel.

24. Fanny Kemble.

25. Frank Johnson was the free African American bandleader from Philadelphia

who was the most widely published native-born American composer in the first half of the nineteenth century. In 1821, Johnson began his annual summer visits to Saratoga Springs, New York, where Samuel Drake hired his group for the house band at the Congress Hall Hotel. Drake later employed Rice for western theatrical tours. Johnson's band toured free as well as slave states throughout the 1830s and played in England in 1837 as "The American Minstrels."

26. Restive.

27. Mordecai Noah (1785–1851), sheriff of the Seventh Ward in New York City when Rice was growing up there. Noah was a popular newspaper editor, playwright, consul, and advocate of Jewish issues.

28. Printer: Noah was then editor of the New York *Evening Star.*

29. Turtle and terrapin dishes were popular saloon fare in these years.

30. New York currency.

31. A coin worth about five pennies.

32. Restive.

33. A hit against both the class divisions then manifest in Philadelphia, where the finer people attended the Chesnut while working people favor the Walnut Street Theatre (where Rice was then performing); and the overseas stars who were bringing their foreign culture into the American scene and charging high prices for it. Jim Crow imagines stinking up the Chesnut scene with his act, or that of his progeny.

34. Before Friedrich Nietzsche applied "Dionysian" (ecstatic abandon) and "Apollonian" (determining order) to Greek dramatic forms in *The Birth of Tragedy (From the Spirit of Music)* (1872), the concepts were street talk in American popular culture.

35. Francis Anne Butler, *Fanny Kemble, Journal* (London: J. Murray, 1835).

"A Faithful Account of the Life of Jim Crow"

1. This street biography is the final item in the songster, *Jim Crow's Vagaries, or, Black Flights of Fancy: Containing a Choice Collection of Nigger Melodies. To Which is Added the Erratic Life of Jim Crow* (London: Orlando Hodgson, [1840]). As such, this biography of Jim Crow gives an English take on American popular culture. The bends of its ethnic and class prejudices, the twists in its genealogy of Jim Crow, and the pamphlet's probable 1840 date all provide useful counterpositions for the earlier American examples.

2. "Improvistory" plays on *Improvisatore,* an Italian category for improvising singer, rhymer, and teller of tales.

3. In England, "black" had long meant "darker than European."

4. The English made several treaties at Lancaster with the Six Iroquois Nations—in 1744, 1748, and 1762, but not in 1774. The English made peace with the Iroquois in October 1774 at Onandaga, agreeing to persuade the Shawnees to settle with the Virginians. (See Barbara Graymont, *The Iroquois in the American Revolution* [Syracuse: Syracuse University Press, 1972], pp. 48–50.)

5. The author may refer here to the smallpox epidemic that Lord Jeffrey Amherst caused when he ordered his British commander to infect the Indians besieging Fort Pitt with a gift of smallpox-infested blankets. Begun in 1763, this epidemic raged throughout the Indian nations from Canada to Georgia.

6. Except for these lines, which are variants on "Jim Crow," all the songs cited here were published in the same English songster that concluded with this "Life of Jim Crow."

7. From "Gumbo Chaff," as is the next quoted line.

8. From "Sich a Gittin' Upstairs," as is the next quote.

9. From "Who Dare."

Acknowledgments

Without the knowledge and encouragement of the librarians and curators at the Harvard Theatre Collection of the Houghton Library at Harvard University, where the songs reprinted here are found, the Library Company of Philadelphia, the American Antiquarian Society, the Billy Rose Collection at the New York Public Library, where *Otello* can be found, the British Library, which houses all the remaining plays reprinted here, and the New York Historical Society, this book would have been impossible. My particular thanks to Phil Lapsansky, Jim Green, and Connie King in Philadelphia; to Annette Fern and Fredric Woodbridge Wilson in Cambridge, Massachusetts; and to Joanne Chaison, Russell Martin, and Nancy Burkett in Worcester, Massachusetts. Such communities make interdisciplinary synthesis possible.

I thank the National Endowment for the Humanities as well as the Houghton Library, the Library Company of Philadelphia, and the American Antiquarian Society for the enabling fellowships they awarded me. The English department at Florida State University granted me summers of research support for several archival trips, as did the university's Committee on Faculty Research and Scholarship. Anna Deveare Smith's Institute for the Arts in Civic Dialogue brought me to Cambridge, Massachusetts for memorable involvement with the issues of blackface in cultural production. Likewise, the African American Studies Department at Harvard University involved me in another week's productive dialogue about stereotypes in painting and collecting; special thanks here to Karen C. C. Dalton, Mike Vazquez, and Dick Newman. At Stanford, Duke, and Indiana Universities, the College of William & Mary, the University of Virginia, the University of Wisconsin–Madison, the University of Pennsylvania, and its McNeil Center for Early American Studies, sharp questioners challenged early drafts of this material and I have tried to adjust where I could.

I have been fortunate to find friends whose conceptual labor opened new ways through the issues I engage. I have noted their influence, but I must emphasize how much I gained from Paul Gilroy's and Peter Linebaugh's separate works on the interracial Atlantic world, Shane White's creative revelation of early black New York's vernacular life, David Waldstreicher's and Dale Cockrell's work on festivity, Michael

[455]

Ray Charles's paintings and Donald Byrd's choreography that upend hateful images, Werner Sollors's wide-ranging analysis of interracial mutuality, and Eric Lott's insistent study of sexuality and class. Conversations I had long ago with Bob Cantwell, as with Roger Abrahams, still affect the way I see and hear American vernacular culture. Chris Looby's support and work on interracial fraternity have both been important to me. Sandy Goennel, T. D. Rice's great-great-granddaughter, shared notes, made pea soup, and has been sending warm regards my way for years. Diane Roberts, at first my student but long since my friend and conspirator in prose, helped me find these plays at the British Library.

An old debt is to two former undergraduate honors students who shucked open *Otello* for me: in 1994 June Piscitelli and Sean Christian coined the term "problem child" for Young Otello and showed me his radicality. I thank all the students in my blackface seminars for their skeptical interest in, and sometimes outright resistance to, fetishes, masks, gestural transmission, and duck-rabbit phenomena. I have had three excellent research assistants while working on this project: Doug Ford, Peter Reed, and Becky Godlasky.

My editor, Lindsay Waters, has provided enthusiastic support since we met at this project's onset. His energy, vision, and problem-solving repeatedly sustained it.

And to Fita Ferguson, thanks for her critical readings. Her spirit infused every part of this book.

Index